HowToDraw

BOATS, TRAINS & PLANES

Written and Illustrated by **Michael LaPlaca**

Watermill Press

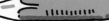

Materials

The first things you will need are some pencils. Number 2 pencils are best. Next, you'll need some white paper—a pad is good to have—an eraser, a felt-tip pen, and some crayons.

Basic Shapes

Here are a few basic shapes you should practice drawing before you start. You'll find that you will use these shapes again and again to draw each of the boats, trains, and planes in this book.

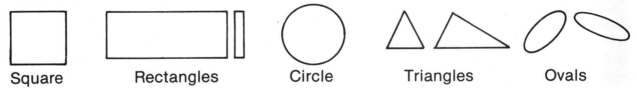

| Square | Rectangles | Circle | Triangles | Ovals |

You will also be drawing some three-dimensional shapes:

Each of the drawings in this book is broken down into several easy steps for you to follow. Look at all the details in each step, and take your time as you work. Begin your drawing in pencil. When it looks the way you want it, go over your pencil lines with a felt-tip pen. Then erase any unwanted pencil lines. Use your crayons to color your boats, trains, and planes. Work carefully as you draw, but most important of all—have fun!

Sloop

A sloop is a small boat that has one mast.

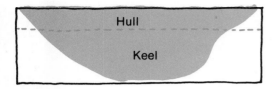
Hull
Keel

1. Start with a rectangle. Then draw the shape of the boat. The part above the dotted line is called the *hull*. The part below the line is called the *keel.* The keel is what keeps the boat from tipping over.

This sloop has two sails.

Jib →

Mainsail ←

← Mast

Boom →

2. Next, draw the cabin. The cabin of this sloop is made from rectangles. Add the portholes.

3. Draw the mast and the sails. The mainsail is attached to the boom. The boom swings from side to side, so it can catch the strongest wind. Add a rudder. The rudder is needed to steer the boat. Almost all boats have rudders, as you will see in the drawings that follow.

4. Add the final details, and you have drawn a sloop.

← Rudder

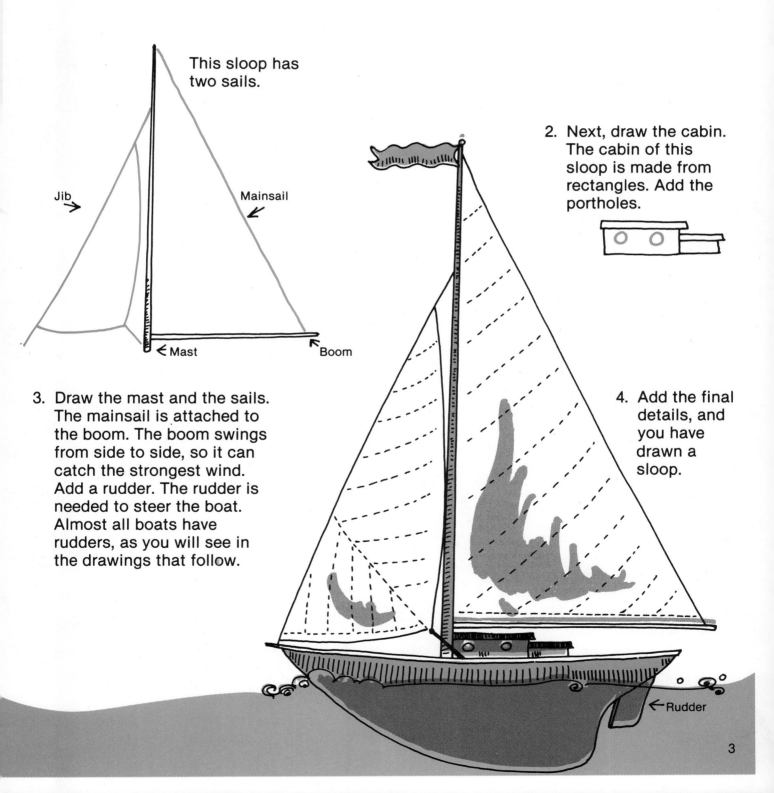

3

Viking Ship

This ship is also known as a *long ship.* Long ago, it was used in the North Atlantic Ocean by bands of Vikings.

1. First, draw a canoe-shaped boat. Then add the planks and ribs.

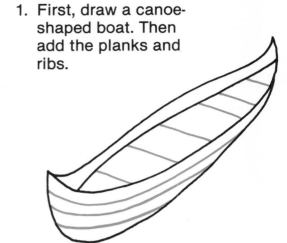

2. Add the front and rear ends of the boat. The *prow* is the front end of the boat. This is a simple prow, but if you like, you can try one of the ones at the top of the next page, instead.

Prow

3. Draw the mast. The sail is attached to two *yards.*

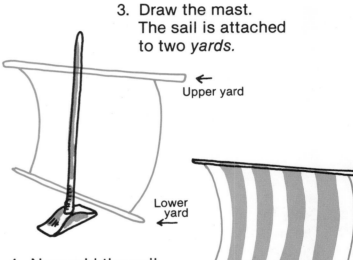

Upper yard

Lower yard

4. Now add the sail. Draw bold stripes. Then color them with your crayons.

5. Add the steering oar. The steering oar serves the same function as a rudder.

When there was no wind to push the Viking ships, the sailors used oars that looked like this. Some oars were eighteen feet (5.4 meters) long.

The Vikings often carved the prows of their ships to look like dragons. Here are several prows you might like to add to your Viking ship.

5

Spanish Galleon

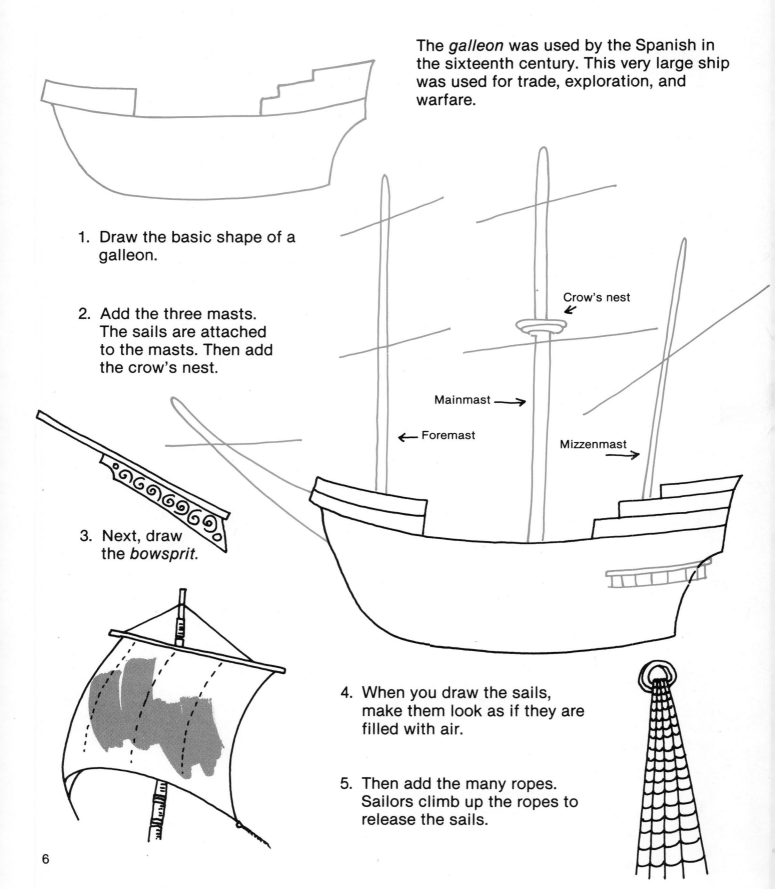

The *galleon* was used by the Spanish in the sixteenth century. This very large ship was used for trade, exploration, and warfare.

1. Draw the basic shape of a galleon.

2. Add the three masts. The sails are attached to the masts. Then add the crow's nest.

Crow's nest

Mainmast →

← Foremast

Mizzenmast →

3. Next, draw the *bowsprit.*

4. When you draw the sails, make them look as if they are filled with air.

5. Then add the many ropes. Sailors climb up the ropes to release the sails.

6. Now add the final details.

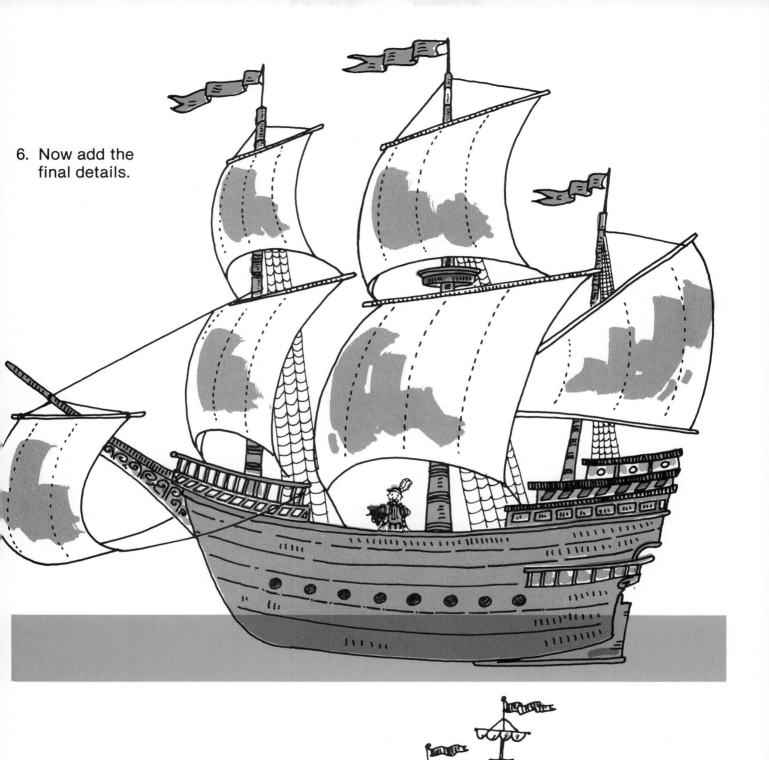

This is the *Santa Maria,* the ship that Columbus sailed to America in 1492. It is a type of ship called a *carrack.* It looked very much like a Spanish galleon.

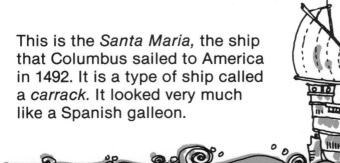

River Boat

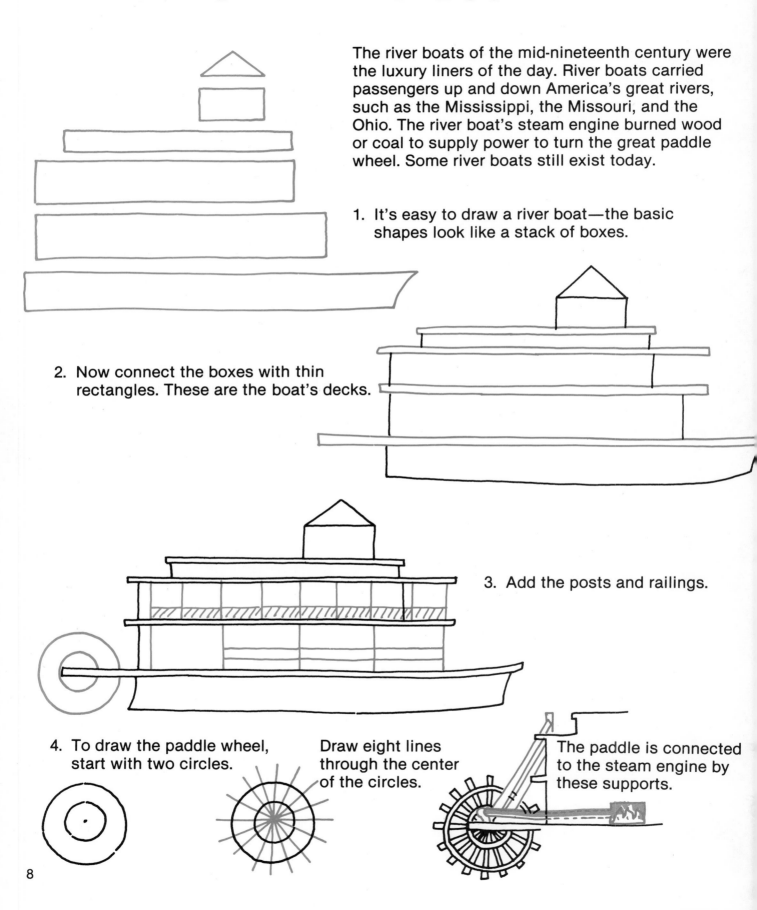

The river boats of the mid-nineteenth century were the luxury liners of the day. River boats carried passengers up and down America's great rivers, such as the Mississippi, the Missouri, and the Ohio. The river boat's steam engine burned wood or coal to supply power to turn the great paddle wheel. Some river boats still exist today.

1. It's easy to draw a river boat—the basic shapes look like a stack of boxes.

2. Now connect the boxes with thin rectangles. These are the boat's decks.

3. Add the posts and railings.

4. To draw the paddle wheel, start with two circles.

Draw eight lines through the center of the circles.

The paddle is connected to the steam engine by these supports.

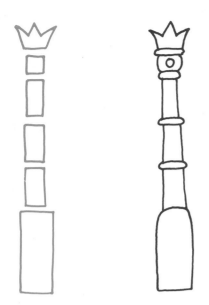

6. Next, draw the pilot-house. It has windows all around it, so the captain and navigator can see up and down the river.

7. The railings on the second level are easy to draw.

5. To draw the smokestack, start with five box shapes and top them off with a crown.

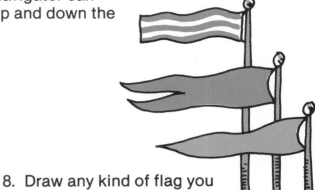

8. Draw any kind of flag you like. Use bright colors.

Luxury Liner

This is a very big boat. It is longer than three football fields.

1. To begin, stack three long box shapes on top of each other.

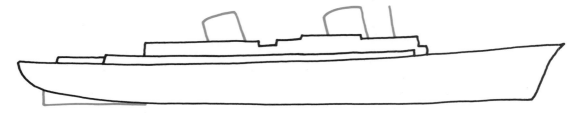

2. Add the smokestacks, rudder, and radar tower.

3. Then add the lifeboats, propellers, and the stern (rear) and bow (front) masts.

Mast

Boom

The function of the masts on a luxury liner is much different than on a sailing ship. Here the masts are used to raise and lower cargo. The crosspiece is called a *boom.*

Tugboat

Tugboats are small, but they are very powerful boats. One of their jobs is to guide big luxury liners into dock.

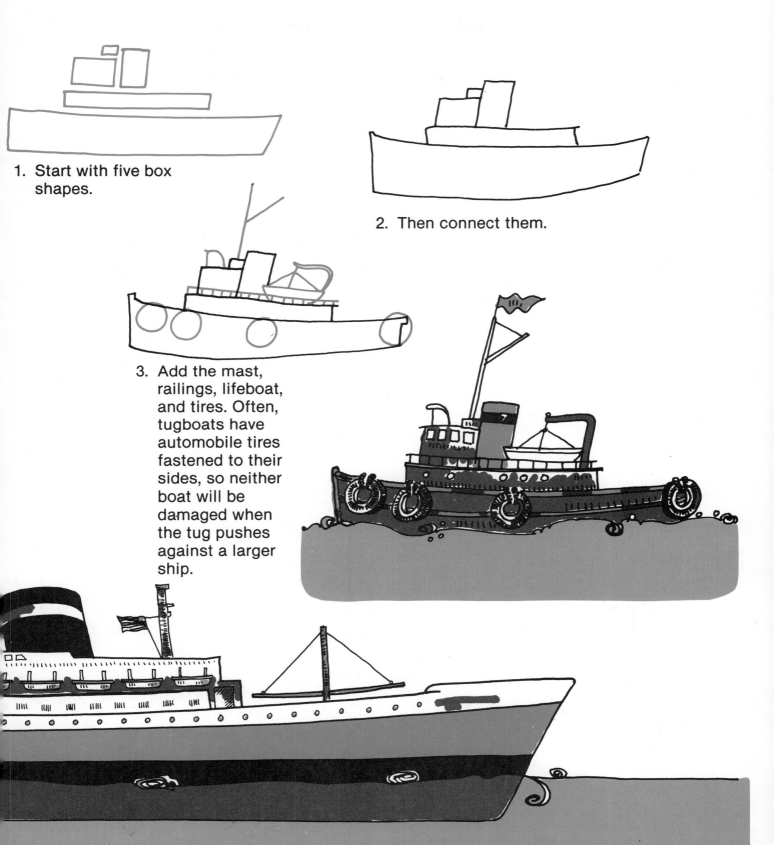

1. Start with five box shapes.

2. Then connect them.

3. Add the mast, railings, lifeboat, and tires. Often, tugboats have automobile tires fastened to their sides, so neither boat will be damaged when the tug pushes against a larger ship.

Submarine

Submarines are ships that go under water. They are used by the Navy and by scientists to study the ocean.

1. To draw a submarine, start with two oval shapes.

2. Add the four rudders and the conning tower.

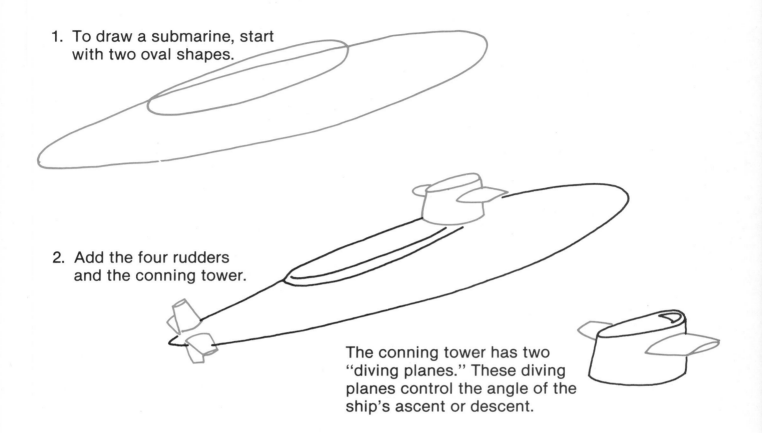

The conning tower has two "diving planes." These diving planes control the angle of the ship's ascent or descent.

This is a nuclear-powered submarine. It can travel great distances under the water on very little fuel. This one could go around the world without coming up at all. Submarines take water into special tanks in order to sink. When the sub is ready to surface, air pressure is used to blow the water out of the tanks.

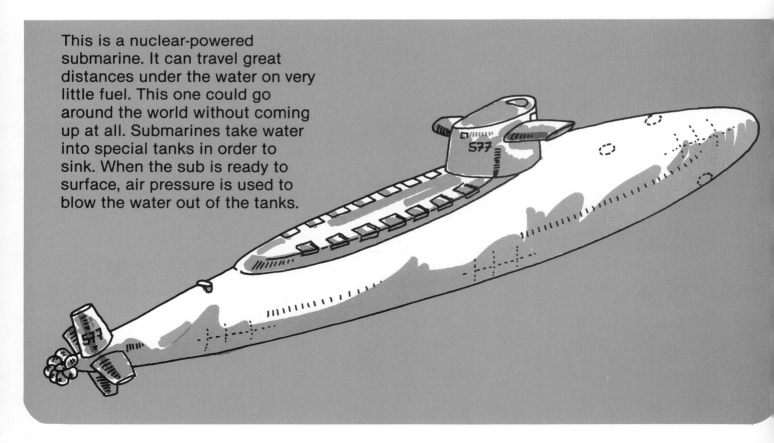

Bathyscaphe

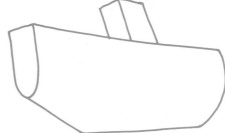

A bathyscaphe is another type of submarine. It is used by scientists to study and explore the deepest parts of the ocean. It is made of very strong steel and can go much deeper than other submarines.

1. Start with two three-dimensional shapes.

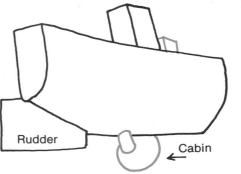

Rudder

Cabin ←

2. Add the rudder. Next, add the cabin that holds the scientists.

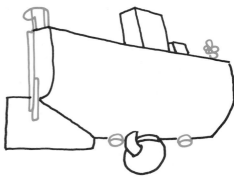

3. Then add the final details.

Bathysphere

The bathysphere is also used to study the ocean. It cannot move by itself, so it must be connected to a ship.

1. Start with a circle.

2. Add the porthole and some details.

3. To draw the top of the bathysphere, connect a stack of boxes like this.

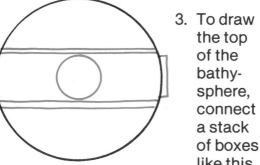

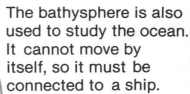

Steam Engine

1. Start with three rectangles.

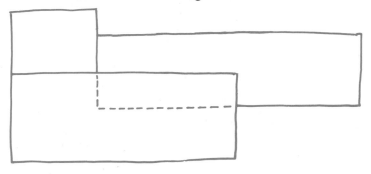

The first successful steam-engine locomotive was completed in 1829. It was called the *Rocket* and was built in England. Railroads were first used in Europe and England as early as the sixteenth century. At that time, they were used to transport coal and minerals from mines, and they were pulled by horses. It wasn't until the nineteenth century, and the invention of the steam engine, that railroads were used for passenger travel. The engine you are learning to draw is an American engine built in 1869.

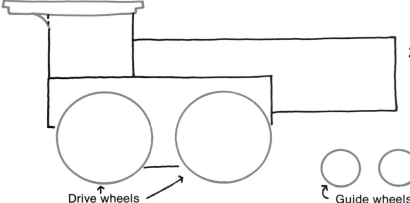

2. Add the roof of the cab and the wheels. This type of engine was also known as an *eight-wheeler*.

Drive wheels

Guide wheels

Piston

The front wheels are called the *guide wheels.* Above them is the piston, which is attached to the larger *drive wheels.*

Light

3. Now add the piston and the rest of the locomotive.

4. Draw the drive wheels like this:

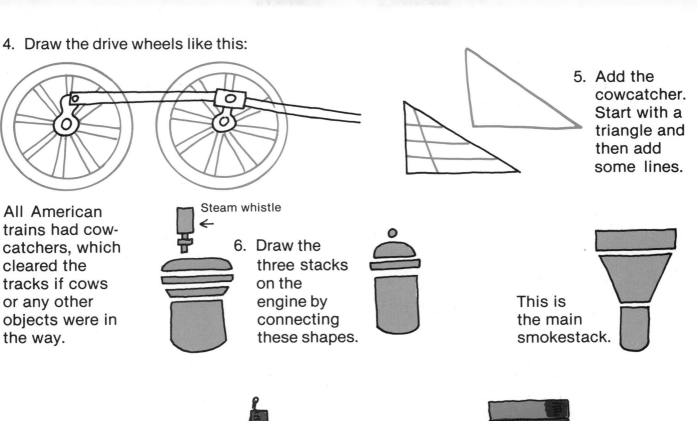

All American trains had cowcatchers, which cleared the tracks if cows or any other objects were in the way.

5. Add the cowcatcher. Start with a triangle and then add some lines.

Steam whistle

6. Draw the three stacks on the engine by connecting these shapes.

This is the main smokestack.

7. Finish the details and color the train. Don't forget the bell!

Engine 382: This was the famous locomotive driven by Casey Jones in 1900.

The Burlington Zephyr

The *Zephyr* was the first streamlined diesel-engine, passenger train built in the United States. "Streamlined" means that it was designed to offer less resistance to the wind, so it could move very fast. The *Zephyr* was built in 1934. The more efficient diesel-engine locomotive soon replaced the steam-engine locomotive on important railroad lines.

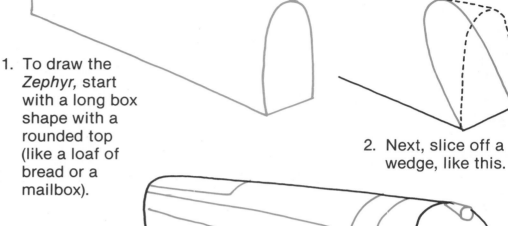

1. To draw the *Zephyr,* start with a long box shape with a rounded top (like a loaf of bread or a mailbox).

2. Next, slice off a wedge, like this.

3. Now you have the basic shape of the engine. Add the light and these few lines.

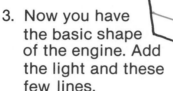

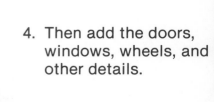

4. Then add the doors, windows, wheels, and other details.

Electric Engine

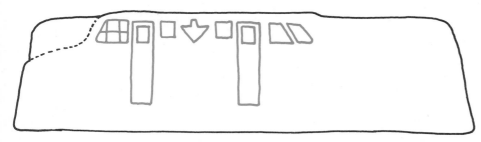

1. Start with a long rectangular shape and add doors and windows.

Electric engines were first developed in the 1930s. Usually, these engines get their power from a power plant by means of overhead wires. Electric engines are very fast and strong. They are also much quieter than diesel or steam engines and do not give off exhaust fumes. Electric engines that travel in long tunnels, and especially in subway systems, have a third rail, which supplies electric current to run the train.

2. This engine has ten wheels on each side. Add them.

3. Draw the *pantograph.* It connects the train to the electric wires that run overhead.

The wheels on this engine are similar to the guide wheels of the steam engine on page 14. The springs are shock absorbers.

PENNSYLVANIA 4777 4777

Light

To draw all the cars on these two pages, start with a rectangle like this. If you look carefully, you'll see that they are all made from this basic shape.

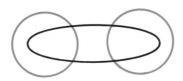

To draw the wheels, start with two circles and an oval.

Turn the oval into this shape.

boxcar

A boxcar is the easiest car to draw. Add the ladder and wheels. Then draw the designs on the outside. Boxcars carry everything from boxes to boats.

auto-carrier

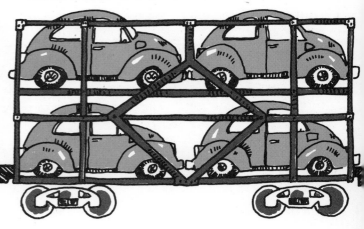

An auto-carrier car does just that! This is one way new cars are shipped across the country.

hopper car

A hopper car carries coal, gravel, or other types of ore. This one is open, but many hopper cars have tops to cover cargo that can't be exposed to the weather.

refrigerator car

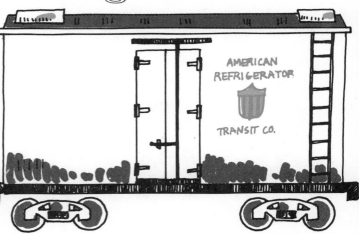

A refrigerator car carries food and other perishable cargo.

stock car

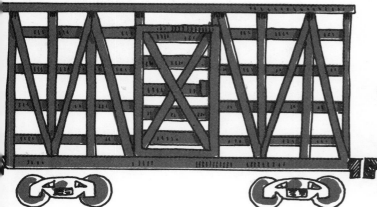

A stock car carries animals. It has openings in the sides so the animals can breathe. This car carries cattle.

tank car

A tank car carries liquids. It can carry milk, water, or oil.

passenger car

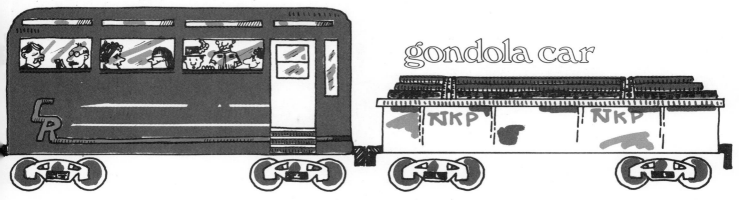

A passenger car carries people. It can take people on long trips across the country or on short trips back and forth to work every day.

gondola car

A gondola car carries cargo that can be exposed to the weather. This one is carrying pipes.

caboose

The caboose is always the last car on the train. The brightly colored caboose serves as a small apartment for the crew of the train. The crew eats and sleeps there.

Now that you know all about the many different cars, draw a long train showing them all.

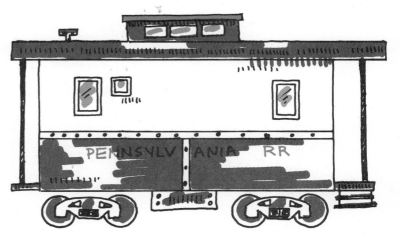

Monorail

1. To draw a monorail, start with a series of three-dimensional box shapes. Practice drawing the boxes until they look like they are coming toward you.

2. Next, round off the corners of the cars and make the front look like this.

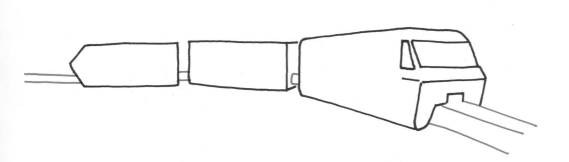

3. Remember, a monorail runs on one rail. Draw the rail and make sure that all the cars are attached to it.

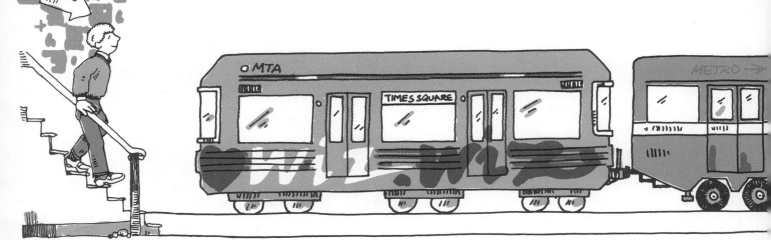

The New York City subway system is the largest in the world. It was first opened in 1904.

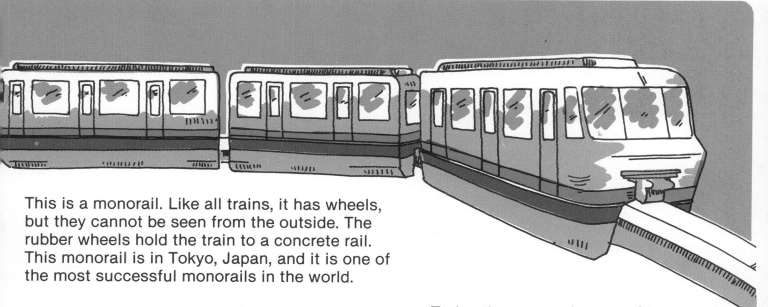

This is a monorail. Like all trains, it has wheels, but they cannot be seen from the outside. The rubber wheels hold the train to a concrete rail. This monorail is in Tokyo, Japan, and it is one of the most successful monorails in the world.

Subways

Trains that run underground are called subway trains. The first subway was opened in London in 1863. It was pulled by steam locomotives. Today, all subways run on electricity.

To draw a subway train, start with a rectangle. For the San Francisco train shown below, add a triangle to the rectangle. Then add the windows, doors, and wheels.

Some subway trains have rubber wheels (very much like a car's), which make the train run quietly and smoothly on a concrete track. If anything happens to one of the tires, the train can also run on metal wheels.

Rubber Wheels

The San Francisco subway system has very sleek, streamlined trains. They are painted silver, and they are faster and quieter than most other trains.

21

A *biplane* is a plane that has two sets of wings, one over the other. (A plane with one set of wings is called a *monoplane*.) Biplanes were first developed in the early 1900s, and they were used in World War I.

1. To draw a biplane, start with a three-dimensional shape like this.

2. Then draw the cockpit, where the pilot sits. Add the windshield.

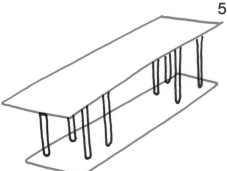

3. Add the tail assembly.

4. Next, draw the wheels.

Practice drawing some ovals for the propeller.

5. To draw the wings, start with two slanted rectangles and add the supports.

Spirit of St. Louis

In his small plane, the *Spirit of St. Louis,* Charles Lindbergh was the first person to make a nonstop solo flight across the Atlantic Ocean. On May 20, 1927, he left New York. In 33½ hours, he arrived in Paris— 3,600 miles (5,760 kilometers) away.

1. To draw the *Spirit of St. Louis,* start with a rectangular wing shape.

2. Then add a body shape like this.

3. Add the wing supports and the wheels.

4. Planes, like boats, have rudders. Add the rudder and the elevators.

5. Now draw a series of boxes around the nose of the plane. On this type of plane, part of the engine is exposed. This helps to cool the engine.

6. In your final drawing, draw a circle around the nose of the plane to show the propeller in motion.

23

Douglas DC-4

Many major developments in the design of airplanes were due to the airplane's importance during World Wars I and II. After World War II, many passenger airlines bought planes from the Air Force and changed the planes slightly. The Douglas DC-4 was one of the first large-body passenger planes. It was used from 1945 until the mid-1950s.

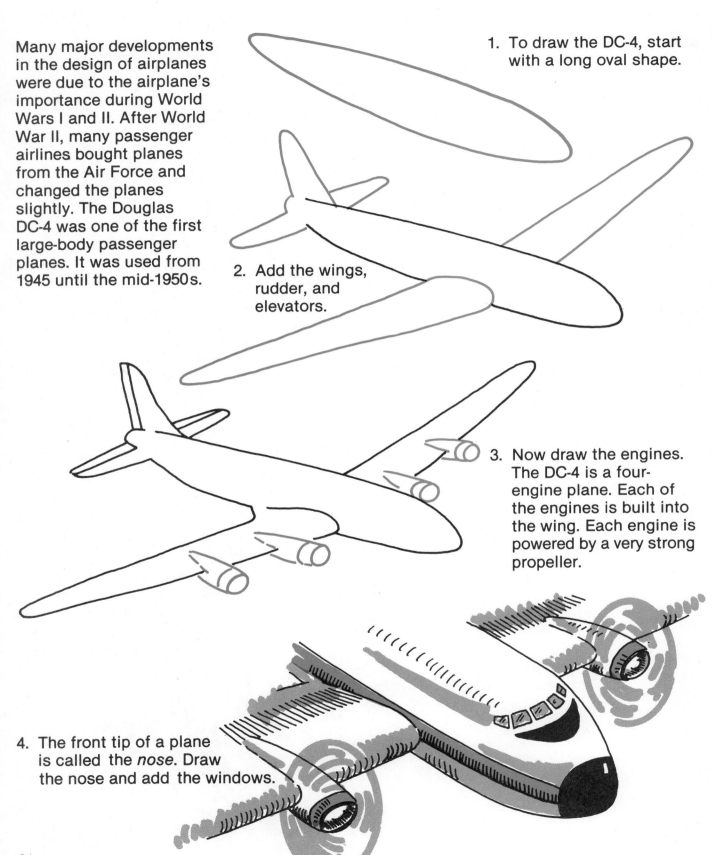

1. To draw the DC-4, start with a long oval shape.

2. Add the wings, rudder, and elevators.

3. Now draw the engines. The DC-4 is a four-engine plane. Each of the engines is built into the wing. Each engine is powered by a very strong propeller.

4. The front tip of a plane is called the *nose*. Draw the nose and add the windows.

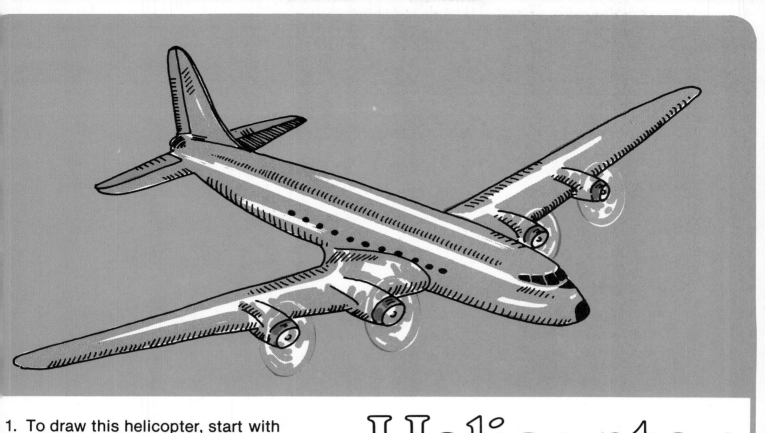

1. To draw this helicopter, start with two ovals for the cockpit, and a long triangle for the tail boom.

Helicopter

Cockpit

2. Next, add the engine, tail rotor, landing gear, and supports on tail boom.

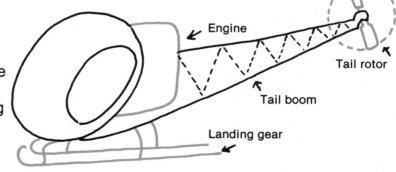

Engine

Tail rotor

Tail boom

Landing gear

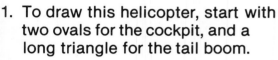

3. Draw these shapes. They are the main rotor and the mast of the helicopter.

A helicopter is called a "VTOL" (Vertical Takeoff and Landing). It can go straight up and down in the air, and requires no runway, as airplanes do.

Helicopters have many uses. They can be used to spray crops, to help stop forest fires, to rescue people from boats, to give traffic reports to commuters, or just to tour places of interest.

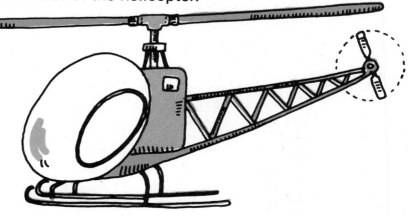

Boeing 747

This is a Boeing 747. It is known as a jumbo-jet because it is one of the largest passenger planes. The 747 can carry 374 passengers

1. Start with this basic shape.

2. Now add the tail fin, or rudder, and the elevators. Notice how the front of the plane slants in and up. This is where the pilot and crew sit.

3. Add the wing.

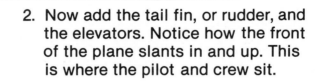

4. Add the turbojets. A 747 has four turbojets. Two are mounted under each wing.

Boeing 727

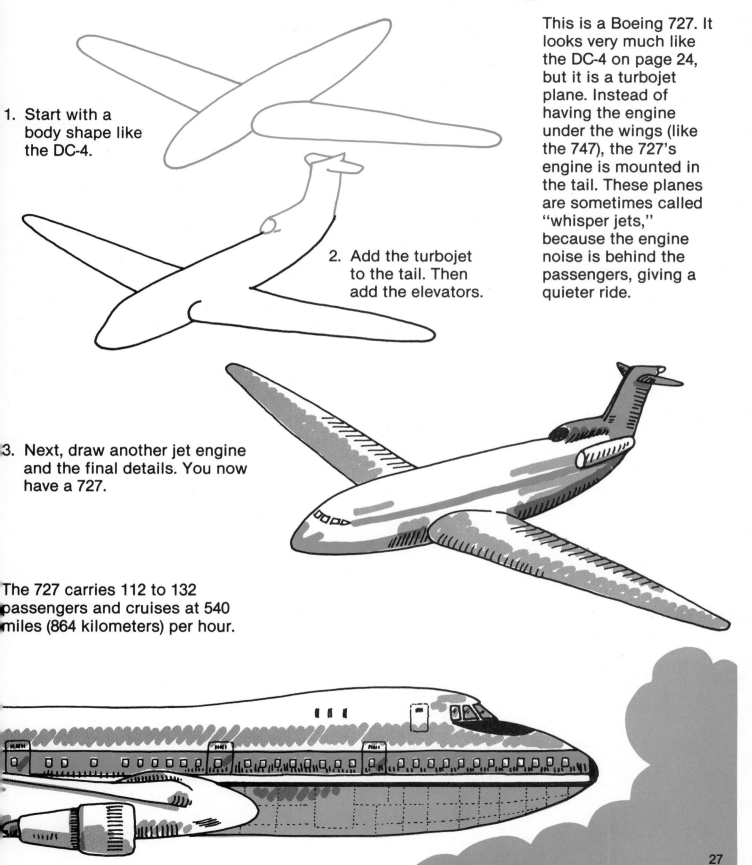

This is a Boeing 727. It looks very much like the DC-4 on page 24, but it is a turbojet plane. Instead of having the engine under the wings (like the 747), the 727's engine is mounted in the tail. These planes are sometimes called "whisper jets," because the engine noise is behind the passengers, giving a quieter ride.

1. Start with a body shape like the DC-4.

2. Add the turbojet to the tail. Then add the elevators.

3. Next, draw another jet engine and the final details. You now have a 727.

The 727 carries 112 to 132 passengers and cruises at 540 miles (864 kilometers) per hour.

Concorde-SST

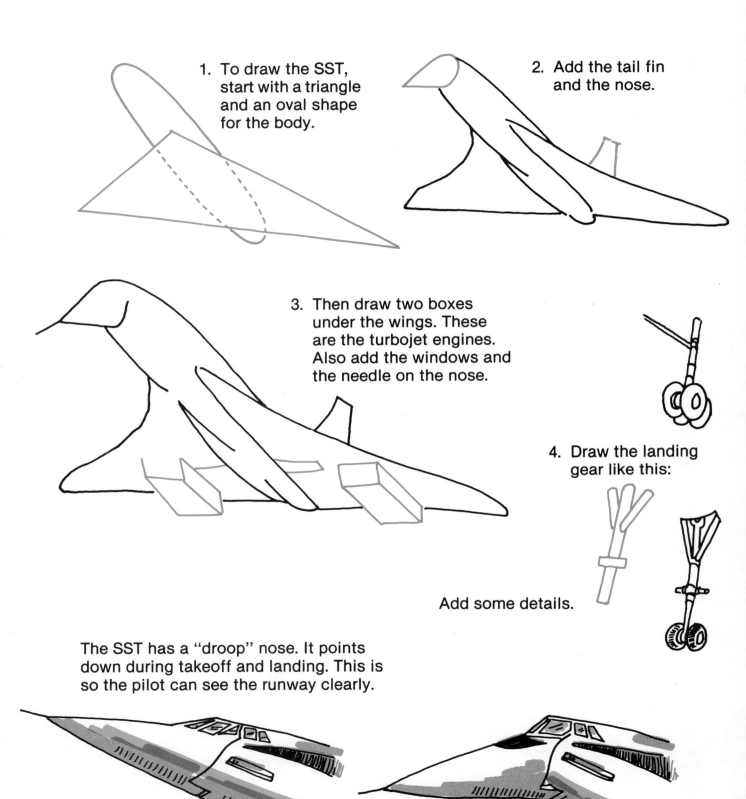

1. To draw the SST, start with a triangle and an oval shape for the body.

2. Add the tail fin and the nose.

3. Then draw two boxes under the wings. These are the turbojet engines. Also add the windows and the needle on the nose.

4. Draw the landing gear like this:

Add some details.

The SST has a "droop" nose. It points down during takeoff and landing. This is so the pilot can see the runway clearly.

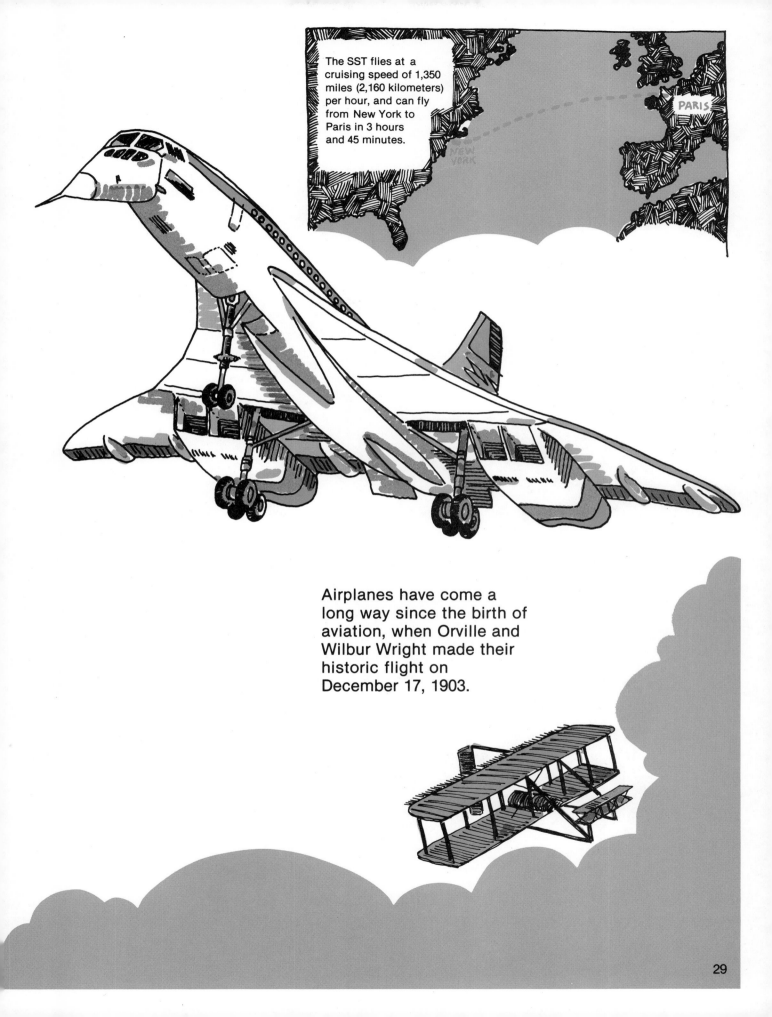

The SST flies at a cruising speed of 1,350 miles (2,160 kilometers) per hour, and can fly from New York to Paris in 3 hours and 45 minutes.

PARIS

NEW YORK

Airplanes have come a long way since the birth of aviation, when Orville and Wilbur Wright made their historic flight on December 17, 1903.

Now that you've learned how to draw so many kinds of boats, trains, and planes, it's time to draw a boat, train, or plane of your very own. Then make up a story to go with it.

Imagine you are Christopher Columbus sailing across the ocean ...or Mark Twain cruising the Mississippi on a river boat...or perhaps you are making a voyage to the bottom of the sea.

Flying high above the clouds, imagine that you are making the first, solo transatlantic flight...or that you are flying over the North Pole...or that you are the pilot of an SST.

Draw a train and imagine you are riding across the country in the year of 1887. What would you see along the way? You might have to stop the train because a cow is on the tracks...or you might be attacked by a band of outlaws. Let your imagination guide you as you create your own boats, planes, and trains—and have fun as you draw!

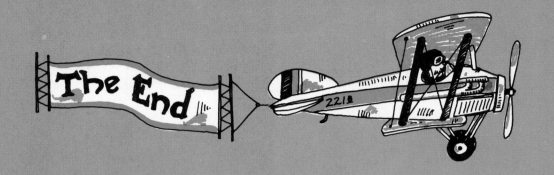

uppermost cartilage. During swallowing, the larynx is elevated, and the epiglottis closes over the top to prevent the entry of food into the larynx.

The mucosa of the larynx is ciliated epithelium, except for the vocal cords (stratified squamous epithelium). The cilia of the mucosa sweep upward to remove mucus and trapped dust and microorganisms.

The **vocal cords** (or vocal folds) are on either side of the **glottis,** the opening between them. During breathing, the vocal cords are held at the sides of the glottis, so that air passes freely into and out of the trachea (Fig. 15–3). During speaking, the intrinsic muscles of the larynx pull the vocal cords across the glottis, and exhaled air vibrates the vocal cords to produce sounds which can be turned into speech. It is also physically possible to speak while inhaling, but this is not what we are used to. The cranial nerves that are motor nerves to the larynx for speaking are the vagus and accessory nerves.

TRACHEA AND BRONCHIAL TREE

The **trachea** is about 4 to 5 inches (10 to 13 cm) long and extends from the larynx to the primary bronchi. The wall of the trachea contains 16 to 20

C-shaped pieces of cartilage, wh chea open. The gaps in these incor rings are posterior, to permit the exp esophagus when food is swallowed. The the trachea is ciliated epithelium with gob As in the larynx, the cilia sweep upward towa pharynx.

The right and left **primary bronchi** (Fig. 15– are the branches of the trachea that enter the lungs. Within the lungs, each primary bronchus branches into secondary bronchi leading to the lobes of each lung (three right, two left). The further branching of the bronchial tubes is often called the **bronchial tree.** Imagine the trachea as the trunk of an upside-down tree with extensive branches that become smaller and smaller; these smaller branches are the **bronchioles.** No cartilage is present in the walls of the bronchioles; this becomes clinically important in asthma (see Box 15–1: Asthma). The smallest bronchioles terminate in clusters of alveoli, the air sacs of the lungs.

LUNGS AND PLEURAL MEMBRANES

The **lungs** are located on either side of the heart in the chest cavity and are encircled and protected

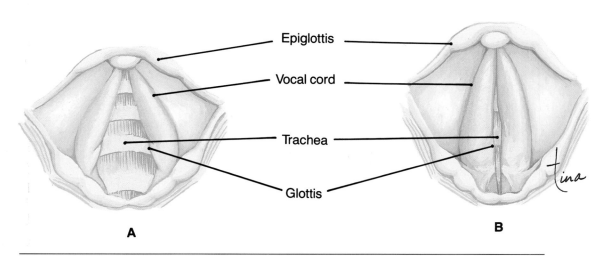

Epiglottis

Vocal cord

Trachea

Glottis

A

B

Figure 15–3 Vocal cords and glottis. **(A),** Position of the vocal cords during breathing. **(B),** Position of the vocal cords during speaking.

...ich keep the tra-
...plete cartilage
...nsion of the
...mucosa of
...let cells.
...d the

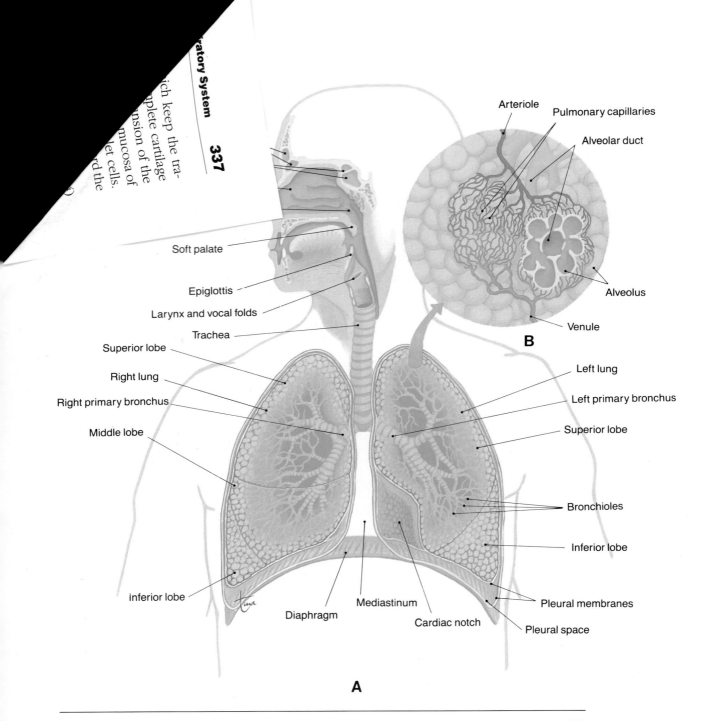

Figure 15-4 Respiratory system. **(A)**, Anterior view of the upper and lower respiratory tracts. **(B)**, Microscopic view of alveoli and pulmonary capillaries. (The colors represent the vessels, not the oxygen content of the blood within the vessel.)

Box 15–1 ASTHMA

Asthma is usually triggered by an allergic reaction that affects the smooth muscle and glands of the bronchioles. Allergens include foods and inhaled substances such as dust and pollen. Wheezing and dyspnea (difficult breathing) characterize an asthma attack, which may range from mild to fatal.

As part of the allergic response, the smooth muscle of the bronchioles constricts. Since there is no cartilage present in their walls, the bronchioles may close completely. The secretion of mucus increases, perhaps markedly, so the already constricted bronchioles may become clogged or completely obstructed with mucus.

Chronic asthma is a predisposing factor for emphysema. When obstructed bronchioles prevent ventilation of alveoli, the walls of the alveoli begin to deteriorate and break down, leaving large cavities that do not provide much surface area for gas exchange.

by the rib cage. The base of each lung rests on the diaphragm below; the apex (superior tip) is at the level of the clavicle. On the medial surface of each lung is an indentation called the **hilus,** where the primary bronchus and the pulmonary artery and veins enter the lung.

The pleural membranes are the serous membranes of the thoracic cavity. The **parietal pleura** lines the chest wall, and the **visceral pleura** is on the surface of the lungs. Between the pleural membranes is serous fluid, which prevents friction and keeps the two membranes together during breathing.

Alveoli

The functional units of the lungs are the **alveoli,** which are made of simple squamous epithelium. In the spaces between clusters of alveoli is elastic connective tissue, which is important for exhalation. There are millions of alveoli in each lung, and each alveolus is surrounded by a network of pulmonary capillaries (see Fig 15–4). Recall that capillaries are also made of simple squamous epithelium, so there are only two cells between the air in the

alveoli and the blood in the pulmonary capillaries, which permits efficient diffusion of gases (Fig. 15–5).

Each alveolus is lined with a thin layer of tissue fluid, which is essential for the diffusion of gases, because a gas must dissolve in a liquid in order to enter or leave a cell (the earthworm principle—an earthworm breathes through its moist skin, and will suffocate if its skin dries out). Although this tissue fluid is necessary, it creates a potential problem in that it would make the walls of an alveolus stick together internally. Imagine a plastic bag that is wet inside; its walls would stick together because of the surface tension of the water. This is just what would happen in alveoli, and inflation would be very difficult.

This problem is overcome by **pulmonary surfactant,** a lipoprotein secreted by alveolar cells. Surfactant mixes with the tissue fluid within the alveoli and decreases its surface tension, permitting inflation of the alveoli (see Box 15–2: Hyaline Membrane Disease). Normal inflation of the alveoli in turn permits the exchange of gases, but before we discuss this process, we will first see how air gets into and out of the lungs.

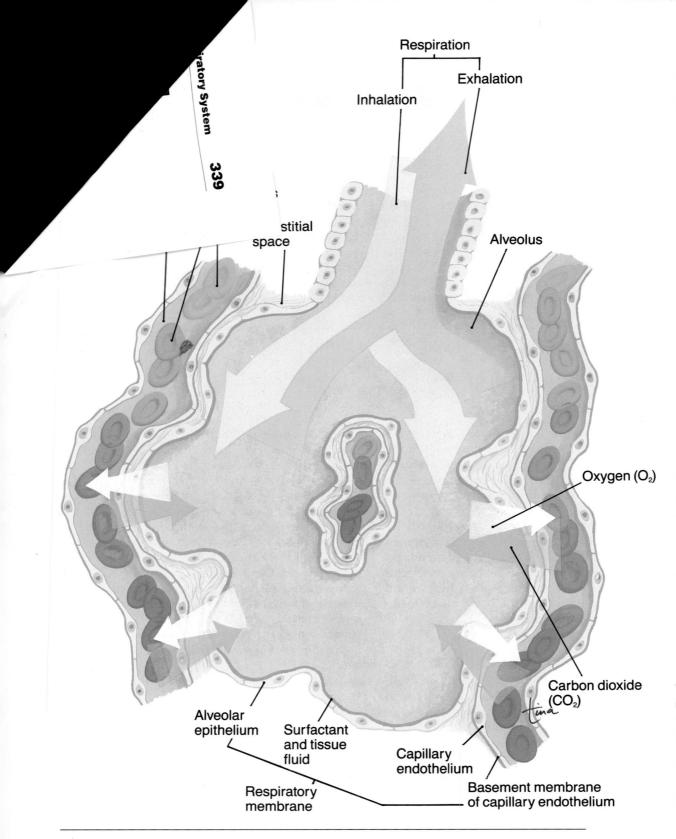

Respiration

Inhalation

Exhalation

...stitial space

Alveolus

Oxygen (O₂)

Carbon dioxide (CO₂)

Alveolar epithelium

Surfactant and tissue fluid

Capillary endothelium

Respiratory membrane

Basement membrane of capillary endothelium

Figure 15–5 The respiratory membrane: the structures and substances through which gases must pass as they diffuse from air to blood (oxygen) or from blood to air (CO₂).

Box 15–2   HYALINE MEMBRANE DISEASE

Hyaline membrane disease is also called Respiratory Distress Syndrome (RDS) of the Newborn, and most often affects premature infants whose lungs have not yet produced sufficient quantities of pulmonary surfactant.

The first few breaths of a newborn inflate most of the previously collapsed lungs, and the presence of surfactant permits the alveoli to remain open. The following breaths become much easier, and normal breathing is established.

Without surfactant, the surface tension of the tissue fluid lining the alveoli causes the air sacs to collapse after each breath rather than remain inflated. Each breath, therefore, is difficult, and the newborn must expend a great deal of energy just to breathe.

Premature infants may require respiratory assistance until their lungs are mature enough to produce surfactant. Recent clinical trials of a synthetic surfactant have shown that some infants are helped significantly, and because they can breathe more normally, their dependence on respirators is minimized. Still undergoing evaluation are the effects of the long-term use of this surfactant in the most premature babies, who may require it for much longer periods of time.

MECHANISM OF BREATHING

Ventilation is the term for the movement of air to and from the alveoli. The two aspects of ventilation are inhalation and exhalation, which are brought about by the nervous system and the respiratory muscles. The respiratory centers are located in the medulla and pons. Their specific functions will be covered in a later section, but it is the medulla that generates impulses to the respiratory muscles.

These muscles are the diaphragm and the external and internal intercostal muscles (Fig. 15–6). The **diaphragm** is a dome-shaped muscle below the lungs; when it contracts, the diaphragm flattens and moves downward. The intercostal muscles are found between the ribs. The **external intercostal muscles** pull the ribs upward and outward, and the **internal intercostal muscles** pull the ribs downward and inward. Ventilation is the result of the respiratory muscles producing changes in the pressure within the alveoli and bronchial tree.

With respect to breathing, the important pressures are these three:

1. **Atmospheric Pressure**—the pressure of the air around us. At sea level, atmospheric pressure is 760 mmHg. At higher altitudes, of course, atmospheric pressure is lower.

2. **Intrapleural Pressure**—the pressure within the potential pleural space between the parietal pleura and visceral pleura. This is a potential rather than a real space. A thin layer of serous fluid causes the two pleural membranes to adhere to one another. Intrapleural pressure is always slightly below atmospheric pressure (about 756 mmHg). This is called a "negative" pressure because the elastic lungs are always tending to collapse and pull the visceral pleura away from the parietal pleura. The serous fluid, however, prevents separation of the pleural membranes (see Box 15–3: Pneumothorax).

3. **Intrapulmonic Pressure**—the pressure within the bronchial tree and alveoli. This pressure fluctuates below and above atmospheric pressure during each cycle of breathing.

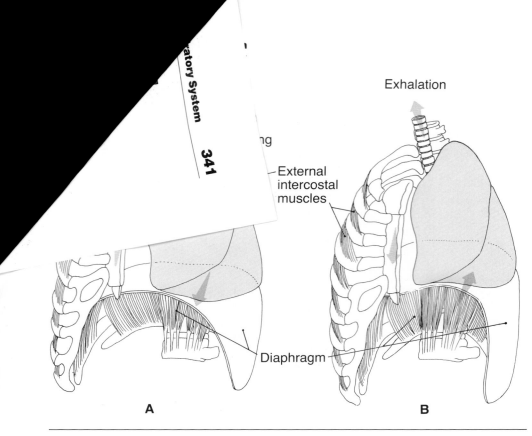

Exhalation

External
intercostal
muscles

ng

Diaphragm

A

B

Figure 15–6   Actions of the respiratory muscles. **(A)**, Inhalation: diaphragm contracts downward; external intercostal muscles pull rib cage upward and outward; lungs are expanded. **(B)**, Normal exhalation: diaphragm relaxes upward; rib cage falls down and in as external intercostal muscles relax; lungs are compressed.

Box 15–3   PNEUMOTHORAX

Pneumothorax is the presence of air in the pleural space, which causes collapse of the lung on that side. Recall that the pleural space is only a potential space because the serous fluid keeps the pleural membranes adhering to one another, and the intrapleural pressure is always slightly below atmospheric pressure. Should air at atmospheric pressure enter the pleural cavity, the suddenly higher pressure outside the lung will contribute to its collapse (the other factor is the normal elasticity of the lungs).

A spontaneous pneumothorax, without apparent trauma, may result from rupture of weakened alveoli on the lung surface. Pulmonary diseases such as emphysema may weaken alveoli.

Puncture wounds of the chest wall also allow air into the pleural space, with resulting collapse of a lung. In severe cases, large amounts of air push the heart, great vessels, trachea, and esophagus toward the opposite side (mediastinal shift), putting pressure on the other lung and making breathing difficult. This is called tension pneumothorax, and requires rapid medical intervention to remove the trapped air.

INHALATION

Inhalation, also called **inspiration,** is a precise sequence of events that may be described as follows:

Motor impulses from the medulla travel along the **phrenic nerves** to the diaphragm and along the **intercostal nerves** to the external intercostal muscles. The diaphragm contracts, moves downward, and expands the chest cavity from top to bottom. The external intercostal muscles pull the ribs up and out, which expands the chest cavity from side to side and front to back.

As the chest cavity is expanded, the parietal pleura expands with it. Intrapleural pressure becomes even more negative as a sort of suction is created between the pleural membranes. The adhesion created by the serous fluid, however, permits the visceral pleura to be expanded too, and this expands the lungs as well.

As the lungs expand, intrapulmonic pressure falls below atmospheric pressure, and air enters the nose and travels through the respiratory passages to the alveoli. Entry of air continues until intrapulmonic pressure is equal to atmospheric pressure; this is a normal inhalation. Of course, inhalation can be continued beyond normal, that is, a deep breath.

This requires a more forceful con piratory muscles to further expand mitting the entry of more air.

EXHALATION

Exhalation may also be called **expiration** and begins when motor impulses from the medulla decrease, and the diaphragm and external intercostal muscles relax. As the chest cavity becomes smaller, the lungs are compressed, and their elastic connective tissue, which was stretched during inhalation, recoils and also compresses the alveoli. As intrapulmonic pressure rises above atmospheric pressure, air is forced out of the lungs until the two pressures are again equal.

Notice that inhalation is an active process that requires muscle contraction, but normal exhalation is a passive process, depending to a great extent on the normal elasticity of healthy lungs. In other words, under normal circumstances we must expend energy to inhale but not to exhale (see Box 15–4: Emphysema).

We can, however, go beyond a normal exhalation and expel more air, as when talking, singing,

---

Box 15–4 EMPHYSEMA

Emphysema is a degenerative disease in which the alveoli lose their elasticity and cannot recoil. Perhaps the most common (and avoidable) cause is cigarette smoking; other causes are long-term exposure to severe air pollution or industrial dusts, or chronic asthma. Inhaled irritants damage the alveolar walls and cause deterioration of the elastic connective tissue surrounding the alveoli. As the alveoli break down, larger air cavities are created that are not efficient in gas exchange.

In progressive emphysema, damaged lung tissue is replaced by fibrous connective tissue (scar tissue), which further limits the diffusion of gases. Blood oxygen level decreases, and blood carbon dioxide level increases. Accumulating carbon dioxide decreases the pH of body fluids; this is a respiratory acidosis.

One of the most characteristic signs of emphysema is that the affected person must make an effort to exhale. The loss of lung elasticity makes normal exhalation an active process, rather than the passive process it usually is. The person must expend energy to exhale in order to make room in the lungs for inhaled air. This extra "work" required for exhalation may be exhausting for the person and contribute to the debilitating nature of emphysema.

...raction of the res-
... the lungs, per-

...NEUVER

...eceived much well-deserved publicity in recent
...g technique.
...gn object (such as food) lodged in the pharynx or
...utilized to remove the object. The physiology of

...uver stands behind the choking victim and puts
... One hand forms a fist that is placed between
...(below the diaphragm), and the other hand covers the
...ant to place hands correctly, in order to avoid breaking the victim's ribs. With both hands, a quick, forceful upward thrust is made and repeated if necessary. This forces the diaphragm upward to compress the lungs and force air out. The forcefully expelled air is often sufficient to dislodge the foreign object.

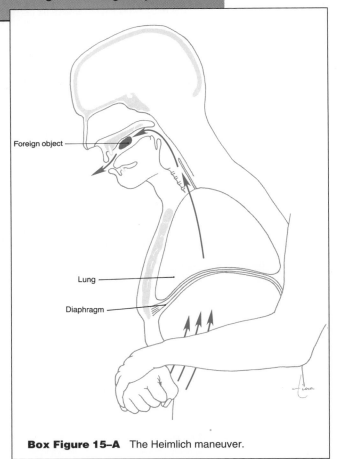

Box Figure 15–A The Heimlich maneuver.

or blowing up a balloon. Such a forced exhalation is an active process that requires contraction of other muscles. Contraction of the internal intercostal muscles pulls the ribs down and in and squeezes even more air out of the lungs. Contraction of abdominal muscles, such as the rectus abdominus, compresses the abdominal organs and pushes the diaphragm upward, which also forces more air out of the lungs (see Box 15–5: The Heimlich Maneuver).

EXCHANGE OF GASES

There are two sites of exchange of oxygen and carbon dioxide: the lungs and the tissues of the body. The exchange of gases between the air in the alveoli and the blood in the pulmonary capillaries is called **external respiration.** This term may be a bit confusing at first, because we often think of "external" as being outside the body. In this case, however, "external" means the exchange that involves air from the external environment. **Internal respiration** is the exchange of gases between the blood in the systemic capillaries and the tissue fluid (cells) of the body.

The air we inhale (the earth's atmosphere) is approximately 21% oxygen and 0.04% carbon dioxide. Although most (78%) of the atmosphere is nitrogen, this gas is not physiologically available to us, and we simply exhale it. This exhaled air also contains about 16% oxygen and 4.5% carbon dioxide, so it is apparent that some oxygen is retained within the body, and the carbon dioxide produced by cells is exhaled.

DIFFUSION OF GASES— PARTIAL PRESSURES

Within the body, a gas will diffuse from an area of greater concentration to an area of lesser concentration. The concentration of each gas in a particular site (alveolar air, pulmonary blood, and so on) is expressed in a value called **partial pressure.** The partial pressure of a gas, measured in mmHg, is the pressure it exerts within a mixture of gases,

whether the mixture is actually in a or is in a liquid such as blood. The pa of oxygen and carbon dioxide in the and in the sites of exchange in the body in Table 15–1. The abbreviation for partial is "P," which is used, for example, on hospi slips for blood gases and will be used here.

The partial pressures of oxygen and carbon oxide at the sites of external respiration (lungs) and internal respiration (body) are shown in Fig. 15–7. Since partial pressure reflects concentration, a gas will diffuse from an area of higher partial pressure to an area of lower partial pressure.

The air in the alveoli has a high P_{O_2} and a low P_{CO_2}. The blood in the pulmonary capillaries, which has just come from the body, has a low P_{O_2} and a high P_{CO_2}. Therefore, in external respiration, oxygen diffuses from the air in the alveoli to the blood, and carbon dioxide diffuses from the blood to the air in the alveoli. The blood that returns to the heart now has a high P_{O_2} and a low P_{CO_2} and is pumped by the left ventricle into systemic circulation.

The arterial blood that reaches systemic capillar-

Table 15–1 PARTIAL PRESSURES

Site	P_{O_2} (mmHg)	P_{CO_2} (mmHg)
Atmosphere	160	0.15
Alveolar air	104	40
Pulmonary blood (venous)	40	45
Systemic blood (arterial)	100	40
Tissue fluid	40	50

Partial pressure is calculated as follows:
% of the gas in the mixture × total pressure = Pgas

Example: **O_2 in the atmosphere**
21% × 760 mmHg = 160 mmHg (P_{O_2})
Example: **CO_2 in the atmosphere**
0.04% × 760 mmHg = 0.15 mmHg (P_{CO_2})

Notice that alveolar partial pressures are not exactly those of the atmosphere. Alveolar air contains significant amounts of water vapor and the CO_2 diffusing in from the blood. Oxygen also diffuses readily from the alveoli into the pulmonary capillaries. Therefore, alveolar P_{O_2} is lower than atmospheric P_{O_2}, and alveolar P_{CO_2} is significantly higher than atmospheric P_{CO_2}.

ry System

em

345

gaseous state
tial pressures
atmosphere
are listed
pressure
al lab
di-

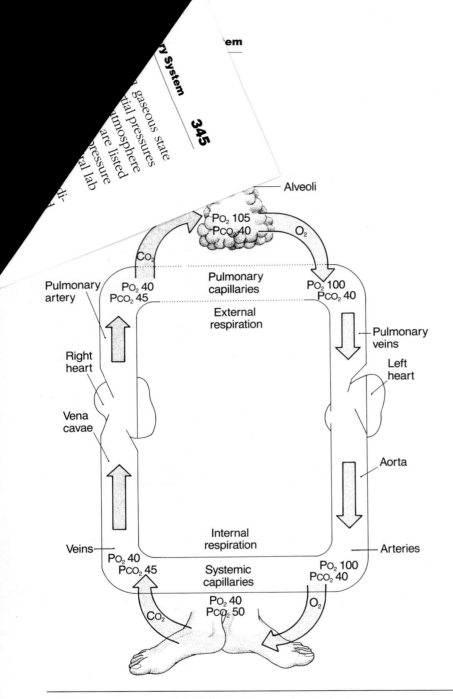

Alveoli

PO$_2$ 105
PCO$_2$ 40   O$_2$

CO$_2$

Pulmonary
artery

PO$_2$ 40   Pulmonary
PCO$_2$ 45   capillaries   PO$_2$ 100
PCO$_2$ 40

External
respiration

Pulmonary
veins

Right
heart

Left
heart

Vena
cavae

Aorta

Internal
respiration

Veins   Arteries

PO$_2$ 40
PCO$_2$ 45   Systemic   PO$_2$ 100
capillaries   PCO$_2$ 40

PO$_2$ 40
PCO$_2$ 50

CO$_2$ O$_2$

Figure 15–7 External respiration in the lungs and internal respiration in the body. The partial pressures of oxygen and carbon dioxide are shown at each site.

Box 15–6   PULMONARY EDEMA

Pulmonary edema is the accumulation of fluid in the alveoli. This is often a consequence of congestive heart failure in which the left side of the heart (or the entire heart) is not pumping efficiently. If the left ventricle does not pump strongly, the chamber does not empty as it should and cannot receive all the blood flowing in from the left atrium. Blood flow, therefore, is "congested," and blood backs up in the pulmonary veins and then in the pulmonary capillaries. As blood pressure increases in the pulmonary capillaries, filtration creates tissue fluid that collects in the alveoli.

Fluid-filled alveoli are no longer sites of efficient gas exchange, and the resulting hypoxia leads to the symptoms of **dyspnea** and increased respiratory rate. The most effective treatment is that which restores the pumping ability of the heart to normal.

---

ies has a high P_{O_2} and a low P_{CO_2}. The body cells and tissue fluid have a low P_{O_2} and a high P_{CO_2} because cells continuously use oxygen in cell respiration (energy production) and produce carbon dioxide in this process. Therefore, in internal respiration, oxygen diffuses from the blood to tissue fluid (cells), and carbon dioxide diffuses from tissue fluid to the blood. The blood that enters systemic veins to return to the heart now has a low P_{O_2} and a high P_{CO_2} and is pumped by the right ventricle to the lungs to participate in external respiration.

Disorders of gas exchange often involve the lungs, that is, external respiration (see Box 15–6: Pulmonary Edema and Box 15–7: Pneumonia).

Box 15–7   PNEUMONIA

Pneumonia is a bacterial infection of the lungs. Although there are many bacteria that can cause pneumonia, the most common one is probably *Streptococcus pneumoniae.* This species is estimated to cause at least 500,000 cases of pneumonia every year in the United States, with 50,000 deaths.

S. pneumoniae is a transient inhabitant of the upper respiratory tract, but in otherwise healthy people, the ciliated epithelium and the immune system prevent infection. Most cases of pneumonia occur in elderly people following a primary infection such as influenza.

When the bacteria are able to establish themselves in the alveoli, the alveolar cells secrete fluid that accumulates in the air sacs. Many neutrophils migrate to the site of infection and attempt to phagocytize the bacteria. The alveoli become filled with fluid, bacteria, and neutrophils (this is called consolidation); this decreases the exchange of gases.

Pneumovax is a vaccine for this type of pneumonia. It contains only the capsules of *S. pneumoniae* and cannot cause the disease. This vaccine is recommended for people over the age of 60 years, and for those with chronic pulmonary disorders or any debilitating disease.

TRANSPORT OF GASES IN THE BLOOD

As you already know, most oxygen is carried in the blood bonded to the **hemoglobin** in red blood cells (although some oxygen is dissolved in blood plasma, it is not enough to sustain life). The mineral iron is part of hemoglobin and gives this important protein its oxygen-carrying ability.

The oxygen-hemoglobin bond is formed in the lungs where Po_2 is high. This bond, however, is relatively unstable, and when blood passes through tissues with a low Po_2, the bond breaks, and oxygen is released to the tissues. The lower the oxygen concentration in a tissue, the more oxygen hemoglobin will release. This ensures that active tissues, such as exercising muscles, receive as much oxygen as possible to continue cell respiration. Other factors that increase the release of oxygen from hemoglobin are a high Pco_2 (actually a lower pH) and a high temperature, both of which are also characteristic of active tissues (see Box 15–8: Carbon Monoxide).

Carbon dioxide transport is a little more complicated. Some carbon dioxide is dissolved in the plasma, and some is carried by hemoglobin (carbaminohemoglobin), but these account for only 10% to 30% of total CO_2 transport. Most carbon dioxide is carried in the plasma in the form of bicarbonate ions (HCO_3^-). Let us look at the reactions that transform CO_2 into a bicarbonate ion.

When carbon dioxide enters the blood, most diffuses into red blood cells, which contain the enzyme **carbonic anhydrase.** This enzyme (which contains zinc) catalyzes the reaction of carbon dioxide and water to form carbonic acid:

$$CO_2 + H_2O \rightarrow H_2CO_3.$$

The carbonic acid then dissociates:

$$H_2CO_3 \rightarrow H^+ + HCO_3^-$$

The bicarbonate ions diffuse out of the red blood cells into the plasma, leaving the hydrogen ions (H^+) in the red blood cells. The many H^+ ions would tend to make the red blood cells too acidic, but hemoglobin acts as a buffer to prevent acidosis.

Box 15–8 CARBON MONOXIDE

Carbon monoxide (CO) is a colorless, odorless gas that is produced during the combustion of fuels such as gasoline, coal, oil, and wood. As you know, CO is a poison that may cause death if inhaled in more than very small quantities or for more than a short period of time.

The reason CO is so toxic is that it forms a very strong and stable bond with the hemoglobin in RBCs. Hemoglobin with CO bonded to it cannot bond to and transport oxygen. The effect of CO, therefore, is to drastically decrease the amount of oxygen carried in the blood. As little as 0.1% CO in inhaled air can saturate half the total hemoglobin with CO.

Lack of oxygen is often apparent in people with light skin as **cyanosis,** a bluish cast to the skin, lips, and nail beds. This is because hemoglobin is dark red unless something (usually oxygen) is bonded to it. When hemoglobin bonds to CO, however, it becomes a bright, cherry red. This color may be seen in light skin and may be very misleading; the person with CO poisoning is in a severely hypoxic state.

Although CO is found in cigarette smoke, it is present in such minute quantities that it is not lethal. Heavy smokers, however, may be in a mild but chronic hypoxic state since much of their hemoglobin is firmly bonded to CO. As a compensation, RBC production may increase, and a heavy smoker may have a hematocrit over 50%.

To maintain an ionic equilibrium, chloride ions (Cl^-) from the plasma enter the red blood cells; this is called the chloride shift. Where is the CO_2? In the plasma as part of HCO_3^- ions. When the blood reaches the lungs, an area of lower P_{CO_2}, these reactions are reversed, CO_2 is reformed and diffuses into the alveoli to be exhaled.

PULMONARY VOLUMES

The capacity of the lungs varies with the size and age of the person. Taller people have larger lungs than do shorter people. Also, as we get older our lung capacity diminishes as lungs lose their elasticity and the respiratory muscles become less efficient. For the following pulmonary volumes, the values given are those for healthy young adults. These are also shown in Fig. 15–8.

1. **Tidal Volume**—the amount of air involved in one normal inhalation and exhalation. The average tidal volume is 500 ml, but many people often have lower tidal volumes due to shallow breathing.
2. **Minute Respiratory Volume** (MRV)—the amount of air inhaled and exhaled in 1 minute.

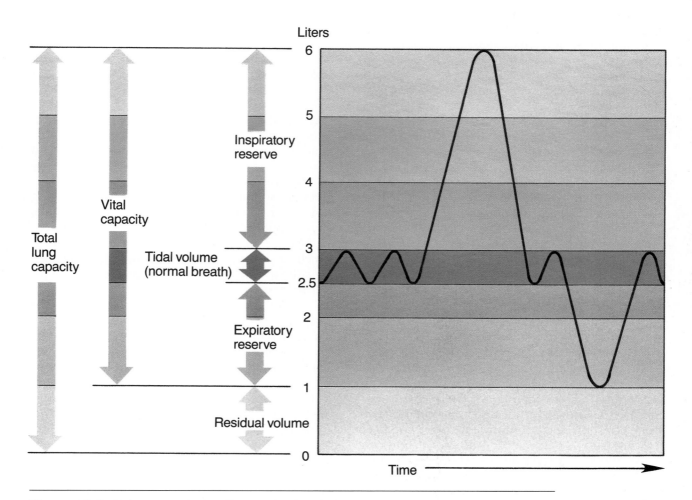

Figure 15–8 Pulmonary volumes. See text for description.

MRV is calculated by multiplying tidal volume by the number of respirations per minute (average range: 12 to 20 per minute). If tidal volume is 500 ml and the respiratory rate is 12 breaths per minute, the MRV is 6000 ml, or 6 liters of air per minute, which is average. Shallow breathing usually indicates a smaller than average tidal volume, and would thus require more respirations per minute to obtain the necessary MRV.

3. **Inspiratory Reserve**—the amount of air, beyond tidal volume, that can be taken in with the deepest possible inhalation. Normal inspiratory reserve ranges from 2000 to 3000 ml.

4. **Expiratory Reserve**—the amount of air, beyond tidal volume, that can be expelled with the most forceful exhalation. Normal expiratory reserve ranges from 1000 to 1500 ml.

5. **Vital Capacity**—the sum of tidal volume, inspiratory reserve, and expiratory reserve. Stated another way, vital capacity is the amount of air involved in the deepest inhalation followed by the most forceful exhalation. Average range of vital capacity is 3500 to 5000 ml.

6. **Residual Air**—the amount of air that remains in the lungs after the most forceful exhalation; the average range is 1000 to 1500 ml. Residual air is important to ensure that there is some air in the lungs at all times, so that exchange of gases is a continuous process, even between breaths.

Some of the volumes described above can be determined with instruments called spirometers, which measure movement of air. Trained singers and musicians who play wind instruments often have vital capacities much larger than would be expected for their height and age, because their respiratory muscles have become more efficient with "practice." The same is true for athletes who exercise regularly. A person with emphysema, however, must "work" to exhale, and vital capacity and expiratory reserve volume are often much lower than average.

REGULATION OF RESPIRATION

There are two types of mechanisms that regulate breathing: nervous mechanisms and chemical mechanisms. Since any changes in the rate or depth of breathing are ultimately brought about by nerve impulses, we will consider nervous mechanisms first.

NERVOUS REGULATION

The respiratory centers are located in the **medulla** and **pons,** which are parts of the brain stem. Within the medulla are the inspiration center and expiration center; each generates impulses in spurts or bursts. These two centers function on the principle of reciprocal inhibition, which means that when one center becomes active, it depresses the other.

When the **inspiration center** generates impulses, some of them travel along nerves to the respiratory muscles to stimulate their contraction, and some of these impulses depress the expiration center. The result is inhalation. As the lungs inflate, baroreceptors in lung tissue detect this stretching and generate sensory impulses to the medulla; these impulses begin to depress the inspiration center. This is called the Hering-Breuer inflation reflex, which helps prevent overinflation of the lungs.

As the inspiration center is depressed, the **expiration center** becomes more active, and its impulses further depress the inspiration center. The result is a decrease in impulses to the respiratory muscles, which relax to bring about exhalation. Then the inspiration center becomes more active again to begin another cycle of breathing.

The two respiratory centers in the pons work with the medullary centers to produce a normal rhythm of breathing. The **apneustic center** prolongs inhalation, and is then interrupted by impulses from the **pneumotaxic center,** which contributes to exhalation. In normal breathing, inhalation lasts 1 to 2 seconds, followed by a slightly longer (2 to 3 seconds) exhalation, producing the normal range of respiratory rate of 12 to 20 breaths per minute.

What has just been described is normal breathing, but variations are possible and quite common. Emotions often affect respiration; a sudden fright may bring about a gasp or a scream, and anger usually increases the respiratory rate. In these situations, impulses from the **hypothalamus** modify the output from the medulla. The **cerebral cortex** enables us to voluntarily change our breathing rate or rhythm to talk, sing, breathe faster or slower, or even to stop breathing for 1 or 2 minutes. Such changes cannot be continued indefinitely, however, and the medulla will eventually resume control.

Coughing and **sneezing** are reflexes that remove irritants from the respiratory passages; the medulla contains the centers for both of these reflexes. Sneezing is stimulated by an irritation of the nasal mucosa, and coughing is stimulated by irritation of the mucosa of the pharynx, larynx, or trachea. The reflex action is essentially the same for both: an inhalation is followed by exhalation beginning with the glottis closed to build up pressure. Then the glottis opens suddenly, and the exhalation is explosive. A cough directs the exhalation out the mouth, while a sneeze directs the exhalation out the nose.

Yet another respiratory reflex is yawning. Most of us yawn when we are tired, but the stimulus for and purpose of yawning are not known with certainty. There are several possibilities, such as lack of oxygen or accumulation of carbon dioxide, but we really do not know. Nor do we know why yawning is contagious, but seeing someone yawn is almost sure to elicit a yawn of one's own. You may even have yawned while reading this paragraph about yawning!

CHEMICAL REGULATION

Chemical regulation refers to the effect on breathing of blood pH and blood levels of oxygen and carbon dioxide. **Chemoreceptors** that detect changes in blood gases and pH are located in the carotid and aortic bodies and in the medulla itself.

A decrease in the blood level of oxygen (hypoxia) is detected by the chemoreceptors in the **ca-** **rotid** and **aortic bodies.** The sensory impulses generated by these receptors travel along the glossopharyngeal and vagus nerves to the medulla, which responds by increasing respiratory rate or depth (or both). This response will bring more air into the lungs so that more oxygen can diffuse into the blood to correct the hypoxic state.

Carbon dioxide becomes a problem when it is present in excess in the blood, because excess CO_2 lowers the pH when it reacts with water to form carbonic acid (a source of H^+ ions). That is, excess CO_2 makes the blood or other body fluids less alkaline (or more acidic). The **medulla** contains **chemoreceptors** that are very sensitive to changes in pH, especially decreases. If accumulating CO_2 lowers blood pH, the medulla responds by increasing respiration. This is not for the purpose of inhaling, but rather to exhale more CO_2 to raise the pH back to normal.

Of the two respiratory gases, which is the more important as a regulator of respiration? Our guess might be oxygen, because it is essential for energy production in cell respiration. However, the respiratory system can maintain a normal blood level of oxygen even if breathing decreases to half the normal rate or stops for a few moments. Recall that exhaled air is 16% oxygen. This oxygen did not enter the blood but was available to do so if needed. Also, the residual air in the lungs supplies oxygen to the blood even if breathing rate slows.

Therefore, carbon dioxide must be the major regulator of respiration, and the reason is that carbon dioxide affects the pH of the blood. As was just mentioned, an excess of CO_2 causes the blood pH to decrease, a process that must not be allowed to continue. Therefore, any increase in blood CO_2 level is quickly compensated for by increased breathing to exhale more CO_2. If, for example, you hold your breath, what is it that makes you breathe again? Have you run out of oxygen? Probably not, for the reasons mentioned above. What has happened is that accumulating CO_2 has lowered blood pH enough to stimulate the medulla to start the breathing cycle again.

In some situations, oxygen does become the major regulator of respiration. People with severe, chronic pulmonary diseases such as emphysema have decreased exchange of both oxygen and carbon dioxide in the lungs. The decrease in pH caused by accumulating CO_2 is corrected by the kidneys, but the blood oxygen level keeps decreasing. Eventually, the oxygen level may fall so low that it does provide a very strong stimulus to increase the rate and depth of respiration.

RESPIRATION AND ACID-BASE BALANCE

As you have just seen, respiration affects the pH of body fluids because it regulates the amount of carbon dioxide in these fluids. Remember that CO_2 reacts with water to form carbonic acid (H_2CO_3), which ionizes into H^+ ions and HCO_3^- ions. The more hydrogen ions present in a body fluid, the lower the pH, and the fewer hydrogen ions present, the higher the pH.

The respiratory system may be the cause of a pH imbalance, or it may help correct a pH imbalance created by some other cause.

RESPIRATORY ACIDOSIS AND ALKALOSIS

Respiratory acidosis occurs when the rate or efficiency of respiration decreases, permitting carbon dioxide to accumulate in body fluids. The excess CO_2 results in the formation of more H^+ ions, which decrease the pH. Holding one's breath can bring about a mild respiratory acidosis, which will soon stimulate the medulla to initiate breathing again. More serious causes of respiratory acidosis are pulmonary diseases, such as pneumonia and emphysema, or severe asthma. Each of these impairs gas exchange and allows excess CO_2 to remain in body fluids.

Respiratory alkalosis occurs when the rate of respiration increases, and CO_2 is very rapidly exhaled. Less CO_2 decreases H^+ ion formation, which increases the pH. Breathing faster for a few minutes can bring about a mild state of respiratory alkalosis. Babies who cry for extended periods (crying is a noisy exhalation) experience this condition. In general, however, respiratory alkalosis is not a common

occurrence. Certain states of mental and/or emotional anxiety may be accompanied by hyperventilation and also result in respiratory alkalosis. In addition, traveling to a higher altitude (less oxygen in the atmosphere) may cause a temporary increase in breathing rate before compensation occurs (increased rate of RBC production—see Chapter 11).

RESPIRATORY COMPENSATION

If a pH imbalance is caused by something other than a change in respiration, it is called a metabolic acidosis or alkalosis. In either case, the change in pH stimulates a change in respiration that may help restore the pH of body fluids to normal.

Metabolic acidosis may be caused by untreated diabetes mellitus (ketoacidosis), kidney disease, or severe diarrhea. In such situations, the H^+ ion concentration of body fluids is increased. Respiratory compensation involves an increase in the rate and depth of respiration to exhale more CO_2 to decrease H^+ ion formation, which will raise the pH toward the normal range.

Metabolic alkalosis is not a common occurrence but may be caused by ingestion of excessive amounts of alkaline medications such as those used to relieve gastric disturbances. Another possible cause is vomiting of stomach contents only. In such situations, the H^+ ion concentration of body fluids is decreased. Respiratory compensation involves a decrease in respiration to retain CO_2 in the body to increase H^+ ion formation, which will lower the pH toward the normal range.

Respiratory compensation for an ongoing metabolic pH imbalance cannot be complete, because there are limits to the amounts of CO_2 that may be exhaled or retained. At most, respiratory compensation is only about 75% effective. A complete discussion of acid-base balance will be found in Chapter 19.

SUMMARY

As you have learned, respiration is much more than the simple mechanical actions of breathing. Inhalation provides the body with the oxygen that is necessary for the production of ATP in the process of cell respiration. Exhalation removes the CO_2 that is a product of cell respiration. Breathing also regulates the level of CO_2 within the body, and this contributes to the maintenance of the acid-base balance of body fluids. Although the respiratory gases do not form structural components of the body, their role in the chemical level of organization is essential to the functioning of the body at every level.

STUDY OUTLINE

The respiratory system moves air into and out of the lungs, which are the site of exchange for O_2 and CO_2 between the air and the blood. The functioning of the respiratory system is directly dependent on the proper functioning of the circulatory system.

1. The upper respiratory tract consists of those parts outside the chest cavity.
2. The lower respiratory tract consists of those parts within the chest cavity.

Nose—made of bone and cartilage covered with skin

1. Hairs inside the nostrils block the entry of dust.

Nasal Cavities—within the skull; separated by the nasal septum (see Fig. 15–1)

1. Nasal mucosa is ciliated epithelium with goblet cells; surface area is increased by the conchae.
2. Nasal mucosa warms and moistens the incoming air; dust and microorganisms are trapped on mucus and swept by the cilia to the pharynx.
3. Olfactory receptors respond to vapors in inhaled air.
4. Paranasal sinuses in the maxillae, frontal, sphenoid, and ethmoid bones open into the nasal cavities: functions are to lighten the skull and provide resonance for the voice.

Pharynx—posterior to nasal and oral cavities (see Fig. 15–1)

1. Nasopharynx—above the level of the soft palate, which blocks it during swallowing; a passageway for air only. The eustachian tubes from the middle ears open into it. The adenoid is a lymph nodule on the posterior wall.

2. Oropharynx—behind the mouth; a passageway for both air and food. Palatine tonsils are on the lateral walls.
3. Laryngopharynx—a passageway for both air and food; opens anteriorly into the larynx and posteriorly into the esophagus.

Larynx—the voice box and the airway between the pharynx and trachea (see Fig. 15–2)

1. Made of nine cartilages; the thyroid cartilage is the largest and most anterior.
2. The epiglottis is the uppermost cartilage; covers the larynx during swallowing.
3. The vocal cords are lateral to the glottis, the opening for air (see Fig. 15–3).
4. During speaking, the vocal cords are pulled across the glottis and vibrated by exhaled air, producing sounds which may be turned into speech.
5. The cranial nerves for speaking are the vagus and accessory.

Trachea—extends from the larynx to the primary bronchi (see Fig. 15–4)

1. 16 to 20 C-shaped cartilages in the tracheal wall keep the trachea open.
2. Mucosa is ciliated epithelium with goblet cells; cilia sweep mucus, trapped dust, and microorganisms upward to the pharynx.

Bronchial Tree—extends from the trachea to the alveoli (see Fig. 15–4)

1. The right and left primary bronchi are branches of the trachea; one to each lung.
2. Secondary bronchi: to the lobes of each lung (three right, two left)
3. Bronchioles—no cartilage in their walls.

Pleural Membranes—serous membranes of the thoracic cavity
1. Parietal pleura lines the chest wall.
2. Visceral pleura covers the lungs.
3. Serous fluid between the two layers prevents friction and keeps the membranes together during breathing.

Lungs—on either side of the heart in the chest cavity; extend from the diaphragm below up to the level of the clavicles
1. The rib cage protects the lungs from mechanical injury.
2. Hilus—indentation on the medial side: primary bronchus and pulmonary artery and veins enter (also bronchial vessels).

Alveoli—the sites of gas exchange in the lungs
1. Made of simple squamous epithelium; thin to permit diffusion of gases.
2. Surrounded by pulmonary capillaries, which are also made of simple squamous epithelium (see Fig. 15–4).
3. Elastic connective tissue between alveoli is important for normal exhalation.
4. A thin layer of tissue fluid lines each alveolus; essential to permit diffusion of gases (see Fig. 15–5).
5. Pulmonary surfactant mixes with the tissue fluid lining to decrease surface tension to permit inflation of the alveoli.

Mechanism of Breathing
1. Ventilation is the movement of air into and out of the lungs: inhalation and exhalation.
2. Respiratory centers are in the medulla and pons.
3. Respiratory muscles are the diaphragm and external and internal intercostal muscles (see Fig. 15–6).
   - Atmospheric pressure is air pressure: 760 mmHg at sea level.
   - Intrapleural pressure is within the potential pleural space; always slightly below atmospheric pressure ("negative").
   - Intrapulmonic pressure is within the bronchial tree and alveoli; fluctuates during breathing.

Inhalation (inspiration)
1. Motor impulses from medulla travel along phrenic nerves to diaphragm, which contracts and moves down. Impulses along intercostal nerves to external intercostal muscles, which pull ribs up and out.
2. The chest cavity is expanded and expands the parietal pleura.
3. The visceral pleura adheres to the parietal pleura and is also expanded and in turn expands the lungs.
4. Intrapulmonic pressure decreases, and air rushes into the lungs.

Exhalation (expiration)
1. Motor impulses from the medulla decrease, and the diaphragm and external intercostals relax.
2. The chest cavity becomes smaller and compresses the lungs.
3. The elastic lungs recoil and further compress the alveoli.
4. Intrapulmonic pressure increases, and air is forced out of the lungs.
5. Forced exhalation: contraction of the internal intercostal muscles pulls the ribs down and in; contraction of the abdominal muscles forces the diaphragm upward.

Exchange of Gases
1. External respiration is the exchange of gases between the air in the alveoli and the blood in the pulmonary capillaries.
2. Internal respiration is the exchange of gases between blood in the systemic capillaries and tissue fluid (cells).
3. Inhaled air (atmosphere) is 21% O_2 and 0.04% CO_2. Exhaled air is 16% O_2 and 4.5% CO_2.
4. Diffusion of O_2 and CO_2 in the body occurs because of pressure gradients (see Table 15–1). A gas will diffuse from an area of higher partial pressure to an area of lower partial pressure.
5. External respiration: Po_2 in the alveoli is high, and Po_2 in the pulmonary capillaries is low, so O_2 diffuses from the air to the blood. Pco_2 in the alveoli is low, and Pco_2 in the pulmonary capillaries is high, so CO_2 diffuses from the blood to the air and is exhaled (see Fig. 15–7).

6. Internal respiration: P_{O_2} in the systemic capillaries is high, and P_{O_2} in the tissue fluid is low, so O_2 diffuses from the blood to the tissue fluid and cells. P_{CO_2} in the systemic capillaries is low, and P_{CO_2} in the tissue fluid is high, so CO_2 diffuses from the tissue fluid to the blood (see Fig. 15–7).

Transport of Gases in the Blood

1. Oxygen is carried by the iron of hemoglobin (Hb) in the RBCs. The O_2-Hb bond is formed in the lungs where the P_{O_2} is high.
2. In tissues, Hb releases much of its O_2; the important factors are low P_{O_2} in tissues, high P_{CO_2} in tissues, and a high temperature in tissues.
3. Most CO_2 is carried as HCO_3^- ions in blood plasma. CO_2 enters the RBCs and reacts with H_2O to form carbonic acid (H_2CO_3). Carbonic anhydrase is the enzyme that catalyzes this reaction. H_2CO_3 dissociates to H^+ ions and HCO_3^- ions. The HCO_3^- ions leave the RBCs and enter the plasma; Hb buffers the H^+ ions that remain in the RBCs. Cl^- ions from the plasma enter the RBCs to maintain ionic equilibrium (the chloride shift).
4. When blood reaches the lungs, CO_2 is reformed, diffuses into the alveoli, and is exhaled.

Pulmonary Volumes (see Fig. 15–8)

1. Tidal volume—the amount of air in one normal inhalation and exhalation.
2. Minute Respiratory Volume—the amount of air inhaled and exhaled in 1 minute.
3. Inspiratory Reserve—the amount of air beyond tidal in a maximal inhalation.
4. Expiratory Reserve—the amount of air beyond tidal in the most forceful exhalation.
5. Vital Capacity—the sum of tidal volume, inspiratory and expiratory reserves.
6. Residual volume—the amount of air that remains in the lungs after the most forceful exhalation; provides for continuous exchange of gases.

Nervous Regulation of Respiration

1. The medulla contains the inspiration center and expiration center, which work on the principle of reciprocal inhibition.

2. Impulses from the inspiration center to the respiratory muscles cause their contraction; the chest cavity is expanded.
3. Baroreceptors in lung tissue detect stretching and send impulses to the medulla to depress the inspiration center. This is the Hering-Breuer inflation reflex, which prevents overinflation of the lungs.
4. The expiration center becomes more active and depresses the inspiration center, which decreases impulses to the respiratory muscles, which relax and bring about exhalation.
5. In the pons: the apneustic center prolongs inhalation, and the pneumotaxic center helps bring about exhalation. These centers work with those in the medulla to produce a normal breathing rhythm.
6. The hypothalamus influences changes in breathing in emotional situations. The cerebral cortex permits voluntary changes in breathing.
7. Coughing and sneezing remove irritants from the upper respiratory tract; the centers for these reflexes are in the medulla.

Chemical Regulation of Respiration

1. Decreased blood O_2 is detected by chemoreceptors in the carotid body and aortic body. Response: increased respiration to take more air into the lungs.
2. Increased blood CO_2 level is detected by chemoreceptors in the medulla. Response: increased respiration to exhale more CO_2.
3. CO_2 is the major regulator of respiration because excess CO_2 decreases the pH of body fluids ($CO_2 + H_2O \rightarrow H_2CO_3 \rightarrow H^+ + HCO_3$ . . . and excess H^+ ions lower pH).
4. Oxygen becomes a major regulator of respiration when blood level is very low, as may occur with severe, chronic pulmonary disease.

Respiration and Acid-Base Balance

1. Respiratory acidosis: a decrease in the rate or efficiency of respiration permits excess CO_2 to accumulate in body fluids, resulting in the formation of excess H^+ ions, which lower pH. Occurs in severe pulmonary disease.
2. Respiratory alkalosis: an increase in the rate of

respiration increases the CO_2 exhaled, which decreases the formation of H^+ ions and raises pH. Occurs during hyperventilation or when first at a high altitude.

3. Respiratory compensation for metabolic acidosis: increased respiration to exhale CO_2 to decrease H^+ ion formation to raise pH to normal.

4. Respiratory compensation for metabolic alkalosis: decreased respiration to retain CO_2 to increase H^+ ion formation to lower pH to normal.

REVIEW QUESTIONS

1. State the three functions of the nasal mucosa. (p. 334)

2. Name the three parts of the pharynx; state whether each is an air passage only or an air and food passage. (pp. 334, 336)

3. Name the tissue that lines the larynx and trachea, and describe its function. State the function of the cartilage of the larynx and trachea. (pp. 336–337)

4. Name the pleural membranes, state the location of each, and describe the functions of serous fluid. (p. 339)

5. Name the tissue of which the alveoli and pulmonary capillaries are made, and explain the importance of this tissue in these locations. Explain the function of pulmonary surfactant. (p. 339)

6. Name the respiratory muscles, and describe how they are involved in normal inhalation and exhalation. Define these pressures and relate them to a cycle of breathing: atmospheric pressure, intrapulmonic pressure. (pp. 341, 343)

7. Describe external respiration in terms of partial pressures of oxygen and carbon dioxide. (p. 345)

8. Describe internal respiration in terms of partial pressures of oxygen and carbon dioxide. (pp. 345, 347)

9. Name the cell, protein, and mineral that transport oxygen in the blood. State the three factors that increase the release of oxygen in tissues. (p. 348)

10. Most carbon dioxide is transported in what part of the blood, and in what form? Explain the function of hemoglobin with respect to carbon dioxide transport. (p. 348)

11. Name the respiratory centers in the medulla and pons, and explain how each is involved in a breathing cycle. (p. 350)

12. State the location of chemoreceptors affected by a low blood oxygen level; describe the body's response to hypoxia and its purpose. State the location of chemoreceptors affected by a high blood CO_2 level; describe the body's response and its purpose. (p. 351)

13. For respiratory acidosis and alkalosis: state a cause and explain what happens to the pH of body fluids. (p. 352)

14. Explain how the respiratory system may compensate for metabolic acidosis or alkalosis. For an ongoing pH imbalance, what is the limit of respiratory compensation? (p. 352)

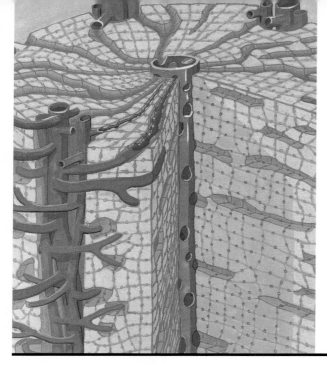

Chapter 16

Chapter Outline

Student Objectives

- Describe the general functions of the digestive system, and name its major divisions.
- Explain the difference between mechanical and chemical digestion, and name the end products of digestion.
- Describe the structure and functions of the teeth and tongue.
- Explain the functions of saliva.
- Describe the location and function of the pharynx and esophagus.
- Describe the structure and function of each of the four layers of the alimentary tube.
- Describe the location, structure, and function of the stomach, liver, gallbladder, pancreas, and small intestine.
- Describe absorption in the small intestine.
- Describe the location and functions of the large intestine.
- Explain the functions of the normal flora of the colon.
- Describe the functions of the liver.

The Digestive System

New Terminology

Alimentary tube (AL–i–**MEN**–tah–ree TOOB)
Chemical digestion (**KEM**–i–kuhl dye–**JES**–chun)
Common bile duct (**KOM**–mon BYL DUKT)
Defecation reflex (DEF–e–**KAY**–shun)
Duodenum (dew–**AH**–den–um)
Emulsify (e–**MULL**–si–fye)
Enamel (e–**NAM**–uhl)
Essential amino acids (e–**SEN**–shul ah–**ME**–noh **ASS**–ids)
External anal sphincter (eks–**TER**–nuhl **AY**–nuhl **SFINK**–ter)
Ileocecal valve (ILL–ee–oh–**SEE**–kuhl VALV)
Internal anal sphincter (in–**TER**–nuhl **AY**–nuhl **SFINK**–ter)
Lower esophageal sphincter (e–SOF–uh–**JEE**–uhl **SFINK**–ter)
Mechanical digestion (muh–**KAN**–i–kuhl dye–**JES**–chun)

Non-essential amino acids (NON e–**SEN**–shul ah–**ME**–noh **ASS**–ids)
Normal flora (**NOR**–muhl **FLOOR**–ah)
Periodontal membrane (PER–ee–oh–**DON**–tal)
Pyloric sphincter (pye–**LOR**–ik **SFINK**–ter)
Rugae (**ROO**–gay)
Villi (**VILL**–eye)

Related Clinical Terminology

Appendicitis (uh–PEN–di–**SIGH**–tis)
Diverticulitis (DYE–ver–TIK–yoo–**LYE**–tis)
Gastric ulcer (**GAS**–trik **UL**–ser)
Hepatitis (HEP–uh–**TIGH**–tis)
Lactose intolerance (**LAK**–tohs in–**TAHL**–er–ense)
Lithotripsy (LITH–oh–**TRIP**–see)
Paralytic ileus (**PAR**–uh–LIT–ik **ILL**–ee–us)
Peritonitis (per–i–toh–**NIGH**–tis)
Pyloric stenosis (pye–**LOR**–ik ste–**NOH**–sis)

Terms that appear in **bold type** in the chapter text are defined in the glossary, which begins on page 549.

A hurried breakfast when you are late for work or school . . . Thanksgiving dinner . . . going on a diet to lose 5 pounds . . . what do these experiences all have in common? Food. We may take food for granted, celebrate with it, or wish we wouldn't eat quite so much of it. Although food is not as immediate a need for human beings as is oxygen, it is a very important part of our lives. Food provides the raw materials or nutrients that cells use to reproduce and to build new tissue. The energy needed for cell reproduction and tissue building is released from food in the process of cell respiration. In fact, a supply of nutrients from regular food intake is so important, that the body can even store any excess for use later. Those "extra 5 pounds" are often stored fat in adipose tissue.

The food we eat, however, is not in a form that our body cells can use. A turkey sandwich, for example, consists of complex proteins, fats, and carbohydrates. The function of the **digestive system** is to change these complex organic nutrient molecules into simple organic and inorganic molecules that can then be absorbed into the blood or lymph to be transported to cells. In this chapter we will discuss the organs of digestion and the contribution each makes to digestion and absorption.

DIVISIONS OF THE DIGESTIVE SYSTEM

The two divisions of the digestive system are the alimentary tube and the accessory organs (Fig. 16–1). The **alimentary tube** extends from the mouth to the anus. It consists of the oral cavity, pharynx, esophagus, stomach, small intestine, and large intestine. Digestion takes place within the oral cavity, stomach, and small intestine; most absorption of nutrients takes place in the small intestine. Undigestable material, primarily cellulose, is eliminated by the large intestine (also called the colon).

The **accessory organs** of digestion are the teeth, tongue, salivary glands, liver, gallbladder, and pancreas. Digestion does not take place *within* these organs, but each contributes something *to* the digestive process.

TYPES OF DIGESTION

The food we eat is broken down in two complementary processes: mechanical digestion and chemical digestion. **Mechanical digestion** is the physical breaking up of food into smaller pieces. Chewing is an example of this. As food is broken up, more of its surface area is exposed for the action of digestive enzymes. Enzymes are discussed in Chapter 2. The work of the digestive enzymes is the **chemical digestion** of broken up food particles, in which complex chemical molecules are changed into much simpler chemicals that the body can utilize. Such enzymes are specific with respect to the fat, protein, or carbohydrate food molecules each can digest. For example, protein-digesting enzymes work only on proteins, not on carbohydrates or fats. Each enzyme is produced by a particular digestive organ and functions at a specific site. However, the enzyme's site of action may or may not be its site of production. These digestive enzymes and their functions will be discussed in later sections.

END PRODUCTS OF DIGESTION

Before we describe the actual organs of digestion, let us see where the process of digestion will take us, or rather, will take our food. The three types of complex organic molecules found in food are carbohydrates, proteins, and fats. Each of these complex molecules is then digested to a much more simple substance which the body can then use. Carbohydrates, such as starches and disaccharides, are digested to monosaccharides such as glucose, fruc-

Figure 16–1 The digestive organs shown in anterior view of the trunk and left lateral view of the head. (The spleen is not a digestive organ but is included to show its location relative to the stomach, pancreas, and colon.)

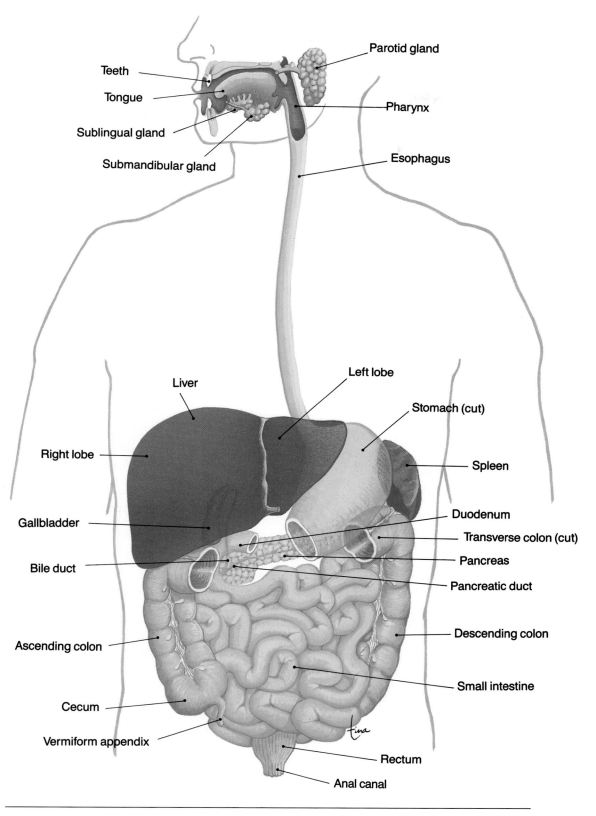

Figure 16–1 See legend on facing page.

tose, and galactose. Proteins are digested to amino acids, and fats are digested to fatty acids and glycerol. Also part of food, and released during digestion, are vitamins, minerals, and water.

We will now return to the beginning of the alimentary tube and consider the digestive organs and the process of digestion.

ORAL CAVITY

Food enters the **oral cavity** (or **buccal cavity**) by way of the mouth. The boundaries of the oral cavity are the hard and soft palates, superiorly; the cheeks, laterally; and the floor of the mouth, inferiorly. Within the oral cavity are the teeth and tongue and the openings of the ducts of the salivary glands.

TEETH

The function of the **teeth** is, of course, chewing. This is the process which mechanically breaks food into smaller pieces and mixes it with saliva. An individual develops two sets of teeth: deciduous and permanent. The **deciduous teeth** begin to erupt through the gums at about 6 months of age, and the set of 20 teeth is usually complete by the age of 2 years. These teeth are gradually lost throughout childhood and replaced by the **permanent teeth,** the first of which are molars that emerge around the age of 6 years. A complete set of permanent teeth consists of 32 teeth; the types of teeth are incisors, canines, premolars, and molars. The wisdom teeth are the third molars on either side of each jawbone. In some people, the wisdom teeth may not emerge from the jawbone because there is no room for them along the gum line. These wisdom teeth are said to be impacted and may put pressure on the roots of the second molars. In such cases, extraction of a wisdom tooth may be necessary to prevent damage to other teeth.

The structure of a tooth is shown in Fig. 16–2. The crown is visible above the gum **(gingiva).** The root is enclosed in a socket in the mandible or maxillae. The **periodontal membrane** lines the socket

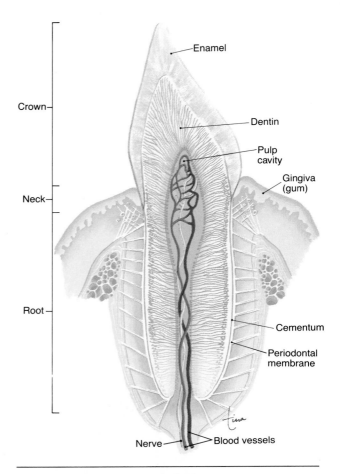

Figure 16–2 Tooth structure. Longitudinal section of a tooth showing internal structure.

and produces a bone-like cement that anchors the tooth. The outermost layer of the crown is **enamel,** which is made by cells called ameloblasts. Enamel provides a hard chewing surface and is more resistant to decay than are other parts of the tooth. Within the enamel is **dentin,** which is very similar to bone and is produced by cells called odontoblasts. Dentin also forms the roots of a tooth. The innermost portion of a tooth is the **pulp cavity,** which contains blood vessels and nerve endings of the trigeminal nerve (5th cranial). Erosion of the enamel and dentin layers by bacterial acids (dental caries or cavities) may result in bacterial invasion of the pulp cavity and a very painful toothache.

TONGUE

The **tongue** is made of skeletal muscle that is innervated by the hypoglossal nerves (12th cranial). On the upper surface of the tongue are small projections called **papillae,** many of which contain taste buds (see also Chapter 9). The sensory nerves for taste are also cranial nerves: the facial (7th) and glossopharyngeal (9th). As you know, the sense of taste is important because it makes eating enjoyable, but the tongue has other functions as well.

Chewing is efficient because of the action of the tongue in keeping the food between the teeth and mixing it with saliva. Elevation of the tongue is the first step in swallowing. This is a voluntary action, in which the tongue contracts and meets the resist-ance of the hard palate. The mass of food, called a bolus, is thus pushed backward toward the pharynx. The remainder of swallowing is a reflex, which will be described in the section on the pharynx.

SALIVARY GLANDS

The digestive secretion in the oral cavity is **saliva,** produced by three pairs of **salivary glands,** which are shown in Fig. 16–3. The **parotid glands** are just below and in front of the ears. The **submandibular** (also called submaxillary) glands are at the posterior corners of the mandible, and the **sublingual** glands are below the floor of the mouth. Each gland has at least one duct that takes saliva to the oral cavity.

Figure 16–3 The salivary glands shown in left lateral view.

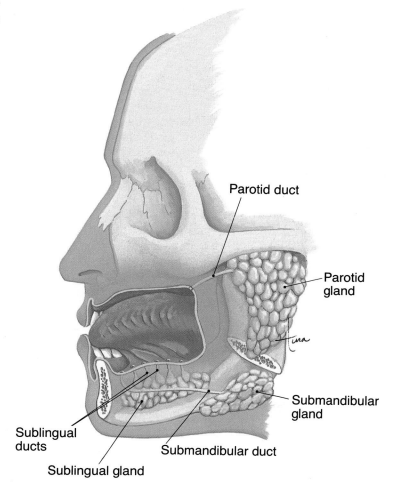

Parotid duct

Parotid gland

Submandibular gland

Submandibular duct

Sublingual gland

Sublingual ducts

Table 16–1 THE PROCESS OF DIGESTION

Organ	Enzyme or Other Secretion	Function	Site of Action
Salivary Glands	• Amylase	• Converts starch to maltose	Oral Cavity
Stomach	• Pepsin • HCl	• Converts proteins to polypeptides • Changes pepsinogen to pepsin; maintains pH 1–2; destroys pathogens	Stomach Stomach
Liver	• Bile salts	• Emulsify fats	Small Intestine
Pancreas	• Amylase • Trypsin • Lipase	• Converts starch to maltose • Converts polypeptides to peptides • Converts emulsified fats to fatty acids and glycerol	Small Intestine Small Intestine Small Intestine
Small Intestine	• Peptidases • Sucrase • Maltase • Lactase	• Convert peptides to amino acids • Converts sucrose to glucose and fructose • Converts maltose to glucose (2) • Converts lactose to glucose and galactose	Small Intestine Small Intestine Small Intestine Small Intestine

Secretion of saliva is continuous, but the amount varies in different situations. The presence of food (or anything else) in the mouth increases saliva secretion. This is a parasympathetic response mediated by the facial and glossopharyngeal nerves. The sight or smell of food also increases secretion of saliva. Sympathetic stimulation in stress situations decreases secretion, making the mouth dry and swallowing difficult.

Saliva is mostly water, which is important to dissolve food for tasting and to moisten food for swallowing. The digestive enzyme in saliva is salivary amylase, which breaks down starch molecules to shorter chains of glucose molecules, or to maltose, a dissacharide. Most of us, however, do not chew our food long enough for the action of salivary amylase to be truly effective. As you will see, another amylase from the pancreas is also available to digest starch. Table 16–1 summarizes the functions of digestive secretions.

necting the oral cavity to the esophagus. No digestion takes place in the pharynx. Its only function is swallowing, the mechanical movement of food. When the bolus of food is pushed backward by the tongue, the constrictor muscles of the pharynx contract as part of the swallowing reflex. The reflex center for swallowing is in the medulla, which coordinates the many actions that take place: constriction of the pharynx, cessation of breathing, elevation of the soft palate to block the nasopharynx, elevation of the larynx and closure of the epiglottis, and peristalsis of the esophagus. As you can see, swallowing is rather complicated, but because it is a reflex we don't have to think about making it happen correctly. Talking or laughing while eating, however, may interfere with the reflex and cause food to go into the "wrong pipe," the larynx. When that happens, the cough reflex is usually effective in clearing the airway.

PHARYNX

As described in the last chapter, the oropharynx and laryngopharynx are food passageways con-

ESOPHAGUS

The **esophagus** is a muscular tube that takes food from the pharynx to the stomach; no digestion

takes place here. Peristalsis of the esophagus propels food in one direction and ensures that food gets to the stomach even if the body is horizontal or upside down. At the junction with the stomach, the lumen (cavity) of the esophagus is surrounded by the **lower esophageal sphincter** (LES or cardiac sphincter), a circular smooth muscle. The LES relaxes to permit food to enter the stomach, then contracts to prevent the backup of stomach contents. If the LES does not close completely, gastric juice may splash up into the esophagus; this is a painful condition we call heartburn.

STRUCTURAL LAYERS OF THE ALIMENTARY TUBE

Before we continue with our discussion of the organs of digestion, we will first examine the structure of the alimentary tube. When viewed in cross section, the alimentary tube has four layers (Fig. 16–4): the mucosa, submucosa, external muscle layer, and serosa. Each layer has a specific structure, and its functions contribute to the functioning of the organs of which it is a part.

MUCOSA

The **mucosa,** or lining, of the alimentary tube is made of epithelial tissue. In the esophagus the mucosa is stratified squamous epithelium; the mucosa of the stomach and intestines is simple columnar epithelium. The mucosa secretes mucus, which lubricates the passage of food, and also secretes the digestive enzymes of the stomach and small intestine. Just below the epithelium are lymph nodules which contain macrophages to phagocytize bacteria or other foreign material that get through the epithelium.

SUBMUCOSA

The **submucosa** is made of areolar connective tissue with many blood vessels and lymphatic vessels. Autonomic nerve networks called **Meissner's plexus** (or submucosal plexus) innervate the mucosa to regulate secretions. Parasympathetic impulses increase secretions, while sympathetic impulses decrease secretions.

EXTERNAL MUSCLE LAYER

This layer typically contains two layers of smooth muscle: an inner, circular layer and an outer, longitudinal layer. Variations from the typical do occur, however. In the esophagus, this layer is striated muscle in the upper third, which gradually changes to smooth muscle in the lower portions. The stomach has three layers of smooth muscle, rather than two.

Contractions of this muscle layer help break up food and mix it with digestive juices. The one-way contractions of **peristalsis** move the food toward the anus. **Auerbach's plexus** (or myenteric plexus) is the autonomic network in this layer: sympathetic impulses decrease contractions and peristalsis, while parasympathetic impulses increase contractions and peristalsis. The parasympathetic nerves are the vagus (10th cranial) nerves; they truly live up to the meaning of "vagus," which is "wanderer."

SEROSA

Above the diaphragm, for the esophagus, the serosa, the outermost layer, is fibrous connective tissue. Below the diaphragm, the serosa is the **mesentery** or visceral peritoneum, a serous membrane. Lining the abdominal cavity is the parietal peritoneum, usually simply called the **peritoneum.** The peritoneum-mesentery is actually one continuous membrane (see Fig. 16–4). The serous fluid between the peritoneum and mesentery prevents friction when the alimentary tube contracts and the organs slide against one another.

The above descriptions are typical of the layers of the alimentary tube. As noted, variations are possible, and any important differences will be mentioned in the sections that follow on specific organs.

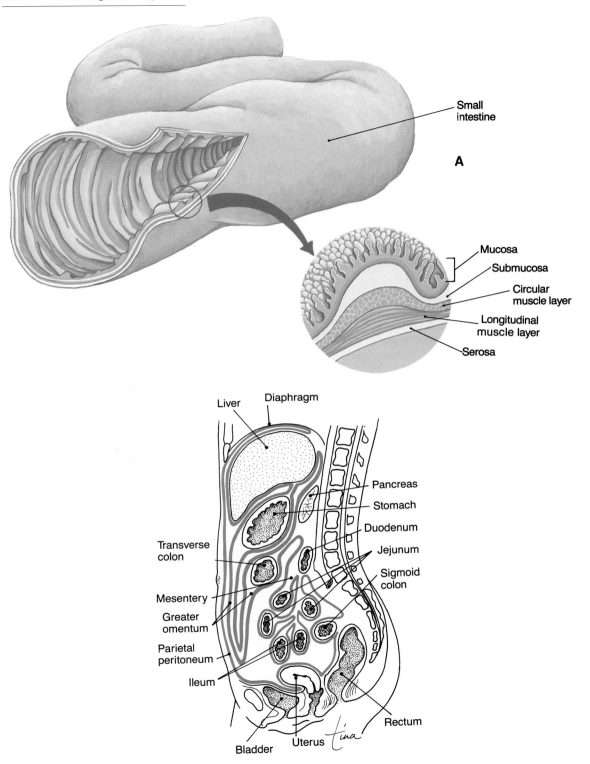

Small intestine

A

Mucosa
Submucosa
Circular muscle layer
Longitudinal muscle layer
Serosa

Liver
Diaphragm
Pancreas
Stomach
Duodenum
Jejunum
Transverse colon
Sigmoid colon
Mesentery
Greater omentum
Parietal peritoneum
Ileum
Rectum
Bladder
Uterus

B

Figure 16–4 See legend on facing page.

STOMACH

The **stomach** is located in the upper left quadrant of the abdominal cavity, to the left of the liver and in front of the spleen. Although part of the alimentary tube, the stomach is not a tube, but rather a sac that extends from the esophagus to the small intestine. Because it is a sac, the stomach serves as a reservoir for food, so that digestion proceeds gradually and we do not have to eat constantly. Both mechanical and chemical digestion take place in the stomach.

The parts of the stomach are shown in Fig. 16–5. The cardiac orifice is the opening of the esophagus, and the fundus is the portion above the level of this opening. The body of the stomach is the large central portion, bounded laterally by the greater curvature and medially by the lesser curvature. The pylorus is adjacent to the duodenum of the small intestine, and the **pyloric sphincter** surrounds the junction of the two organs. The fundus and body are mainly storage areas, while most digestion takes place in the pylorus.

When the stomach is empty, the mucosa appears wrinkled or folded. These folds are called **rugae;** they flatten out as the stomach is filled and permit expansion of the lining without tearing it. The **gastric pits** are the glands of the stomach and consist of several types of cells; their collective secretions are called gastric juice. **Mucous cells** secrete mucus, which coats the stomach lining and helps prevent erosion by the gastric juice. **Chief cells** secrete **pepsinogen,** an inactive form of the enzyme **pepsin. Parietal cells** secrete hydrochloric acid (HCl), which converts pepsinogen to pepsin, which then begins the digestion of proteins to polypeptides. Hydrochloric acid also gives gastric juice its pH of 1 to 2. This very acidic pH is necessary for pepsin to function and also kills most microorganisms that enter the stomach.

Gastric juice is secreted in small amounts at the sight or smell of food. This is a parasympathetic response that ensures that some gastric juice will be present in the stomach when food arrives. The presence of food in the stomach causes the gastric mucosa to secrete the hormone gastrin, which stimulates the secretion of greater amounts of gastric juice.

The external muscle layer of the stomach consists of three layers of smooth muscle: circular, longitudinal, and oblique layers. These three layers provide for very efficient mechanical digestion to change food into a thick liquid called chyme. The pyloric sphincter is usually contracted when the stomach is churning food; it relaxes at intervals to permit small amounts of chyme to pass into the duodenum. This sphincter then contracts again to prevent the backup of intestinal contents into the stomach (see Box 16–1: Disorders of the Stomach).

SMALL INTESTINE

The **small intestine** is about 1 inch (2.5 cm) in diameter and approximately 20 feet (6 meters) long and extends from the stomach to the cecum of the large intestine. Within the abdominal cavity, the large intestine encircles the coils of the small intestine (see Fig. 16–1).

The **duodenum** is the first 10 inches (25 cm) of the small intestine. The common bile duct enters the duodenum at the ampulla of Vater (or hepatopancreatic ampulla). The **jejunum** is about 8 feet long, and the **ileum** is about 11 feet in length. In a living person, however, the small intestine is always contracted and is therefore somewhat shorter.

Digestion is completed in the small intestine, and the end products of digestion are absorbed into the blood and lymph. The external muscle layer has the typical circular and longitudinal smooth muscle lay-

Figure 16–4 **(A)**, The four layers of the wall of the alimentary tube. A small part of the wall of the small intestine has been magnified to show the four layers typical of the alimentary tube. **(B)**, Sagittal section through the abdomen showing the relationship of the peritoneum and mesentery to the abdominal organs.

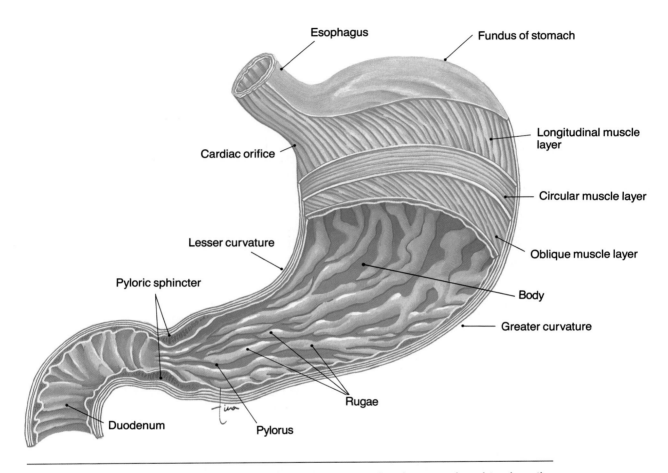

Figure 16–5 The stomach in anterior view. The stomach wall has been sectioned to show the muscle layers and the rugae of the mucosa.

Box 16–1 DISORDERS OF THE STOMACH

Vomiting is the expulsion of stomach and intestinal contents through the esophagus and mouth. Stimuli include irritation of the stomach, motion sickness, food poisoning, or diseases such as meningitis. The vomiting center is in the medulla, which coordinates the simultaneous contraction of the diaphragm and the abdominal muscles. This squeezes the stomach and upper intestine, expelling their contents. As part of the reflex, the lower esophageal sphincter relaxes, and the glottis closes. If the glottis fails to close, as may happen in alcohol intoxication, aspiration of vomitus may occur and result in fatal obstruction of the respiratory passages.

Pyloric stenosis means that the opening of the pyloric sphincter is narrowed, and emptying of the stomach is impaired. This is most often a congenital disorder caused by hypertrophy of the pyloric sphincter. For reasons unknown, this condition is more common in male infants than in female infants. When the stomach does not empty efficiently, its internal pressure increases. Vomiting relieves the pressure; this is a classic symptom of pyloric stenosis. Correcting this condition requires surgery to widen the opening in the sphincter.

A **gastric ulcer** is an erosion of the mucosa of the stomach. Since the normal stomach lining is adapted to resist the corrosive action of gastric juice, ulcer formation is the result of oversecretion of HCl or undersecretion of mucus. Possible contributing factors include cigarette smoking and ingestion of alcohol or caffeine.

As erosion reaches the submucosa, small blood vessels are ruptured and bleed. If vomiting occurs, the vomitus has a "coffee-ground" appearance due to the presence of blood acted on by gastric juice. A more serious complication is perforation of the stomach wall, with leakage of gastric contents into the abdominal cavity, and **peritonitis.**

There are a number of medications that decrease the secretion of HCl; these are often very effective in the treatment of ulcers. It is also important, however, to eliminate any of the contributing factors mentioned above.

Recent clinical studies have confirmed that a bacterium called *Helicobacter pylori* may also be a cause of gastric ulcers. For some patients, a few weeks of antibiotic therapy to eradicate this bacterium has produced rapid healing of their ulcers. Other researchers have proposed a link between this bacterium and stomach cancer, and these investigations are continuing.

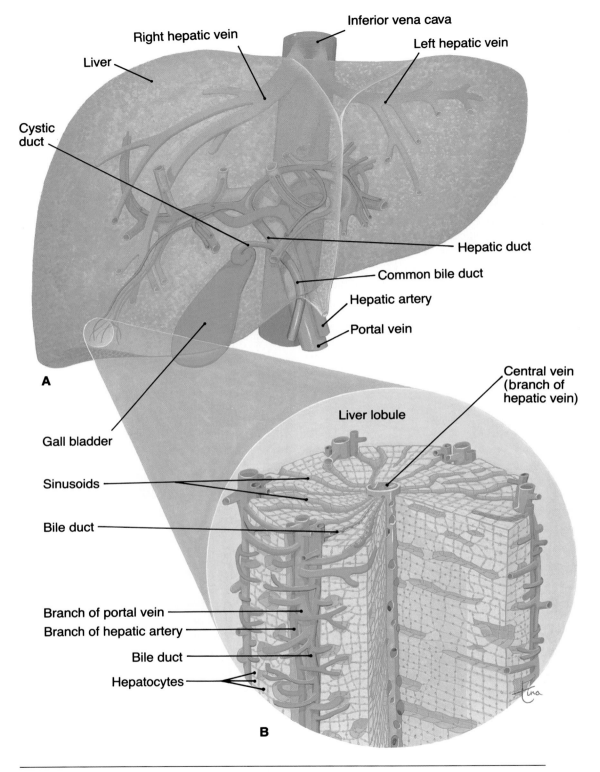

Figure 16–6 **(A)**, The liver and gallbladder with blood vessels and bile ducts. **(B)**, Magnified view of one liver lobule. See text for description.

ers that mix the chyme with digestive secretions and propel the chyme toward the colon.

There are three sources of digestive secretions that function within the small intestine: the liver, the pancreas, and the small intestine itself. We will return to the small intestine after considering these other organs.

LIVER

The **liver** consists of two large lobes, right and left and fills the upper right and center of the abdominal cavity, just below the diaphragm. The cells of the liver have many functions (which will be discussed in a later section), but their only digestive function is the production of **bile.** Bile enters the small bile ducts, called bile canaliculi, on the liver cells, which unite to form larger ducts and finally merge to form the **hepatic duct** which takes bile out of the liver (Fig. 16–6). The hepatic duct unites with the cystic duct of the gall bladder to form the **common bile duct,** which takes bile to the duodenum.

Bile is mostly water and has an excretory function in that it carries bilirubin and excess cholesterol to the intestines for elimination in feces. The digestive function of bile is accomplished by **bile salts,** which **emulsify** fats in the small intestine. Emulsification means that large fat globules are broken into smaller globules. This is mechanical, not chemical, digestion; the fat is still fat but now has more surface area to facilitate chemical digestion.

Production of bile is stimulated by the hormone **secretin,** which is produced by the duodenum when food enters the small intestine. Table 16–2 summarizes the regulation of secretion of all the digestive secretions.

GALLBLADDER

The **gallbladder** is a sac about 3 to 4 inches (7.5 to 10 cm) long located on the undersurface of the

Table 16–2   REGULATION OF DIGESTIVE SECRETIONS

Secretion	Nervous Regulation	Chemical Regulation
Saliva	Presence of food in mouth or sight of food; parasympathetic impulses along 7th and 9th cranial nerves	• None
Gastric juice	Sight or smell of food; parasympathetic impulses along 10th cranial nerves	• Gastrin—produced by the gastric mucosa when food is present in the stomach
Bile		
Secretion by the liver	None	• Secretin—produced by the duodenum when chyme enters
Contraction of the gallbladder	None	• Cholecystokinin—produced by the duodenum when chyme enters
Enzyme pancreatic juice	None	• Cholecystokinin—from the duodenum
Bicarbonate pancreatic juice	None	• Secretin—from the duodenum
Intestinal juice	Presence of chyme in the duodenum; parasympathetic impulses along 10th cranial nerves	• None

Box 16–2 GALLSTONES

One of the functions of the gallbladder is to concentrate bile by absorbing water. If the bile contains a high concentration of cholesterol, absorption of water may lead to precipitation and the formation of cholesterol crystals. These crystals are **gallstones.**

If the gallstones are small, they will pass through the cystic duct and common bile duct to the duodenum without causing symptoms. If large, however, the gallstones cannot pass out of the gallbladder, and may cause mild to severe pain that often radiates to the right shoulder. Obstructive jaundice may occur if bile backs up into the liver and bilirubin is reabsorbed into the blood.

There are several possible treatments for gallstones. Medications that dissolve gallstones work slowly, over the course of several months, and are useful if biliary obstruction is not severe. An instrument that generates shock waves (called a lithotripter) may be used to pulverize the stones into smaller pieces that may easily pass into the duodenum; this procedure is called **lithotripsy.** Surgery to remove the gallbladder (cholecystectomy) is required in some cases. The hepatic duct is then connected directly to the common bile duct, and dilute bile flows into the duodenum. Following such surgery, the patient should avoid meals high in fats.

right lobe of the liver. Bile in the hepatic duct of the liver flows through the **cystic duct** into the gallbladder (see Fig. 16–6), which stores bile until it is needed in the small intestine. The gallbladder also concentrates bile by absorbing water (see Box 16–2: Gallstones).

When fatty foods enter the duodenum, the duodenal mucosa secretes the hormone **cholecystokinin.** It is this hormone which stimulates contraction of the smooth muscle in the wall of the gallbladder, which forces bile into the cystic duct, then into the common bile duct, and on into the duodenum.

PANCREAS

The **pancreas** is located in the upper left abdominal quadrant between the curve of the duodenum and the spleen and is about 6 inches (15 cm) in length. The endocrine functions of the pancreas were discussed in Chapter 10, so only the exocrine functions will be considered here. The exocrine glands of the pancreas are called acini. They pro-

duce enzymes that are involved in the digestion of all three types of complex food molecules.

The pancreatic enzyme **amylase** digests starch to maltose. You may recall that this is the "backup" enzyme for salivary amylase. **Lipase** converts emulsified fats to fatty acids and glycerol. The emulsifying or fat-separating action of bile salts increases the surface area of fats so that lipase works effectively. Trypsinogen is an inactive enzyme that is changed to active **trypsin** in the duodenum. Trypsin digests polypeptides to shorter chains of amino acids.

The pancreatic enzyme juice is carried by small ducts that unite to form larger ducts, then finally the main **pancreatic duct.** An accessory duct may also be present. The main pancreatic duct emerges from the medial side of the pancreas and joins the common bile duct to the duodenum (Fig. 16–7).

The pancreas also produces a **bicarbonate juice** (containing sodium bicarbonate), which is alkaline. Since the gastric juice that enters the duodenum is very acidic, it must be neutralized to prevent damage to the duodenal mucosa. This neutralizing is accomplished by the sodium bicarbonate in pancreatic juice, and the pH of the duodenal chyme is raised to about 7.5.

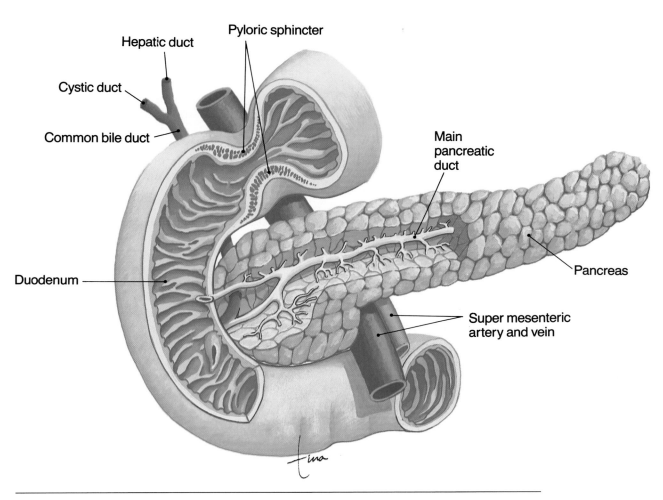

Figure 16–7 The pancreas, sectioned to show the pancreatic ducts. The main pancreatic duct joins the common bile duct.

Secretion of pancreatic juice is stimulated by the hormones secretin and cholecystokinin, which are produced by the duodenal mucosa when chyme enters the small intestine. **Secretin** stimulates the production of bicarbonate juice by the pancreas, and **cholecystokinin** stimulates the secretion of the pancreatic enzymes.

COMPLETION OF DIGESTION AND ABSORPTION

SMALL INTESTINE

The secretion of the intestinal glands (or crypts of Lieberkühn) is stimulated by the presence of food in the duodenum. The intestinal enzymes are the peptidases and sucrase, maltase, and lactase. **Peptidases** complete the digestion of protein by breaking down short polypeptide chains to amino acids. **Sucrase, maltase,** and **lactase,** respectively, digest the disaccharides sucrose, maltose, and lactose to monosaccharides.

A summary of the digestive secretions and their functions is found in Table 16–1. Regulation of these secretions is shown in Table 16–2.

ABSORPTION

Most absorption of the end products of digestion takes place in the small intestine (although the stomach does absorb water and alcohol). The process of absorption requires a large surface area, which is provided by several structural modifications of the small intestine; these are shown in Fig. 16–8. **Plica circulares** are macroscopic folds of the mucosa and submucosa, somewhat like accordian pleats. The mucosa is further folded into projections called **villi,** which give the inner surface of the intestine a velvet-like appearance. Each columnar cell (except the mucus-secreting goblet cells) of the villi also has **microvilli** on its free surface. Microvilli are microscopic folds of the cell membrane. All of these folds greatly increase the surface area of the intestinal lining. It is estimated that if the intestinal mucosa could be flattened out, it would cover more than 2000 square feet (half a basketball court).

The absorption of nutrients takes place from the lumen of the intestine into the vessels within the villi. Refer back to Fig. 16–8 and notice that within each villus is a **capillary network** and a **lacteal,** which is a dead-end lymph capillary. Water-soluble nutrients are absorbed into the blood in the capillary networks. Monosaccharides, amino acids, positive ions, and the water-soluble vitamins (vitamin C and the B vitamins) are absorbed by active transport. Negative ions may be absorbed by either passive or active transport mechanisms. Water is absorbed by osmosis following the absorption of minerals, especially sodium. Certain nutrients have additional special requirements for their absorption: for example, vitamin B_{12} requires the intrinsic factor produced by the gastric mucosa, and the efficient absorption of calcium ions requires parathyroid hormone and vitamin D.

Fat-soluble nutrients are absorbed into the lymph in the lacteals of the villi. Bile salts are necessary for the efficient absorption of fatty acids and the fat-soluble vitamins (A, D, E, K). Once absorbed, fatty acids are recombined with glycerol to form triglycerides. These triglycerides then form globules that include cholesterol and protein; these lipid-protein complexes are called **chylomicrons.** In the form of chylomicrons, most absorbed fat is transported by the lymph and eventually enters the blood in the left subclavian vein.

Blood from the capillary networks in the villi does not return directly to the heart but first travels through the portal vein to the liver. You may recall the importance of portal circulation, discussed in Chapter 13. This pathway enables the liver to regulate the blood levels of glucose and amino acids, store certain vitamins, and remove potential poisons from the blood (see Box 16–3: Disorders of the Intestines).

LARGE INTESTINE

The **large intestine,** also called the **colon,** is approximately 2.5 inches (6.3 cm) in diameter and 5 feet (1.5 m) in length. It extends from the ileum of the small intestine to the anus, the terminal opening. The parts of the colon are shown in Fig. 16–9.

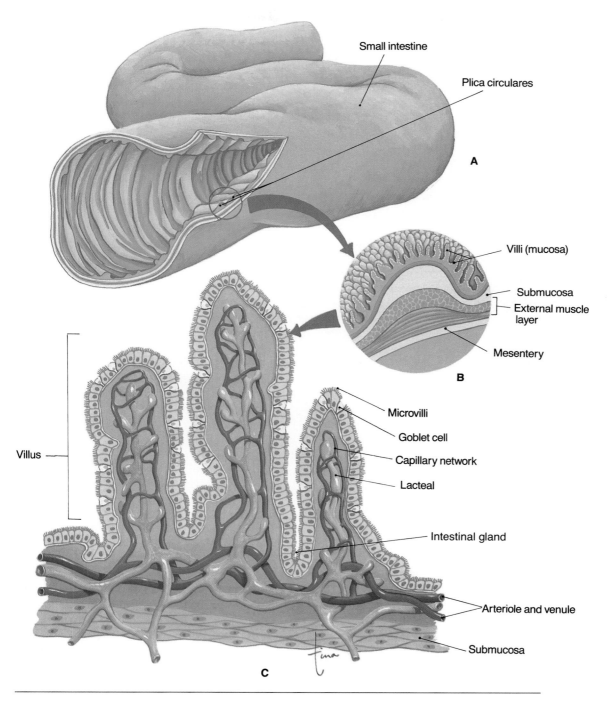

Figure 16–8 The small intestine. **(A)**, Section through the small intestine showing plica circulares. **(B)**, Magnified view of a section of the intestinal wall showing the villi and the four layers. **(C)**, Microscopic view of three villi showing the internal structure.

Box 16–3 DISORDERS OF THE INTESTINES

Duodenal ulcers are erosions of the duodenal wall caused by the gastric juice that enters from the stomach (see Box 16–1).

Paralytic ileus is the cessation of contraction of the smooth muscle layer of the intestine. This is a possible complication of abdominal surgery, but it may also be the result of peritonitis or inflammation elsewhere in the abdominal cavity. In the absence of peristalsis, intestinal obstruction may occur. Bowel movements cease, and vomiting occurs to relieve the pressure within the alimentary tube. Treatment involves suctioning the intestinal contents to eliminate any obstruction and allow the intestine to regain its normal motility.

Lactose intolerance is the inability to digest lactose because of deficiency of the enzyme lactase. Lactase deficiency may be congenital, a consequence of prematurity, or acquired later in life. The delayed form is quite common among people of African or Asian ancestry, and in part is probably genetic. When lactose, or milk sugar, is not digested, it undergoes fermentation in the intestine. Symptoms include diarrhea, abdominal pain, bloating, and flatulence (gas formation).

Salmonella food poisoning is caused by bacteria in the genus *Salmonella.* These are part of the intestinal flora of animals, and animal foods such as meat and eggs may be sources of infection. These bacteria are not normal for people, and they cause the intestines to secrete large amounts of fluid. Symptoms include diarrhea, abdominal cramps, and vomiting and usually last only a few days. For elderly or debilitated people, however, salmonella food poisoning may be very serious or even fatal.

Diverticula are small outpouchings through weakened areas of the intestinal wall. They are more likely to occur in the colon than in the small intestine and may exist for years without causing any symptoms. The presence of diverticula is called **diverticulosis.** Inflammation of diverticula is called **diverticulitis,** which is usually the result of entrapment of feces and bacteria. Symptoms include abdominal pain and tenderness and fever. If uncomplicated, diverticulitis may be treated with antibiotics and modifications in diet. The most serious complication is perforation of diverticula, allowing fecal material into the abdominal cavity, causing peritonitis. A diet high in fiber is believed to be an important aspect of prevention, to provide bulk in the colon and prevent weakening of its wall.

The **cecum** is the first portion, and at its junction with the ileum is the **ileocecal valve,** which is not a sphincter but serves the same purpose. After undigested food (which is now mostly cellulose) and water pass from the ileum into the cecum, closure of the ileocecal valve prevents the backflow of fecal material.

Attached to the cecum is the **appendix,** a small, dead-end tube with abundant lymphatic tissue. The appendix seems to be a **vestigial organ,** that is,

one whose size and function seem to be reduced. Although there is abundant lymphatic tissue in the wall of the appendix, the possibility that the appendix is concerned with immunity is not known with certainty. **Appendicitis** refers to inflammation of the appendix, which may occur if fecal material becomes impacted within it. This usually necessitates an **appendectomy,** the surgical removal of the appendix.

The remainder of the colon consists of the as-

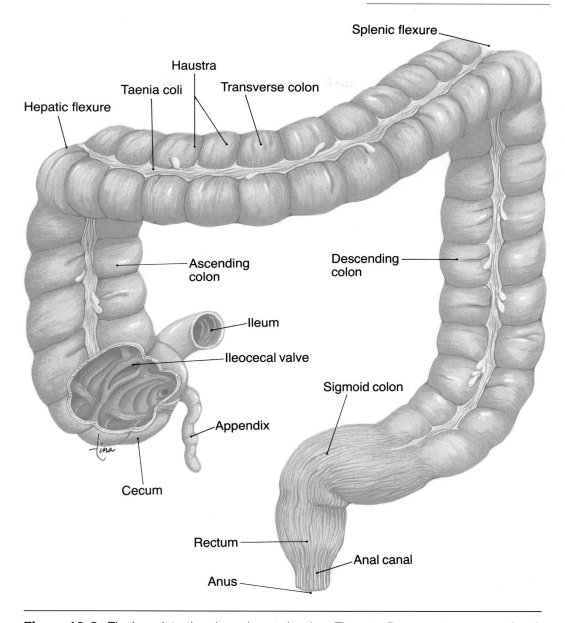

Splenic flexure

Haustra

Taenia coli

Transverse colon

Hepatic flexure

Ascending colon

Descending colon

Ileum

Ileocecal valve

Sigmoid colon

Appendix

Cecum

Rectum

Anal canal

Anus

Figure 16–9 The large intestine shown in anterior view. The term *flexure* means a turn or bend.

cending, transverse, and descending colon which encircle the small intestine; the sigmoid colon, which turns medially and downward; the rectum; and the anal canal. The rectum is about 6 inches long, and the anal canal is the last inch of the colon that surrounds the anus. Clinically, however, the terminal end of the colon is usually referred to as the rectum.

No digestion takes place in the colon. The only secretion of the colonic mucosa is mucus, which lubricates the passage of fecal material. The longitudinal smooth muscle layer of the colon is in three bands called **taeniae coli.** The rest of the colon is "gathered" to fit these bands. This gives the colon a puckered appearance; the puckers or pockets are called **haustra,** which provide for more surface area within the colon.

The functions of the colon are the absorption of water, minerals, and vitamins and the elimination of undigestable material. About 80% of the water that enters the colon is absorbed (400 to 800 ml per day). Positive and negative ions are also absorbed. The vitamins absorbed are those produced by the **normal flora,** the trillions of bacteria that live in the colon. Vitamin K is produced and absorbed in amounts usually sufficient to meet a person's daily need. Other vitamins produced in smaller amounts include riboflavin, thiamin, biotin, and folic acid. Everything absorbed by the colon circulates first to the liver by way of portal circulation. Yet another function of the normal colon flora is to inhibit the growth of pathogens (see Box 16–4: Infant Botulism).

ELIMINATION OF FECES

Feces consist of cellulose and other undigestable material, dead and living bacteria, and water. Elim-ination of feces is accomplished by the **defecation reflex,** a spinal cord reflex that may be controlled voluntarily. The rectum is usually empty until peristalsis of the colon pushes feces into it. These waves of peristalsis tend to occur after eating, especially when food enters the duodenum. The wall of the rectum is stretched by the entry of feces, and this is the stimulus for the defecation reflex.

Stretch receptors in the smooth muscle layer of the rectum generate sensory impulses that travel to the spinal cord. The returning motor impulses cause the smooth muscle of the rectum to contract. Surrounding the anus is the **internal anal sphincter,** which is made of smooth muscle. As part of the reflex this sphincter relaxes, permitting defecation to take place.

The **external anal sphincter** is made of skeletal muscle and surrounds the internal anal sphincter (Fig. 16–10). If defecation must be delayed, the external sphincter may be voluntarily contracted to close the anus. The awareness of the need to defecate passes as the stretch receptors of the rectum adapt. These receptors will be stimulated again when the next wave of peristalsis reaches the rectum (see Box 16–5: Fiber).

Box 16–4 INFANT BOTULISM

Botulism is most often acquired from food. When the spores of the botulism bacteria are in an anaerobic (without oxygen) environment such as a can of food, the spores germinate into active bacteria that produce a neurotoxin. If people ingest food containing this toxin, they will develop the paralysis that is characteristic of botulism.

For infants less than 1 year of age, however, ingestion of just the bacterial spores may be harmful. The infant's stomach does not produce much HCl, so ingested botulism spores may not be destroyed. Of equal importance, the infant's normal colon flora is not yet established. Without the normal population of colon bacteria to provide competition, spores of the botulism bacteria may germinate and produce their toxin.

An affected infant becomes lethargic and weak; paralysis may progress slowly or rapidly. Treatment (antitoxin) is available, but may be delayed if botulism is not suspected. Many cases of infant botulism have been traced to honey which was found to contain botulism spores. Such spores are not harmful to older children and adults, who have a normal colon flora that prevents the botulism bacteria from becoming established.

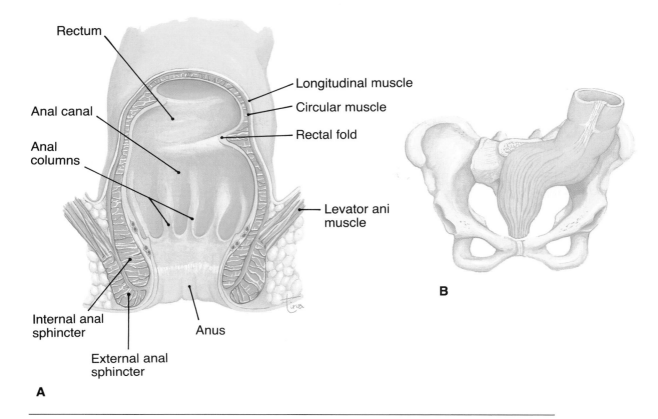

A

B

Labels (A): Rectum, Longitudinal muscle, Circular muscle, Rectal fold, Anal canal, Anal columns, Levator ani muscle, Internal anal sphincter, Anus, External anal sphincter

Figure 16–10 **(A)**, Internal and external anal sphincters shown in a frontal section through the lower rectum and anal canal. **(B)**, Position of rectum and anal canal relative to pelvic bone.

Box 16–5   FIBER

Fiber is a term we use to refer to the organic materials in the cell walls of plants. These are mainly cellulose and pectins. The role of dietary fiber, and possible benefits that a high-fiber diet may provide, are currently the focus of much research. It is important to differentiate what is known from what is, at present, merely speculation.

Many studies have shown that populations (large groups of people) who consume high-fiber diets tend to have a lower frequency of certain diseases. These include diverticulitis, colon cancer, coronary artery disease, diabetes, and hypertension. Such diseases are much more common among populations whose diets are low in vegetables, fruits, and whole grains, and high in meat, dairy products, and processed foods.

Recent claims that high-fiber diets directly lower blood levels of cholesterol and fats are not yet supported by definitive clinical or experimental studies. One possible explanation may be that a person whose diet consists largely of high-fiber foods simply eats less of foods high in cholesterol and fats, and this is the reason for their lower blood levels of fats and cholesterol.

Should people try to make great changes in their diets? Probably not, not if they are careful to limit fat intake and to include significant quantities of vegetables and fruits. Besides the possible benefits of fiber, unprocessed plant foods provide important amounts of vitamins and minerals.

OTHER FUNCTIONS OF THE LIVER

The **liver** is a remarkable organ, and only the brain is capable of a greater variety of functions. The liver cells (hepatocytes) produce many enzymes that catalyze many different chemical reactions. These reactions are the functions of the liver. As blood flows through the sinusoids (capillaries) of the liver (see Fig. 16–6), materials are removed by the liver cells, and the products of the liver cells are secreted into the blood. Some of the liver functions will already be familiar to you. Others will be mentioned again and discussed in more detail in the next chapter. Since the liver has such varied effects on so many body systems, we will use the categories below to summarize the liver functions.

1. Carbohydrate metabolism—As you know, the liver regulates the blood glucose level. Excess glucose is converted to glycogen (glycogenesis) when blood glucose is high; the hormones insulin and cortisol facilitate this process. During hypoglycemia or stress situations, glycogen is converted back to glucose (glycogenolysis) to raise the blood glucose level. Epinephrine and glucagon are the hormones that facilitate this process.

   The liver also changes other monosaccharides to glucose. Fructose and galactose, for example, are end products of the digestion of sucrose and lactose. Because most cells, however, cannot readily use fructose and galactose as energy sources, they are converted by the liver to glucose, which is easily used by cells.

2. Amino Acid Metabolism—The liver regulates blood levels of amino acids based on tissue needs for protein synthesis. Of the 20 different amino acids needed for the production of human proteins, the liver is able to synthesize 12, called the **non-essential amino acids.** The chemical process by which this is done is called **transamination,** the transfer of an amino group (NH_2) from an amino acid present in excess to a free carbon chain which forms a complete, new amino acid molecule. The other eight amino acids, which the liver cannot synthesize, are called the **essential amino acids.** In this case, "essential" means that the amino acids must be supplied by our food, since the liver cannot manufacture them. Similarly, "non-essential" means that the amino acids do not have to be supplied in our food because the liver *can* make them. All 20 amino acids are required in order to make our body proteins.

   Excess amino acids, those not needed right away for protein synthesis, cannot be stored. However, they do serve another useful purpose. By the process of **deamination,** which also occurs in the liver, the NH_2 group is removed from an amino acid, and the remaining carbon chain may be converted to a simple carbohydrate molecule or to fat. Thus, excess amino acids are utilized for energy production: either for immediate energy or for the potential energy stored as fat in adipose tissue. The NH_2 groups that were detached from the original amino acids are combined to form urea, a waste product that will be removed from the blood by the kidneys and excreted in urine.

3. Lipid Metabolism—The liver forms lipoproteins, which as their name tells us, are molecules of lipids and proteins, for the transport of fats in the blood to other tissues. The liver also synthesizes cholesterol and excretes excess cholesterol into bile to be eliminated in feces.

   Fatty acids are a potential source of energy, but in order to be used in cell respiration they must be broken down to smaller molecules. In the process of **beta-oxidation,** the long carbon chains of fatty acids are split into two-carbon molecules called acetyl groups, which are simple carbohydrates. These acetyl groups may be used by the liver cells to produce ATP or may be combined to form ketones to be transported in the blood to other cells. These other cells then use the ketones to produce ATP in cell respiration.

4. Synthesis of Plasma Proteins—This is a liver function that you will probably remember from Chapter 11. The liver synthesizes many of the proteins that circulate in the blood. **Albumin,** the most abundant plasma protein,

Box 16–6   HEPATITIS

Hepatitis is inflammation of the liver caused by any of several viruses. The most common of these hepatitis viruses have been designated A, B, and C, although there are others. Symptoms of hepatitis include anorexia, nausea, fatigue, and possibly jaundice. Severity of disease ranges from very mild (even asymptomatic) to fatal. Hundreds of thousands of cases of hepatitis occur in the United States every year, and although liver inflammation is common to all of them, the three hepatitis viruses have different modes of transmission and different consequences for affected people.

Hepatitis A is an intestinal virus that is spread by the fecal-oral route. Contaminated food is the usual vehicle of transmission, although shellfish harvested from water contaminated with human sewage are another possible source of this virus. Hepatitis A is most often mild, recovery provides lifelong immunity, and the carrier state is not known to occur. A vaccine is being developed, but people who have been exposed to hepatitis A may receive gamma globulin by injection to prevent the disease.

Hepatitis B is contracted by exposure to the body fluids of an infected person; these fluids include blood and semen. It is important to mention, however, that neither hepatitis A nor B is spread by blood transfusions, since donated blood is tested for both these viruses. Hepatitis B may be severe or even fatal, and approximately 10% of those who recover become carriers of the virus. Possible consequences of the carrier state are chronic hepatitis progressing to cirrhosis or primary liver cancer. Of equal importance, carriers are sources of the virus for others, especially their sexual partners.

A vaccine is available for hepatitis B, and although it is expensive, healthcare workers who have contact with blood, even occasionally, should receive it. Other potential recipients of the vaccine are the sexual partners of carriers, and infants born to carrier mothers.

The **hepatitis C** virus is also present in body fluids and is spread in the same ways as is hepatitis B. The range of severity of hepatitis C is also very similar to that of hepatitis B, and the carrier state is possible after recovery. Until very recently, there was no serological (blood) test to detect this virus in donated blood, and the hepatitis C virus was responsible for several hundred thousand cases of post-transfusion hepatitis every year. The now standard testing done in blood banks has significantly reduced the number of new cases of hepatitis C.

helps maintain blood volume by pulling tissue fluid into capillaries.

The **clotting factors** are also produced by the liver. These, as you recall, include prothrombin, fibrinogen, and Factor 8, which circulate in the blood until needed in the chemical clotting mechanism. The liver also synthesizes alpha and beta **globulins,** which are proteins that serve as carriers for other molecules, such as fats, in the blood.

5. Formation of Bilirubin—This is another familiar function: the liver contains fixed macrophages that phagocytize old RBCs. Bilirubin is then formed from the heme portion of the hemoglobin. The liver also removes from the blood the bilirubin formed in the spleen and red bone marrow, and excretes it into bile to be eliminated in feces.

6. Phagocytosis by **Kupffer Cells**—The fixed macrophages of the liver are called Kupffer cells (or stellate reticuloendothelial cells). Besides destroying old RBCs, Kupffer cells phagocytize pathogens or other foreign material that circulate through the liver. Many of the bacteria that get to the liver come from the colon. These bacteria are part of the normal flora of the colon but would be very harmful elsewhere in the body. The bacteria that enter the blood with the water absorbed by the colon are carried to the liver by way of portal circulation. The Kupffer cells in the liver phagocytize and destroy these bacteria, removing them from the blood before the blood returns to the heart.

7. Storage—The liver stores the fat-soluble vitamins A, D, E, and K, and the water-soluble vitamin B_{12}. Up to a 6- to 12-month supply of vitamins A and D may be stored, and liver is an excellent dietary source of these vitamins.

Also stored by the liver are the minerals iron and copper. You already know that iron is needed for hemoglobin and myoglobin and enables these proteins to bond to oxygen. Copper is part of some of the proteins needed for cell respiration.

8. Detoxification—The liver is capable of synthesizing enzymes that will detoxify harmful substances, that is, change them to less harmful ones. Alcohol, for example, is changed to acetate, which is a two-carbon molecule that can be used in cell respiration.

Medications are all potentially toxic, but the liver produces enzymes that break them down or change them. When given in a proper dosage, a medication exerts its therapeutic effect but is then changed to less active substances that are usually excreted by the kidneys. An overdose of a drug means that there is too much of it for the liver to detoxify in a given time, and the drug will remain in the body with possibly harmful effects. This is why alcohol should never be consumed when taking medication. Such a combination may cause the liver's detoxification ability to be overworked and ineffective, with the result that both the alcohol and the medication will remain toxic for a longer time. Barbiturates taken as sleeping pills after consumption of alcohol have too often proved fatal for just this reason.

Ammonia is a toxic substance produced by the bacteria in the colon. Since it is soluble in water, some ammonia is absorbed into the blood, but it is carried first to the liver by portal circulation. The liver converts ammonia to urea, a less toxic substance, before the ammonia can circulate and damage other organs, especially the brain. The urea formed is excreted by the kidneys (see Box 16–6: Hepatitis).

SUMMARY

The processes of the digestion of food and the absorption of nutrients enable the body to use complex food molecules for many purposes. Much of the food we eat literally becomes part of us. The body synthesizes proteins and lipids for the growth and repair of tissues and produces enzymes to catalyze all the reactions that contribute to homeostasis. Some of our food provides the energy required for growth, repair, movement, sensation, and thinking. In the next chapter we will discuss the chemical basis of energy production from food and consider the relationship of energy production to the maintenance of body temperature.

STUDY OUTLINE

Function of the Digestive System—to break down food into simple chemicals that can be absorbed into the blood and lymph and utilized by cells

Divisions of the Digestive System

1. Alimentary tube: oral cavity, pharynx, esophagus, stomach, small intestine, large intestine. Digestion takes place in the oral cavity, stomach, and small intestine.
2. Accessory Organs: salivary glands, teeth and tongue, liver and gallbladder, pancreas. Each contributes to digestion.

Types of Digestion

1. Mechanical: breaks food into smaller pieces to increase the surface area for the action of enzymes.
2. Chemical: enzymes break down complex organics into simpler organics and inorganics; each enzyme is specific for the food it will digest.

End Products of Digestion

1. Carbohydrates are digested to monosaccharides.
2. Fats are digested to fatty acids and glycerol.
3. Proteins are digested to amino acids.
4. Other end products are vitamins, minerals, and water.

Oral Cavity—food enters by way of the mouth

1. Teeth and tongue break up food and mix it with saliva.
2. Tooth structure (see Fig. 16–2): enamel covers the crown and provides a hard chewing surface; dentin is within the enamel and forms the roots; the pulp cavity contains blood vessels and endings of the trigeminal nerve; the periodontal membrane produces cement to anchor the tooth in the jawbone.
3. The tongue is skeletal muscle innervated by the hypoglossal nerves. Papillae on the upper surface contain taste buds (facial and glossopharyngeal nerves). Functions: taste, keeps food between the teeth when chewing, elevates to push food backward for swallowing.
4. Salivary Glands—parotid, submandibular, and sublingual (see Fig. 16–3); ducts take saliva to the oral cavity.

5. Saliva—amylase digests starch to maltose; water dissolves food for tasting and moistens food for swallowing; lysozyme inhibits the growth of bacteria (see Tables 16–1 and 16–2).

Pharynx—food passageway from the oral cavity to the esophagus

1. No digestion takes place.
2. Contraction of pharyngeal muscles is part of swallowing reflex, regulated by the medulla.

Esophagus—food passageway from pharynx to stomach

1. No digestion takes place.
2. Lower esophageal sphincter (LES) at junction with stomach prevents backup of stomach contents.

Structural Layers of the Alimentary Tube (see Fig. 16–4)

1. Mucosa (lining)—made of epithelial tissue which produces the digestive secretions; lymph nodules contain macrophages to phagocytize pathogens that penetrate the mucosa.
2. Submucosa—areolar connective tissue with blood vessels and lymphatic vessels; Meissner's plexus is an autonomic nerve network that innervates the mucosa.
3. External Muscle Layer—typically an inner circular layer and an outer longitudinal layer of smooth muscle; function is mechanical digestion and peristalsis; innervated by Auerbach's plexus: sympathetic impulses decrease motility; parasympathetic impulses increase motility.
4. Serosa—outermost layer; above the diaphragm is fibrous connective tissue; below the diaphragm is the mesentery (serous). The peritoneum (serous) lines the abdominal cavity; serous fluid prevents friction between the serous layers.

Stomach—in upper left abdominal quadrant; a muscular sac that extends from the esophagus to the small intestine (see Fig. 16–5)

1. Reservoir for food; begins the digestion of protein.
2. Gastric juice is secreted by gastric pits (see Tables 16–1 and 16–2).

3. The pyloric sphincter at the junction with the duodenum prevents backup of intestinal contents.

Liver—consists of two lobes in the upper right and center of the abdominal cavity (see Figs. 16–1 and 16–6)

1. The only digestive secretion is bile; the hepatic duct takes bile out of the liver and unites with the cystic duct of the gallbladder to form the common bile duct to the duodenum.
2. Bile salts emulsify fats, a type of mechanical digestion (see Table 16–2).
3. Excess cholesterol and bilirubin are excreted by the liver into bile.

Gallbladder—on undersurface of right lobe of liver (see Fig. 16–6)

1. Stores and concentrates bile until needed in the duodenum (see Table 16–2).
2. The cystic duct joins the hepatic duct to form the common bile duct.

Pancreas—in upper left abdominal quadrant between the duodenum and the spleen (see Fig. 16–1)

1. Pancreatic juice is secreted by acini, carried by pancreatic duct to the common bile duct to the duodenum (see Fig. 16–7).
2. Enzyme pancreatic juice contains enzymes for the digestion of all three food types (see Tables 16–1 and 16–2).
3. Bicarbonate pancreatic juice neutralizes HCl from the stomach in the duodenum.

Small Intestine—coiled within the center of the abdominal cavity (see Fig. 16–1); extends from stomach to colon

1. Duodenum—first 10 inches; the common bile duct brings in bile and pancreatic juice. Jejunum (8 feet) and ileum (11 feet).
2. Enzymes secreted by the intestinal glands complete digestion (see Tables 16–1 and 16–2).
3. Surface area for absorption is increased by plica circulares, villi, and microvilli (see Fig. 16–8).
4. The villi contain capillary networks for the absorption of water-soluble nutrients: monosaccharides, amino acids, vitamin C and B vitamins, minerals, and water. Blood from the small intestine goes to the liver first by way of portal circulation.
5. The villi contain lacteals (lymph capillaries) for the absorption of fat-soluble nutrients: vitamins A, D, E, and K, fatty acids and glycerol, which are combined to form chylomicrons. Lymph from the small intestine is carried back to the blood in the left subclavian vein.

Large Intestine (colon)—extends from the small intestine to the anus

1. Colon—parts (see Fig. 16–9): cecum, ascending colon, transverse colon, descending colon, sigmoid colon, rectum, anal canal.
2. Ileocecal Valve—at the junction of the cecum and ileum; prevents backup of fecal material into the small intestine.
3. Colon—functions: absorption of water, minerals, vitamins; elimination of undigestible material.
4. Normal Flora—the bacteria of the colon; produce vitamins, especially vitamin K, and inhibit the growth of pathogens.
5. Defecation Reflex—stimulus: stretching of the rectum when peristalsis propels feces into it. Sensory impulses go to the spinal cord, and motor impulses return to the smooth muscle of the rectum, which contracts. The internal anal sphincter relaxes to permit defecation. Voluntary control is provided by the external anal sphincter, made of skeletal muscle (see Fig. 16–10).

Liver—other functions

1. Carbohydrate Metabolism—excess glucose is stored in the form of glycogen and converted back to glucose during hypoglycemia; fructose and galactose are changed to glucose.
2. Amino Acid Metabolism—the non-essential amino acids are synthesized by transamination; excess amino acids are changed to carbohydrates or fats by deamination; the amino groups are converted to urea and excreted by the kidneys.
3. Lipid Metabolism—formation of lipoproteins for transport of fats in the blood; synthesis of cholesterol; excretion of excess cholesterol into bile; beta-oxidation of fatty acids to form two-carbon acetyl groups for energy use.

4. Synthesis of Plasma Proteins—albumin to help maintain blood volume; clotting factors for blood clotting; alpha and beta globulins as carrier molecules.
5. Formation of Bilirubin—old RBCs are phagocytized, and bilirubin is formed from the heme and put into bile to be eliminated in feces.
6. Phagocytosis by Kupffer Cells—fixed macrophages; phagocytize old RBCs and bacteria, especially bacteria absorbed by the colon.
7. Storage—vitamins: B_{12}, A, D, E, K, and the minerals iron and copper.
8. Detoxification—liver enzymes change potential poisons to less harmful substances; examples of toxic substances are alcohol, medications, and ammonia absorbed by the colon.

REVIEW QUESTIONS

1. Name the organs of the alimentary tube, and describe the location of each. Name the accessory digestive organs, and describe the location of each. (pp. 360, 362–364, 367, 371–372, 374)

2. Explain the purpose of mechanical digestion, and give two examples. Explain the purpose of chemical digestion, and give two examples. (pp. 360–364)

3. Name the end products of digestion, and explain how each is absorbed in the small intestine. (pp. 360, 362, 374)

4. Explain the function of teeth and tongue, salivary amylase, enamel of teeth, lysozyme, water of saliva. (pp. 362–363)

5. Describe the function of the pharynx, esophagus, lower esophageal sphincter. (pp. 364–365)

6. Name and describe the four layers of the alimentary tube. (p. 365)

7. State the two general functions of the stomach and the function of the pyloric sphincter. Explain the function of pepsin, HCl, and mucus. (p. 367)

8. Describe the general functions of the small intestine, and name the three parts. Describe the structures that increase the surface area of the small intestine. (pp. 367, 374)

9. Explain how the liver, gallbladder, and pancreas contribute to digestion. (pp. 371–372)

10. Describe the internal structure of a villus, and explain how structure is related to absorption. (p. 374)

11. Name the parts of the large intestine, and describe the function of the ileocecal valve. (pp. 376–377)

12. Describe the functions of the colon and of the normal flora of the colon. (p. 378)

13. With respect to the defecation reflex, explain the stimulus, the part of the CNS directly involved, the effector muscle, the function of the internal anal sphincter, the voluntary control possible. (p. 378)

14. Name the vitamins and minerals stored in the liver. Name the fixed macrophages of the liver, and explain their function. (p. 382)

15. Describe how the liver regulates blood glucose level. Explain the purpose of the processes of deamination and transamination. (p. 380)

16. Name the plasma proteins produced by the liver, and state the function of each. (pp. 380, 382)

17. Name the substances excreted by the liver into bile. (p. 380, 382)

Chapter 17
Body Temperature and Metabolism

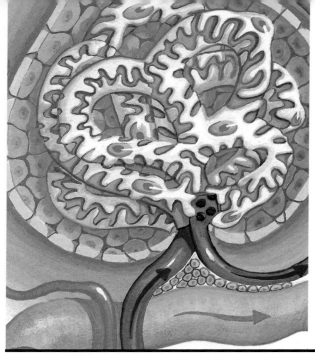

Chapter 17

Student Objectives

- State the normal range of human body temperature.
- Explain how cell respiration produces heat and the factors that affect heat production.
- Describe the pathways of heat loss through the skin and respiratory tract.
- Explain why the hypothalamus is called the thermostat of the body.
- Describe the mechanisms to increase heat loss.
- Describe the mechanisms to conserve heat.
- Explain how a fever is caused and the advantages and disadvantages.
- Define metabolism, anabolism, catabolism.
- Describe what happens to a glucose molecule during the three stages of cell respiration.
- State what happens to each of the products of cell respiration.
- Explain how amino acids and fats may be used for energy production.
- Describe the synthesis uses for glucose, amino acids, and fats.
- Explain what is meant by metabolic rate and kilocalories.
- Describe the factors that affect a person's metabolic rate.

Body Temperature and Metabolism

New Terminology

Anabolism (an–**AB**–uh–lizm)
Catabolism (kuh–**TAB**–uh–lizm)
Coenzyme (ko–**EN**–zime)
Conduction (kon–**DUK**–shun)
Convection (kon–**VEK**–shun)
Cytochromes (**SIGH**–toh–krohms)
Endogenous pyrogen (en–**DOJ**–en–us **PYE**–roh–jen)
Fever (**FEE**–ver)
Glycolysis (gly–**KOL**–ah–sis)
Kilocalorie (KILL–oh–**KAL**–oh–ree)
Krebs cycle (KREBS **SIGH**–kuhl)
Metabolism (muh–**TAB**–uh–lizm)

Minerals (**MIN**–er–als)
Pyrogen (**PYE**–roh–jen)
Radiation (RAY–dee–**AY**–shun)
Vitamins (**VY**–tah–mins)

Related Clinical Terminology

Antipyretic (AN–tigh–pye–**RET**–ik)
Basal metabolic rate (**BAY**–zuhl met–ah–**BAHL**–ik RAYT)
Frostbite (**FRAWST**–bite)
Heat exhaustion (HEET eks–**ZAWS**–chun)
Heat stroke (HEET STROHK)
Hypothermia (HIGH–poh–**THER**–mee–ah)

Terms that appear in **bold type** in the chapter text are defined in the glossary, which begins on page 549.

During every moment of our lives, our cells are breaking down food molecules to obtain ATP for energy-requiring cellular processes. Naturally, we are not aware of the process of cell respiration, but we may be aware of one of the products, energy in the form of heat. The human body is indeed warm, and its temperature is regulated very precisely, even in a wide range of environmental temperatures.

In this chapter we will discuss the regulation of body temperature and also discuss **metabolism,** which is the total of all the reactions that take place within the body. These reactions include the energy-releasing ones of cell respiration and energy-requiring ones such as protein synthesis, or DNA synthesis for mitosis. As you will see, body temperature and metabolism are inseparable.

BODY TEMPERATURE

The normal range of human body temperature is 96.5 to 99.5°F (36 to 38°C), with an average of 98.6°F (37°C). (A 1992 study suggested a slightly lower average temperature: 98.2°F or 36.8°C. Whether these values will replace the more "traditional" average temperatures remains to be seen.) Within a 24-hour period, an individual's temperature fluctuates 1 to 2°F, with the lowest temperatures occurring during sleep.

At either end of the age spectrum, however, temperature regulation may not be as precise as it is in older children or younger adults. Infants have more surface area (skin) relative to volume and are likely to lose heat more rapidly. In the elderly, the mechanisms that maintain body temperature may not function as efficiently as they once did, and changes in environmental temperature may not be compensated for as quickly or effectively. This is especially important to remember when caring for patients who are very young or very old.

HEAT PRODUCTION

Cell respiration, the process that releases energy from food to produce ATP, also produces heat as one of its energy products. Although cell respiration

takes place constantly, there are many factors that influence the rate of this process:

1. The hormone **thyroxine** (and T_3), produced by the thyroid gland, increases the rate of cell respiration and heat production. The secretion of thyroxine is regulated by the body's rate of energy production, the metabolic rate itself (see Chapter 10 for the feedback mechanism involving the hypothalamus and anterior pituitary gland). When the metabolic rate decreases, the thyroid gland is stimulated to secrete more thyroxine. As thyroxine increases the rate of cell respiration, a negative feedback mechanism inhibits further secretion until metabolic rate decreases again. Thus, thyroxine is secreted whenever there is a need for increased cell respiration and is probably the most important regulator of day-to-day energy production.

2. In stress situations, **epinephrine** and norepinephrine are secreted by the adrenal medulla, and the **sympathetic** nervous system becomes more active. Epinephrine increases the rate of cell respiration, especially in organs such as the heart, skeletal muscles, and liver. Sympathetic stimulation also increases the activity of these organs. The increased production of ATP to meet the demands of the stress situation also means that more heat will be produced.

3. Organs that are normally active (producing ATP) are significant sources of heat when the body is at rest. The skeletal muscles, for example, are usually in a state of slight contraction called muscle tone. Since even slight contraction requires ATP, the muscles are also producing heat. This amounts to about 25% of the total body heat at rest and much more during exercise when more ATP is produced.

The liver is another organ that is continually active, producing ATP to supply energy for its many functions. As a result, the liver produces as much as 20% of the total body heat at rest.

The heat produced by these active organs is dispersed throughout the body by the blood. As the relatively cooler blood flows through organs such as the muscles and liver, the heat they produce is transferred to the blood, warming it. The warmed blood circulates to other areas of the body, distributing this heat.

4. The intake of food also increases heat production, because the metabolic activity of the digestive tract is increased. Heat is generated as the digestive organs produce ATP for peristalsis and for the synthesis of digestive enzymes.

5. Changes in body temperature also have an effect on metabolic rate and heat production. This becomes clinically important when a person has a **fever,** an abnormally high body temperature. The higher temperature increases the metabolic rate, which increases heat production and elevates body temperature further. Thus, a high fever may trigger a vicious cycle of ever-increasing heat production. Fever will be discussed later in this chapter.

The factors that affect heat production are summarized in Table 17–1.

HEAT LOSS

The pathways of heat loss from the body are the skin, respiratory tract, and to a lesser extent, the urinary and digestive tracts.

Heat Loss through the Skin

Since the skin covers the body, most body heat is lost from the skin to the environment. When the environment is cooler than body temperature (as it usually is), heat loss is unavoidable. The amount of heat that is lost is determined by blood flow through the skin and by the activity of sweat glands.

Blood flow through the skin influences the amount of heat lost by the processes of radiation, conduction, and convection. **Radiation** means that heat from the body is lost to cooler air, much as a radiator warms the air within a room (radiation starts to become less effective when the environmental temperature rises above 88°F). **Conduction** is the loss of heat to cooler objects, such as clothing, that touch the skin. **Convection** means that air currents move the warmer air away from the skin surface and facilitate the loss of heat; this is why a fan makes us feel cooler on hot days.

Table 17–1 FACTORS THAT AFFECT HEAT PRODUCTION

Factor	Effect
Thyroxine	• The most important regulator of day-to-day metabolism; increases use of foods for ATP production, thereby increasing heat production
Epinephrine and sympathetic stimulation	• Important in stress situations; increases the metabolic activity of many organs; increases ATP and heat production
Skeletal muscles	• Normal muscle tone requires ATP; the heat produced is about 25% of the total body heat at rest
Liver	• Always metabolically active; produces as much as 20% of total body heat at rest
Food intake	• Increases activity of the GI tract; increases ATP and heat production
Higher body temperature	• Increases metabolic rate, which increases heat production, which further increases metabolic rate and heat production. May become detrimental during high fevers.

The temperature of the skin and the subsequent loss of heat is determined by blood flow through the skin. The arterioles in the dermis may constrict or dilate to decrease or increase blood flow. **Vasoconstriction** decreases blood flow through the dermis and thereby decreases heat loss. **Vasodilation** in the dermis increases blood flow to the body surface and loss of heat to the environment.

The other mechanism by which heat is lost from the skin is sweating. The **eccrine sweat glands** secrete sweat (water) onto the skin surface, and excess body heat evaporates the sweat. Think of running water into a hot frying pan; the pan is rapidly cooled as its heat vaporizes the water. Although sweating is not quite as dramatic (no visible steam), the principle is just the same.

Sweating is most efficient when the humidity of the surrounding air is low. Humidity is the percentage of the maximum amount of water vapor the atmosphere can contain. A humidity reading of 90% means that the air is already 90% saturated with water vapor and can hold little more. In such a situation, sweat does not readily evaporate, but rather, remains on the skin even as more sweat is secreted. If the humidity is 40%, however, the air can hold a great deal more water vapor, and sweat evaporates quickly from the skin surface, removing excess body heat. In air that is completely dry, a person may tolerate a temperature of 200°F for nearly 1 hour.

Although sweating is a very effective mechanism of heat loss, it does have a disadvantage in that it requires the loss of water in order to also lose heat. Water loss during sweating may rapidly lead to dehydration, and the water lost must be replaced by drinking fluids (see Box 17–1: Heat-Related Disorders).

Small amounts of heat are also lost in what is called "insensible water loss." Since the skin is not like a plastic bag, but is somewhat permeable to water, a small amount of water diffuses through the skin and is evaporated by body heat. Compared to sweating, however, insensible water loss is a minor source of heat loss.

Heat Loss through the Respiratory Tract

Heat is lost from the respiratory tract as the warmth of the respiratory mucosa evaporates some water from the living epithelial surface. The water vapor formed is exhaled, and a small amount of heat is lost.

Animals such as dogs that do not have numerous sweat glands often pant in warm weather. Panting is the rapid movement of air into and out of the upper respiratory passages, where the warm sur-

---

Box 17–1 HEAT-RELATED DISORDERS

Heat exhaustion is caused by excessive sweating with loss of water and salts, especially NaCl. The affected person feels very weak, and the skin is usually cool and clammy (moist). Body temperature is normal or slightly below normal, the pulse is often rapid and weak, and blood pressure may be low because of fluid loss. Other symptoms may include dizziness, vomiting, and muscle cramps. Treatment involves rest and consumption of salty fluids or fruit juices (in small amounts at frequent intervals).

Heat stroke is a life-threatening condition that may affect elderly or chronically ill people on hot, humid days, or otherwise healthy people who exercise too strenuously during such weather. High humidity makes sweating an ineffective mechanism of heat loss, but in high heat the sweating process continues. As fluid loss increases, sweating stops to preserve body fluid, and body temperature rises rapidly (over 105°F, possibly as high as 110°F).

The classic symptom of heat stroke is hot, dry skin. The affected person often loses consciousness, reflecting the destructive effect of such a high body temperature on the brain. Treatment should involve hospitalization so that IV fluids may be administered and body temperature lowered under medical supervision. A first-aid measure would be the application of cool (not ice cold) water to as much of the skin as possible. Fluids should never be forced on an unconscious person, since the fluid may be aspirated into the respiratory tract.

faces evaporate large amounts of water. In this way the animal may lose large amounts of heat.

Heat Loss through the Urinary and Digestive Tracts

When excreted, urine and feces are at body temperature, and their elimination results in a very small amount of heat loss. The pathways of heat loss are summarized in Table 17–2.

REGULATION OF BODY TEMPERATURE

The **hypothalamus** is responsible for the regulation of body temperature and is considered the "thermostat" of the body. As the thermostat, the hypothalamus maintains the "setting" of body temperature by balancing heat production and heat loss to keep the body at the set temperature.

In order to do this, the hypothalamus must receive information about the temperature within the

body and about the environmental temperature. Specialized neurons of the hypothalamus detect changes in the temperature of the blood that flows through the brain. The temperature receptors in the skin provide information about the external temperature changes the body is exposed to. The hypothalamus then integrates this sensory information and promotes the necessary responses to maintain body temperature within the normal range.

Mechanisms to Increase Heat Loss

In a warm environment or during exercise, the body temperature tends to rise, and greater heat loss is needed. This is accomplished by vasodilation in the dermis and an increase in sweating. Vasodilation brings more warm blood close to the body surface, and heat is lost to the environment. However, if the environmental temperature is close to or higher than body temperature, this mechanism becomes ineffective. The second mechanism is increased sweating, in which excess body heat evaporates the sweat on the skin surface. As mentioned previously, sweating becomes inefficient when the atmospheric humidity is high.

On hot days, heat production may also be decreased by a decrease in muscle tone. This is why we may feel very sluggish on hot days; our muscles are even less slightly contracted than usual and are slower to respond.

Mechanisms to Conserve Heat

In a cold environment, heat loss from the body is unavoidable but may be minimized to some extent. Vasoconstriction in the dermis shunts blood away from the body surface, so that more heat is kept in the core of the body. Sweating decreases, and will stop completely if the temperature of the hypothalamus falls below about 98.6°F.

If these mechanisms are not sufficient to prevent the body temperature from dropping, more heat may be produced by increasing muscle tone. When this greater muscle tone becomes noticeable and rhythmic it is called shivering and may increase heat production as much as five times the normal.

People also have behavioral responses to cold,

Table 17–2   PATHWAYS OF HEAT LOSS

Pathway	Mechanism
Skin (major pathway)	• Radiation and Conduction—heat is lost from the body to cooler air or objects that touch the skin. • Convection—air currents move warm air away from the skin. • Sweating—excess body heat evaporates sweat on the skin surface.
Respiratory tract (secondary pathway)	• Evaporation—body heat evaporates water from the respiratory mucosa, and water vapor is exhaled.
Urinary tract (minor pathway)	• Urination—urine is at body temperature when eliminated.
Digestive tract (minor pathway)	• Defecation—feces are at body temperature when eliminated.

and these too are important to prevent heat loss. Such things as putting on a sweater or going indoors reflect our awareness of the discomfort of being cold. For people (we do not have thick fur as do some other mammals), these voluntary activities are of critical importance to the prevention of excessive heat loss when it is very cold (see Box 17–2: Cold-Related Disorders).

FEVER

A fever is an abnormally high body temperature and may accompany infectious diseases, extensive physical trauma, cancer, or damage to the CNS. The substances that may cause a fever are called **pyrogens.** Pyrogens include bacteria, foreign proteins, and chemicals released during inflammation **(endogenous pyrogens).** It is believed that py-

rogens chemically affect the hypothalamus and "raise the setting" of the hypothalamic thermostat. The hypothalamus will then stimulate responses by the body to raise body temperature to this higher setting.

Let us use as a specific example a child who has a strep throat. The bacterial and endogenous pyrogens reset the hypothalamic thermostat upward, to 102°F. At first, the body is "colder" than the setting of the hypothalamus, and the heat conservation and production mechanisms are activated. The child feels cold and begins to shiver (chills). Eventually, sufficient heat is produced to raise the body temperature to the hypothalamic setting of 102°F. At this time, the child will feel neither too warm nor too cold, because the body temperature is what the hypothalamus wants.

As the effects of the pyrogens diminish, the hy-

Box 17–2 COLD-RELATED DISORDERS

Frostbite is the freezing of part of the body. Fingers, toes, the nose, and ears are most often affected by prolonged exposure to cold, since these areas have little volume in proportion to their surface.

At first the skin tingles, then becomes numb. If body fluids freeze, ice crystals may destroy capillaries and tissues (because water expands when it freezes), and blisters form. In the most severe cases gangrene develops, that is, tissue dies because of lack of oxygen.

Treatment of frostbite includes rewarming the affected area. If skin damage is apparent, it should be treated as if it were a burn injury.

Hypothermia is an abnormally low body temperature (below 95°F) that is most often the result of prolonged exposure to cold. Although the affected person certainly feels cold at first, this sensation may pass and be replaced by confusion, slurred speech, drowsiness, and lack of coordination. At this stage, people often do not realize the seriousness of their condition, and if outdoors (ice skating or skiing) may not seek a warmer environment. In progressive hypothermia, breathing and heart rate slow, and coma and death follow.

Other people at greater risk for hypothermia include the elderly, whose temperature-regulating mechanisms are no longer effective, and quadriplegics, who have no sensation of cold in the body. For both these groups, heat production is or may be low because of inactivity of skeletal muscles.

Artificial hypothermia may be induced during some types of cardiovascular or neurological surgery. This carefully controlled lowering of body temperature decreases the metabolic rate and need for oxygen and makes possible prolonged surgery without causing extensive tissue death in the patient.

pothalamic setting decreases, perhaps close to normal again, 99°F. Now the child will feel warm, and the heat loss mechanisms will be activated. Vasodilation in the skin and sweating will occur until the body temperature drops to the new hypothalamic setting. This is sometimes referred to as the "crisis," but actually the crisis has passed, since sweating indicates that the body temperature is returning to normal. The sequence of temperature changes during a fever is shown in Fig. 17–1.

You may be wondering if a fever serves a useful purpose. For low fevers that are the result of infec-

tion, the answer seems to be yes. White blood cells increase their activity at moderately elevated temperatures, and the metabolism of some pathogens is inhibited. Thus, a fever may be beneficial in that it may shorten the duration of an infection by accelerating the destruction of the pathogen.

High fevers, however, may have serious consequences. When the body temperature rises above 106°F, the hypothalamus begins to lose its ability to regulate temperature. The enzymes of cells are also damaged by such high temperatures. Enzymes become denatured, that is, lose their shape and do not

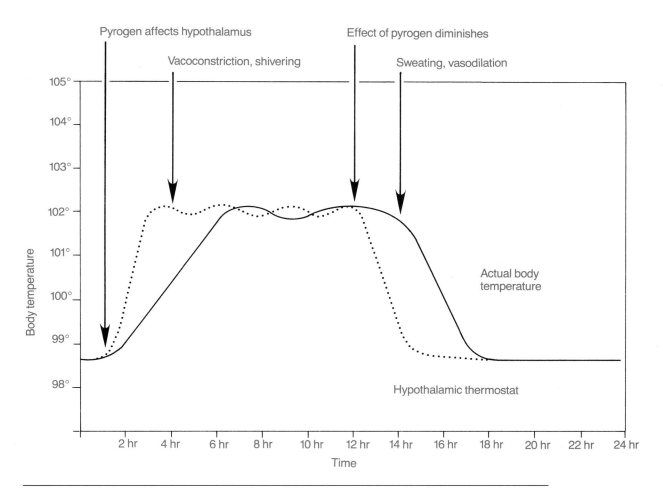

Figure 17–1 Changes in body temperature during an episode of fever. The body temperature *(solid line)* changes lag behind the changes in the hypothalamic thermostat *(dotted line)* but eventually reach whatever the thermostat has called for.

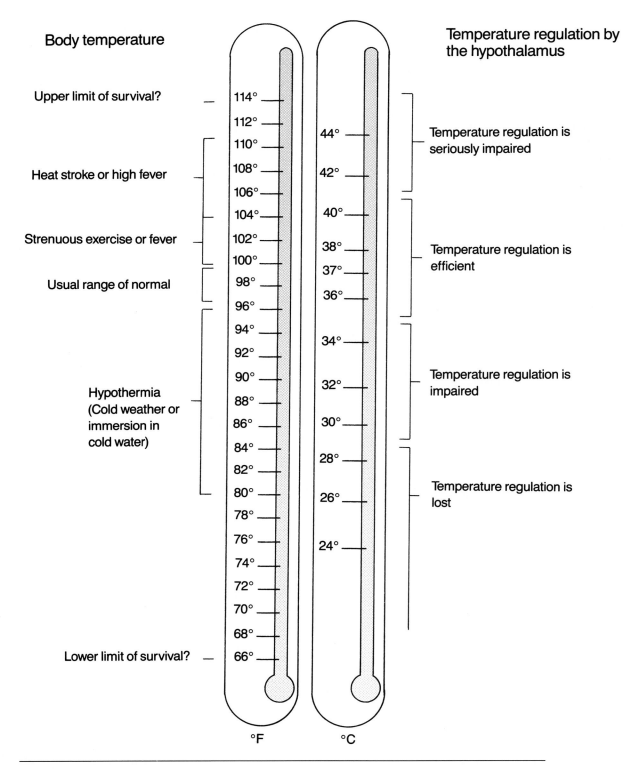

Figure 17–2 Effects of changes in body temperature on the temperature-regulating ability of the hypothalamus. Body temperature is shown in degrees Fahrenheit and degrees Celsius.

catalyze the reactions necessary within cells. As a result, cells begin to die. This is most serious in the brain, since neurons cannot be replaced and is the cause of brain damage that may follow a prolonged high fever. The effects of changes in body temperature on the hypothalamus are shown in Fig. 17–2.

A medication such as aspirin is called an **antipyretic** because it lowers a fever, probably by affecting the hypothalamic thermostat. To help lower a very high fever, the body may be cooled by sponging with alcohol or cold water. The excessive body heat will cause these fluids to evaporate, thus reducing temperature.

METABOLISM

The term **metabolism** encompasses all the reactions that take place in the body. Everything that happens within us is part of our metabolism. The reactions of metabolism may be divided into two major categories: anabolism and catabolism.

Anabolism means synthesis or "formation" reactions, the bonding together of smaller molecules to form larger ones. The synthesis of hemoglobin by cells of the red bone marrow, synthesis of glycogen by liver cells, and synthesis of fat to be stored in adipose tissue are all examples of anabolism. Such reactions require energy, usually in the form of ATP.

Catabolism means decomposition, the breaking of bonds of larger molecules to form smaller molecules. Cell respiration is a series of catabolic reactions that break down food molecules to carbon dioxide and water. During catabolism, energy is often released and used to synthesize ATP (the heat energy released was discussed in the previous section). The ATP formed during catabolism is then used for energy-requiring anabolic reactions.

Most of our anabolic and catabolic reactions are catalyzed by enzymes. Enzymes are proteins that enable reactions to take place rapidly at body temperature (see Chapter 2 to review the active site theory of enzyme functioning). The body has thousands of enzymes, and each is specific, that is, will catalyze only one type of reaction. As you read

the discussions that follow, keep in mind the essential role of enzymes.

CELL RESPIRATION

You are already familiar with the summary equation of cell respiration,

$$C_6H_{12}O_6 + O_2 \rightarrow CO_2 + H_2O + ATP + Heat$$
(glucose)

the purpose of which is to produce ATP. Glucose contains potential energy, and when it is broken down to CO_2 and H_2O, this energy is released in the forms of ATP and heat. The oxygen that is required comes from breathing, and the CO_2 formed is circulated to the lungs to be exhaled. The water formed is called metabolic water, and helps to meet our daily need for water. Energy in the form of heat gives us a body temperature, and the ATP formed is used for energy-requiring reactions. Synthesis of ATP means that energy is used to bond a free phosphate molecule to ADP (adenosine diphosphate). ADP and free phosphates are present in cells after ATP has been broken down for energy-requiring processes.

The breakdown of glucose summarized above is not quite that simple, however, and involves a complex series of reactions. Glucose is broken down "piece by piece," with the removal of hydrogens and the splitting of carbon-carbon bonds. This releases the energy of glucose gradually, so that a significant portion (about 40%) is available to synthesize ATP.

Cell respiration of glucose involves three major stages: glycolysis, the Krebs citric acid cycle, and the cytochrome (or electron) transport system. Although all the details of each stage are beyond the scope of this book, we will summarize the most important aspects of each, and then relate to them the use of amino acids and fats for energy.

Glycolysis

The enzymes for the reactions of **glycolysis** are found in the cytoplasm of cells, and oxygen is not required (glycolysis is an anaerobic process). Refer now to Fig. 17–3 as you read the following. In glycolysis, a six-carbon glucose molecule is broken

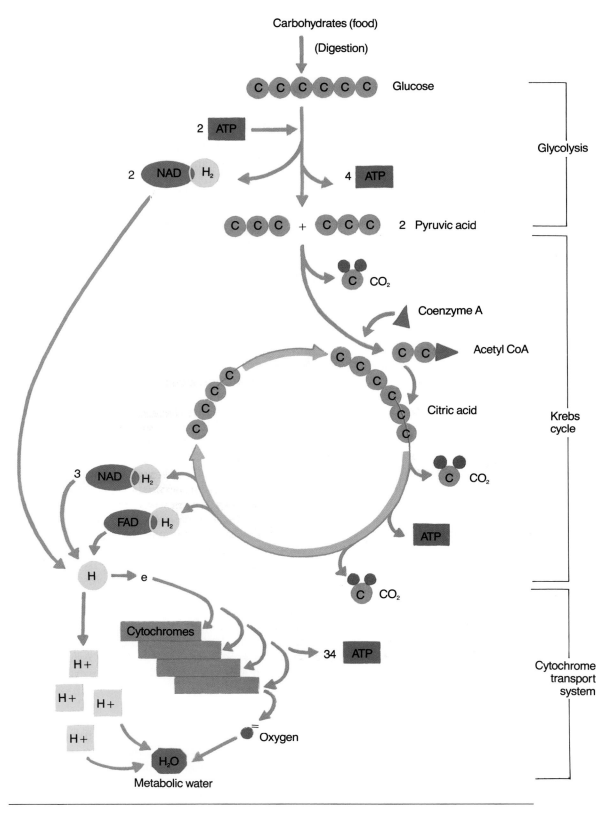

Figure 17–3 Schematic representation of one glucose molecule being broken down in the process of cell respiration. See text for description.

down to two three-carbon molecules of pyruvic acid. Two molecules of ATP are necessary to start the process. The energy they supply is called energy of activation and is necessary to make glucose unstable enough to begin to break down. As a result of these reactions, enough energy is released to synthesize four molecules of ATP, for a net gain of two ATP molecules per glucose molecule. Also during glycolysis, two pairs of hydrogens are removed by NAD, a carrier molecule that contains the vitamin **niacin.** Two NAD molecules thus become 2NADH$_2$, and these attached hydrogen pairs will be transported to the cytochrome transport system (stage 3).

If no oxygen is present in the cell, as may happen in muscle cells during exercise, pyruvic acid is converted to lactic acid, which causes muscle fatigue. If oxygen *is* present, however, pyruvic acid continues into the next stage, the Krebs citric acid cycle (or, more simply, the Krebs cycle).

Krebs Citric Acid Cycle

The enzymes for the **Krebs cycle** (or citric acid cycle) are located in the mitochondria of cells. This second stage of cell respiration is aerobic, meaning that oxygen is required. In a series of reactions, a pyruvic acid molecule is "taken apart," and its carbons are converted to CO$_2$. The first CO$_2$ molecule is removed by an enzyme that contains the vitamin **thiamine.** This leaves a two-carbon molecule called an acetyl group, which combines with a molecule called Coenzyme A to form acetyl coenzyme A (acetyl CoA). As acetyl CoA continues in the Krebs cycle, two more carbons are removed as CO$_2$, and more pairs of hydrogens are picked up by NAD and FAD (another carrier molecule that contains the vitamin **riboflavin**). NADH$_2$ and FADH$_2$ will carry their hydrogens to the cytochrome transport system.

During the Krebs cycle, a small amount of energy is released, enough to synthesize one molecule of ATP (two per glucose). Notice also that a four-carbon molecule (oxaloacetic acid) is regenerated after the formation of CO$_2$. This molecule will react with the next acetyl CoA, which is what makes the Krebs cycle truly a self-perpetuating cycle. The results of all the stages of cell respiration are listed in Table 17–3. Before you continue here you may wish to look at that table to see just where the process has gotten thus far.

Table 17–3 SUMMARY OF CELL RESPIRATION

Stage	Molecules That Enter the Process	Results	Vitamins or Minerals Needed
Glycolysis (cytoplasm)	Glucose—ATP needed as energy of activation	• 2 ATP (net) • 2 NADH$_2$ (to cytochrome transport system) • 2 pyruvic acid (aerobic: to Krebs cycle; anaerobic: lactic acid formation)	• niacin (part of NAD)
Krebs Citric Acid Cycle (mitochondria)	Pyruvic acid—from glucose or glycerol or excess amino acids *or* Acetyl CoA—from fatty acids or excess amino acids	• CO$_2$ (exhaled) • ATP (2 per glucose) • 3 NADH$_2$ and 1 FADH$_2$ (to cytochrome transport system) • A 4-carbon molecule is regenerated for the next cycle	• thiamine (thiamin) (for removal of CO$_2$) • niacin (part of NAD) • riboflavin (part of FAD) • pantothenic acid (part of CoenzymeA)
Cytochrome Transport System (mitochondria)	NADH$_2$ and FADH$_2$—from glycolysis or the Krebs cycle	• 34 ATP • metabolic water	• iron and copper (part of some cytochromes)

Cytochrome Transport System

Cytochromes are proteins that contain either **iron** or **copper** and are found in the mitochondria of cells. The pairs of hydrogens that were once part of glucose are brought to the cytochromes by the carrier molecules NAD and FAD. Each hydrogen atom is then split into its proton (H^+ ion) and its electron. The electrons of the hydrogens are passed from one cytochrome to the next, and finally to oxygen. The reactions of the electrons with the cytochromes release most of the energy that was contained in the glucose molecule, enough to synthesize 34 molecules of ATP. As you can see, most of the ATP produced in cell respiration comes from this third stage.

Finally, and very importantly, each oxygen atom that has gained two electrons (from the cytochromes) reacts with two of the H^+ ions (protons) to form water. The formation of metabolic water contributes to the necessary intracellular fluid, and also prevents acidosis. If H^+ ions accumulated, they would rapidly lower the pH of the cell. This does not happen, however, because the H^+ ions react with oxygen to form water, and a decrease in pH is prevented.

The summary of the three stages of cell respiration in Table 17–3 also includes the vitamins and minerals that are essential for this process. An important overall concept is the relationship between eating and breathing. Eating provides us with a potential energy source (often glucose) and with necessary vitamins and minerals. However, to release the energy from food, we must breathe. This is *why* we breathe. The oxygen we inhale is essential for the completion of cell respiration, and the CO_2 produced is exhaled.

Proteins and Fats as Energy Sources

Although glucose is the preferred energy source for cells, proteins and fats also contain potential energy and are alternative energy sources in certain situations.

As you know, proteins are made of the smaller molecules called **amino acids,** and the primary use for the amino acids we obtain from food is the synthesis of new proteins. Excess amino acids, how-ever, those not needed immediately for protein synthesis, may be used for energy production. In the liver, excess amino acids are **deaminated,** that is, the amino group (NH_2) is removed. The remaining portion is converted to a molecule that will fit into the Krebs Cycle. For example, a deaminated amino acid may be changed to a three-carbon pyruvic acid or to a two-carbon acetyl group. When these molecules enter the Krebs Cycle, the results are just the same as if they had come from glucose. This is diagrammed in Fig. 17–4.

Fats are made of glycerol and fatty acids, which are the end products of fat digestion. These molecules may also be changed to ones that will take part in the Krebs Cycle, and the reactions that change them usually take place in the liver. Glycerol is a three-carbon molecule that can be converted to the three-carbon pyruvic acid, which enters the Krebs Cycle. In the process of beta-oxidation, the long carbon chains of fatty acids are split into two-carbon acetyl groups, which enter a later step in the Krebs Cycle (Fig. 17–5).

Both amino acids and fatty acids may be converted by the liver to **ketones** which are two- or four-carbon molecules such as acetone and acetoacetic acid. Although body cells can use ketones in cell respiration, they do so slowly. In situations in which fats or amino acids have become the primary energy sources, a state called **ketosis** may develop; this is described in Box 17–3: Ketosis. Excess amino acids may also be converted to glucose; this is important to supply the brain when dietary intake of carbohydrates is low. The effects of hormones on the metabolism of food are summarized in Table 17–4.

Energy Available from the Three Nutrient Types

The potential energy in food is measured in units called **Calories** or **kilocalories.** A calorie (lower case "c") is the amount of energy needed to raise the temperature of 1 gram of water 1°C. A kilocalorie or Calorie (capital "C") is 1000 times that amount of energy.

One gram of carbohydrate yields about 4 kilocalories. A gram of protein also yields about 4 kilocalories. A gram of fat, however, yields 9 kilocalo-

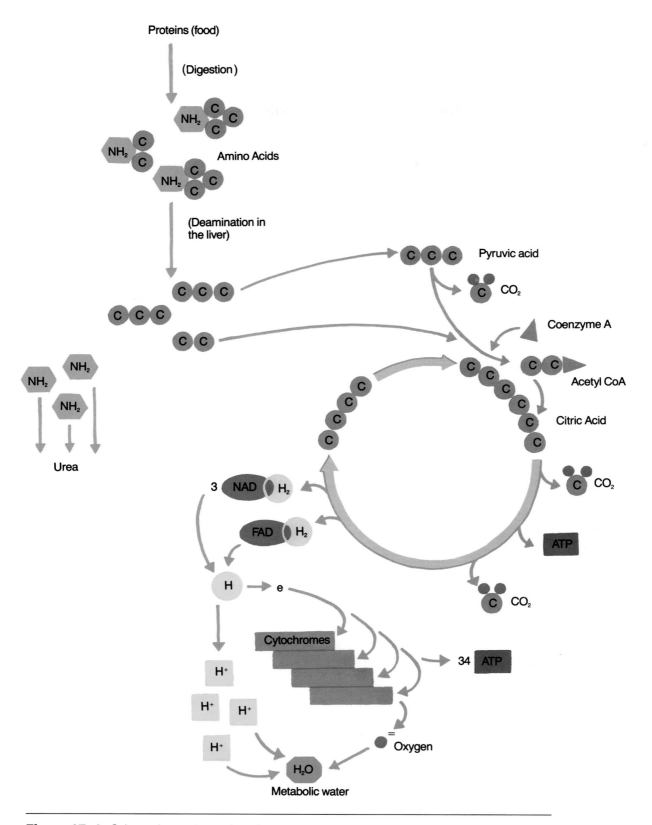

Figure 17–4 Schematic representation of the use of excess amino acids for energy production in cell respiration. An amino acid is deaminated and the carbon chain then enters some phase of the Krebs cycle.

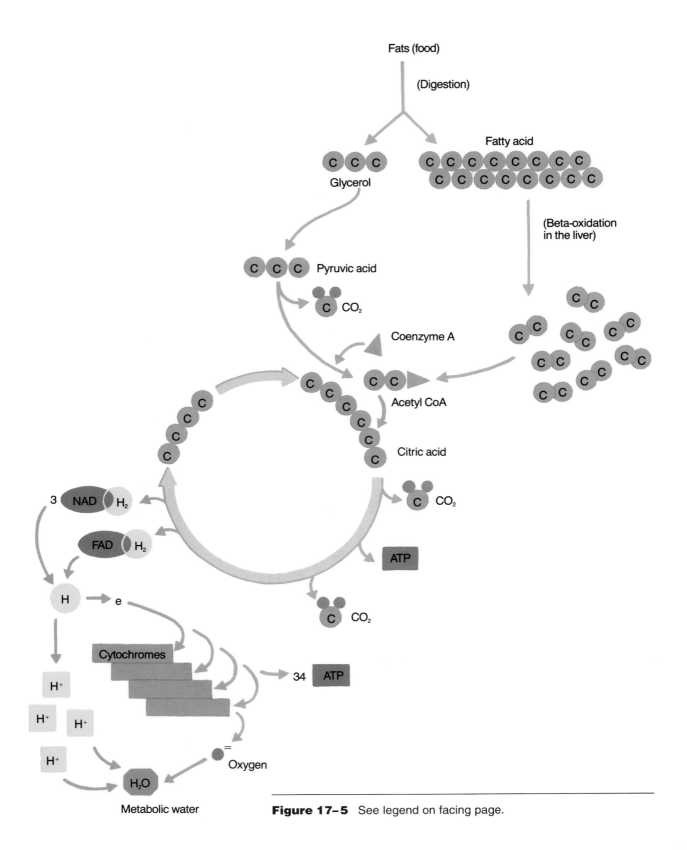

Figure 17-5 See legend on facing page.

Box 17–3 KETOSIS

When fats and amino acids are to be used for energy, they are often converted by the liver to ketones. Ketones are organic molecules such as acetone that may be changed to acetyl CoA and enter the Krebs cycle. Other cells are able to use ketones as an energy source, but they do so slowly. When ketones are produced in small amounts, as they usually are between meals, the blood level does not rise sharply.

A state of **ketosis** exists when fats and proteins become the primary energy sources, and ketones accumulate in the blood faster than cells can utilize them. Since ketones are organic acids, they lower the pH of the blood. As the blood ketone level rises, the kidneys excrete ketones, but they must also excrete more water as a solvent, which leads to dehydration.

Ketosis is clinically important in diabetes mellitus, starvation, and eating disorders such as anorexia nervosa. Diabetics whose disease is poorly controlled may progress to **ketoacidosis,** a form of metabolic acidosis that may lead to confusion, coma, and death. Reversal of this state requires a carbohydrate energy source and the insulin necessary to utilize it.

---

ries, and a gram of alcohol yields 7 kilocalories. This is why a diet high in fat is more likely to result in weight gain if the calories are not expended in energy-requiring activities.

You may have noticed that calorie content is part of the nutritional information on food labels. Here, however, the term "calorie" actually means Calorie or kilocalories but is used for the sake of simplicity.

SYNTHESIS USES OF FOODS

Besides being available for energy production, each of the three food types is used in anabolic reactions to synthesize necessary materials for cells and tissues.

Glucose

Glucose is the raw material for the synthesis of another essential monosaccharide, the **pentose sugars** that are part of nucleic acids. Deoxyribose is the five-carbon sugar found in DNA, and ribose is found in RNA. This function of glucose is very important, for without the pentose sugars our cells could neither produce new chromosomes for cell division nor carry out the process of protein synthesis.

Any glucose in excess of immediate energy needs or the need for pentose sugars is converted to **glycogen** in the liver and skeletal muscles. Glycogen is then an energy source during states of hypoglycemia or during exercise.

Amino Acids

As mentioned previously, the primary uses for amino acids are the synthesis of the **non-essential amino acids** by the liver and the synthesis of new **proteins** in all tissues. By way of review, we can mention some proteins with which you are already familiar: keratin and melanin in the epidermis; collagen in the dermis, tendons, and ligaments; myosin, actin, and myoglobin in muscle cells; hemoglobin in RBCs; antibodies produced by WBCs;

Figure 17–5 Use of glycerol and fatty acids for energy production in cell respiration. Gycerol is changed to pyruvic acid, and a fatty acid is converted to acetyl groups, which then enter the Krebs cycle.

Table 17–4 HORMONES THAT REGULATE METABOLISM

Hormone (gland)	Effects
Thyroxine (thyroid gland)	• Increases use of all three food types for energy (glucose, fats, amino acids) • Increases protein synthesis
Growth Hormone (anterior pituitary)	• Increases amino acid transport into cells • Increases protein synthesis • Increases use of fats for energy
Insulin (pancreas)	• Increases glucose transport into cells and use for energy • Increases conversion of glucose to glycogen in liver and muscles • Increases transport of amino acids and fatty acids into cells to be used for synthesis (*not* energy production)
Glucagon (pancreas)	• Increases conversion of glycogen to glucose • Increases use of amino acids and fats for energy
Cortisol (adrenal cortex)	• Increases conversion of glucose to glycogen in liver • Increases use of amino acids and fats for energy • Decreases protein synthesis except in liver and GI tract
Epinephrine (adrenal medulla)	• Increases conversion of glycogen to glucose • Increases use of fats for energy

prothrombin and fibrinogen for clotting; albumin to maintain blood volume; pepsin and amylase for digestion; growth hormone and insulin; and the thousands of enzymes needed to catalyze reactions within the body.

The amino acids we obtain from the proteins in our food are used by our cells to synthesize all of these proteins in the amounts needed by the body. Only when the body's needs for new proteins have been met are amino acids used for energy production.

Fatty Acids and Glycerol

The end products of fat digestion that are not needed immediately for energy production may be stored as fat (triglycerides) in **adipose tissue.** Most adipose tissue is found subcutaneously and is potential energy for times when food intake decreases.

Fatty acids and glycerol are also used for the synthesis of **phospholipids,** which are essential components of all cell membranes. Myelin, for example, is a phospholipid of the membranes of Schwann cells which form the myelin sheath of peripheral neurons.

When fatty acids are broken down in the process of beta-oxidation, the resulting acetyl groups may also be used for the synthesis of **cholesterol,** a steroid. This takes place primarily in the liver, although all cells are capable of synthesizing cholesterol for their cell membranes. The liver uses cholesterol to synthesize bile salts for the emulsification of fats in digestion. The **steroid hormones** are also synthesized from cholesterol. Cortisol and aldosterone are produced by the adrenal cortex; estrogen and progesterone by the ovaries, and testosterone by the testes.

VITAMINS AND MINERALS

Vitamins are organic molecules needed in very small amounts for normal body functioning. Some vitamins are **coenzymes,** that is, they are necessary for the functioning of certain enzymes. Table 17–5 summarizes some important metabolic and nutritional aspects of the vitamins we need.

Minerals are simple inorganic chemicals and have a variety of functions. Table 17–6 lists some important aspects of minerals. We will return to the minerals as part of fluid-electrolyte balance in Chapter 19.

METABOLIC RATE

Although the term **metabolism** is used to describe all of the chemical reactions that take place within the body, **metabolic rate** is usually expressed as an amount of heat production. This is because many body processes that utilize ATP also

Table 17–5 VITAMINS

Vitamin	Functions	Food Sources	Comment
Water Soluble			
Thiamine (B$_1$)	• Conversion of pyruvic acid to acetylCoA in cell respiration • Synthesis of pentose sugars • Synthesis of acetylcholine	• Meat, eggs, legumes, green leafy vegetables, grains	Rapidly destroyed by heat
Riboflavin (B$_2$)	• Part of FAD in cell respiration	• Meat, milk, cheese, grains	Small amounts produced by GI bacteria
Niacin (nicotinamide)	• Part of NAD in cell respiration • Metabolism of fat for energy	• Meat, fish, grains, legumes	
Pyridoxine (B$_6$)	• Part of enzymes needed for amino acid metabolism and protein synthesis, nucleic acid synthesis, synthesis of antibodies	• Meat, fish, grains, yeast, yogurt	Small amounts produced by GI bacteria
B$_{12}$ (cyanocobalamin)	• Synthesis of DNA, especially in RBC production • Metabolism of amino acids for energy	• Liver, meat, fish, eggs, milk, cheese	Contains cobalt; intrinsic factor required for absorption
Biotin	• Synthesis of nucleic acids • Metabolism of fatty acids and amino acids	• Yeast, liver, eggs	Small amounts produced by GI bacteria
Folic Acid (folacin)	• Synthesis of DNA, especially in blood cell production	• Liver, grains, legumes, leafy green vegetables	Small amounts produced by GI bacteria
Pantothenic Acid	• Part of coenzymeA in cell respiration, use of amino acids and fats for energy	• Meat, fish, grains, legumes, vegetables	Small amounts produced by GI bacteria
Vitamin C (ascorbic acid)	• Synthesis of collagen, especially for wound healing • Metabolism of amino acids • Absorption of iron	• Citrus fruits, tomatoes, potatoes	Rapidly destroyed by heat
Fat Soluble			
Vitamin A	• Synthesis of rhodopsin • Calcification of growing bones • Maintenance of epithelial tissues	• Yellow and green vegetables, liver, milk, eggs	Stored in liver; bile salts required for absorption
Vitamin D	• Absorption of calcium and phosphorus in the small intestine	• Fortified milk, egg yolks, fish liver oils	Produced in skin exposed to UV rays; stored in liver; bile salts required for absorption
Vitamin E	• An antioxidant—prevents destruction of cell membranes • Contributes to wound healing and detoxifying ability of the liver	• Nuts, wheat germ, seed oils	Stored in liver and adipose tissue; bile salts required for absorption
Vitamin K	• Synthesis of prothrombin and other clotting factors	• Liver, spinach, cabbage	Large amounts produced by GI bacteria; bile salts required for absorption; stored in liver

Table 17–6 MINERALS

Mineral	Functions	Food Sources	Comment
Calcium	• Formation of bones and teeth • Neuron and muscle functioning • Blood clotting	• Milk, cheese, yogurt, shellfish, leafy green vegetables	Vitamin D required for absorption; stored in bones
Phosphorus	• Formation of bones and teeth • Part of DNA, RNA, and ATP • Part of phosphate buffer system	• Milk, cheese, fish, meat	Vitamin D required for absorption; stored in bones
Sodium	• Contributes to osmotic pressure of body fluids • Nerve impulse transmission and muscle contraction • Part of bicarbonate buffer system	• Table salt, almost all foods	Most abundant cation (+) in extracellular fluid
Potassium	• Contributes to osmotic pressure of body fluids • Nerve impulse transmission and muscle contraction	• Virtually all foods	Most abundant cation in intracellular fluid
Chlorine	• Contributes to osmotic pressure of body fluids • Part of HCl in gastric juice	• Table salt	Most abundant anion (−) in extracellular fluid
Iron	• Part of hemoglobin and myoglobin • Part of some cytochromes in cell respiration	• Meat, shellfish, dried apricots, legumes, eggs	Stored in liver
Iodine	• Part of thyroxine and T_3	• Iodized salt, seafood	
Sulfur	• Part of some amino acids • Part of thiamine and biotin	• Meat, eggs	Insulin and keratin require sulfur
Magnesium	• Formation of bone • Metabolism of ATP–ADP	• Green vegetables, legumes, seafood, milk	Part of chlorophyll in green plants
Manganese	• Formation of urea • Synthesis of fatty acids and cholesterol	• Legumes, grains, nuts, leafy green vegetables	Some stored in liver
Copper	• Synthesis of hemoglobin • Part of some cytochromes in cell respiration • Synthesis of melanin	• Liver, seafood, grains, nuts, legumes	Stored in liver
Cobalt	• Part of vitamin B_{12}	• Liver, meat, fish	
Zinc	• Part of carbonic anhydrase needed for CO_2 transport • Part of peptidases needed for protein digestion • Necessary for normal taste sensation • Involved in wound healing	• Meat, seafood, grains, legumes	

produce heat. These processes include the contraction of skeletal muscle, the pumping of the heart, and the normal breakdown of cellular components. Therefore, it is possible to quantify heat production as a measure of metabolic activity.

As mentioned previously, the energy available from food is measured in kilocalories (kcal). Kilocalories are also the units used to measure the energy expended by the body. During sleep, for example, energy expended by a 150-pound person is about 60 to 70 kcal per hour. Getting up and preparing breakfast increases energy expenditure 80 to 90 kcal per hour. For mothers with several small

children, this value may be significantly higher. Clearly, greater activity results in greater energy expenditure.

The energy required for merely living (lying quietly in bed) is the **basal metabolic rate** (BMR). See Box 17–4: Metabolic Rate for a formula to estimate your own metabolic rate. There are a number of factors that affect the metabolic rate of an active person.

1. Exercise—Contraction of skeletal muscle increases energy expenditure and raises metabolic rate (see Box 17–5: Weight Loss).
2. Age—Metabolic rate is highest in young chil-

Box 17–4 METABOLIC RATE

To estimate your own **basal metabolic rate** (BMR), calculate kilocalories (kcal) used per hour as follows:

    For women: use the factor of 0.9 kcal per kilogram (kg) of body weight
    For men: use the factor of 1.0 kcal per kg of body weight
    Then multiply kcal/hour by 24 hours to determine kcal per day.

Example: A **120-pound woman**
  1. Change pounds to kilograms:
    120 lb at 2.2 lb/kg = 55 kg
  2. Multiply kg weight by the BMR factor:
    55 kg × 0.9 kcal/kg/hr = 49.5 kcal/hr
  3. Multiply kcal/hr by 24:
    49.5 kcal/hr × 24 = 1188 kcal/day*
    *This is an approximate BMR, about 1200 kcal/day
Example: **A 160-pound man**
  1. 160 lb at 2.2 lb/kg = 73 kg
  2. 73 kg × 1.0 kcal/kg/hr = 73 kcal/hr
  3. 73 kcal/hr × 24 = 1752 kcal/day

To approximate the amount of energy actually expended during an average day (24 hours), the following percentages may be used:
    Sedentary Activity: add 40% to 50% of the BMR to the BMR
    Light Activity: add 50% to 65% of the BMR to the BMR
    Moderate Activity: add 65% to 75% of the BMR to the BMR
    Strenuous Activity: add 75% to 100% of the BMR to the BMR
Using our example of the 120-pound woman with a BMR of 1200 kcal/day:
    Sedentary: 1680 to 1800 kcal/day
    Light: 1800 to 1980 kcal/day
    Moderate: 1980 to 2100 kcal/day
    Strenuous: 2100 to 2400 kcal/day

Box 17–5 WEIGHT LOSS

Although diet books are often found on the best-seller lists, there is no magic method that will result in weight loss. Losing weight depends on one simple fact: calorie expenditure in activity must exceed calorie intake in food (the term calorie here will be used to mean kilocalorie).

In order to lose 1 pound of body fat, which consists of fat, water, and protein, 3500 calories of energy must be expended. While any form of exercise requires calories, the more strenuous the exercise, the more calories expended. Some examples are as follows:

Activity	*Calories per 10 minutes* (average for a 150-lb person)
Walking slowly	30
Walking briskly	45
Walking up stairs	170 (remember, this is *10 minutes* of walking up stairs)
Dancing (slow)	40
Dancing (fast)	65
Running (8 mph)	120
Cycling (10 mph)	70
Cycling (15 mph)	115
Swimming	100

Most food packaging contains nutritional information, including the calories per serving of the food. Keeping track of daily caloric intake is an important part of a decision to try to lose weight. It is also important to remember that sustained loss of fat usually does not exceed 1 to 2 pounds per week. In part this is so because as calorie intake decreases, the metabolic rate decreases. There will also be loss of some body protein so that amino acids can be converted to glucose to supply the brain.

A sensible weight-loss diet will include carbohydrate to supply energy needs, will have sufficient protein (40 to 45 grams per day), and will be low in fat. Including vegetables and fruits will supply vitamins, minerals, and fiber.

---

dren and decreases with age. The energy requirements for growth and the greater heat loss by a smaller body contribute to the higher rate in children. After growth has stopped, metabolic rate decreases about 2% per decade. If a person becomes less active, the total decrease is almost 5% per decade.

3. Body Configuration of Adults—Tall, thin people usually have higher metabolic rates than do short, stocky people of the same weight. This is so because the tall, thin person has a larger surface area (proportional to weight) through which heat is continuously lost. The metabolic rate, therefore, is slightly higher to compensate for the greater heat loss. The variance of surface to weight ratios for different body configurations is illustrated in Fig. 17–6.

4. Sex Hormones—Testosterone increases metabolic activity to a greater degree than does estrogen, giving men a slightly higher metabolic rate than women. Also, men tend to have more muscle, an active tissue, whereas women tend to have more fat, a relatively inactive tissue.

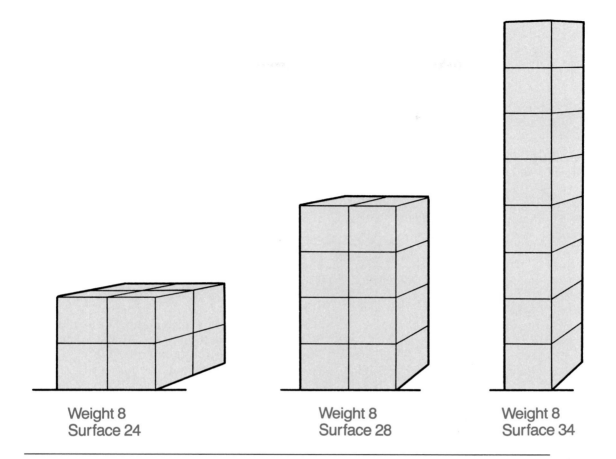

Weight 8
Surface 24

Weight 8
Surface 28

Weight 8
Surface 34

Figure 17–6 Surface to weight ratios. Imagine that the three shapes are people who all weigh the same amount. The "tall, thin person" on the right has about 50% more surface area than does the "short, stocky person" on the left. The more surface area (where heat is lost), the higher the metabolic rate.

5. Sympathetic Stimulation—In stress situations, the metabolism of many body cells is increased. Also contributing to this are the hormones epinephrine and norepinephrine. As a result, metabolic rate increases.

6. Decreased Food Intake—If the intake of food decreases for a prolonged period of time, metabolic rate also begins to decrease. It is as if the body's metabolism is "slowing down" to conserve whatever energy sources may still be available.

7. Climate—People who live in cold climates may have metabolic rates 10% to 20% higher than people who live in tropical regions. This is believed to be due to the variations in the secretion of thyroxine, the hormone most responsible for regulation of metabolic rate. In a cold climate, the necessity for greater heat production brings about an increased secretion of thyroxine and a higher metabolic rate.

SUMMARY

Food is needed for the synthesis of new cells and tissues, or is utilized to produce the energy required for such synthesis reactions. As a consequence of metabolism, heat energy is released to provide a constant body temperature and permit the continuation of metabolic activity. The metabolic pathways described in this chapter are only a small portion of the body's total metabolism. Even this simple presentation, however, suggests the great chemical complexity of the functioning human being.

STUDY OUTLINE

Body Temperature
1. Normal range is 96.5 to 99.5°F (36 to 38°C), with an average of 98.6° F (37°C).
2. Normal fluctuation in 24 hours is 1 to 2°F.
3. Temperature regulation in infants and the elderly is not as precise as it is at other ages.

Heat Production
Heat is one of the energy products of cell respiration. Many factors affect the total heat actually produced (see Table 17–1).
1. Thyroxine from the thyroid gland—the most important regulator of daily heat production. As metabolic rate decreases, more thyroxine is secreted to increase the rate of cell respiration.
2. Stress—sympathetic impulses and epinephrine and norepinephrine increase the metabolic activity of many organs, increasing the production of ATP and heat.
3. Active organs continuously produce heat. Skeletal muscle tone produces 25% of the total body heat at rest. The liver provides up to 20% of the resting body heat.
4. Food intake increases the activity of the digestive organs and increases heat production.
5. Changes in body temperature affect metabolic rate. A fever increases the metabolic rate, and more heat is produced; this may become detrimental during very high fevers.

Heat Loss (see Table 17–2)
1. Most heat is lost through the skin.
2. Blood flow through the dermis determines the amount of heat that is lost by radiation, conduction, and convection.
3. Vasodilation in the dermis increases blood flow and heat loss; radiation and conduction are effective only if the environment is cooler than the body.
4. Vasoconstriction in the dermis decreases blood flow and conserves heat in the core of the body.
5. Sweating is a very effective heat loss mechanism; excess body heat evaporates sweat on the skin surface; sweating is most effective when the atmospheric humidity is low.
6. Sweating also has a disadvantage in that water is lost and must be replaced to prevent serious dehydration.
7. Heat is lost from the respiratory tract by the evaporation of water from the warm respiratory mucosa; water vapor is part of exhaled air.
8. A very small amount of heat is lost as urine and feces are excreted at body temperature.

Regulation of Heat Loss
1. The hypothalamus is the thermostat of the body and regulates body temperature by balancing heat production and heat loss.
2. The hypothalamus receives information from its own neurons (blood temperature) and from the temperature receptors in the dermis.
3. Mechanisms to increase heat loss are vasodilation in the dermis and increased sweating. Decreased muscle tone will decrease heat production.
4. Mechanisms to conserve heat are vasoconstriction in the dermis and decreased sweating. Increased muscle tone (shivering) will increase heat production.

Fever—an abnormally elevated body temperature
1. Pyrogens are substances that cause a fever: bacteria, foreign proteins, or chemicals released during inflammation (endogenous pyrogens).

2. Pyrogens raise the setting of the hypothalamic thermostat; the person feels cold and begins to shiver to produce heat.
3. When the pyrogen has been eliminated, the hypothalamic setting returns to normal; the person feels warm, and sweating begins to lose heat to lower the body temperature.
4. A low fever may be beneficial because it increases the activity of WBCs and inhibits the activity of some pathogens.
5. A high fever may be detrimental because enzymes are denatured at high temperatures. This is most critical in the brain, where cells that die cannot be replaced.

Metabolism—all the reactions within the body

1. Anabolism—synthesis reactions that usually require energy in the form of ATP.
2. Catabolism—decomposition reactions that often release energy in the form of ATP.
3. Enzymes catalyze most anabolic and catabolic reactions.

Cell Respiration—the breakdown of food molecules to release their potential energy and synthesize ATP

1. Glucose + oxygen yields CO_2 + H_2O + ATP + heat.
2. The breakdown of glucose involves three stages: glycolysis, Krebs cycle, and the cytochrome transport system (see Table 17–3 and Fig. 17–3).
3. The oxygen necessary comes from breathing.
4. The water formed becomes part of intracellular fluid; CO_2 is exhaled; ATP is used for energy-requiring reactions; heat provides a body temperature.

Proteins and Fats—as energy sources (see Table 17–4 for hormonal regulation)

1. Excess amino acids are deaminated in the liver and converted to pyruvic acid or acetyl groups to enter the Krebs cycle. Amino acids may also be converted to glucose to supply the brain (Fig. 17–4).
2. Glycerol is converted to pyruvic acid to enter the Krebs cycle.

3. Fatty acids, in the process of beta-oxidation in the liver, are split into acetyl groups to enter the Krebs cycle; ketones are formed for transport to other cells (see Fig. 17–5).

Energy Available from Food

1. Energy is measured in kilocalories (Calories): kcal.
2. There are 4 kcal per gram of carbohydrate, 4 kcal per gram of protein, 9 kcal per gram of fat.

Synthesis Uses of Foods

1. Glucose—used to synthesize the pentose sugars for DNA and RNA; used to synthesize glycogen to store energy in liver and muscles.
2. Amino acids—used to synthesize new proteins and the non-essential amino acids.
3. Fatty acids and glycerol—used to synthesize phospholipids for cell membranes, triglycerides for fat storage in adipose tissue, and cholesterol and other steroids.
4. Vitamins and minerals—see Tables 17–5 and 17–6.

Metabolic Rate—the heat production by the body; measured in kcal

1. Basal Metabolic Rate (BMR) is the energy required to maintain life (see Box 17–4); several factors influence the metabolic rate of an active person.
2. Age—metabolic rate is highest in young children and decreases with age.
3. Body configuration—more surface area proportional to weight (tall and thin) means a higher metabolic rate.
4. Sex hormones—men usually have a higher metabolic rate than do women; men have more muscle proportional to fat than do women.
5. Sympathetic stimulation—metabolic activity increases in stress situations.
6. Decreased food intake—metabolic rate decreases to conserve available energy sources.
7. Climate—people who live in cold climates usually have higher metabolic rates because of a greater need for heat production.

REVIEW QUESTIONS

1. State the normal range of human body temperature in °F and °C. (p. 390)

2. State the summary equation of cell respiration, and state what happens to (or the purpose of) each of the products. (p. 397)

3. Describe the role of each on heat production: thyroxine, skeletal muscles, stress situations, the liver. (p. 390)

4. Describe the two mechanisms of heat loss through the skin, and explain the role of blood flow. Describe how heat is lost through the respiratory tract. (pp. 391–392)

5. Explain the circumstances when sweating and vasodilation in the dermis are not effective mechanisms of heat loss. (pp. 391–392)

6. Name the part of the brain that regulates body temperature, and explain what is meant by a thermostat. (p. 393)

7. Describe the responses by the body to a warm environment and to a cold environment. (pp. 393–394)

8. Explain how pyrogens are believed to cause a fever, and give two examples of pyrogens. (p. 394)

9. Define metabolism, anabolism, catabolism, kilocalorie, metabolic rate. (pp. 397, 404)

10. Name the three stages of the cell respiration of glucose and state where in the cell each takes place and whether or not oxygen is required. (pp. 397, 399–400)

11. For each, state the molecules that enter the process and the results of the process: glycolysis, Krebs cycle, cytochrome transport system. (pp. 397–400)

12. Explain how fatty acids, glycerol, and excess amino acids are used for energy production in cell respiration. (pp. 400–402)

13. Describe the synthesis uses for glucose, amino acids, fatty acids. (pp. 403–404)

14. Describe four factors that affect the metabolic rate of an active person. (pp. 407–409)

15. If lunch consists of 60 grams of carbohydrate, 15 grams of protein, and 10 grams of fat, how many kilocalories are provided by this meal? (p. 400)

Chapter 18
The Urinary System

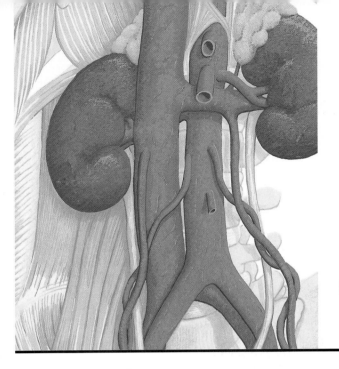

Chapter 18

Chapter Outline

Student Objectives

- Describe the location and general function of each organ of the urinary system.
- Name the parts of a nephron and the important blood vessels associated with them.
- Explain how the following are involved in urine formation: glomerular filtration, tubular reabsorption, tubular secretion, blood flow through the kidney.
- Describe the mechanisms of tubular reabsorption, and explain the importance of tubular secretion.
- Describe how the kidneys help maintain normal blood volume and blood pressure.
- Name and state the functions of the hormones that affect the kidneys.
- Describe how the kidneys help maintain normal pH of blood and tissue fluid.
- Describe the urination reflex, and explain how voluntary control is possible.
- Describe the characteristics of normal urine.

The Urinary System

New Terminology

Bowman's capsule (**BOW**–manz **KAP**–suhl)

Detrusor muscle (de–**TROO**–ser)

External urethral sphincter (yoo–**REE**–thruhl **SFINK**–ter)

Glomerular filtration rate (gloh-**MER**–yoo–ler fill–**TRAY**–shun RAYT)

Glomerulus (gloh–**MER**–yoo–lus)

Internal urethral sphincter (yoo–**REE**–thruhl **SFINK**–ter)

Juxtaglomerular cells (JUKS–tah–gloh–**MER**–yoo–ler SELLS)

Micturition (MIK–tyoo–**RISH**–un)

Nephron (**NEFF**–ron)

Nitrogenous wastes (nigh–**TRAH**–jen–us)

Peritubular capillaries (PER–ee–**TOO**–byoo–ler)

Renal corpuscle (**REE**–nuhl **KOR**–pus'l)

Renal filtrate (**REE**–nuhl **FILL**–trayt)

Renal tubule (**REE**–nuhl **TOO**–byoo'l)

Retroperitoneal (RE–troh–PER–i–toh–**NEE**–uhl)

Specific gravity (spe–**SIF**–ik **GRA**–vi–tee)

Threshold level (**THRESH**–hold **LE**–vuhl)

Trigone (**TRY**–gohn)

Ureter (**YOOR**–uh–ter)

Urethra (yoo–**REE**–thrah)

Urinary bladder (**YOOR**–i–NAR–ee **BLA**–der)

Related Clinical Terminology

Cystitis (sis–**TIGH**–tis)

Dysuria (dis–**YOO**–ree–ah)

Hemodialysis (HEE–moh–dye–**AL**–i–sis)

Nephritis (ne–**FRY**–tis)

Oliguria (AH–li–**GYOO**–ree–ah)

Polyuria (PAH–li–**YOO**–ree–ah)

Renal calculi (**REE**–nuhl **KAL**–kew–lye)

Renal failure (**REE**–nuhl **FAYL**–yer)

Uremia (yoo–**REE**–me–ah)

Terms that appear in **bold type** in the chapter text are defined in the glossary, which begins on page 549.

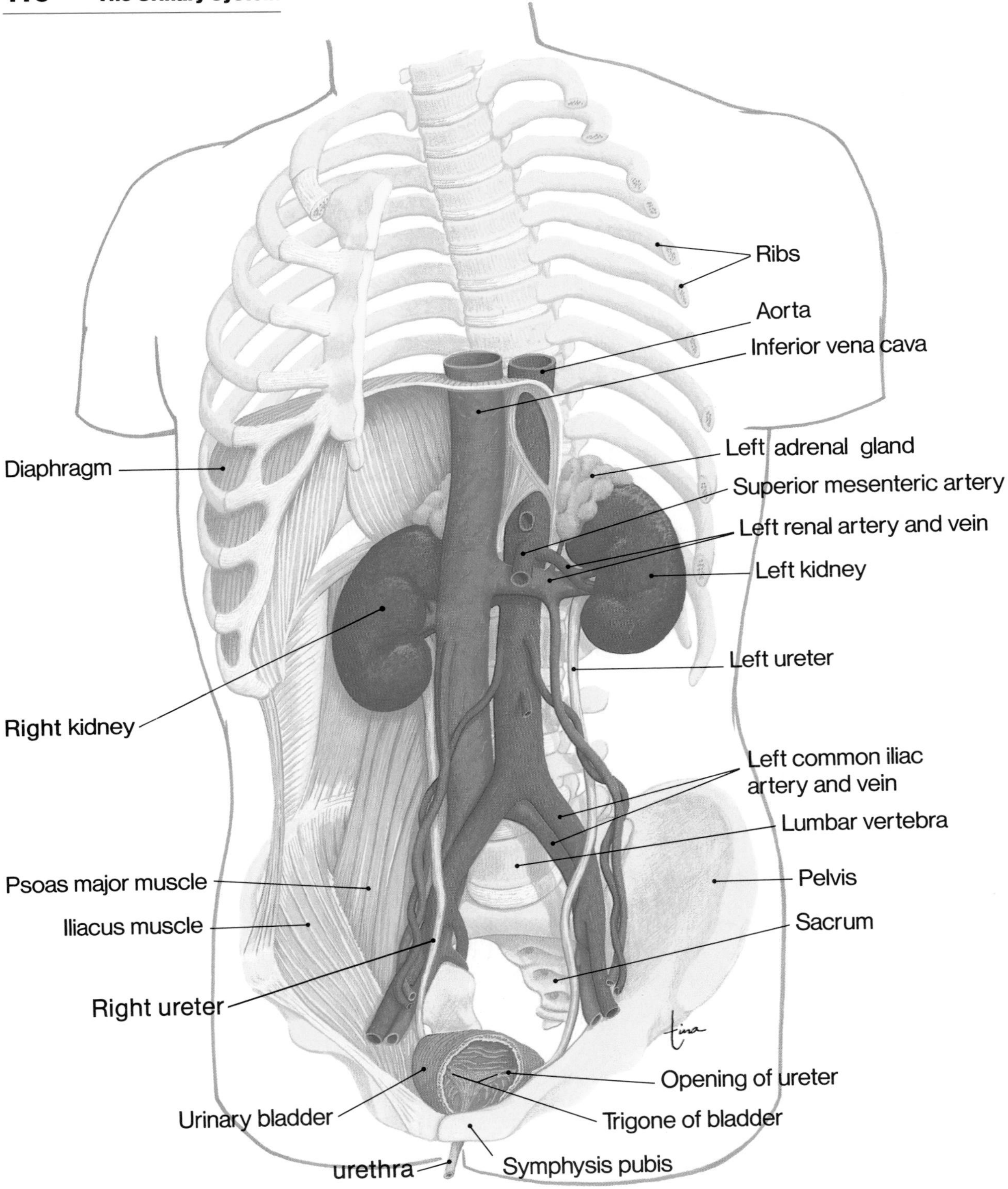

Figure 18–1 The urinary system shown in anterior view.

The first successful human organ transplant was a kidney transplant performed in 1953. Since the donor and recipient were identical twins, rejection was not a problem. Thousands of kidney transplants have been performed since then, and the development of immunosuppressive medications has permitted many people to live a normal life with a donated kidney. Although a person usually has two kidneys, it is clear that one kidney can carry out the complex work required to maintain homeostasis of the body fluids.

The urinary system consists of two kidneys, two ureters, the urinary bladder, and the urethra (Fig. 18–1). The formation of urine is the function of the kidneys, and the rest of the system is responsible for eliminating the urine.

Body cells produce waste products such as urea, creatinine, and ammonia, which must be removed from the blood before they accumulate to toxic levels. As the kidneys form urine to excrete these waste products, they also accomplish several other important functions:

1. regulation of the volume of blood by excretion or conservation of water
2. regulation of the electrolyte content of the blood by the excretion or conservation of minerals
3. regulation of the acid-base balance of the blood by excretion or conservation of ions such as H^+ ions or HCO_3^- ions
4. regulation of all of the above in tissue fluid

The process of urine formation, therefore, helps maintain the normal composition, volume, and pH of both blood and tissue fluid by removing those substances that would upset the normal constancy and balance of these extracellular fluids.

KIDNEYS

The two **kidneys** are located in the upper abdominal cavity on either side of the vertebral column, behind the peritoneum (retroperitoneal). The upper portions of the kidneys rest on the lower surface of the diaphragm and are enclosed and protected by the lower rib cage (see Fig. 18–1). The kidneys are embedded in adipose tissue that acts as a cushion and is in turn covered by a fibrous connective tissue membrane called the **renal fascia,** which helps hold the kidneys in place (see Box 18–1: Floating Kidney).

Each kidney has an indentation called the **hilus** on its medial side. At the hilus, the renal artery enters the kidney, and the renal vein and ureter emerge. The renal artery is a branch of the abdominal aorta, and the renal vein returns blood to the inferior vena cava (see Fig. 18–1). The ureter carries urine from the kidney to the urinary bladder.

INTERNAL STRUCTURE OF THE KIDNEY

In a coronal or frontal section of the kidney, three areas can be distinguished (Fig. 18–2). The outermost area is called the **renal cortex;** it is made of renal corpuscles and convoluted tubules. These are parts of the nephron and will be described in the next section. The middle area is the **renal medulla,**

Box 18–1 FLOATING KIDNEY

A floating kidney is one that has moved out of its normal position. This may happen in very thin people whose renal cushion of adipose tissue is thin, or it may be the result of a sharp blow to the back that dislodges a kidney.

A kidney can function in any position; the problem with a floating kidney is that the ureter may become twisted or kinked. If urine cannot flow through the ureter, the urine backs up and collects in the renal pelvis. Incoming urine from the renal tubules then backs up as well. If the renal filtrate cannot flow out of Bowman's capsules, the pressure within Bowman's capsules increases, opposing the blood pressure in the glomeruli. Glomerular filtration then cannot take place efficiently. If uncorrected, this may lead to permanent kidney damage.

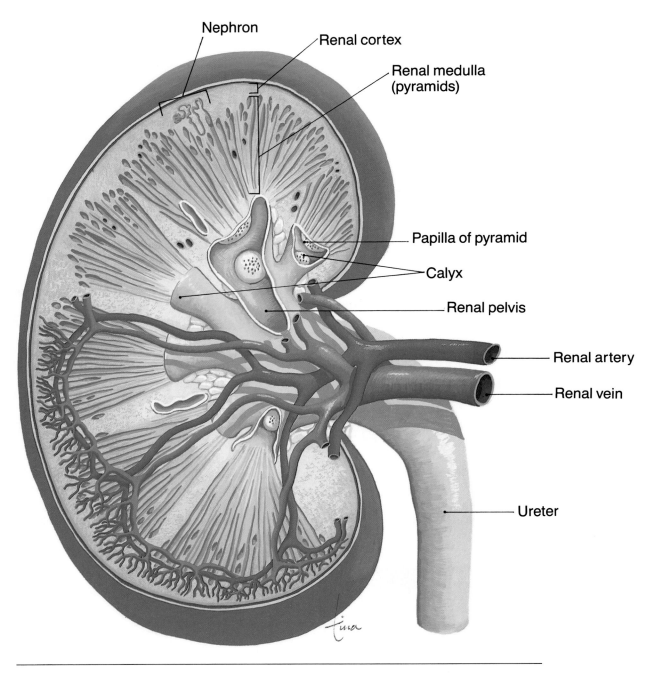

Nephron

Renal cortex

Renal medulla
(pyramids)

Papilla of pyramid

Calyx

Renal pelvis

Renal artery

Renal vein

Ureter

Figure 18–2 Frontal section of the right kidney showing internal structure and blood vessels. An individual nephron is depicted in the upper part of the kidney.

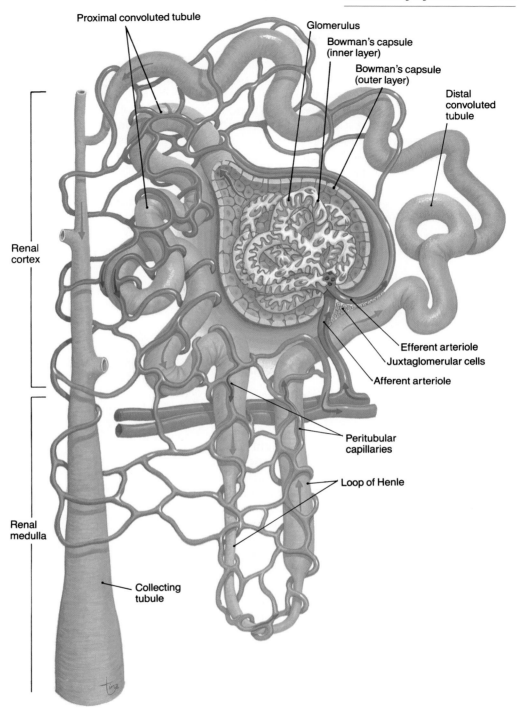

Proximal convoluted tubule

Glomerulus

Bowman's capsule (inner layer)

Bowman's capsule (outer layer)

Distal convoluted tubule

Renal cortex

Efferent arteriole

Juxtaglomerular cells

Afferent arteriole

Peritubular capillaries

Renal medulla

Loop of Henle

Collecting tubule

Figure 18–3 A nephron with its associated blood vessels. The arrows indicate the direction of blood flow. See text for description.

which is made of loops of Henle and collecting tubules (also parts of the nephron). The renal medulla consists of wedge-shaped pieces called **renal pyramids.** The tip of each pyramid is its apex or papilla.

The third area is the **renal pelvis;** this is not a layer of tissues, but rather a cavity formed by the expansion of the ureter within the kidney at the hilus. Funnel-shaped extensions of the renal pelvis, called **calyces** (singular, **calyx**), enclose the papillae of the renal pyramids. Urine flows from the renal pyramids into the calyces, then to the renal pelvis and out into the ureter.

THE NEPHRON

The **nephron** is the structural and functional unit of the kidney. Each kidney contains approximately 1 million nephrons. It is in the nephrons, with their associated blood vessels, that urine is formed. Each nephron has two major portions: a renal corpuscle and a renal tubule. Each of these major parts has further subdivisions, which are shown with their blood vessels in Fig. 18–3.

Renal Corpuscle

A **renal corpuscle** consists of a glomerulus surrounded by a Bowman's capsule. The **glomerulus** is a capillary network that arises from an **afferent arteriole** and empties into an **efferent arteriole.** The diameter of the efferent arteriole is smaller than that of the afferent arteriole, which helps maintain a fairly high blood pressure in the glomerulus.

Bowman's capsule (or glomerular capsule) is the expanded end of a renal tubule; it encloses the glomerulus. The inner layer of Bowman's capsule has pores and is very permeable; the outer layer has no pores and is not permeable. The space between the inner and outer layers of Bowman's capsule contains renal filtrate, the fluid that is formed from the blood in the glomerulus and will eventually become urine.

Renal Tubule

The **renal tubule** continues from Bowman's capsule and consists of the following parts: **proximal convoluted tubule** (in the renal cortex), **loop of Henle** (or loop of the nephron, in the renal medulla), and **distal convoluted tubule** (in the renal cortex). The distal convoluted tubules from several nephrons empty into a **collecting tubule.** Several collecting tubules then unite to form a papillary duct that empties urine into a calyx of the renal pelvis. A single nephron is depicted in Fig. 18–2 so that you may see its placement within the kidney.

All the parts of the renal tubule are surrounded by **peritubular capillaries,** which arise from the efferent arteriole. The peritubular capillaries will receive the materials reabsorbed by the renal tubules; this will be described in the section on urine formation.

BLOOD VESSELS OF THE KIDNEY

The pathway of blood flow through the kidney is an essential part of the process of urine formation. Blood from the abdominal aorta enters the **renal artery,** which branches extensively within the kidney into smaller arteries (see Fig. 18–2). The smallest arteries give rise to afferent arterioles in the renal cortex (see Fig. 18–3). From the afferent arterioles, blood flows into the glomeruli (capillaries), to efferent arterioles, to peritubular capillaries, to veins within the kidney, to the **renal vein,** and finally to the inferior vena cava. Notice that in this pathway there are two sets of capillaries, and recall that it is in capillaries that exchanges take place between the blood and surrounding tissues. Therefore, in the kidneys there are two sites of exchanges. The exchanges that take place in the capillaries of the kidneys will form urine from blood plasma.

FORMATION OF URINE

The formation of urine involves three major processes. The first is glomerular filtration, which takes place in the renal corpuscles. The second and third are tubular reabsorption and tubular secretion, which take place in the renal tubules.

GLOMERULAR FILTRATION

You may recall that filtration is the process in which blood pressure forces plasma and dissolved material out of capillaries. In **glomerular filtration,** blood pressure forces plasma, dissolved substances and small proteins out of the glomeruli and into Bowman's capsules. This fluid is no longer plasma but is called **renal filtrate.**

The blood pressure in the glomeruli, compared to that in other capillaries, is relatively high, about 60 mmHg. The pressure in Bowman's capsule is very low, and its inner layer is very permeable, so that approximately 20% to 25% of the blood that enters glomeruli becomes renal filtrate in Bowman's capsules. The blood cells and larger proteins are too large to be forced out of the glomeruli, so they remain in the blood. Waste products are dissolved in blood plasma, so they pass into the renal filtrate. Useful materials such as nutrients and minerals are also dissolved in plasma and are also present in renal filtrate. Therefore, renal filtrate is very much like blood plasma, except that there is far less protein, and no blood cells are present.

The **Glomerular Filtration Rate** (GFR) is the amount of renal filtrate formed by the kidneys in 1 minute, and averages 100 to 125 ml per minute. GFR may be altered if the rate of blood flow through the kidney changes. If blood flow increases, the GFR increases, and more filtrate is formed. If blood flow decreases (as may happen following a severe hemorrhage), the GFR decreases, less filtrate is formed, and urinary output decreases (see Box 18–2: Renal Failure and Hemodialysis).

Box 18–2   RENAL FAILURE AND HEMODIALYSIS

Renal failure, the inability of the kidneys to function properly, may be the result of three general causes, which may be called: prerenal, renal, and postrenal.

Prerenal means that the problem is "before" the kidneys, that is, in the blood flow to the kidneys. Any condition that decreases blood flow to the kidneys may result in renal damage and failure. Examples are severe hemorrhage or very low blood pressure following a heart attack (MI).

Renal means that the problem is in the kidneys themselves. Bacterial infections of the kidneys or exposure to chemicals (certain antibiotics) may cause this type of damage. Polycystic kidney disease is a genetic disorder in which the kidney tubules dilate and become nonfunctional. Severe damage may not be apparent until age 40 to 60 years but may then progress to renal failure.

Postrenal means that the problem is "after" the kidneys, somewhere in the rest of the urinary tract. Obstruction of urine flow may be caused by kidney stones, a twisted ureter, or prostatic hypertrophy.

Treatment of renal failure involves correcting the specific cause, if possible. If not possible, and kidney damage is permanent, the person is said to have chronic renal failure. **Hemodialysis** is the use of an artificial kidney machine to do what the patient's nephrons can no longer do. The patient's blood is passed through minute tubes surrounded by fluid (dialysate) with the same chemical composition as plasma. Waste products and excess minerals diffuse out of the patient's blood into the fluid of the machine.

Although hemodialysis does prolong life for those with chronic renal failure, it does not fully take the place of functioning kidneys. The increasing success rate of kidney transplants, however, does indeed provide the possibility of a normal life for people with chronic renal failure.

TUBULAR REABSORPTION

Tubular reabsorption takes place from the renal tubules into the peritubular capillaries. In a 24-hour period, the kidneys form 150 to 180 liters of filtrate, and normal urinary output in that time is 1 to 2 liters. Therefore, it becomes apparent that most of the renal filtrate does not become urine. Approximately 99% of the filtrate is reabsorbed back into the blood in the peritubular capillaries. Only about 1% of the filtrate will enter the renal pelvis as urine.

Most reabsorption and secretion (about 65%) take place in the proximal convoluted tubules, whose cells have **microvilli** that greatly increase their surface area. The distal convoluted tubules and collecting tubules are also important sites for the reabsorption of water (Fig. 18–4).

Mechanisms of Reabsorption

1. **Active Transport**—the cells of the renal tubule use ATP to transport most of the useful materials from the filtrate to the blood. These useful materials include glucose, amino acids, vitamins, and positive ions.

   For many of these substances, the renal tubules have a **threshold level** of reabsorption. This means that there is a limit to how much the tubules can remove from the filtrate. For example, if the filtrate level of glucose is normal (reflecting a normal blood glucose level), the tubules will reabsorb all the glucose, and none will be found in the urine. If, however, the blood glucose level is above normal, the amount of glucose in the filtrate will also be above normal and will exceed the threshold level of reabsorption. In this situation, therefore, some glucose will be present in urine.

   The reabsorption of Ca^{+2} ions is increased by parathyroid hormone (PTH). The parathyroid glands secrete PTH when the blood calcium level decreases. The reabsorption of Ca^{+2} ions by the kidneys is one of the mechanisms by which the blood calcium level is raised back to normal.

   The hormone aldosterone, secreted by the adrenal cortex, increases the reabsorption of Na$^+$ ions and the excretion of K$^+$ ions. Besides regulating the blood levels of sodium and potassium, aldosterone also affects the volume of blood.

2. **Passive Transport**—many of the negative ions that are returned to the blood are reabsorbed following the reabsorption of positive ions, since unlike charges attract.

3. **Osmosis**—the reabsorption of water follows the reabsorption of minerals, especially sodium ions. The hormones that affect reabsorption of water will be discussed in the next section.

4. **Pinocytosis**—small proteins are too large to be reabsorbed by active transport. They become adsorbed to the membranes of the cells of the proximal convoluted tubules. The cell membrane then sinks inward and folds around the protein to take it in. Normally all proteins in the filtrate are reabsorbed; none are found in urine.

TUBULAR SECRETION

This mechanism also changes the composition of urine. In **tubular secretion,** substances are actively secreted from the blood in the peritubular capillaries into the filtrate in the renal tubules. Waste products such as ammonia and some creatinine, and the metabolic products of medications may be secreted into the filtrate to be eliminated in urine. Hydrogen ions (H$^+$) may be secreted by the tubule cells to help maintain the normal pH of blood.

HORMONES THAT INFLUENCE REABSORPTION OF WATER

Aldosterone is secreted by the adrenal cortex in response to a high blood potassium level, to a low blood sodium level, or to a decrease in blood pressure. When aldosterone stimulates the reabsorption of Na$^+$ ions, water follows from the filtrate back to the blood. This helps maintain normal blood volume and blood pressure.

You may recall that the antagonist to aldosterone

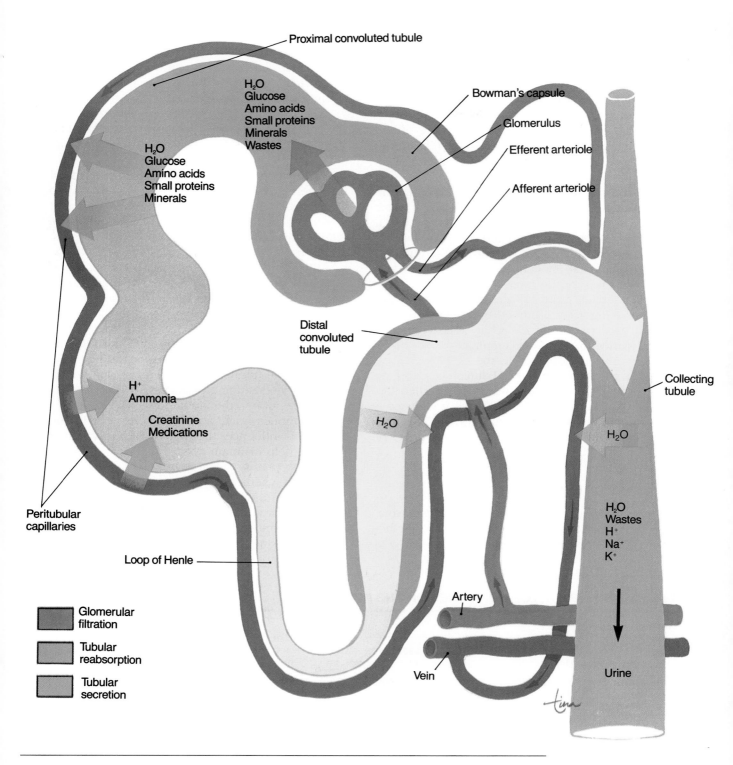

Figure 18–4 Schematic representation of glomerular filtration, tubular reabsorption, and tubular secretion. The renal tubule has been uncoiled, and the peritubular capillaries are shown adjacent to the tubule.

is **atrial natriuretic hormone** (ANH), which is secreted by the atria of the heart when the atrial walls are stretched by high blood pressure or greater blood volume. ANH decreases the reabsorption of Na^+ ions by the kidneys; these remain in the filtrate, as does water, and are excreted. By increasing the elimination of sodium and water, ANH lowers blood volume and blood pressure.

Antidiuretic hormone (ADH) is released by the posterior pituitary gland when the amount of water in the body decreases. Under the influence of ADH, the distal convoluted tubules and collecting tubules are able to reabsorb more water from the renal filtrate. This helps maintain normal blood volume and blood pressure, and also permits the kidneys to produce urine that is more concentrated than body fluids. Producing a concentrated urine is essential to prevent excessive water loss while still excreting all the substances that must be eliminated.

If the amount of water in the body increases, however, the secretion of ADH diminishes, and the kidneys will reabsorb less water. Urine then becomes dilute, and water is eliminated until its concentration in the body returns to normal. This may occur following ingestion of excessive quantities of fluids.

SUMMARY OF URINE FORMATION

1. The kidneys form urine from blood plasma. Blood flow through the kidneys is a major factor in determining urinary output.

2. Glomerular filtration is the first step in urine formation. Filtration is not selective in terms of usefulness of materials; it is selective only in terms of size. High blood pressure in the glomeruli forces plasma, dissolved materials, and small proteins into Bowman's capsules; the fluid is now called renal filtrate.

3. Tubular reabsorption is selective in terms of usefulness. Nutrients such as glucose, amino acids, and vitamins are reabsorbed by active transport and may have renal threshold levels. Positive ions are reabsorbed by active transport and negative ions most often by passive transport. Water is reabsorbed by osmosis, and small proteins are reabsorbed by pinocytosis.

   Reabsorption takes place from the filtrate in the renal tubules to the blood in the peritubular capillaries.

4. Tubular secretion takes place from the blood in the peritubular capillaries to the filtrate in the renal tubules and can ensure that wastes such as creatinine or excess H^+ ions are actively put into the filtrate to be excreted.

5. Hormones such as aldosterone, ANH, and ADH influence the reabsorption of water and help maintain normal blood volume and blood pressure. The secretion of ADH determines whether a concentrated or dilute urine will be formed.

6. Waste products remain in the renal filtrate and are excreted in urine. The effects of hormones on the kidneys are summarized in Table 18–1.

Table 18–1 EFFECTS OF HORMONES ON THE KIDNEYS

Hormone (gland)	Function
Parathyroid Hormone (PTH) (parathyroid glands)	• Promotes reabsorption of Ca^{+2} ions from filtrate to the blood and excretion of phosphate ions into the filtrate.
Antidiuretic Hormone (ADH) (posterior pituitary)	• Promotes reabsorption of water from the filtrate to the blood.
Aldosterone (adrenal cortex)	• Promotes reabsorption of Na^+ ions from the filtrate to the blood and excretion of K^+ ions into the filtrate. Water is reabsorbed following the reabsorption of sodium.
Atrial Natriuretic Hormone (ANH) (atria of heart)	• Decreases reabsorption of Na^+ ions, which remain in the filtrate. More sodium and water are eliminated in urine.

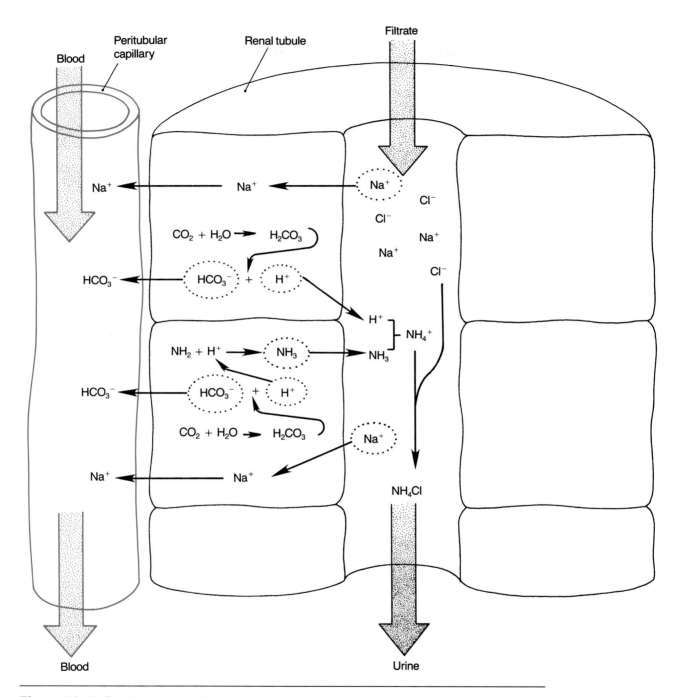

Figure 18–5 Renal regulation of acid-base balance. The cells of the renal tubule secrete H^+ ions and ammonia into the filtrate and return Na^+ ions and HCO_3^- ions to the blood in the peritubular capillaries. See text for further description.

THE KIDNEYS AND ACID–BASE BALANCE

The kidneys are the organs most responsible for maintaining the pH of blood and tissue fluid within normal ranges. They have the greatest ability to compensate for the pH changes that are a normal part of body functioning or the result of disease and to make the necessary corrections.

This regulatory function of the kidneys is complex, but at its simplest it may be described as follows. If body fluids are becoming too acidic, the kidneys will secrete more H^+ ions into the renal filtrate and will return more HCO_3^- ions to the blood. This will help raise the pH of the blood back to normal. The reactions involved in such a mechanism are shown in Fig. 18–5, and we will return to it later. First however, let us briefly consider how the kidneys will compensate for body fluids that are becoming too alkaline. You might expect the kidneys to do just the opposite of what is described above, and that is just what happens. The kidneys will return H^+ ions to the blood and excrete HCO_3^- ions in urine. This will help lower the pH of the blood back to normal.

Since the natural tendency is for body fluids to become more acidic, let us look at the pH raising mechanism in more detail (see Fig. 18–5). The cells of the renal tubules can secrete H^+ ions or ammonia in exchange for Na^+ ions, and by doing so, influence the reabsorption of other ions. Hydrogen ions are obtained from the reaction of CO_2 and water (or other processes). An amine group from an amino acid is combined with a H^+ ion to form ammonia.

The tubule cell secretes the H^+ ion and the ammonia into the renal filtrate, and two Na^+ ions are reabsorbed in exchange. In the filtrate, the H^+ ion and ammonia form NH_4^+ (an ammonium radical), which reacts with a chloride ion (Cl^-) to form NH_4Cl (ammonium chloride) that is excreted in urine.

As the Na^+ ions are returned to the blood in the peritubular capillaries, HCO_3^- ions follow. Notice what has happened: two H^+ ions have been excreted in urine, and two Na^+ ions and two HCO_3^- ions have been returned to the blood. As reactions like these take place, the body fluids are prevented from becoming too acidic.

Another mechanism used by the cells of the kidney tubules to regulate pH is the phosphate buffer system, which will be described in Chapter 19.

OTHER FUNCTIONS OF THE KIDNEYS

In addition to the functions described thus far, the kidneys have other functions, some of which are not directly related to the formation of urine. These functions are secretion of renin (which does influence urine formation), production of erythropoietin, and activation of vitamin D.

1. Secretion of Renin—When blood pressure decreases, the **juxtaglomerular** (juxta means "next to") cells in the walls of the afferent arterioles secrete the enzyme **renin**. Renin then initiates the Renin-Angiotensin mechanism to raise blood pressure. This was first described in Chapter 13, and the sequence of events is presented in Table 18–2. The end product of this mechanism is **angiotensin II,** which causes vasoconstriction and increases the secretion of aldosterone, both of which help raise blood pressure.

   A normal blood pressure is essential to normal body functioning. Perhaps the most serious change is a sudden, drastic decrease in

Table 18–2   THE RENIN–ANGIOTENSIN MECHANISM

Sequence

1. Decreased blood pressure stimulates the kidneys to secrete renin.
2. Renin splits the plasma protein angiotensinogen (synthesized by the liver) to angiotensin I.
3. Angiotensin I is converted to angiotensin II by an enzyme found primarily in lung tissue.
4. Angiotensin II causes vasoconstriction and stimulates the adrenal cortex to secrete aldosterone.

Box 18–3 ERYTHROPOIETIN

Anemia is one of the most debilitating consequences of renal failure, one that hemodialysis cannot reverse. Diseased kidneys stop producing erythropoietin, a natural stimulus for RBC production. Recently, however, erythropoietin has been produced by genetic engineering and is now available for hemodialysis patients. Until now, their anemia could only be treated with transfusions, which exposed these patients to possible immunologic complications of repeated exposure to donated blood or to viral diseases such as hepatitis C. The synthetic erythropoietin eliminates such risks. Others who may benefit from this new medication are cancer patients and AIDS patients with severe anemia.

---

blood pressure, as would follow a severe hemorrhage. In response to such a decrease, the kidneys will decrease filtration and urinary output and will initiate the formation of angiotensin II. In these ways the kidneys help ensure that the heart has enough blood to pump to maintain cardiac output and blood pressure.

2. Secretion of **erythropoietin**—This hormone is secreted whenever the blood oxygen level decreases (a state of hypoxia). Erythropoietin stimulates the red bone marrow to increase the rate of RBC production. With more RBCs in circulation, the oxygen-carrying capacity of the blood is greater, and the hypoxic state may be corrected (see also Box 18–3: Erythropoietin).

3. Activation of vitamin D—This vitamin exists in several structural forms which are converted to **calciferol** (D_2) by the kidneys. Calciferol is the most active form of vitamin D, which increases the absorption of calcium and phosphorus in the small intestine.

ELIMINATION OF URINE

The ureters, urinary bladder, and urethra do not change the composition or amount of urine, but are responsible for the periodic elimination of urine.

URETERS

Each **ureter** extends from the hilus of a kidney to the lower, posterior side of the urinary bladder (see Fig. 18–1). Like the kidneys, the ureters are retroperitoneal, that is, behind the peritoneum of the dorsal abdominal cavity.

The smooth muscle in the wall of the ureter contracts in peristaltic waves to propel urine toward the urinary bladder. As the bladder fills, it expands and compresses the lower ends of the ureters to prevent backflow of urine.

URINARY BLADDER

The **urinary bladder** is a muscular sac below the peritoneum and behind the pubic bones. In women, the bladder is inferior to the uterus; in men, the bladder is superior to the prostate gland. The bladder is a reservoir for accumulating urine, and it contracts to eliminate urine.

The mucosa of the bladder is **transitional epithelium,** which permits expansion without tearing the lining. When the bladder is empty the mucosa appears wrinkled; these folds are **rugae,** which also permit expansion. On the floor of the bladder is a triangular area called the **trigone,** which has no rugae and does not expand. The points of the triangle are the openings of the two ureters and that of the urethra (Fig. 18–6).

The smooth muscle layer in the wall of the blad-

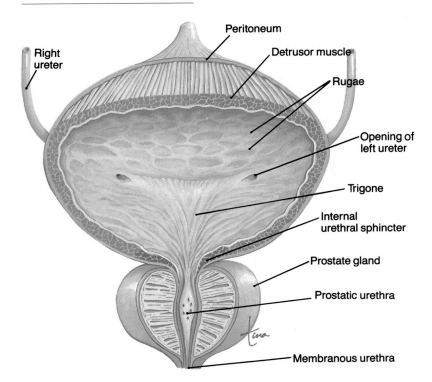

Peritoneum

Right ureter

Detrusor muscle

Rugae

Opening of left ureter

Trigone

Internal urethral sphincter

Prostate gland

Prostatic urethra

Membranous urethra

Figure 18–6 The urinary bladder and a portion of the urethra in the male. Anterior view of a frontal section.

der is called the **detrusor muscle.** It is a muscle in the form of a sphere; when it contracts it becomes a smaller sphere, and its volume diminishes. Around the opening of the urethra the muscle fibers of the detrusor form the **internal urethral sphincter** (or sphincter of the bladder), which is involuntary.

URETHRA

The urethra carries urine from the bladder to the exterior. Within its wall is the **external urethral sphincter,** which is made of skeletal muscle and is under voluntary control.

In women, the urethra is 1 to 1.5 inches (2.5 to 4 cm) long and is anterior to the vagina. In men, the urethra is 7 to 8 inches (17 to 20 cm) long and extends through the prostate gland and penis. The male urethra carries semen as well as urine.

THE URINATION REFLEX

Urination may also be called **micturition** or **voiding.** This reflex is a spinal cord reflex over which voluntary control may be exerted. The stimulus for the reflex is stretching of the detrusor muscle of the bladder. The bladder can hold as much as 800 ml of urine, or even more, but the reflex is activated long before the maximum is reached.

When urine volume reaches 200 to 400 ml, the stretching is sufficient to generate sensory impulses that travel to the sacral spinal cord. Motor impulses return along parasympathetic nerves to the detrusor muscle, causing contraction. At the same time, the internal urethral sphincter relaxes. If the external urethral sphincter is voluntarily relaxed, urine flows into the urethra, and the bladder is emptied.

Urination can be prevented by voluntary contraction of the external urethral sphincter. However, if the bladder continues to fill and be stretched, voluntary control eventually becomes no longer possible.

CHARACTERISTICS OF URINE

The characteristics of urine include the physical and chemical aspects that are often evaluated as part of a urinalysis. Some of these are described in this section, and others are included in Appendix D: Normal Values for Some Commonly Used Urine Tests.

Amount—normal urinary output per 24 hours is 1 to 2 liters. There are many factors that can significantly change output. Excessive sweating or loss of fluid through diarrhea will decrease urinary output to conserve body water. Excessive fluid intake will increase urinary output. Consumption of alcohol will also increase output because alcohol inhibits the secretion of ADH, and the kidneys will reabsorb less water.

Color—the typical yellow color of urine is often referred to as "straw" or "amber." Concentrated urine is a deeper yellow (amber) than is dilute urine. Freshly voided urine is also clear rather than cloudy.

Specific gravity—the normal range is 1.010 to 1.025; this is a measure of the dissolved materials in urine. The specific gravity of distilled water is 1.000, meaning that there are no solutes present. Therefore, the higher the specific gravity number, the more dissolved material is present. Someone who has been exercising strenuously and has lost body water in sweat will usually produce less urine, which will be more concentrated and have a higher specific gravity.

The specific gravity of the urine is an indicator of the concentrating ability of the kidneys: the kidneys must excrete the waste products that are constantly formed in as little water as possible.

pH—the pH range of urine can vary between 4.6 and 8.0, with an average value of 6.0. Diet has the greatest influence on urine pH. A vegetarian diet will result in a more alkaline urine, while a high protein diet will result in a more acidic urine.

Constituents—urine is approximately 95% water, which is the solvent for waste products and salts. Salts are not considered true waste products since they may well be utilized by the body when needed, but excess amounts will be excreted in urine (see Box 18–4: Kidney Stones).

Nitrogenous wastes—as their name indicates, all contain nitrogen. Urea is formed by liver cells when excess amino acids are deaminated to be used for energy production. Creatinine comes

---

Box 18–4 KIDNEY STONES

Kidney stones, or **renal calculi,** are crystals of the salts that are normally present in urine. A very high concentration of salts in urine may trigger precipitation of the salt and formation of crystals, which can range in size from microscopic to 10 to 20 mm in diameter. The most common type of kidney stone is made of calcium salts; a less common type is made of uric acid.

Kidney stones are most likely to form in the renal pelvis. Predisposing factors include decreased fluid intake or overingestion of minerals (as in mineral supplements), both of which lead to the formation of a very concentrated urine.

The entry of a kidney stone into a ureter may cause intense pain (renal colic) and bleeding. Obstruction of a ureter by a stone may cause backup of urine and possible kidney damage. Treatments include surgery to remove the stone, or lithotripsy, the use of shock waves to crush the stone into pieces small enough to be eliminated without damage to the urinary tract.

Box 18–5   BLOOD TESTS AND KIDNEY FUNCTION

Waste products are normally present in the blood, and the concentration of each varies within a normal range. As part of the standard lab work called Blood Chemistry, the levels of the three nitrogenous waste products are determined (urea, creatinine, and uric acid).

If blood levels of these three substances are within normal ranges, it may be concluded that the kidneys are excreting these wastes at normal rates. If, however, these blood levels are elevated, one possible cause is that kidney function has been impaired. Of the three, the creatinine level is probably the most reliable indicator of kidney functioning. Blood urea nitrogen (BUN) may vary considerably in certain situations not directly related to the kidneys. For example, BUN may be elevated as a consequence of a high-protein diet or of starvation when body protein is being broken down at a faster rate. Uric acid levels may also vary according to diet. However, elevated blood levels of all three nitrogenous wastes usually indicate impaired glomerular filtration.

---

from the metabolism of creatine phosphate, an energy source in muscles. Uric acid comes from the metabolism of nucleic acids, that is, the breakdown of DNA and RNA. Although these are waste products, there is always a certain amount of each in the blood. Box 18–5: Blood Tests and Kidney Function describes the relationship between blood levels of these waste products and kidney function.

Other non-nitrogenous waste products may include the metabolic products of medications. Table 18–3 summarizes the characteristics of urine.

When a substance not normally found in urine does appear there, there is a reason for it. The reason may be quite specific or more general. Table 18–4 lists some abnormal constituents of urine and possible reasons for each (see Box 18–6: Urinary Tract Infections).

Table 18–3   CHARACTERISTICS OF NORMAL URINE

Characteristic	Description
Amount	• 1–2 liters per 24 hours; highly variable depending on fluid intake and water loss through the skin and GI tract
Color	• Straw or amber; darker means more concentrated; should be clear not cloudy
Specific gravity	• 1.010–1.025; a measure of the dissolved material in urine; the lower the value, the more dilute the urine
pH	• Average 6; range 4.6–8.0; diet has the greatest effect on urine pH
Composition	• 95% water; 5% salts and waste products
Nitrogenous wastes	• Urea—from amino acid metabolism • Creatinine—from muscle metabolism • Uric acid—from nucleic acid metabolism

Table 18–4   ABNORMAL CONSTITUENTS IN URINE

Characteristic	Reason(s)
Glycosuria (the presence of glucose)	As long as blood glucose levels are within normal limits, filtrate levels will also be normal and will not exceed the threshold level for reabsorption. In an untreated diabetic, for example, blood glucose is too high; therefore the filtrate glucose level is too high. The kidneys reabsorb glucose up to their threshold level, but the excess remains in the filtrate and is excreted in urine.
Proteinuria (the presence of protein)	Most plasma proteins are too large to be forced out of the glomeruli, and the small proteins that enter the filtrate are reabsorbed by pinocytosis. The presence of protein in the urine indicates that the glomeruli have become too permeable, as occurs in some types of kidney disease.
Hematuria (the presence of blood—RBCs)	The presence of RBCs in urine may also indicate that the glomeruli have become too permeable. Another possible cause might be bleeding somewhere in the urinary tract. Pinpointing the site of bleeding would require specific diagnostic tests.
Bacteriuria (the presence of bacteria)	Bacteria give urine a cloudy rather than clear appearance; WBCs may be present also. The presence of bacteria means that there is an infection somewhere in the urinary tract. Further diagnostic tests would be needed to determine the precise location.
Ketonuria (the presence of ketones)	Ketones are formed from fats and proteins that are used for energy production. A trace of ketones in urine is normal. Higher levels of ketones indicate an increased use of fats and proteins for energy. This may be the result of malfunctioning carbohydrate metabolism (as in diabetes mellitus) or simply the result of a high protein diet.

Box 18–6   URINARY TRACT INFECTIONS

Infections may occur anywhere in the urinary tract and are most often caused by the microbial agents of sexually-transmitted diseases (see Chapter 20) or by the bacteria that are part of the normal flora of the colon. In women especially, the urinary and anal openings are in close proximity, and colon bacteria on the skin of the perineum may invade the urinary tract. The use of urinary catheters in hospitalized or bed-ridden patients may also be a factor if sterile technique is not carefully followed.

Cystitis is inflammation of the urinary bladder. Symptoms include frequency of urination, painful voiding, and low back pain. **Nephritis** (or pyelonephritis) is inflammation of the kidneys. Although this may be the result of a systemic bacterial infection, nephritis is a common complication of untreated lower urinary tract infections such as cystitis. Possible symptoms are fever and flank pain (in the area of the kidneys). Untreated nephritis may result in severe damage to nephrons and progress to renal failure.

SUMMARY

The kidneys are the principal regulators of the internal environment of the body. The composition of all body fluids is either directly or indirectly regulated by the kidneys as they form urine from blood plasma. The kidneys are also of great importance in the regulation of the pH of the body fluids. These topics are the subject of the next chapter.

STUDY OUTLINE

The urinary system consists of two kidneys, two ureters, the urinary bladder, and the urethra.
1. The kidneys form urine to excrete waste products and to regulate the volume, electrolytes, and pH of blood and tissue fluid.
2. The other organs of the system are concerned with elimination of urine.

Kidneys (see Fig. 18–1)
1. Retroperitoneal on either side of the backbone in the upper abdominal cavity; partially protected by the lower rib cage.
2. Adipose tissue and the renal fascia cushion the kidneys and help hold them in place.
3. Hilus—an indentation on the medial side; renal artery enters, renal vein and ureter emerge.

Kidney—internal structure (see Fig. 18–2)
1. Renal Cortex—outer area, made of renal corpuscles and convoluted tubules.
2. Renal Medulla (pyramids)—middle area, made of loops of Henle and collecting tubules.
3. Renal Pelvis—a cavity formed by the expanded end of the ureter within the kidney; extensions around the papillae of the pyramids are called calyces, which collect urine.

The Nephron—the functional unit of the kidney (see Fig. 18–3); 1 million per kidney
1. Renal Corpuscle—consists of a glomerulus surrounded by a Bowman's capsule.
   - Glomerulus—a capillary network between an afferent arteriole and an efferent arteriole.
   - Bowman's Capsule—the expanded end of a renal tubule that encloses the glomerulus; inner layer has pores and is very permeable; contains renal filtrate (potential urine).

2. Renal Tubule—consists of the proximal convoluted tubule, loop of Henle, distal convoluted tubule, and collecting tubule. Collecting tubules unite to form papillary ducts that empty urine into the calyces of the renal pelvis.
   - Peritubular capillaries—arise from the efferent arteriole and surround all parts of the renal tubule.

Blood Vessels of the Kidney (see Figs. 18–1, 18–2, and 18–3)
1. Pathway: abdominal aorta → renal artery → small arteries in the kidney → afferent arterioles → glomeruli → efferent arterioles → peritubular capillaries → small veins in the kidney → renal vein → inferior vena cava.
2. Two sets of capillaries provide for two sites of exchanges between the blood and tissues in the process of urine formation.

Formation of Urine (see Fig. 18–4)
1. Glomerular Filtration—takes place from the glomerulus to Bowman's capsule. High blood pressure (60 mmHg) in the glomerulus forces plasma, dissolved materials and small proteins out of the blood and into Bowman's capsule. The fluid is now called filtrate. Filtration is selective only in terms of size; blood cells and large proteins remain in the blood.
2. GFR is 100 to 125 ml per minute. Increased blood flow to the kidney increases GFR; decreased blood flow decreases GFR.
3. Tubular Reabsorption—takes place from the filtrate in the renal tubule to the blood in the peritubular capillaries; 99% of the filtrate is reabsorbed; only 1% becomes urine.
   - Active Transport—reabsorption of glucose, amino acids, vitamins, and positive ions;

threshold level is a limit to the quantity that can be reabsorbed.
- Passive Transport—most negative ions follow the reabsorption of positive ions.
- Osmosis—water follows the reabsorption of minerals, especially sodium.
- Pinocytosis—small proteins are engulfed by proximal tubule cells.
4. Tubular Secretion—takes place from the blood in the peritubular capillaries to the filtrate in the renal tubule; creatinine and other waste products may be secreted into the filtrate to be excreted in urine; secretion of H$^+$ ions helps maintain pH of blood.
5. Hormones that Affect Reabsorption—aldosterone, atrial natriuretic hormone, antidiuretic hormone, parathyroid hormone—see Table 18–1.

The Kidneys and Acid-Base Balance
1. The kidneys have the greatest capacity to compensate for normal and abnormal pH changes.
2. If the body fluids are becoming too acidic, the kidneys excrete H$^+$ ions and return HCO$_3^-$ ions to the blood (see Fig. 18–5).
3. If the body fluids are becoming too alkaline, the kidneys return H$^+$ ions to the blood and excrete HCO$_3^-$ ions.

Other Functions of the Kidneys
1. Secretion of renin by juxtaglomerular cells when blood pressure decreases (see Table 18–2). Angiotensin II causes vasoconstriction and increases secretion of aldosterone.
2. Secretion of erythropoietin in response to hypoxia; stimulates RBM to increase rate of RBC production.
3. Activation of vitamin D—conversion of inactive forms to the active form.

Elimination of urine—the function of the ureters, urinary bladder, and urethra
Ureters (see Figs. 18–1 and 18–6)
1. Each extends from the hilus of a kidney to the lower posterior side of the urinary bladder.

2. Peristalsis of smooth muscle layer propels urine toward bladder.

Urinary Bladder (see Figs. 18–1 and 18–6)
1. A muscular sac below the peritoneum and behind the pubic bones; in women, below the uterus; in men, above the prostate gland.
2. Mucosa—transitional epithelial tissue folded into rugae; permit expansion without tearing.
3. Trigone—triangular area on bladder floor; no rugae, does not expand; bounded by openings of ureters and urethra.
4. Detrusor Muscle—the smooth muscle layer, a spherical muscle; contracts to expel urine (reflex).
5. Internal Urethral Sphincter—involuntary; formed by detrusor muscle fibers around the opening of the urethra.

Urethra—takes urine from the bladder to the exterior
1. In women—1 to 1.5 inches long; anterior to vagina.
2. In men—7 to 8 inches long; passes through the prostate gland and penis.
3. Contains the external urethral sphincter: skeletal muscle (voluntary).

The Urination Reflex—also called micturition or voiding
1. Stimulus: stretching of the detrusor muscle by accumulating urine.
2. Sensory impulses to spinal cord, motor impulses return to detrusor muscle, which contracts; internal urethral sphincter relaxes.
3. Voluntary control is provided by the external urethral sphincter.

Characteristics of Urine (see Table 18–3)

Abnormal Constituents of Urine (see Table 18–4)

REVIEW QUESTIONS

1. Describe the location of the kidneys, ureters, urinary bladder, and urethra. (pp. 417, 427, 428)

2. Name the three areas of the kidney, and state what each consists of. (pp. 417, 420)

3. Name the two major parts of a nephron. State the general function of nephrons. (p. 420)

4. Name the parts of a renal corpuscle. What process takes place here? Name the parts of a renal tubule. What processes take place here? (pp. 420–422)

5. State the mechanism of tubular reabsorption of each of the following: (pp. 422)
   a. water
   b. glucose
   c. small proteins
   d. positive ions
   e. negative ions
   f. amino acids
   g. vitamins
   Explain what is meant by a threshold level of reabsorption.

6. Explain the importance of tubular secretion. (p. 422)

7. Describe the pathway of blood flow through the kidney from the abdominal aorta to the inferior vena cava. (p. 420)

8. Name the two sets of capillaries in the kidney, and state the processes that take place in each. (pp. 420–422)

9. Name the hormone that has each of these effects on the kidneys: (p. 422, 424)
   a. promotes reabsorption of Na^+ ions
   b. promotes direct reabsorption of water
   c. promotes reabsorption of Ca^{+2} ions
   d. promotes excretion of K^+ ions
   e. decreases reabsorption of Na^+ ions

10. In what circumstances will the kidneys excrete H^+ ions? What ions will be returned to the blood? How will this affect the pH of blood? (p. 426)

11. In what circumstances do the kidneys secrete renin, and what is its purpose? (p. 426)

12. In what circumstances do the kidneys secrete erythropoietin, and what is its purpose? (p. 427)

13. Describe the function of the ureters and that of the urethra. (pp. 427–428)

14. With respect to the urinary bladder, describe the function of rugae, the detrusor muscle. (pp. 427–428)

15. Describe the urination reflex in terms of stimulus, part of the CNS involved, effector muscle, internal urethral sphincter, voluntary control. (p. 428)

16. Describe the characteristics of normal urine in terms of appearance, amount, pH, specific gravity, and composition. (pp. 429–430)

17. State the source of each of the nitrogenous waste products: creatinine, uric acid, and urea. (pp. 429–430)

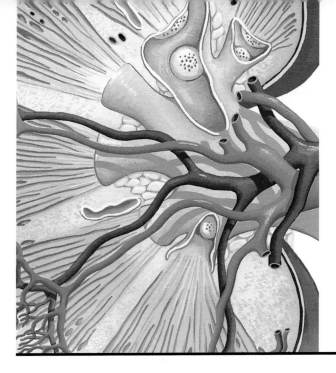

Chapter 19

Chapter Outline

Student Objectives

- Describe the water compartments and the name for the water in each.
- Explain how water moves between compartments.
- Explain the regulation of the intake and output of water.
- Name the major electrolytes in body fluids, and state their functions.
- Explain the regulation of the intake and output of electrolytes.
- Describe the three buffer systems in body fluids.
- Explain why the respiratory system has an effect on pH, and describe respiratory compensating mechanisms.
- Explain the renal mechanisms for pH regulation of extracellular fluid.
- Describe the effects of acidosis and alkalosis.

Fluid-Electrolyte and Acid-Base Balance

New Terminology

Amine group (ah–**MEE**–n)
Anions (**AN**–eye–ons)
Carboxyl group (kar–**BAHK**–sul)
Cations (**KAT**–eye–ons)
Electrolytes (ee–**LEK**–troh–lites)
Osmolarity (ahs–moh–**LAR**–i–tee)
Osmoreceptors (AHS–moh–re–**SEP**–ters)

Related Clinical Terminology

Edema (uh–**DEE**–muh)
Hypercalcemia (HIGH–per–kal–**SEE**–me–ah)
Hyperkalemia (HIGH–per–kuh–**LEE**–me–ah)
Hypernatremia (HIGH–per–nuh–**TREE**–me–ah)
Hypocalcemia (HIGH–poh–kal–**SEE**–me–ah)
Hypokalemia (HIGH–poh–kuh–**LEE**–me–ah)
Hyponatremia (HIGH–poh–nuh–**TREE**–me–ah)

Terms that appear in **bold type** in the chapter text are defined in the glossary, which begins on page 549.

The fluid medium of the human body is, of course, water. Water makes up 60% to 75% of the total body weight. Electrolytes are the positive and negative ions present in body fluids. Many of these ions are minerals that are already familiar to you. They each have specific functions in body fluids, and some of them are also involved in the maintenance of the normal pH of the body fluids. In this chapter we will first discuss fluid-electrolyte balance, then review and summarize the mechanisms involved in acid-base balance.

WATER COMPARTMENTS

Most of the water of the body, about two thirds of the total water volume, is found within individual cells and is called **intracellular fluid** (ICF). The remaining third is called **extracellular fluid** (ECF) and includes blood plasma, lymph, tissue fluid, and the specialized fluids such as cerebrospinal fluid, synovial fluid, aqueous humor, and serous fluid.

Water constantly moves from one fluid site in the body to another by the processes of filtration and osmosis. These fluid sites are called **water compartments** (Fig. 19–1). The chambers of the heart and all of the blood vessels comprise one compartment, and the water within is called plasma. By the process of filtration in capillaries, some plasma is forced out into tissue spaces (another compartment) and is then called tissue fluid. When tissue fluid enters cells by the process of osmosis, it has moved to still another compartment and is called intracellular fluid. The tissue fluid that enters lymph

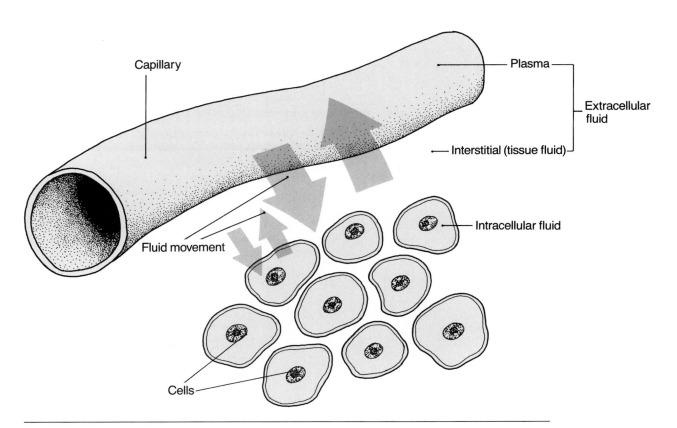

Figure 19–1 Water compartments. The name given to water in each of its locations is indicated.

Box 19–1   EDEMA

Edema is an abnormal increase in the amount of tissue fluid, which may be localized or systemic. Sometimes edema is inapparent, and sometimes it is apparent as swelling.

Localized edema follows injury and inflammation of a body part. Spraining an ankle, for example, damages tissues which then release histamine. Histamine increases the permeability of capillaries, and more tissue fluid is formed. As tissue fluid accumulates, the ankle may become swollen.

Systemic edema is the result of an imbalance between the movement of water out of and into capillaries, that is, between filtration and osmosis. Excessive filtration will occur when capillary pressure rises. This may be caused by venous obstruction due to blood clots or by congestive heart failure. Edema of this type is often apparent in the lower extremities (pulmonary edema was described in Chapter 15).

Systemic bacterial infections may increase capillary permeability, and loss of plasma to tissue spaces is one aspect of septicemia. In this situation, however, the edema is of secondary importance to the hypotension, which may be life threatening.

Insufficient osmosis, the return of tissue fluid into capillaries, is a consequence of a decrease in plasma proteins, especially albumin. This may occur in severe liver diseases such as cirrhosis, kidney disease involving loss of protein in urine, malnutrition, or severe burn injuries.

Since edema is a symptom rather than a disease, treatment is aimed at correcting the specific cause. If that is not possible, the volume of tissue fluid may be diminished by a low-salt diet and the use of diuretics.

capillaries is in yet another compartment and is called lymph.

The other process (besides filtration) by which water moves from one compartment to another is osmosis, which you may recall, is the diffusion of water through a semi-permeable membrane. Water will move through cell membranes from the area of its greater concentration to the area of its lesser concentration. Another way of expressing this is to say that water will diffuse to an area with a greater concentration of dissolved material. The concentration of electrolytes present in the various water compartments determines just how osmosis will take place. Therefore, if water is in balance in all the compartments, the electrolytes are also in balance. Although water and ions are constantly moving, their relative proportions in the compartments remain constant; this is fluid-electrolyte homeostasis, and its maintenance is essential for life (see Box 19–1: Edema).

WATER INTAKE AND OUTPUT

Most of the water the body requires comes from the ingestion of liquids; this amount averages 1600 ml per day. The food we eat also contains water. Even foods we think of as somewhat dry, such as bread, contain significant amounts of water. The daily water total from food averages 700 ml. The last source of water, about 200 ml per day, is the metabolic water that is a product of cell respiration. The total intake of water per day, therefore, is about 2500 ml, or 2.5 liters.

Most of the water lost from the body is in the form of urine produced by the kidneys; this averages 1500 ml per day. About 500 ml per day is lost in the form of sweat, another 300 ml per day is in the form of water vapor in exhaled air, and another 200 ml per day is lost in feces. The total output of water is thus about 2500 ml per day.

Naturally, any increase in water output must be compensated for by an increase in intake. Someone who exercises strenuously, for example, may lose 1 to 2 liters of water in sweat and must replace that water by drinking more fluids. In a healthy individual, water intake equals water output, even though the amounts of each may vary greatly from the averages used above (Fig. 19–2 and Table 19–1).

REGULATION OF WATER INTAKE AND OUTPUT

The hypothalamus in the brain contains **osmoreceptors** that detect changes in the osmolarity of body fluids. **Osmolarity** is the concentration of dissolved materials present in a fluid. Dehydration raises the osmolarity of the blood; that is, there is

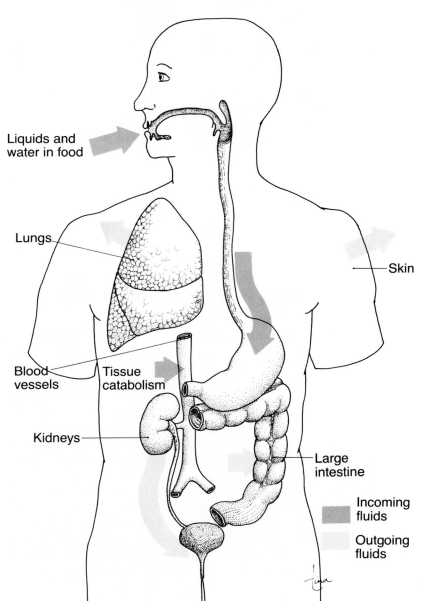

Liquids and water in food

Lungs

Skin

Blood vessels

Tissue catabolism

Kidneys

Large intestine

Incoming fluids

Outgoing fluids

Figure 19–2 Water intake and output. See text for description.

Table 19–1 WATER INTAKE AND OUTPUT

Form	Average Amount per 24 Hours
Intake	
Liquids	1600 ml
Food	700 ml
Metabolic Water	200 ml
Output	
Urine	1500 ml
Sweat (and insensible water loss)	500 ml
Exhaled Air (water vapor)	300 ml
Feces	200 ml

less water in proportion to the amount of dissolved materials. Another way to express this is to simply say that the blood is now a more concentrated solution. When dehydrated, we experience the sensation of thirst, characterized by dryness of the mouth and throat, as less saliva is produced. Thirst is an uncomfortable sensation, and we drink fluids to relieve it. The water we drink is readily absorbed by the mucosa of the stomach and small intestine and has the effect of decreasing the osmolarity of the blood. In other words, we can say that the water we just drank is causing the blood to become a more dilute solution, and, as the serum osmolarity returns to normal, the sensation of thirst diminishes.

As you may recall, the hypothalamus is also involved in water balance because of its production of antidiuretic hormone (ADH), which is stored in the posterior pituitary gland. In a state of dehydration, the hypothalamus stimulates the release of ADH from the posterior pituitary. Antidiuretic hormone then increases the reabsorption of water by the kidney tubules. Water is returned to the blood to preserve blood volume, and urinary output decreases.

The hormone aldosterone, from the adrenal cortex, also helps regulate water output. Aldosterone increases the reabsorption of Na^+ ions by the kidney tubules, and water from the renal filtrate follows the Na^+ ions back to the blood. Aldosterone is secreted when the Na^+ ion concentration of the blood decreases or whenever there is a significant decrease in blood pressure (the Renin-Angiotensin mechanism).

Several other factors may also contribute to water loss. These include excessive sweating, hemorrhage, diarrhea or vomiting, severe burns, and fever. In these circumstances, the kidneys will conserve water, but water must also be replaced by increased consumption. Following hemorrhage or during certain disease states, fluids may also be replaced by intravenous administration.

A less common occurrence is that of too much water in the body. This may happen following overconsumption of fluids. The osmolarity of the blood decreases, and there is too much water in proportion to electrolytes (or, the blood is too dilute). Atrial natriuretic hormone (ANH) is secreted by the atria when blood volume or blood pressure increase. ANH then decreases the reabsorption of Na^+ ions by the kidneys, which increases urinary output of sodium and water. Also, secretion of ADH will diminish, which also will contribute to a greater urinary output that will return the blood osmolarity to normal.

ELECTROLYTES

Electrolytes are chemicals that dissolve in water and dissociate into their positive and negative ions. Most electrolytes are the inorganic salts, acids, and bases found in all body fluids.

Most organic compounds are non-electrolytes, that is, they do not ionize when in solution. Glucose, for example, dissolves in water but does not ionize; it remains as intact glucose molecules. Some proteins, however, do form ionic bonds and when in solution dissociate into ions.

Positive ions are called **cations.** Examples are Na^+, K^+, Ca^{+2}, Mg^{+2}, Fe^{+2}, and H^+. Negative ions are called **anions,** and examples are Cl^-, HCO_3^-, SO_4^{-2} (sulfate), HPO_4^{-2} (phosphate), and protein anions.

Electrolytes help create the osmolarity of body fluids and, therefore, help regulate the osmosis of water between water compartments. Some electrolytes are involved in acid-base regulatory mechanisms, or they are part of structural components of tissues or part of enzymes.

ELECTROLYTES IN BODY FLUIDS

The three principal fluids in the body are intracellular fluid and the extracellular fluids, plasma and tissue fluid. The relative concentrations of the most important electrolytes in these fluids are depicted in Fig. 19–3. The major differences may be summarized as follows. In intracellular fluid, the most abundant cation is K^+, the most abundant anion is HPO_4^{-2}, and protein anions are also abundant. In both tissue fluid and plasma, the most abundant cation is Na^+, and the most abundant anion is Cl^-. Protein anions form a significant part of plasma but not of tissue fluid. The functions of the major electrolytes are described in Table 19–2.

INTAKE, OUTPUT, AND REGULATION

Electrolytes are part of the food and beverages we consume, are absorbed by the GI tract into the blood, and become part of body fluids. The ECF concentrations of some electrolytes are regulated by hormones. Aldosterone increases the reabsorption of Na^+ ions and the excretion of K^+ ions by the kidneys. The blood sodium level is thereby raised, and the blood potassium level is lowered. Atrial natriuretic hormone (ANH) increases the excretion of Na^+ ions by the kidneys and lowers the blood sodium level. Parathyroid hormone (PTH) and calcitonin regulate the blood levels of calcium and phosphate. PTH increases the reabsorption of these minerals from bones, and increases their absorption from food in the small intestine (vitamin D is also necessary). Calcitonin promotes the removal of calcium and phosphate from the blood to form bone matrix.

Electrolytes are lost in urine, sweat, and feces. Urine contains the electrolytes that are not reabsorbed by the kidney tubules; the major one is Na^+ ions. Other electrolytes are present in urine when

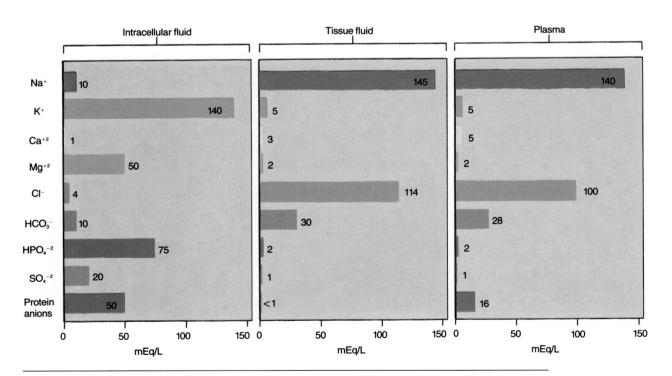

Figure 19–3 Electrolyte concentrations in intracellular fluid, tissue fluid, and plasma. Concentrations are expressed in milliequivalents per liter. See text for summary of major differences among these fluids.

Table 19–2　MAJOR ELECTROLYTES

Electrolyte	Plasma Level mEq/L*	ICF Level mEq/L	Functions
Sodium (Na^+)	136–142	10	• Creates much of the osmotic pressure of ECF; the most abundant cation in ECF • Essential for electrical activity of neurons and muscle cells
Potassium (K^+)	3.8–5.0	141	• Creates much of the osmotic pressure in ICF; the most abundant cation in ICF • Essential for electrical activity of neurons and muscle cells
Calcium (Ca^{+2})	4.6–5.5	1	• Most (98%) is found in bones and teeth • Maintains normal excitability of neurons and muscle cells • Essential for blood clotting
Magnesium (Mg^{+2})	1.3–2.1	58	• Most (50%) is found in bone • More abundant in ICF than in ECF • Essential for ATP production and activity of neurons and muscle cells
Chloride (Cl^-)	95–103	4	• Most abundant anion in ECF; diffuses easily into and out of cells; helps regulate osmotic pressure • Part of HCl in gastric juice
Bicarbonate (HCO_3^-)	28	10	• Part of the bicarbonate buffer system
Phosphate (HPO_4^{-2})	1.7–2.6	75	• Most (85%) is found in bones and teeth • Primarily an ICF anion • Part of DNA, RNA, ATP, phospholipids • Part of phosphate buffer system
Sulfate (SO_4^{-2})	1	2	• Part of some amino acids and proteins

*The concentration of an ion is often expressed in milliequivalents per liter, abbreviated mEq/L, which is the number of electrical charges in each liter of solution.

Box 19–2 ELECTROLYTE IMBALANCES

Imbalances of Sodium
Hyponatremia—a consequence of excessive sweating, diarrhea, or vomiting. Characterized by dizziness, confusion, weakness, low BP, shock.
Hypernatremia—a consequence of excessive water loss or sodium ingestion. Characterized by loss of ICF and extreme thirst and agitation.

Imbalances of Potassium
Hypokalemia—a consequence of vomiting or diarrhea or kidney disease. Characterized by fatigue, confusion, possible cardiac failure.
Hyperkalemia—a consequence of Addison's disease. Characterized by weakness, abnormal sensations, cardiac arrhythmias, and possible cardiac arrest.

Imbalances of Calcium
Hypocalcemia—a consequence of hypoparathyroidism or decreased calcium intake. Characterized by muscle spasms leading to tetany.
Hypercalcemia—a consequence of hyperparathyroidism. Characterized by muscle weakness, bone fragility, possible kidney stones.

---

their concentrations in the blood exceed the body's need for them.

The most abundant electrolytes in sweat are Na^+ ions and Cl^- ions. Electrolytes lost in feces are those that are not absorbed in either the small intestine or colon.

Some of the major imbalances of electrolyte levels are described in Box 19–2: Electrolyte Imbalances.

ACID–BASE BALANCE

You have already learned quite a bit about the regulation of the pH of body fluids in the chapters on chemistry, the respiratory system, and the urinary system. In this section, we will put all that information together. You may first wish to review the pH scale, described in Chapter 2.

The normal pH range of blood is 7.35 to 7.45. The pH of tissue fluid is similar but can vary slightly above or below this range. The intracellular fluid has a pH range of 6.8 to 7.0. Notice that these ranges of pH are quite narrow; they must be maintained in order for enzymatic reactions and other processes to proceed normally.

Maintenance of acid-base homeostasis is accomplished by the buffer systems in body fluids, respirations, and the kidneys.

BUFFER SYSTEMS

The purpose of a **buffer system** is to prevent drastic changes in the pH of body fluids by chemically reacting with strong acids or bases that would otherwise greatly change the pH. A buffer system consists of a weak acid and a weak base. These molecules react with strong acids or bases that may be produced and change them to substances that do not have a great effect on pH.

The Bicarbonate Buffer System

The two components of this buffer system are carbonic acid (H_2CO_3), a weak acid, and sodium bicarbonate ($NaHCO_3$), a weak base. Each of these molecules participates in a specific type of reaction.

If a potential pH change is created by a strong acid, the following reaction takes place:

$$\underset{\text{(strong acid)}}{\text{HCl}} + \text{NaHCO}_3 \rightarrow \text{NaCl} + \underset{\text{(weak acid)}}{\text{H}_2\text{CO}_3}$$

The strong acid has reacted with the sodium bicarbonate to produce a salt (NaCl) that has no effect on pH and a weak acid that has little effect on pH.

If a potential pH change is created by a strong base, the following reaction takes place:

$$\underset{\text{(strong base)}}{\text{NaOH}} + \text{H}_2\text{CO}_3 \rightarrow \text{H}_2\text{O} + \underset{\text{(weak base)}}{\text{NaHCO}_3}$$

The strong base has reacted with the carbonic acid to produce water, which has no effect on pH and a weak base that has little effect on pH.

The bicarbonate buffer system is important in both the blood and tissue fluid. During normal metabolism, these fluids tend to become more acidic, so more sodium bicarbonate than carbonic acid is needed. The usual ratio of these molecules to each other is about 20 to 1 (NaHCO_3 to H_2CO_3).

The Phosphate Buffer System

The two components of this buffer system are sodium dihydrogen phosphate (NaH_2PO_4), a weak acid, and sodium monohydrogen phosphate (Na_2HPO_4), a weak base. Let us use specific reactions to show how this buffer system works.

If a potential pH change is created by a strong acid, the following reaction takes place:

$$\underset{\text{(strong acid)}}{\text{HCl}} + \text{Na}_2\text{HPO}_4 \rightarrow \text{NaCl} + \underset{\text{(weak acid)}}{\text{NaH}_2\text{PO}_4}$$

The strong acid has reacted with the sodium monohydrogen phosphate to produce a salt that has no effect on pH and a weak acid that has little effect on pH.

If a potential pH change is created by a strong base, the following reaction takes place:

$$\underset{\text{(strong base)}}{\text{NaOH}} + \text{NaH}_2\text{PO}_4 \rightarrow \text{H}_2\text{O} + \underset{\text{(weak base)}}{\text{Na}_2\text{HPO}_4}$$

The strong base has reacted with the sodium dihydrogen phosphate to form water, which has no effect on pH and a weak base that has little effect on pH.

The phosphate buffer system is important in the regulation of the pH of the blood by the kidneys. The cells of the kidney tubules can remove excess hydrogen ions by forming NaH_2PO_4, which is excreted in urine. The retained Na^+ ions are returned to the blood in the peritubular capillaries, along with bicarbonate ions (Fig. 19–4).

The Protein Buffer System

This buffer system is the most important one in the intracellular fluid. The amino acids that make up proteins each have a **carboxyl group** (COOH) and an **amine** (or amino) **group** (NH_2) and may act as either acids or bases.

The carboxyl group may act as an acid because it can donate a hydrogen ion (H^+) to the fluid:

$$\underset{\text{R}}{\overset{\text{H}}{\text{NH}_2-\text{C}-\text{COOH}}} \rightarrow \underset{\text{R}}{\overset{\text{H}}{\text{NH}_2-\text{C}-\text{COO}^-}} + \text{H}^+$$

The amine group may act as a base because it can pick up an excess hydrogen ion from the fluid:

$$\underset{\text{R}}{\overset{\text{H}}{\text{COOH}-\text{C}-\text{NH}_2}} \rightarrow \underset{\text{R}}{\overset{\text{H}}{\text{COOH}-\text{C}-\text{NH}_3^+}}$$

The buffer systems react within a fraction of a second to prevent drastic pH changes. However, they have the least capacity to prevent great changes in pH because there are a limited number of molecules of these buffers present in body fluids. When an ongoing cause is disrupting the normal pH, the respiratory and renal mechanisms will also be needed.

RESPIRATORY MECHANISMS

The respiratory system affects pH because it regulates the amount of CO_2 present in body fluids. As you know, the respiratory system may be the cause of a pH imbalance or may help correct a pH imbalance from some other cause.

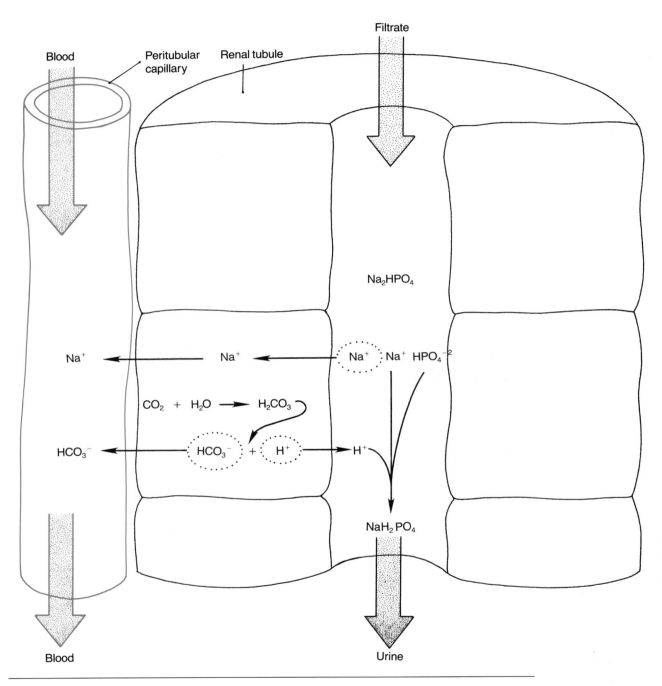

Figure 19–4 The phosphate buffer system. The reactions are shown in a kidney tubule. See text for description.

Respiratory Acidosis and Alkalosis

Respiratory acidosis is caused by anything that decreases the rate or efficiency of respiration. Severe pulmonary diseases are possible causes of respiratory acidosis. When CO_2 cannot be exhaled as fast as it is formed during cell respiration, excess CO_2 results in the formation of excess H^+ ions, as shown in this reaction:

$$CO_2 + H_2O \rightarrow H_2CO_3 \rightarrow H^+ + HCO_3^-$$

The excess H^+ ions lower the pH of body fluids.

Respiratory alkalosis is far less common but is the result of breathing more rapidly, which increases the amount of CO_2 exhaled. Since there are fewer CO_2 molecules in the body fluids, fewer H^+ ions are formed, and pH tends to rise.

Respiratory Compensation for Metabolic pH Changes

Changes in pH caused by other than a respiratory disorder are called metabolic acidosis or alkalosis. In either case, the respiratory system may help prevent a drastic change in pH.

Metabolic acidosis may be caused by kidney disease, uncontrolled diabetes mellitus, excessive diarrhea or vomiting, or the use of some diuretics. When excess H^+ ions are present in body fluids, pH begins to decrease, and this stimulates the respiratory centers in the medulla. The response is to increase the rate of breathing to exhale more CO_2 to decrease H^+ ion formation. This helps raise the pH back toward the normal range.

Metabolic alkalosis is not common, but may be caused by the overuse of antacid medications or the vomiting of stomach contents only. As the pH of body fluids begins to rise, breathing slows and decreases the amount of CO_2 exhaled. The CO_2 retained within the body increases the formation of H^+ ions, which will help lower the pH back toward the normal range.

The respiratory system responds quickly to prevent drastic changes in pH, usually within 1 to 3 minutes. For an ongoing metabolic pH imbalance, however, the respiratory mechanism does not have the capacity to fully compensate. In such cases, respiratory compensation is only 50% to 75% effective.

RENAL MECHANISMS

As just discussed in Chapter 18, the kidneys help regulate the pH of extracellular fluid by excreting or conserving H^+ ions and by reabsorbing (or not) Na^+ ions and HCO_3^- ions. One mechanism was depicted in Fig. 18–5, and another, involving the phosphate buffer system is shown in Fig. 19–4.

The kidneys have the greatest capacity to buffer an ongoing pH change. Although the renal mechanisms do not become fully functional for several hours to days, once they do they continue to be effective far longer than respiratory mechanisms. Let us use as an example a patient with untreated diabetes mellitus who is in ketoacidosis, a metabolic acidosis. As acidic ketones accumulate in the blood, the capacity of the ECF buffer systems is quickly exhausted. Breathing rate then increases, and more CO_2 is exhaled to decrease H^+ ion formation and raise the pH of ECF. There is, however, a limit to how much the respiratory rate can increase, but the renal buffering mechanisms will then become effective. At this time it is the kidneys that are keeping the patient alive by preventing acidosis from reaching a fatal level. Even the kidneys have limits, however, and the cause of the acidosis must be corrected to prevent death.

EFFECTS OF pH CHANGES

A state of **acidosis** is most detrimental to the central nervous system, causing depression of impulse transmission at synapses. A person in acidosis becomes confused and disoriented, then lapses into a coma.

Alkalosis has the opposite effect and affects both the central and peripheral nervous system. Increased synaptic transmission, even without stimuli, is first apparent in irritability and muscle twitches. Progressive alkalosis is characterized by severe muscle spasms and convulsions.

The types of pH changes are summarized in Table 19–3.

Table 19–3   pH CHANGES

Change	Possible Causes	Compensation
Metabolic acidosis	• Kidney disease, ketosis, diarrhea, or vomiting	• Increased respirations to exhale CO_2
Metabolic alkalosis	• Overingestion of bicarbonate medications, gastric suctioning	• Decreased respirations to retain CO_2
Respiratory acidosis	• Decreased rate or efficiency of respiration: emphysema, asthma, pneumonia, paralysis of respiratory muscles	• Kidneys excrete H^+ ions and reabsorb Na^+ ions and HCO_3^- ions
Respiratory alkalosis	• Increased rate of respiration: anxiety, high altitude	• Kidneys retain H^+ ions and excrete Na^+ ions and HCO_3^- ions

STUDY OUTLINE

Fluid-Electrolyte Balance
1. Water makes up 60% to 75% of the total body weight.
2. Electrolytes are the ions found in body fluids; most are minerals.

Water Compartments (see Fig. 19–1)
1. Intracellular Fluid (ICF)—water within cells; about two thirds of total body water.
2. Extracellular Fluid (ECF)—water outside cells; includes plasma, lymph, tissue fluid, and specialized fluids.
3. Water constantly moves from one compartment to another. Filtration: plasma becomes tissue fluid. Osmosis: tissue fluid becomes plasma, or lymph, or ICF.
4. Osmosis is regulated by the concentration of electrolytes in body fluids (osmolarity). Water will diffuse through membranes to areas of greater electrolyte concentration.

Water Intake (see Fig. 19–2)
1. Fluids, food, metabolic water—see Table 19–1.

Water Output (see Fig. 19–2)
1. Urine, sweat, exhaled air, feces—see Table 19–1.

2. Any variation in output must be compensated for by a change in input.

Regulation of Water Intake and Output
1. Hypothalamus contains osmoreceptors that detect changes in osmolarity of body fluids.
2. Dehydration stimulates the sensation of thirst, and fluids are consumed to relieve it.
3. ADH released from the posterior pituitary increases the reabsorption of water by the kidneys.
4. Aldosterone secreted by the adrenal cortex increases the reabsorption of Na^+ ions by the kidneys; water is then reabsorbed by osmosis.
5. If there is too much water in the body, secretion of ADH decreases, and urinary output increases.
6. If blood volume increases, ANH promotes loss of Na^+ ions and water in urine.

Electrolytes
1. Chemicals that dissolve in water and dissociate into ions; most are inorganic.
2. Cations are positive ions such as Na^+ and K^+.
3. Anions are negative ions such as Cl^- and HCO_3^-.
4. By creating osmotic pressure, electrolytes regulate the osmosis of water between compartments.

Electrolytes in Body Fluids (see Fig. 19–3 and Table 19–2)

1. ICF—principal cation is K^+; principal anion is HPO_4^{-2}; protein anions are also abundant.
2. Plasma—principal cation is Na^+; principal anion is Cl^-; protein anions are significant.
3. Tissue fluid—same as plasma except that protein anions are insignificant.

Intake, Output, and Regulation

1. Intake—electrolytes are part of food and beverages.
2. Output—urine, sweat, feces.
3. Hormones involved: aldosterone—Na^+ and K^+; ANH—Na^+; PTH and calcitonin—Ca^{+2} and HPO_4^{-2}.

Acid-Base Balance

1. Normal pH ranges—blood: 7.35 to 7.45; ICF: 6.8 to 7.0; tissue fluid: similar to blood.
2. Normal pH of body fluids is maintained by buffer systems, respirations, and the kidneys.

Buffer Systems

1. Each consists of a weak acid and a weak base; react with strong acids or bases to change them to substances that do not greatly affect pH. React within a fraction of a second, but have the least capacity to prevent pH changes.
2. The bicarbonate buffer system—see text for reactions; important in both blood and tissue fluid; base to acid ratio is 20:1.
3. The phosphate buffer system—see Fig. 19–4 and text for reactions; important in ICF and in the kidneys.
4. The protein buffer system—amino acids may act as either acids or bases. See text for reactions; important in ICF.

Respiratory Mechanisms

1. The respiratory system affects pH because it regulates the amount of CO_2 in body fluids.
2. May be the cause of a pH change or help compensate for a metabolic pH change—see Table 19–3.
3. Respiratory compensation is rapidly effective (within a few minutes), but limited in capacity if the pH imbalance is ongoing.

Renal Mechanisms

1. The kidneys have the greatest capacity to buffer pH changes, but they may take several hours to days to become effective (see Table 19–3).
2. Reactions: see Figs. 18–5 and 19–4.
3. Summary of reactions: in response to acidosis, the kidneys will excrete H^+ ions and retain Na^+ ions and HCO_3^- ions; in response to alkalosis, the kidneys will retain H^+ ions and excrete Na^+ ions and HCO_3^- ions.

Effects of pH Changes

1. Acidosis—depresses synaptic transmission in the CNS; result is confusion, coma, and death.
2. Alkalosis—increases synaptic transmission in the CNS and PNS; result is irritability, muscle spasms, and convulsions.

REVIEW QUESTIONS

1. Name the major water compartments and the name for water in each of them. Name three specialized body fluids and state the location of each. (p. 438)

2. Explain how water moves between compartments; name the processes. (pp. 438–439)

3. Describe the three sources of water for the body and the relative amounts of each. (p. 439)

4. Describe the pathways of water output. Which is the most important? What kinds of variations are possible in water output. (p. 439)

5. Name the hormones that affect fluid volume, and state the function of each. (p. 441)

6. Define electrolyte, cation, anion, osmosis, osmolarity. (pp. 440, 441)

7. Name the major electrolytes in plasma, tissue fluid, and intracellular fluid, and state their functions. (pp. 442–443)

8. Explain how the bicarbonate buffer system will react to buffer a strong acid. (pp. 444–445)

9. Explain how the phosphate buffer system will react to buffer a strong acid. (p. 445)

10. Explain why an amino acid may act as either an acid or a base. (p. 445)

11. Describe the respiratory compensation for metabolic acidosis and for metabolic alkalosis. (p. 447)

12. If the body fluids are becoming too acidic, what ions will the kidneys excrete? What ions will the kidneys return to the blood? (p. 447)

13. Which of the pH regulatory mechanisms works most rapidly? Most slowly? Which of these mechanisms has the greatest capacity to buffer an ongoing pH change? Which mechanism has the least capacity? (pp. 445, 447)

14. Describe the effects of acidosis and alkalosis. (p. 447)

Chapter 20
The Reproductive Systems

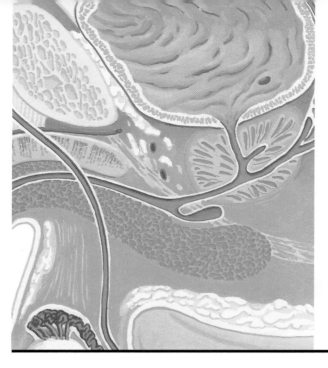

Chapter 20

Chapter Outline

Student Objectives

- Describe the process of meiosis. Define diploid and haploid.
- Describe the differences between spermatogenesis and oogenesis.
- Name the hormones necessary for the formation of gametes, and state the function of each.
- Describe the location and functions of the testes.
- Explain the functions of the epididymis, ductus deferens, ejaculatory duct, and urethra.
- Explain the functions of the seminal vesicles, prostate gland, and bulbourethral glands.
- Describe the composition of semen, and explain why its pH must be alkaline.
- Name the parts of a sperm cell, and state the function of each.
- Describe the functions of the ovaries, fallopian tubes, uterus, and vagina.
- Describe the structure and function of the myometrium and endometrium.
- Describe the structure of the mammary glands and the functions of the hormones involved in lactation.
- Describe the menstrual cycle in terms of the hormones involved and the changes in the ovaries and endometrium.

The Reproductive Systems

New Terminology

Cervix (**SIR**–viks)
Ductus deferens (**DUK**–tus **DEF**–er–enz)
Endometrium (EN–doh–**ME**–tree–uhm)
Fallopian tube (fuh–**LOH**–pee–an TOOB)
Graffian follicle (**GRAF**–ee–uhn **FAH**–li–kuhl)
Inguinal canal (**IN**–gwi–nuhl ka–**NAL**)
Menopause (**MEN**–ah–paws)
Menstrual cycle (**MEN**–stroo–uhl **SIGH**–kuhl)
Myometrium (MY–oh–**ME**–tree–uhm)
Oogenesis (OH–oh–**JEN**–e–sis)
Prostate gland (**PRAHS**–tayt)
Seminiferous tubules (sem–i–**NIFF**–er–us)
Spermatogenesis (SPER–ma–toh–**JEN**–e–sis)
Vulva (**VUHL**–vah)
Zygote (**ZYE**–goat)

Related Clinical Terminology

Amenorrhea (ay–MEN–uh–**REE**–ah)
Down's syndrome (DOWNZ **SIN**–drohm)
Ectopic pregnancy (ek–**TOP**–ik **PREG**–nun–see)
In vitro fertilization (IN **VEE**–troh FER–ti–li–**ZAY**–shun)
Mammography (mah–**MOG**–rah–fee)
Prostatic hypertrophy (prahs–**TAT**–ik high–**PER**–truh–fee)
Trisomy (**TRY**–suh–mee)
Tubal ligation (**TOO**–buhl lye–**GAY**–shun)
Vasectomy (va–**SEK**–tuh–me)

Terms that appear in **bold type** in the chapter text are defined in the glossary, which begins on page 549.

The purpose of the male and female **reproductive systems** is to continue the human species by the production of offspring. How dry and impersonal that sounds, until we remember that each of us is a continuation of our species and that many of us in turn will have our own children. Although some other animals care for their offspring in organized families or societies, the human species is unique, because of cultural influences, in the attention we give to reproduction and to family life.

Yet like other animals, the actual production and growth of offspring is a matter of our anatomy and physiology. The male and female reproductive systems produce **gametes,** that is, sperm and egg cells, and ensure the union of gametes in fertilization following sexual intercourse. In women, the uterus provides the site for the developing embryo/fetus until it is sufficiently developed to survive outside the womb.

In this chapter we will describe the organs of reproduction and the role of each in the creation of new life or the functioning of the reproductive system as a whole. First, however, we will discuss the formation of gametes.

MEIOSIS

The cell division process of **meiosis** produces the gametes, sperm or egg cells. In meiosis, one cell with the diploid number of chromosomes (46 for people) divides twice to form four cells, each with the haploid number of chromosomes. Haploid means half the usual diploid number, so for people the haploid number is 23. Although the process of meiosis is essentially the same in men and women, there are important differences.

SPERMATOGENESIS

Spermatogenesis is the process of meiosis as it takes place in the testes, the site of sperm production. Within each testis are **seminiferous tubules** that contain spermatogonia, or sperm-generating cells. These divide first by mitosis to produce primary spermatocytes (Fig. 20–1). As you may recall from Chapter 10, gamete formation is regulated by

hormones. Follicle stimulating hormone (FSH) from the anterior pituitary gland initiates sperm production, and testosterone, secreted by the testes when stimulated by luteinizing hormone (LH) from the anterior pituitary, promotes the maturation of sperm. Inhibin, also produced by the testes, decreases the secretion of FSH. As you can see in Fig. 20–1, for each primary spermatocyte that undergoes meiosis, four functional sperm cells are produced.

Sperm production begins at **puberty** (10 to 14 years of age), and millions of sperm are formed each day in the testes. Although sperm production diminishes with advancing age, there is usually no complete cessation, as there is of egg production in women at menopause.

OOGENESIS

Oogenesis is the process of meiosis for egg cell formation; it begins in the ovaries and is also regulated by hormones. FSH initiates the growth of **ovarian follicles,** each of which contains an oogonium, or egg-generating cell (Fig. 20–2). This hormone also stimulates the follicle cells to secrete estrogen, which promotes the maturation of the ovum. Notice that for each primary oocyte that undergoes meiosis, only one functional egg cell is produced. The other three cells produced are called polar bodies. They have no function, and will simply deteriorate. A mature ovarian follicle actually contains the secondary oocyte; the second meiotic division will take place if and when the egg is fertilized.

The production of ova begins at puberty (10 to 14 years of age) and continues until **menopause** (45 to 55 years of age), when the ovaries atrophy and no longer respond to pituitary hormones. During this 30- to 40-year span, egg production is cyclical, with a mature ovum being produced approximately every 28 days (the menstrual cycle will be discussed later in this chapter). Actually, *several* follicles usually begin to develop during each cycle. However, the rupturing (ovulation) of the first follicle to mature stops the growth of the others.

The process of meiosis is like other human processes in that "mistakes" may sometimes occur. One of these, trisomy, is discussed in Box 20–1: Trisomy and Down Syndrome.

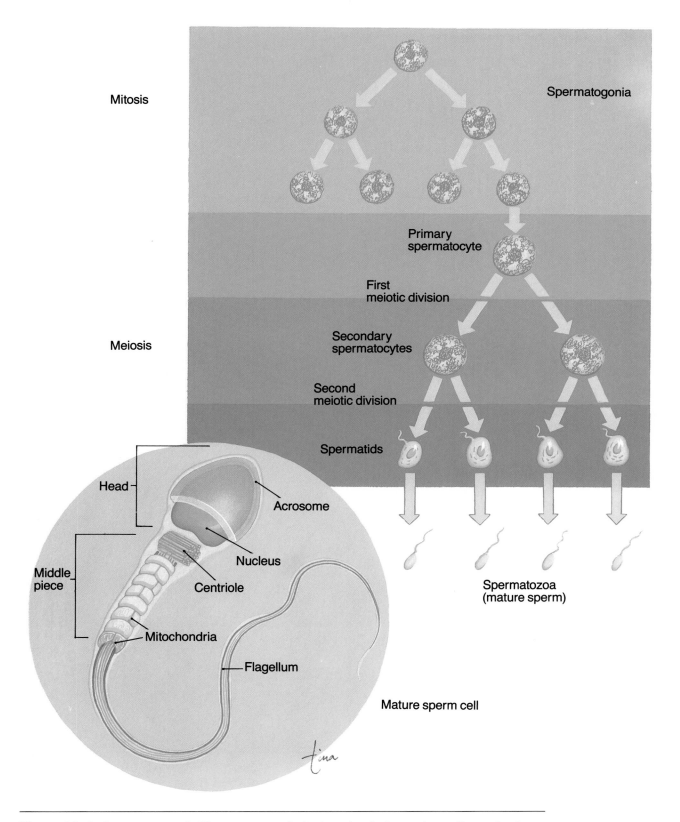

Figure 20–1 Spermatogenesis. The processes of mitosis and meiosis are shown. For each primary spermatocyte that undergoes meiosis, four functional sperm cells are formed. The structure of a mature sperm cell is also shown.

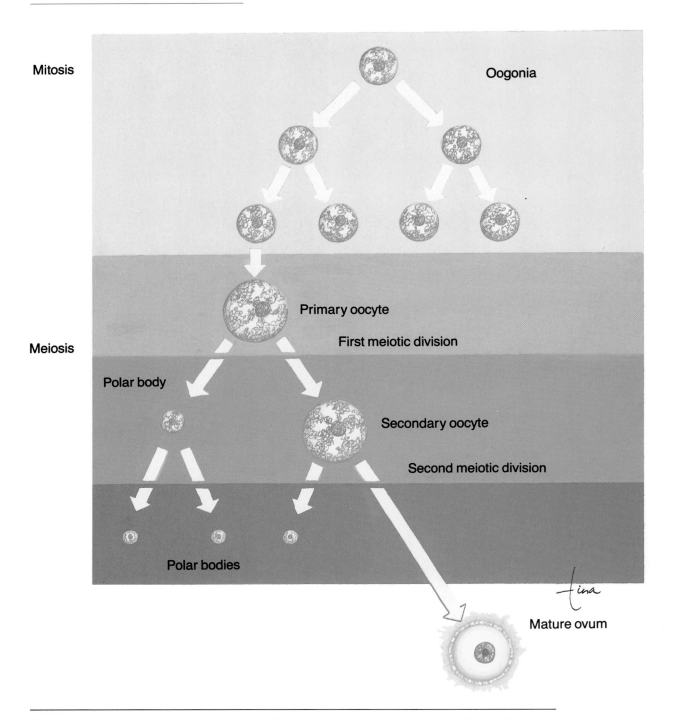

Mitosis

Oogonia

Meiosis

Primary oocyte

First meiotic division

Polar body

Secondary oocyte

Second meiotic division

Polar bodies

Mature ovum

Figure 20–2 Oogenesis. The processes of mitosis and meiosis are shown. For each primary oocyte that undergoes meiosis, only one functional ovum is formed.

Box 20–1   TRISOMY AND DOWN SYNDROME

Trisomy means the presence of three (rather than the normal two) of a particular chromosome in the cells of an individual. This may occur because of non-disjunction (non-separation) of a chromosome pair during the second meiotic division, usually in an egg cell. The egg cell has two of a particular chromosome, and if fertilized by a sperm, will then contain three of that chromosome, and a total of 47 chromosomes.

Most trisomies are probably lethal, that is, the affected embryo will quickly die, even before the woman realizes she is pregnant. When an embryo-fetus survives and a child is born with a trisomy, there are always developmental defects present.

The severity of trisomies may be seen in two of the more rarely occurring ones: Trisomy 13 and Trisomy 18, each of which occurs about once for every 5000 live births. Both of these trisomies are characterized by severe mental and physical retardation, heart defects, deafness, and bone abnormalities. Affected infants usually die within their first year.

Down syndrome (Trisomy 21) is the most common trisomy, with a frequency of about one per 650 live births. Children with Down syndrome are mentally retarded, but there is a great range of mental ability in this group. Physical characteristics include a skin fold above each eye, short stature, poor muscle tone, and heart defects. Again, the degree of severity is highly variable.

Women over the age of 35 are believed to be at greater risk of having a child with Down syndrome. The reason may be that as egg cells age the process of meiosis is more likely to proceed incorrectly.

The haploid egg and sperm cells produced by meiosis each have 23 chromosomes. When fertilization occurs, the nuclei of the egg and sperm merge, and the fertilized egg **(zygote)** has 46 chromosomes, the diploid number. Thus, meiosis maintains the diploid number of the human species by reducing the number of chromosomes by half in the formation of gametes.

MALE REPRODUCTIVE SYSTEM

The male reproductive system consists of the testes and a series of ducts and glands. Sperm are produced in the testes and are transported through the reproductive ducts: epididymis, ductus deferens, ejaculatory duct, and urethra (Fig. 20–3). The reproductive glands produce secretions that become part of semen, the fluid that is ejaculated from the ure-

thra. These glands are the seminal vesicles, prostate gland, and bulbourethral glands.

TESTES

The **testes** are located in the **scrotum,** a sac of skin between the upper thighs. The temperature within the scrotum is about 96°F, slightly lower than body temperature, which is necessary for the production of viable sperm. In the male fetus, the testes develop near the kidneys, then descend into the scrotum just before birth. **Cryptorchidism** is the condition in which the testes fail to descend, and the result is sterility unless the testes are surgically placed in the scrotum.

Each testis is about 1.5 inches long by 1 inch wide (4 cm × 2.5 cm) and is divided internally into lobes (Fig. 20–4). Each lobe contains several **seminiferous tubules,** in which spermatogenesis takes place. Among the spermatogonia of the seminiferous tubules are **sustentacular (Sertoli) cells,**

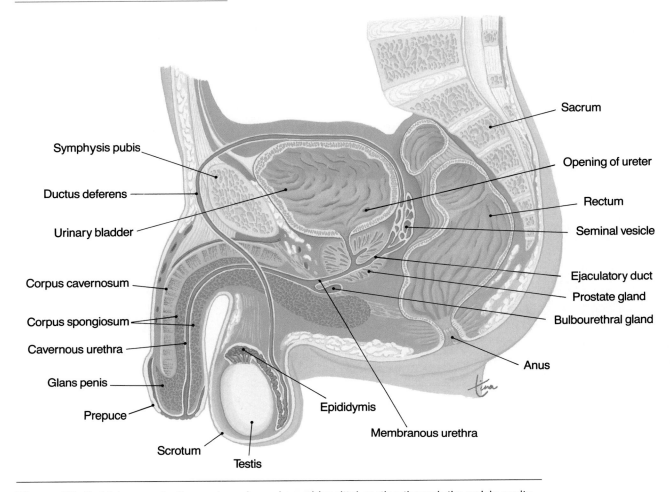

Figure 20–3 Male reproductive system shown in a midsagittal section through the pelvic cavity.

which produce the hormone **inhibin** when stimulated by testosterone. Between the loops of the seminiferous tubules are **interstitial cells,** which produce **testosterone** when stimulated by luteinizing hormone (LH) from the anterior pituitary gland. Besides its role in the maturation of sperm, testosterone is also responsible for the male secondary sex characteristics, which begin to develop at puberty (Table 20–1).

A sperm cell consists of several parts, which are shown in Fig. 20–1. The head contains the 23 chromosomes. On the tip of the head is the **acrosome,** which contains enzymes to digest the membrane of an egg cell. Within the middle piece are mitochondria that produce ATP. The **flagellum** provides mo-

tility, the capability of the sperm cell to move. It is the beating of the flagellum that requires energy from ATP.

Sperm from the seminiferous tubules enter a tubular network called the rete testis, then enter the epididymis, the first of the reproductive ducts.

EPIDIDYMIS

The **epididymis** (plural: epididymides) is a tube about 20 feet (6 m) long that is coiled on the posterior surface of each testis (see Fig. 20–4). Within the epididymis the sperm complete their maturation, and their flagella become functional. Smooth

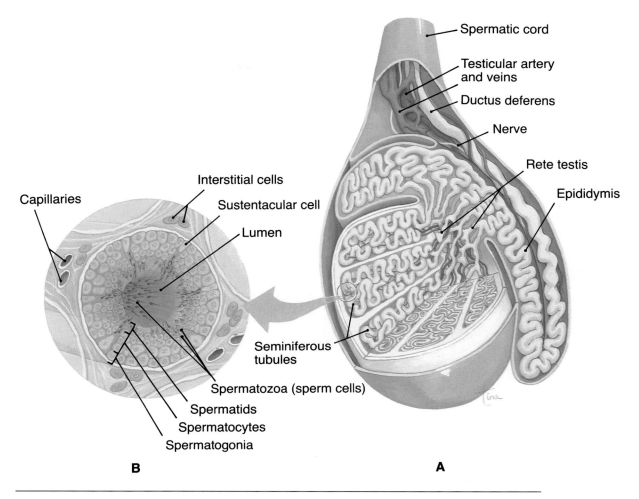

Figure 20–4 (**A**), Midsagittal section of portion of a testis; the epididymis is on the posterior side of the testis. (**B**), Cross section through a seminiferous tubule showing development of sperm.

Table 20–1 MALE HORMONES

Hormone	Secreted By	Functions
FSH	Anterior pituitary	• Initiates production of sperm in the testes
LH (ICSH)	Anterior pituitary	• Stimulates secretion of testosterone by the testes
Testosterone	Testes (Interstitial cells)	• Promotes maturation of sperm • Initiates development of the secondary sex characteristics: —growth of the reproductive organs —growth of the larynx —growth of facial and body hair —increased protein synthesis, especially in skeletal muscles
Inhibin	Testes (Sustentacular cells)	• Decreases secretion of FSH to maintain constant rate of spermatogenesis

muscle in the wall of the epididymis propels the sperm into the ductus deferens.

DUCTUS DEFERENS

Also called the **vas deferens,** the **ductus def-erens** extends from the epididymis in the scrotum on its own side into the abdominal cavity through the **inguinal canal.** This canal is an opening in the abdominal wall for the **spermatic cord,** a connective tissue sheath that contains the ductus deferens, testicular blood vessels, and nerves. Since the inguinal canal is an opening in a muscular wall, it is a natural "weak spot," and it is the most common site of hernia formation in men.

Once inside the abdominal cavity, the ductus deferens extends upward over the urinary bladder, then down the posterior side to join the ejaculatory duct on its own side (see Fig. 20–3). The smooth muscle layer of the ductus deferens contracts in waves of peristalsis as part of ejaculation (see Box 20–2: Contraception).

Box 20–2 CONTRACEPTION

There are several methods of contraception, or birth control; some are more effective than others.

Sterilization—Sterilization in men involves a relatively simple procedure called a **vasectomy.** The ductus (vas) deferens is accessible in the scrotum, in which a small incision is made on either side. The ductus is then sutured and cut. Although sperm are still produced in the testes, they cannot pass the break in the ductus, and they simply die and are reabsorbed.

Sterilization in women is usually accomplished by **tubal ligation,** the suturing and severing of the fallopian tubes. Usually this can be done by way of a small incision in the abdominal wall. Ova can neither pass the break in the tube, nor can sperm pass from the uterine side to fertilize an ovum.

When done properly, these forms of surgical sterilization are virtually 100% effective.

Oral Contraceptives ("the pill")—Birth control pills contain progesterone and estrogen in varying proportions. They prevent ovulation by inhibiting the secretion of FSH and LH from the anterior pituitary gland. When taken according to schedule, birth control pills are about 98% effective. Some women report side effects such as headaches, weight gain, and nausea. Women who use this method of contraception should not smoke, for smoking seems to be associated with abnormal clotting and a greater risk of heart attack or stroke.

Barrier Methods—These include the condom, diaphragm, and cervical cap, which prevent sperm from reaching the uterus and fallopian tubes. The use of a spermacide (sperm-killing chemical) increases the effectiveness of these methods. A condom is a latex or rubber sheath that covers the penis and collects and contains ejaculated semen. Leakage is possible, however, and the condom is considered 80% to 90% effective. This is the only contraceptive method that decreases the spread of sexually transmitted diseases.

The diaphragm and cervical cap are plastic structures that are inserted into the vagina to cover the cervix. They are about 80% effective. These methods should not be used, however, by women with vaginal infections or abnormal Pap smears or who have had toxic shock syndrome.

EJACULATORY DUCTS

Each of the two **ejaculatory ducts** receives sperm from the ductus deferens and the secretion of the seminal vesicle on its own side. Both ejaculatory ducts empty into the single urethra (see Fig. 20–3).

SEMINAL VESICLES

The paired **seminal vesicles** are posterior to the urinary bladder (see Fig. 20–3). Their secretion contains fructose to provide an energy source for sperm and is alkaline to enhance sperm motility. The duct of each seminal vesicle joins the ductus deferens on that side to form the ejaculatory duct.

PROSTATE GLAND

A muscular gland just below the urinary bladder, the **prostate gland** surrounds the first inch of the urethra as it emerges from the bladder (see Fig. 20–3). The glandular tissue of the prostate secretes an alkaline fluid that helps maintain sperm motility. The smooth muscle of the prostate gland contracts during **ejaculation** to contribute to the expulsion of semen from the urethra (see Box 20–3: Prostatic Hypertrophy).

BULBOURETHRAL GLANDS

Also called Cowper's glands, the **bulbourethral glands** are located below the prostate gland and empty into the urethra. Their alkaline secretion coats the interior of the urethra just before ejaculation, which will neutralize any acidic urine that might be present.

You have probably noticed that all the secretions of the male reproductive glands are alkaline. This is important because the cavity of the female vagina has an acidic pH due to the normal flora, the natural bacterial population of the vagina. The alkalinity of seminal fluid helps neutralize the acidic vaginal pH and permits sperm motility in what might otherwise be an unfavorable environment.

URETHRA—PENIS

The **urethra** is the last of the ducts through which semen travels, and its longest portion is enclosed within the penis. The **penis** is an external genital organ; its distal end is called the glans penis and is covered with a fold of skin called the prepuce or foreskin. **Circumcision** is the surgical removal of the foreskin. This is a common procedure performed on male infants, although there is considerable medical debate as to whether circumcision truly has a useful purpose.

Within the penis are three masses of cavernous (erectile) tissue (see Fig. 20–3). Each consists of a framework of smooth muscle and connective tissue that contains blood sinuses, which are large, irregular vascular channels.

When blood flow through these sinuses is mini-

Box 20–3   PROSTATIC HYPERTROPHY

Prostatic hypertrophy is enlargement of the prostate gland. Benign prostatic hypertrophy is a common occurrence in men over the age of 60 years. The enlarged prostate compresses the urethra within it and may make urination difficult or result in urinary retention. A prostatectomy is a surgical procedure to remove part or all of the prostate. A possible consequence is that ejaculation may be impaired. Many experimental surgical procedures are now undergoing clinical trials to determine if they are more likely to preserve sexual function. Other research involves the use of new medications to shrink enlarged prostate tissue.

Cancer of the prostate is the second most common cancer among men (lung cancer is first). Most cases occur in men over the age of 50 years. Treatment may include surgery to remove the prostate, radiation therapy, or hormone therapy to reduce the patient's level of testosterone.

mal, the penis is flaccid. During sexual stimulation, the arteries to the penis dilate, the sinuses fill with blood, and the penis becomes erect and firm. The dilation of penile arteries and the resulting erection are brought about by parasympathetic impulses. The erect penis is capable of penetrating the female vagina to deposit sperm. The culmination of sexual stimulation is ejaculation, which is brought about by peristalsis of all the reproductive ducts and contraction of the prostate gland.

SEMEN

Semen consists of sperm and the secretions of the seminal vesicles, prostate gland, and bulbourethral glands; its average pH is about 7.4. During ejaculation, approximately 2 to 4 ml of semen is expelled. Each milliliter of semen contains about 100 million sperm cells.

FEMALE REPRODUCTIVE SYSTEM

The female reproductive system consists of the paired ovaries and fallopian tubes, the single uterus and vagina, and the external genital structures (Fig. 20–5). Egg cells (ova) are produced in the ovaries and travel through the fallopian tubes to the uterus. The uterus is the site for the growth of the embryo-fetus.

OVARIES

The **ovaries** are a pair of oval structures about 1.5 inches (4 cm) long on either side of the uterus in the pelvic cavity (Fig. 20–6). The ovarian ligament extends from the medial side of an ovary to the uterine wall, and the broad ligament is a fold of the peritoneum that covers the ovaries. These ligaments help keep the ovaries in place.

Within an ovary are several hundred thousand **primary follicles,** which are present at birth. During a woman's childbearing years, only 300 to 400 of these follicles will produce mature ova. As with sperm production in men, the supply of potential gametes far exceeds what is actually needed, but this helps ensure the continuation of the human species.

Each primary ovarian follicle contains an oocyte, a potential ovum or egg cell. Surrounding the oocyte are the follicle cells, which secrete estrogen. Maturation of a follicle, requiring FSH and estrogen, was described previously in the section on oogenesis. A mature follicle may also be called a **graafian follicle,** and the hormone LH from the anterior pituitary gland causes ovulation, that is, rupture of the mature follicle with release of the ovum. At this time, other developing follicles begin to deteriorate; these are called **atretic follicles** and have no further purpose. Under the influence of LH, the ruptured follicle becomes the **corpus luteum** and begins to secrete progesterone as well as estrogen.

FALLOPIAN TUBES

There are two fallopian tubes (also called uterine tubes or oviducts); each is about 4 inches (10 cm) long. The lateral end of a fallopian tube encloses an ovary, and the medial end opens into the uterus. The end of the tube that encloses the ovary has **fimbriae,** fringe-like projections that create currents in the fluid surrounding the ovary to pull the ovum into the fallopian tube.

Since the ovum has no means of self-locomotion (as do sperm) the structure of the fallopian tube ensures that the ovum will be kept moving toward the uterus. The smooth muscle layer of the tube contracts in peristaltic waves that help propel the ovum (or zygote, as you will see in a moment). The mucosa is extensively folded and is made of ciliated epithelial tissue. The sweeping action of the cilia also moves the ovum toward the uterus.

Fertilization usually takes place in the fallopian tube. If not fertilized, an ovum dies within 24 to 48 hours and disintegrates, either in the tube or the uterus. If fertilized, the ovum becomes a zygote and is swept into the uterus; this takes about 4 to 5 days (see Box 20–4: In Vitro Fertilization).

Sometimes the zygote will not reach the uterus but will still continue to develop. This is called an **ectopic pregnancy;** "ectopic" means in an abnormal site. The developing embryo may become implanted in the fallopian tube, the ovary itself, or

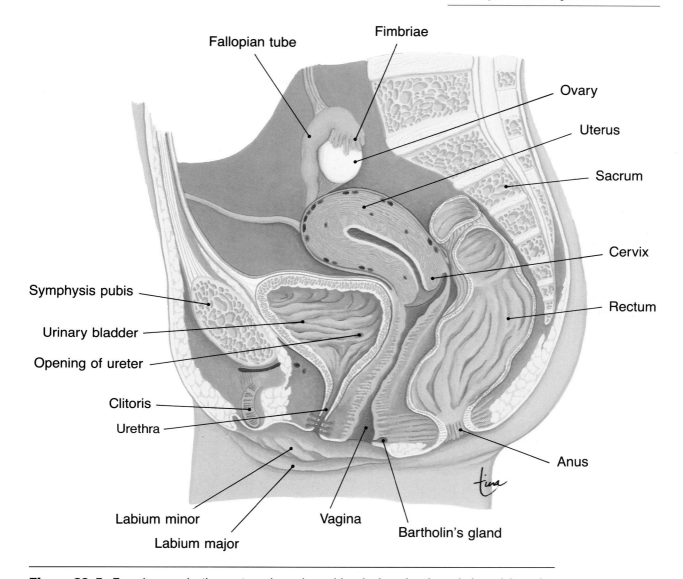

Figure 20–5 Female reproductive system shown in a midsagittal section through the pelvic cavity.

even elsewhere in the abdominal cavity. An ectopic pregnancy usually does not progress very long, since these other sites are not specialized to provide a placenta or to expand to accommodate the growth of a fetus, as the uterus is. The spontaneous termination of an ectopic pregnancy is usually the result of bleeding in the mother, and surgery may be necesssary to prevent maternal death from circulatory shock. Occasionally an ectopic pregnancy does go to full term and produces a healthy baby; such an

event is a credit to the adaptability of the human body and to the advances of medical science.

UTERUS

The **uterus** is shaped like an upside-down pear, about 3 inches long by 2 inches wide (7.5 × 5 cm), superior to the urinary bladder and between the two ovaries in the pelvic cavity (see Fig. 20–5). The

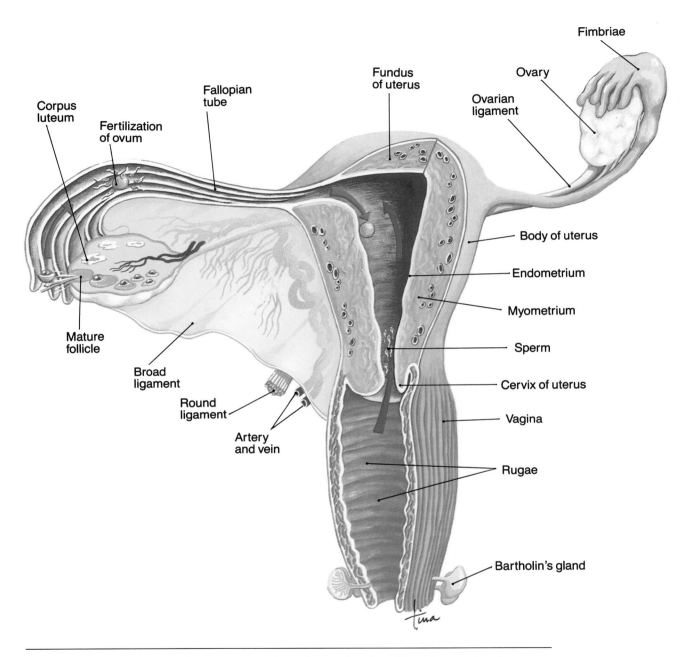

Figure 20–6 Female reproductive system shown in anterior view. The left ovary has been sectioned to show the developing follicles. The left fallopian tube has been sectioned to show fertilization. The uterus and vagina have been sectioned to show internal structures. Arrows indicate the movement of the ovum toward the uterus and the movement of sperm from the vagina toward the fallopian tube.

Box 20–4   IN VITRO FERTILIZATION

In vitro fertilization is fertilization outside the body, usually in a glass dish. A woman who wishes to conceive by this method is given FSH to stimulate the simultaneous development of several ovarian follicles. LH may then be given to stimulate simultaneous ovulation. The ova are removed by way of a small incision in the abdominal wall and are placed in a solution containing the sperm of the woman's partner (or an anonymous donor). After fertilization and the first mitotic divisions of cleavage, the very early embryo is placed in the woman's uterus.

It is also possible to mix the removed ova with sperm and return them almost immediately to the woman's fallopian tube. Development then proceeds as if the ova had been fertilized naturally.

Since the birth of the first "test tube baby" in 1978, more than 25,000 babies have been born following in vitro fertilization. The techniques do not work all the time, and repeated attempts can be very expensive.

broad ligament also covers the uterus (see Fig. 20–6). During pregnancy the uterus increases greatly in size, contains the placenta to nourish the embryo-fetus, and expels the baby at the end of gestation.

The parts and layers of the uterus are shown in Fig. 20–6. The **fundus** is the upper portion above the entry of the fallopian tubes, and the **body** is the large central portion. The narrow, lower end of the uterus is the **cervix,** which opens into the vagina.

The outermost layer of the uterus, the serosa or epimetrium, is a fold of the peritoneum. The **myometrium** is the smooth muscle layer; during pregnancy these cells increase in size to accommodate the growing fetus and contract for labor and delivery at the end of pregnancy.

The lining of the uterus is the **endometrium,** which itself consists of two layers. The **basilar layer,** adjacent to the myometrium, is vascular but very thin and is a permanent layer. The **functional layer** is regenerated and lost during each menstrual cycle. Under the influence of estrogen and progesterone from the ovaries, the growth of blood vessels thickens the functional layer in preparation for a possible embryo. If fertilization does not occur, the functional layer sloughs off in menstruation. During pregnancy, the endometrium forms the maternal portion of the placenta.

VAGINA

The **vagina** is a muscular tube about 4 inches (10 cm) long that extends from the cervix to the vaginal orifice in the **perineum** (pelvic floor). It is posterior to the urethra and anterior to the rectum (see Fig. 20–5). The vaginal opening is usually partially covered by a thin membrane called the **hymen,** which is ruptured by the first sexual intercourse or by the use of tampons during the menstrual period.

The functions of the vagina are to receive sperm from the penis during sexual intercourse, to serve as the exit for the menstrual blood flow, and to serve as the birth canal at the end of pregnancy.

The vaginal mucosa after puberty is stratified squamous epithelium, which is relatively resistant to pathogens. The normal flora (bacteria) of the vagina creates an acidic pH that helps inhibit the growth of pathogens (see Box 20–5: Sexually Transmitted Diseases [STDs]).

EXTERNAL GENITALS

The female external genital structures may also be called the **vulva** (Fig. 20–7), and include the clitoris, labia majora and minora, and the Bartholin's glands (see Fig. 20–5).

Box 20–5 SEXUALLY TRANSMITTED DISEASES (STDs)

Gonorrhea—caused by the bacterium *Neisseria gonorrhoeae*. Infected men have urethritis with painful and frequent urination and pus in the urine. Women are often asymptomatic, and the bacteria may spread from the cervix to other reproductive organs (pelvic inflammatory disease [PID]). The use first of silver nitrate, and more recently antibiotics, in the eyes of all newborns has virtually eliminated neonatal conjunctivitis acquired from an infected mother. Gonorrhea can be treated with antibiotics, but resistant strains of the bacteria complicate treatment. Despite this, the number of reported cases of gonorrhea has been decreasing in recent years.

Syphilis—caused by the bacterium *Treponema pallidum*. Although syphilis can be cured with penicillin, it is a disease that may be ignored by the person who has it since the symptoms may seem minor and often do not last long. If untreated, however, syphilis may cause severe or even fatal damage to the nervous system and heart. In the last few years the number of reported cases of syphilis had increased sharply but is again decreasing.

Genital Herpes—caused by the virus Herpes simplex (usually type 2). Painful lesions in the genital area are the primary symptom. Although the lesions heal within 5 to 9 days, recurrences are possible, perhaps triggered by physiological stresses such as illness. Although herpes is not curable at present, the medication acyclovir has proved useful in treatment. It is estimated that 2 million new cases of genital herpes occur every year.

Neonatal herpes is infection of a newborn during passage through the birth canal. The infant's immune system is too immature to control the herpes virus, and this infection may be fatal or cause brain damage. A pregnant woman with a history of genital herpes may choose to have the baby delivered by cesarean section to avoid this possible outcome.

Chlamydial infection—caused by the very simple bacterium *Chlamydia trachomatis*. This is now the most prevalent STD in the United States, with estimates of 4 million new cases yearly. Infected men may have urethritis or epididymitis. Women often have no symptoms at first but may develop PID that increases the risk of ectopic pregnancy. Infants born to infected women may develop conjunctivitis or pneumonia. Chlamydial infection can be successfully treated with antibiotics such as erythromycin or azithromycin.

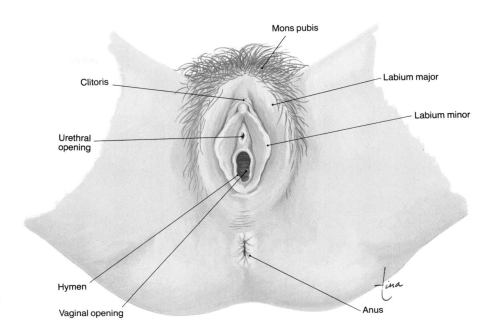

Figure 20–7 Female external genitals (vulva) shown in inferior view of the perineum.

The **clitoris** is a small mass of erectile tissue anterior to the urethral orifice. The only function of the clitoris is sensory, it responds to sexual stimulation, and its vascular sinuses become filled with blood.

The mons pubis is a pad of fat over the pubic symphysis, covered with skin and pubic hair. Extending posteriorly from the mons are the **labia majora** (lateral) and **labia minora** (medial), which are paired folds of skin. The area between the labia minora is called the vestibule and contains the openings of the urethra and vagina. The labia cover these openings and prevent drying of their mucous membranes.

Bartholin's glands, also called vestibular glands (see Figs. 20–5 and 20–6), are within the floor of the vestibule; their ducts open onto the mucosa at the vaginal orifice. The secretion of these glands keeps the mucosa moist and lubricates the vagina during sexual intercourse.

MAMMARY GLANDS

The **mammary glands** are structurally related to the skin but functionally related to the reproductive system because they produce milk for the nourishment of offspring. Enclosed within the breasts, the mammary glands are anterior to the pectoralis major muscles; their structure is shown in Fig. 20–8.

The glandular tissue is surrounded by adipose tissue. The **alveolar glands** produce milk after pregnancy; the milk enters lactiferous ducts which converge at the nipple. The skin around the nipple is a pigmented area called the areola.

The formation of milk is under hormonal control. During pregnancy, high levels of estrogen and progesterone prepare the glands for milk production. **Prolactin** from the anterior pituitary gland causes the actual synthesis of milk after pregnancy. The sucking of the infant on the nipple stimulates the hypothalamus to send nerve impulses to the posterior pituitary gland, which secretes **oxytocin** to cause the release of milk. The effects of these hormones on the mammary glands are summarized in Table 20–2 (see also Box 20–6: Mammography).

THE MENSTRUAL CYCLE

The **menstrual cycle** includes the activity of the hormones of the ovaries and anterior pituitary gland

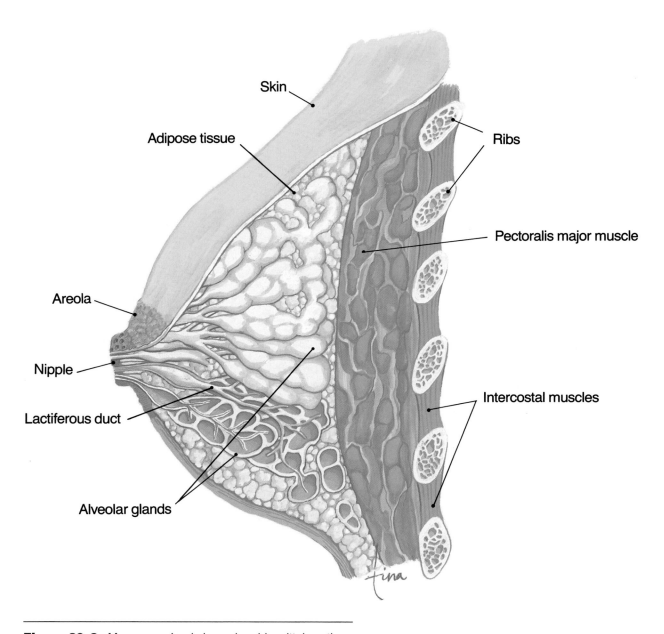

Figure 20–8 Mammary gland shown in midsagittal section.

Table 20–2   HORMONE EFFECTS ON THE MAMMARY GLANDS

Hormone	Secreted By	Functions
Estrogen	• Ovary (follicle) • Placenta	• Promotes growth of duct system
Progesterone	• Ovary (corpus luteum) • Placenta	• Promotes growth of secretory cells
Prolactin	• Anterior pituitary	• Promotes production of milk after birth
Oxytocin	• Posterior pituitary (hypothalamus)	• Promotes release of milk

and the resultant changes in the ovaries and uterus. These are all incorporated into Fig. 20–9, which may look complicated at first, but refer to it as you read the following.

Notice first the four hormones involved: **FSH** and **LH** from the anterior pituitary gland, **estrogen** from the ovarian follicle, and **progesterone** from the corpus luteum. The fluctuations of these hormones are shown as they would occur in an average 28-day cycle. A cycle may be described in terms of three phases: menstrual phase, follicular phase, and luteal phase.

1. **Menstrual phase**—The loss of the functional layer of the endometrium is called **menstruation** or the menses. Although this is actually the end of a menstrual cycle, the onset of menstruation is easily pinpointed and is, therefore, a useful starting point. Menstruation may last 2 to 8 days, with an average of 3 to 6 days. At this time, secretion of FSH is increasing, and several ovarian follicles begin to develop.

2. **Follicular phase**—FSH stimulates growth of ovarian follicles and secretion of estrogen by the follicle cells. The secretion of LH is also increasing but more slowly. FSH and estrogen promote the growth and maturation of the ovum, and estrogen stimulates the growth of blood vessels in the endometrium to regenerate the functional layer.

   This phase ends with ovulation, when a sharp increase in LH causes rupture of a mature ovarian follicle.

3. **Luteal phase**—Under the influence of LH, the ruptured follicle becomes the corpus luteum and begins to secrete progesterone. Progesterone stimulates further growth of blood vessels in the functional layer of the endometrium and promotes the storage of nutrients such as glycogen.

   As progesterone secretion increases, LH secretion decreases, and if the ovum is not fertilized, the secretion of progesterone also begins to decrease. Without progesterone, the

Box 20–6   MAMMOGRAPHY

Mammography is an x-ray technique that is used to evaluate breast tissue for abnormalities. By far the most common usage is to detect breast cancer, which is the most common malignancy in women. If detected early, breast cancer may be cured through a combination of surgery, radiation, and chemotherapy. Women should practice breast self-examination monthly, but mammography can detect lumps that are too small to be felt manually. Women in their 30's may have a mammogram done to serve as a comparison for mammograms later in life.

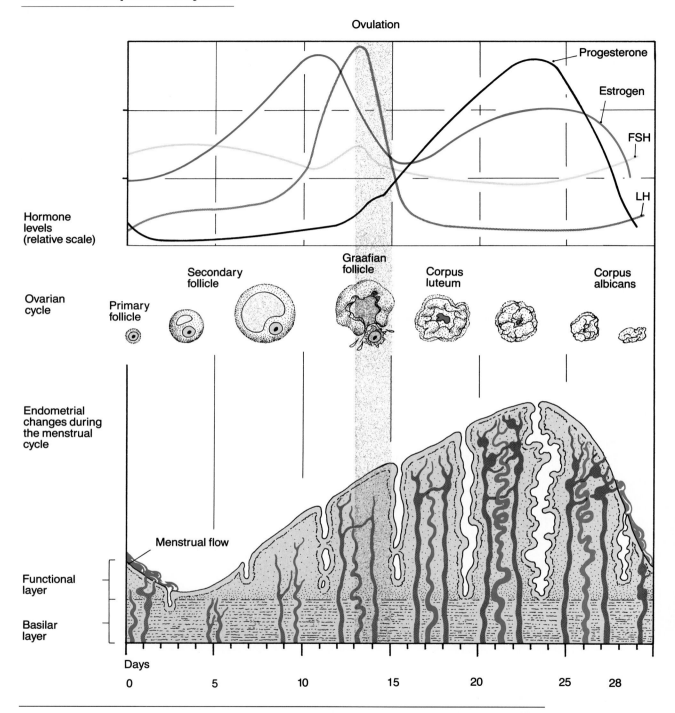

Figure 20–9 The menstrual cycle. The levels of the important hormones are shown relative to one another throughout the cycle. Changes in the ovarian follicle are depicted. The relative thickness of the endometrium is also shown.

Table 20–3 FEMALE HORMONES

Hormone	Secreted By	Functions
FSH	Anterior pituitary	• Initiates development of ovarian follicles • Stimulates secretion of estrogen by follicle cells
LH	Anterior pituitary	• Causes ovulation • Converts the ruptured ovarian follicle into the corpus luteum • Stimulates secretion of progesterone by the corpus luteum
Estrogen	Ovary (follicle)	• Promotes maturation of ovarian follicles • Promotes growth of blood vessels in the endometrium • Initiates development of the secondary sex characteristics: —growth of the uterus and other reproductive organs —growth of the mammary ducts and fat deposition in the breasts —broadening of the pelvic bone —subcutaneous fat deposition in hips and thighs
Progesterone	Ovary (corpus luteum)	• Promotes further growth of blood vessels in the endometrium and storage of nutrients • Inhibits contractions of the myometrium

endometrium cannot be maintained and begins to slough off in menstruation. FSH secretion begins to increase (as estrogen and progesterone decrease), and the cycle begins again.

The 28-day cycle shown in Fig. 20–9 is average. Women may experience cycles of anywhere from 23 to 35 days. Women who engage in strenuous exercise over prolonged periods of time may experience **amenorrhea,** that is, cessation of menses. This seems to be related to reduction of body fat. Apparently the reproductive cycle ceases if a woman does not have sufficient reserves of energy for herself and a developing fetus. The exact mechanism by which this happens is not understood at present. Amenorrhea may also accompany states of physical or emotional stress, anorexia nervosa, or various endocrine disorders.

The functions of the female hormones are summarized in Table 20–3.

SUMMARY

The production of male or female gametes is a process that is regulated by hormones. When fertilization of an ovum by a sperm cell takes place, the zygote, or fertilized egg, has the potential to become a new human being. The development of the zygote to embryo–fetus to newborn infant is also dependent on hormones and is the subject of our next chapter.

STUDY OUTLINE

Reproductive Systems—purpose is to produce gametes (egg and sperm), to ensure fertilization, and in women to provide a site for the embryo-fetus

Meiosis—the cell division process that produces gametes

1. One cell with the diploid number of chromosomes (46) divides twice to form four cells, each with the haploid number of chromosomes (23).

2. Spermatogenesis takes place in the testes; a continuous process from puberty throughout life; each cell produces four functional sperm (see Fig. 20–1). FSH and testosterone are directly necessary (see Table 20–1).

3. Oogenesis takes place in the ovaries; the process is cyclical (every 28 days) from puberty until menopause; each cell produces one functional ovum and three non-functional polar bodies (see Fig. 20–2). FSH, LH, and estrogen, are necessary (see Table 20–3).

Male Reproductive System—consists of the testes and the ducts and glands that contribute to the formation of semen (see Fig. 20–3)

1. Testes (paired)—located in the scrotum between the upper thighs; temperature in the scrotum is 96°F to permit production of viable sperm. Sperm are produced in seminiferous tubules (see Fig. 20–4 and Table 20–1). A sperm cell consists of the head that contains 23 chromosomes, the middle piece that contains mitochondria, the flagellum for motility, and the acrosome on the tip of the head to digest the membrane of the egg cell (see Fig. 20–1).

2. Epididymis (paired)—a long coiled tube on the posterior surface of each testis (see Fig. 20–4). Sperm complete their maturation here.

3. Ductus Deferens (paired)—extends from the epididymis into the abdominal cavity through the inguinal canal, over and down behind the urinary bladder to join the ejaculatory duct (see Fig. 20–3). Smooth muscle in the wall contracts in waves of peristalsis.

4. Ejaculatory Ducts (paired)—receive sperm from the ductus deferens and the secretions from the seminal vesicles (see Fig. 20–3); empty into the urethra.

5. Seminal Vesicles (paired)—posterior to urinary bladder; duct of each opens into ejaculatory duct (see Fig. 20–3). Secretion contains fructose to nourish sperm and is alkaline to enhance sperm motility.

6. Prostate Gland (single)—below the urinary bladder, encloses the first inch of the urethra (see Fig. 20–3); secretion is alkaline to maintain sperm motility; smooth muscle contributes to the force required for ejaculation.

7. Bulbourethral Glands (paired)—below the prostate gland; empty into the urethra (see Fig. 20–3); secretion is alkaline to line the urethra prior to ejaculation.

8. Urethra (single)—within the penis; carries semen to exterior (see Fig. 20–3). The penis contains three masses of erectile tissue that have blood sinuses. Sexual stimulation and parasympathetic impulses cause dilation of the penile arteries and an erection. Ejaculation of semen involves peristalsis of all the male ducts and contraction of the prostate gland.

9. Semen—composed of sperm and the secretions of the seminal vesicles, prostate gland, and bulbourethral glands. The alkaline pH (7.4) neutralizes the acidic pH of the female vagina.

Female Reproductive System—consists of the ovaries, fallopian tubes, uterus, vagina, and external genitals

1. Ovaries (paired)—located on either side of the uterus (see Fig. 20–6). Egg cells are produced in ovarian follicles; each ovum contains 23 chromosomes. Ovulation of a graafian follicle is stimulated by LH (see Table 20–3).

2. Fallopian Tubes (paired)—each extends from an ovary to the uterus (see Fig. 20–6); fimbriae sweep the ovum into the tube; ciliated epithelial tissue and peristalsis of smooth muscle propel the ovum toward the uterus; fertilization usually takes place in the fallopian tube.

3. Uterus (single)—superior to the urinary bladder and between the two ovaries (see Fig. 20–5). Myometrium is the smooth muscle layer that contracts for delivery (see Fig. 20–6). Endometrium is the lining which may become the placenta; basilar layer is permanent; functional layer is lost in menstruation and regenerated. Parts: upper fundus, central body, and lower cervix.
4. Vagina (single)—extends from the cervix to the vaginal orifice (see Figs. 20–5 and 20–6). Receives sperm during intercourse; serves as exit for menstrual blood and as the birth canal during delivery. Normal flora provides an acidic pH that inhibits the growth of pathogens.
5. External Genitals (see Figs. 20–5 and 20–7)—also called the vulva. The clitoris is a small mass of erectile tissue that responds to sexual stimulation; labia majora and minora are paired folds of skin that enclose the vestibule and cover the urethral and vaginal openings; Bartholin's glands open into the vaginal orifice and secrete mucus.

Mammary Glands—anterior to the pectoralis major muscles, surrounded by adipose tissue (see Fig. 20–8)
1. Alveolar glands produce milk; lactiferous ducts converge at the nipple.
2. Hormonal regulation—see Table 20–2.

The Menstrual Cycle—average is 28 days; includes the hormones FSH, LH, estrogen, and progesterone, and changes in the ovaries and endometrium (see Fig. 20–9 and Table 20–3)
1. Menstrual phase—loss of the endometrium.
2. Follicular phase—several ovarian follicles develop; ovulation is the rupture of a mature follicle; blood vessels grow in the endometrium.
3. Luteal phase—the ruptured follicle becomes the corpus luteum; the endometrium continues to develop.
4. If fertilization does not occur, decreased progesterone results in the loss of the endometrium in menstruation.

REVIEW QUESTIONS

1. Describe spermatogenesis and oogenesis in terms of site, number of functional cells produced by each cell that undergoes meiosis, and timing of the process. (p. 454)

2. Describe the functions of FSH, LH, inhibin, and testosterone in spermatogenesis. Describe the functions of FSH and estrogen in oogenesis. (p. 454)

3. Describe the locations of the testes and epididymides, and explain their functions. (pp. 457–458)

4. Name all the ducts, in order, that sperm travel through from the testes to the urethra. (pp. 458, 460–461)

5. Name the male reproductive glands, and state how each contributes to the formation of semen. (p. 461)

6. Explain how the structure of cavernous tissue permits erection of the penis. Name the structures that bring about ejaculation. (pp. 461–462)

7. State the function of each part of a sperm cell: head, middle piece, flagellum, acrosome. (p. 458)

8. Describe the location of the ovaries, and name the hormones produced by the ovaries. (p. 462)

9. Explain how an ovum or zygote is kept moving through the fallopian tube. (p. 462)

10. Describe the function of myometrium, basilar layer of the endometrium, and functional layer of the endometrium. Name the hormones necessary for growth of the endometrium. (p. 465)

11. State the functions of the vagina, labia majora and minora, and Bartholin's glands. (pp. 465, 467)

12. Name the parts of the mammary glands, and state the function of each. (p. 467)

13. Name the hormone that has each of these effects on the mammary glands: (p. 469)
    a. causes release of milk
    b. promotes growth of the ducts
    c. promotes growth of the secretory cells
    d. stimulates milk production

14. Name the phase of the menstrual cycle in which each takes place: (pp. 469, 471)
    a. rupture of a mature follicle
    b. loss of the endometrium
    c. final development of the endometrium
    d. the corpus luteum develops
    e. several ovarian follicles begin to develop

Chapter 21

Human Development and Genetics

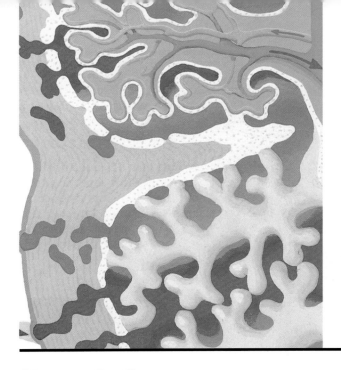

Chapter 21

Chapter Outline

Student Objectives

- Describe the process of fertilization and cleavage to the blastocyst stage.
- Explain when, where, and how implantation of the embryo occurs.
- Describe the functions of the embryonic membranes.
- Describe the structure and functions of the placenta and umbilical cord.
- Name and explain the functions of the placental hormones.
- State the length of the average gestation period, and describe the stages of labor.
- Describe the major changes in the infant at birth.
- Describe some important maternal changes during pregnancy.
- Explain homologous chromosomes, autosomes, sex chromosomes, genes.
- Define alleles, genotype, phenotype, homozygous, heterozygous.
- Explain the following patterns of inheritance: dominant-recessive, multiple alleles, sex-linked traits.

Human Development and Genetics

New Terminology

Alleles (uh–**LEELZ**)
Amnion (**AM**–nee–on)
Amniotic fluid (**AM**–nee–AH–tik **FLOO**–id)
Autosomes (**AW**–toh–sohms)
Cleavage (**KLEE**–vije)
Embryo (**EM**–bree-oh)
Genotype (**JEE**–noh–type)
Gestation (jes–**TAY**–shun)
Heterozygous (HET–er–oh–**ZYE**–gus)
Homologous pair (hoh–**MAHL**–ah–gus PAYR)
Homozygous (HOH–moh–**ZYE**–gus)
Implantation (IM–plan–**TAY**–shun)
Labor (**LAY**–ber)

Parturition (PAR–tyoo–**RISH**–uhn)
Phenotype (**FEE**–noh–type)
Sex chromosome (SEKS **KROH**–muh–sohm)

Related Clinical Terminology

Amniocentesis (AM–nee–oh–sen–**TEE**–sis)
Apgar score (**APP**–gar SKOR)
Cesarean section (se–**SAR**–ee–an **SEK**–shun)
Chorionic villus sampling (KOR–ee–**ON**–ik **VILL**–us)
Congenital (kon–**JEN**–i–tuhl)
Fetal alcohol syndrome (**FEE**–tuhl **AL**–koh–hol)
Teratogen (te–**RAH**–toh–jen)

Terms that appear in **bold type** in the chapter text are defined in the glossary, which begins on page 549.

How often have we heard comments like "She has her mother's eyes" or "That nose is just like his father's"—as people cannot resist comparing a newborn to its parents. Although a child may not resemble either parent, there is a sound basis for such comparisons, because the genetic makeup and many of the traits of a child are the result of the chromosomes inherited from mother and father.

In this chapter, we will cover some of the fundamentals of genetics and inheritance. First, however, we will look at the development of a fertilized egg into a functioning human being.

HUMAN DEVELOPMENT

During the 40 weeks of gestation, the embryo-fetus is protected and nourished in the uterus of the mother. A human being begins life as one cell, a fertilized egg called a zygote, which develops into an individual human being consisting of billions of cells organized into the body systems with whose functions you are now quite familiar.

FERTILIZATION

Although millions of sperm are deposited in the vagina during sexual intercourse, only one will fertilize an ovum. As the sperm swim through the fluid of the uterus and fallopian tube, they undergo a final metabolic change, called **capacitation.** This change involves the **acrosome,** which becomes more fragile and begins to secrete its enzymes. When sperm and egg make contact, these enzymes will digest the layers of cells and membrane around an ovum.

Once a sperm nucleus enters the ovum, changes

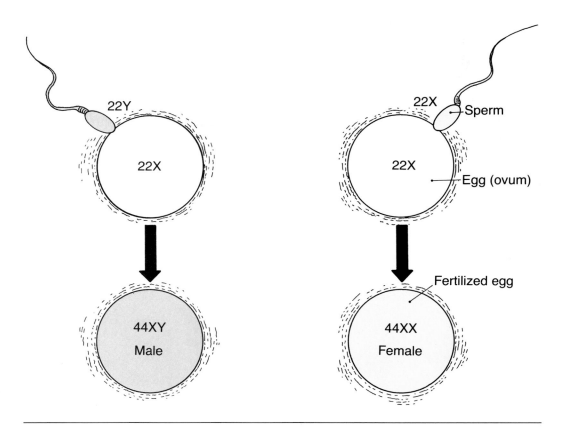

Figure 21–1 Inheritance of gender. Each ovum contains 22 autosomes and an X chromosome. Each sperm contains 22 autosomes and either an X chromosome or a Y chromosome.

in the egg cell membrane block the entry of other sperm. The nucleus of the ovum completes the second meiotic division, and the nuclei of ovum and sperm fuse, restoring the diploid number of chromosomes in the zygote.

The human diploid number of 46 chromosomes is actually 23 pairs of chromosomes; 23 from the sperm and 23 from the egg. These 23 pairs consist of 22 pairs of **autosomes** (designated by the numerals 1 through 22) and one pair of **sex chromosomes.** Women have the sex chromosomes XX, and men have the sex chromosomes XY. Fig. 21–1 shows the inheritance of gender.

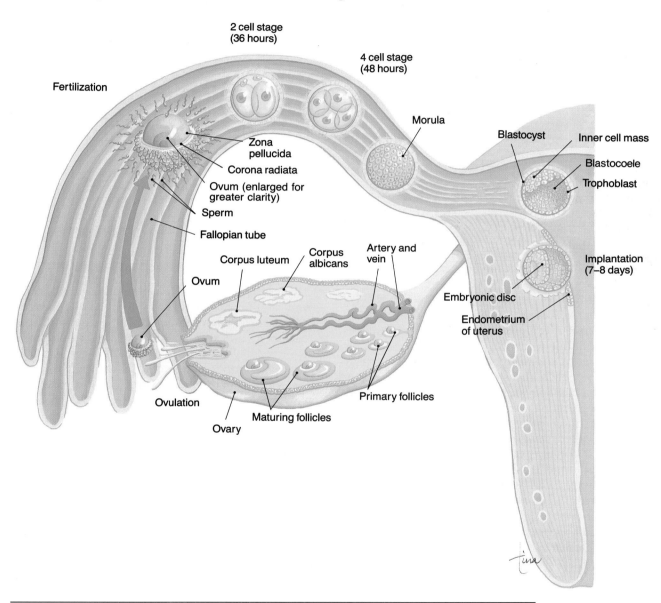

Figure 21–2 Ovulation, fertilization, and early embryonic development. Fertilization takes place in the fallopian tube, and the embryo has reached the blastocyst stage when it becomes implanted in the endometrium of the uterus.

Box 21–1 TWINS

Fraternal twins are the result of two separate ova fertilized by separate sperm. This may occur when two ovarian follicles reach maturity and rupture at the same time. Fraternal twins may be of the same sex or different sexes. Even if of the same sex, however, they are as genetically different as any siblings might be.

Identical twins are the result of the splitting of the very early embryo before the cells start to become specialized. For example, if a 16-cell stage becomes separated into two groups of eight cells each, each group will usually continue to develop in the usual way. Another possible cause is the development of two inner cell masses within the blastocyst. This, too, is before significant specialization has taken place, and each inner cell mass may develop into a complete individual. Twins of this type may be called monozygotic, meaning that they have come from one fertilized egg. Identical twins are always of the same sex, are very much alike in appearance, and in other respects are genetically identical.

IMPLANTATION

Fertilization usually takes place within the fallopian tube, and the zygote begins to divide even as it is being swept toward the uterus. These are mitotic divisions and are called **cleavage.** Refer to Fig. 21–2 as you read the following.

The single-cell zygote divides into a two-cell stage, four-cell stage, eight-cell stage, and so on. Three days after fertilization there are 16 cells, which continue to divide to form a solid sphere of cells called a **morula** (see Box 21–1: Twins). As mitosis proceeds, this sphere becomes hollow and is called a **blastocyst,** which is still about the same size as the original zygote.

A fluid-filled blastocyst consists of an outer layer of cells called the **trophoblast** and an inner cell mass that contains the potential embryo. It is the blastocyst stage that becomes **implanted** in the uterine wall, about 7 to 8 days after fertilization. The trophoblast secretes enzymes to digest the surface of the endometrium, creating a small crater into which the blastocyst sinks. The trophoblast will become the **chorion,** the embryonic membrane that will form the fetal portion of the placenta. Following implantation, the inner cell mass will grow to become the embryo and other membranes.

EMBRYO AND EMBRYONIC MEMBRANES

An **embryo** is the developing human individual, from the time of implanation until the eighth week of gestation. Several stages of early embryonic development are shown in Fig. 21–3. At approximately 12 days, the **embryonic disc** (the potential person) is simply a plate of cells within the blastocyst. Very soon thereafter, three primary layers, or germ layers, begin to develop: the **ectoderm, mesoderm,** and **endoderm.** Each primary layer develops into specific organs or parts of organs. "Ecto" means outer; the epidermis is derived from ectoderm. "Meso" means middle; the skeletal muscles develop from mesoderm. "Endo" means inner; the stomach lining is derived from endoderm. Table 21–1 lists some other structures derived from each of the primary germ layers.

At 20 days the **embryonic membranes** can be clearly distinguished from the embryo itself. The

---

Figure 21–3 Embryonic development at 12 days (after fertilization), 14 days, 20 days, and 4 to 5 weeks. By 5 weeks, the embryo has distinct parts but does not yet look definitely human. See text for description of embryonic membranes.

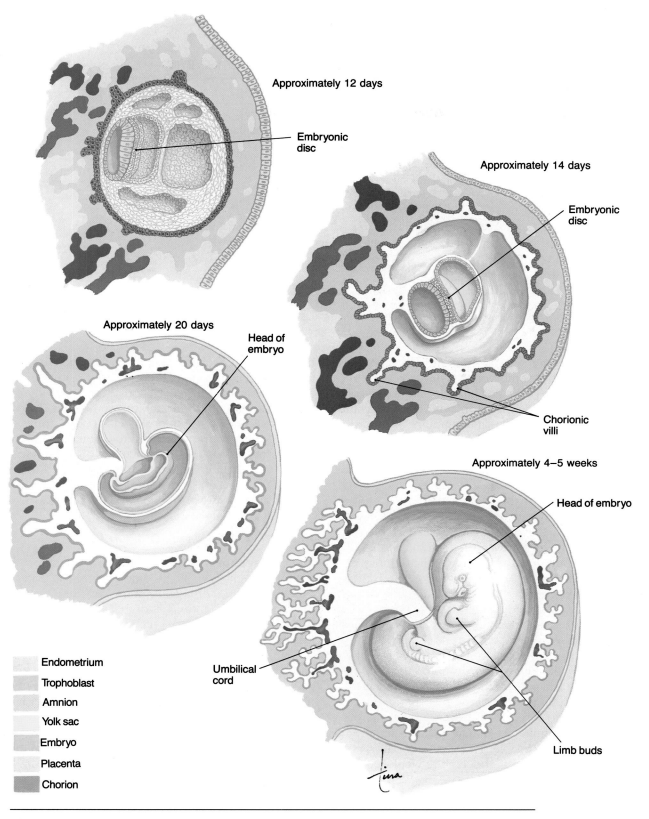

Approximately 12 days

Embryonic disc

Approximately 14 days

Embryonic disc

Chorionic villi

Approximately 20 days

Head of embryo

Approximately 4–5 weeks

Head of embryo

Umbilical cord

Limb buds

Endometrium

Trophoblast

Amnion

Yolk sac

Embryo

Placenta

Chorion

Figure 21–3 See facing page for legend.

Table 21–1   STRUCTURES DERIVED FROM THE PRIMARY GERM LAYERS

Layer	Structures Derived*
Ectoderm	• epidermis; hair and nail follicles; sweat glands • nervous system; pituitary gland; adrenal medulla • lens and cornea; internal ear • mucosa of oral and nasal cavities; salivary glands
Mesoderm	• dermis; bone and cartilage • skeletal muscles; cardiac muscle; most smooth muscle • kidneys and adrenal cortex • bone marrow and blood; lymphatic tissue; lining of blood vessels
Endoderm	• mucosa of esophagus, stomach, and intestines • epithelium of respiratory tract, including lungs • liver and mucosa of gall bladder • thyroid gland; pancreas

*These are representative lists, not all-inclusive ones. Keep in mind also that most organs are combinations of tissues from each of the three germ layers. Related structures are grouped together.

yolk sac does not contain nutrient yolk, as it does for bird and reptile embryos. It is, however, the site for the formation of the first blood cells and the cells that will become spermatogonia or oogonia. As the embryo grows, the yolk sac membrane is incorporated into the umbilical cord.

The **amnion** is a thin membrane that eventually surrounds the embryo and contains **amniotic fluid.** This fluid provides a cushion for the fetus against mechanical injury as the mother moves. When the fetal kidneys become functional, they excrete urine into the amniotic fluid. Also in this fluid are cells that have sloughed off the fetus; this is clinically important in the procedure called amniocentesis (see Box 21–2: Fetal Diagnosis). The rupture of the amnion (sometimes called the "bag of waters") is usually an indication that labor has begun.

The **chorion** is the name given to the trophoblast as it develops further. Once the embryo has become implanted in the uterus, small projections called **chorionic villi** begin to grow into the endometrium. These will contain the fetal blood vessels that become the fetal portion of the placenta.

At about 4 to 5 weeks of development, the embryo shows definite form. The head is apparent, and limb buds are visible. The period of embryonic growth continues until the eighth week. At this time, all of the organ systems have been established. They will continue to grow and mature until the end of gestation. The period of fetal growth extends from the ninth through the 40th week. Table 21–2 lists some of the major aspects of development in the growth of the embryo-fetus. The fetus at 16 weeks and at 28 weeks is depicted in Fig. 21–4 (see Box 21–3: Congenital Fetal Infections, and Box 21–4: Fetal Alcohol Syndrome). Maternal changes during pregnancy are summarized in Table 21–3.

PLACENTA AND UMBILICAL CORD

The **placenta** is made of both fetal and maternal tissue. The chorion of the embryo and the endometrium of the uterus contribute, and the placenta is formed by the third month of gestation (12 weeks). The mature placenta is a flat disc about 7 inches (17 cm) in diameter.

The structure of a small portion of the placenta is shown in Fig. 21–5. Notice that the fetal blood vessels are within maternal blood sinuses, but there is no direct connection between fetal and maternal vessels. Normally, the blood of the fetus does not mix with that of the mother. The placenta has two functions: to serve as the site of exchanges between maternal and fetal blood and to produce hormones

Box 21–2　FETAL DIAGNOSIS

Several procedures are currently available to determine certain kinds of abnormalities in a fetus or to monitor development.

Ultrasound (or Fetal Ultrasonography)

This is a non-invasive procedure; high-frequency sound waves are transmitted through the abdominal wall into the uterus. The reflected sound waves are converted to an image called a sonogram. This method is used to confirm multiple pregnancies, fetal age or position, or to detect fetal abnormalities such as heart defects or malformations of other organs.

Amniocentesis

This procedure is usually performed at 16 to 18 weeks of gestation. A hypodermic needle is inserted through the wall of the abdomen into the amniotic sac, and about 10 to 20 ml of amniotic fluid is removed. Within this fluid are fetal cells, which can be cultured so that their chromosomes may be examined. Through such examination and biochemical tests, a number of genetic diseases or chromosome abnormalities may be detected. Since women over the age of 35 years are believed to have a greater chance of having a child with Down syndrome, amniocentesis is often recommended for this age group. A family history of certain genetic diseases is another reason a pregnant woman may wish to have this procedure.

Chorionic Villus Sampling (CVS)

In this procedure, a biopsy catheter is inserted through the vagina and cervix to collect a small portion of the chorionic villi. These cells are derived from the fetus but are not part of the fetus itself. The information obtained is the same as that for amniocentesis, but CVS may be performed earlier in pregnancy, at about 8 weeks. Although there is a risk that the procedure may cause a miscarriage, CVS is considered comparable in safety to amniocentesis. It is important to remember that no invasive procedure is without risks.

to maintain pregnancy. We will consider the exchanges first.

The fetus is dependent upon the mother for oxygen and nutrients and for the removal of waste products. The **umbilical cord** connects the fetus to the placenta. Within the cord are two umbilical arteries that carry blood from the fetus to the placenta and one umbilical vein that returns blood from the placenta to the fetus.

When blood in the umbilical arteries enters the placenta, CO_2 and waste products in the fetal capillaries diffuse into the maternal blood sinuses. Oxygen diffuses from the maternal blood sinuses into the fetal capillaries; nutrients enter the fetal blood by diffusion and active transport mechanisms. This oxygen and nutrient-rich blood then flows through the umbilical vein back to the fetus. Circulation within the fetus was described in Chapter 13.

When the baby is delivered at the end of gestation, the umbilical cord is cut. The placenta then detaches from the uterine wall and is delivered as the **afterbirth.**

Placental Hormones

The first hormone secreted by the placenta is **human chorionic gonadotropin** (hCG), which is produced by the chorion of the early embryo. The function of hCG is to stimulate the corpus luteum in the maternal ovary, so that it will continue to secrete estrogen and progesterone. The secretion of progesterone is particularly important to prevent contractions of the myometrium, which would oth-

Table 21–2 GROWTH OF THE EMBRYO-FETUS

Month of Gestation	Aspects of Development	Approximate Overall Size in Inches
1	• Heart begins to beat; limb buds form; backbone forms; facial features not distinct	.25
2	• Calcification of bones begins; fingers and toes are apparent on limbs; facial features more distinct; body systems are established	1.25–1.5
3	• Facial features distinct but eyes are still closed; nails develop on fingers and toes; ossification of skeleton continues; fetus is distinguishable as male or female	3
4	• Head still quite large in proportion to body, but the arms and legs lengthen; hair appears on head; body systems continue to develop	5–7
5	• Skeletal muscles become active ("quickening" may be felt by the mother); body grows more rapidly than head; body is covered with fine hair (lanugo)	10–12
6	• Eyelashes and eyebrows form; eyelids open; skin is quite wrinkled	11–14
7	• Head and body approach normal infant proportions; deposition of subcutaneous fat makes skin less wrinkled	13–17
8	• Testes of male fetus descend into scrotum; more subcutaneous fat is deposited; production of pulmonary surfactant begins	16–18
9	• Lanugo is shed; nails are fully developed; cranial bones are ossified with fontanels present; lungs are more mature	19–21

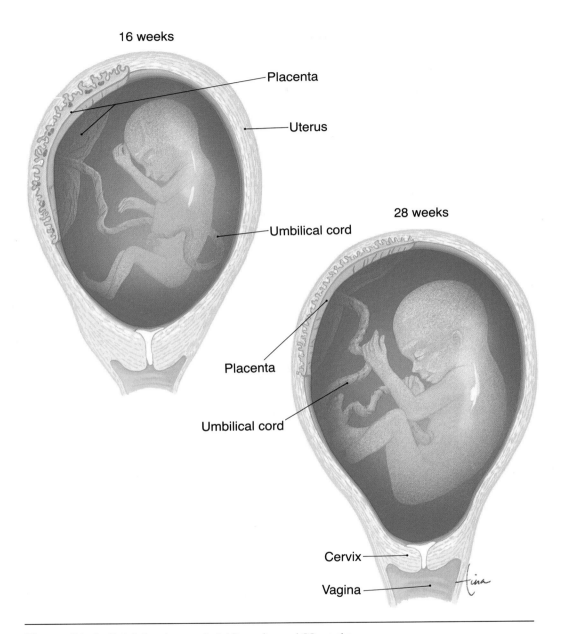

Figure 21–4 Fetal development at 16 weeks and 28 weeks.

Box 21–3 CONGENITAL FETAL INFECTIONS

A **teratogen** is anything that may cause developmental abnormalities in an embryo-fetus. Several infectious microorganisms are known to be teratogenic; they may cross the placenta from maternal blood to fetal blood and damage the fetus.

Congenital Rubella Syndrome—the virus of German measles (rubella) is perhaps the best known of the infectious teratogens. If a woman acquires rubella during pregnancy, there is a 20% chance that her fetus will be affected. Consequences for the fetus may be death (stillborn), heart defects, deafness, or mental retardation. Women who have never had rubella should consider receiving the vaccine before they begin to have children. In this way, congenital rubella syndrome is completely prevented.

Congenital Varicella Syndrome—chickenpox *(Herpes varicella)* is a viral disease that most people have during childhood. If a pregnant woman acquires chickenpox, however, the virus may cross the placenta. Consequences for the fetus include malformed limbs, cutaneous scars, blindness, and mental retardation. Although this is not a common congenital syndrome, women who have never had chickenpox should be educated about it.

Congenital Syphilis—syphilis is a sexually transmitted disease caused by a bacterium *(Treponema pallidum).* These bacteria may cross the placenta after the fourth month of gestation. Consequences of early infection of the fetus are death, malformations of bones and teeth, or cataracts. If infection occurs toward the end of gestation, the child may be born with syphilis. This is most often apparent as a rash on the skin and mucous membranes. Syphilis in adults can be cured by penicillin; prevention of congenital syphilis depends upon good prenatal care for women who may be infected.

Congenital Toxoplasmosis—this condition is caused by the protozoan parasite *Toxoplasma gondii.* For most healthy people, toxoplasmosis has no symptoms at all; it is a harmless infection. Since cats and some other mammals are also hosts for this parasite, pregnant women may acquire infection from contact with cat feces or by eating rare beef or lamb. Consequences for the fetus are death, mental retardation, or blindness. Retinal infection may only become apparent during childhood or adolescence. Prevention now depends upon education of pregnant women to avoid potential sources of infection.

Box 21–4 FETAL ALCOHOL SYNDROME

Fetal alcohol syndrome is the term for a group of characteristics present in infants who were exposed to alcohol during their fetal life. Alcohol is a toxin for adults and even more so for fetal tissues that are immature and growing rapidly. Either alcohol or its toxic intermediate product (acetaldehyde) may pass from maternal to fetal circulation and impair fetal development.

Consequences for infants include low birth weight, small head with facial abnormalities, heart defects, malformation of other organs, and irritability and agitation. The infant often grows slowly, both physically and mentally, and mental retardation is also a possible outcome.

Since there is no way to reverse the damage done by intrauterine exposure to alcohol, the best course is prevention. Education is very important; women should be aware of the consequences their consumption of alcohol may have for a fetus.

Table 21–3 MATERNAL CHANGES DURING PREGNANCY

Aspect	Change
Weight	• Gain of 2–3 pounds for each month of gestation
Uterus	• Enlarges considerably and displaces abdominal organs upward
Thyroid Gland	• Increases secretion of thyroxine, which increases metabolic rate
Skin	• Appearance of striae (stretch marks) on abdomen
Circulatory System	• Heart rate increases, as do stroke volume and cardiac output; blood volume increases; varicose veins may develop in the legs and anal canal
Digestive System	• Nausea and vomiting may occur in early pregnancy (morning sickness); constipation may occur in later pregnancy
Urinary System	• Kidney activity increases; frequency of urination often increases in later pregnancy (bladder is compressed by uterus)
Respiratory System	• Respiratory rate increases; lung capacity decreases as diaphragm is forced upward by compressed abdominal organs in later pregnancy
Skeletal System	• Lordosis may occur with increased weight at front of abdomen; sacroiliac joints and pubic symphysis become more flexible prior to birth

erwise result in miscarriage of the embryo. Once hCG enters maternal circulation, it is excreted in urine, which is the basis for many pregnancy tests. Tests for hCG in maternal blood are even more precise and can determine whether or not a pregnancy has occurred even before a menstrual period is missed.

The corpus luteum is a small structure, however, and cannot secrete sufficient amounts of estrogen and progesterone to maintain a full-term preg-

nancy. The placenta itself begins to secrete **estrogen** and **progesterone** within a few weeks, and the levels of these hormones increase until birth. As the placenta takes over, the secretion of hCG decreases, and the corpus luteum becomes non-functional. During pregnancy, estrogen and progesterone inhibit the anterior pituitary secretion of FSH and LH, so no other ovarian follicles develop. These placental hormones also prepare the mammary glands for lactation.

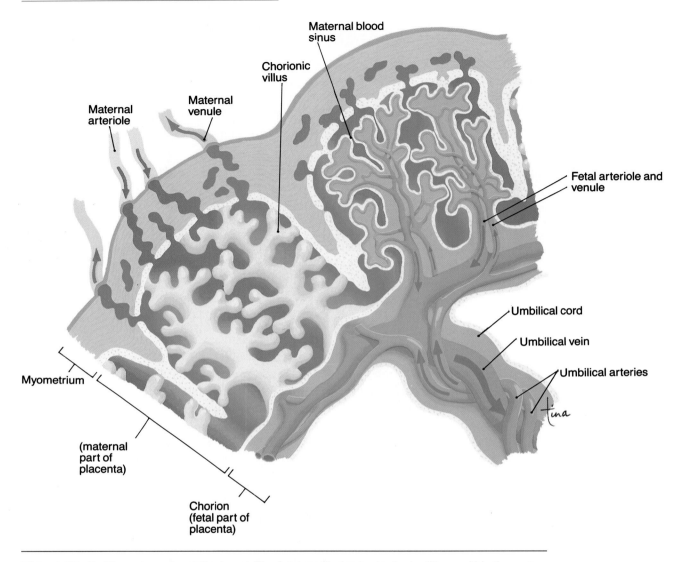

Figure 21–5   Placenta and umbilical cord. The fetal capillaries in chorionic villi are within the maternal blood sinuses. Arrows indicate the direction of blood flow in the umbilical arteries and vein.

PARTURITION AND LABOR

Parturition is the rather formal term for birth, and **labor** is the sequence of events that occurs during birth. The average gestation period is 40 weeks (280 days), with a range of 37 to 42 weeks (see Box 21–5: Premature Birth). Toward the end of gestation, the placental secretion of progesterone decreases while estrogen level remains high, and the myometrium begins to contract weakly at irregular intervals. At this time the fetus is often oriented head down within the uterus (Fig. 21–6). Labor itself may be divided into three stages.

First stage—dilation of the cervix. As the uterus contracts, the amniotic sac is forced into the cervix, which dilates (widens) the cervical opening. At the end of this stage, the amniotic sac breaks (rupture of the "bag of waters") and the fluid leaves through the vagina, which may now be called the **birth canal.** This stage lasts an average of 8 to 12 hours but may vary considerably.

Box 21–5 PREMATURE BIRTH

A premature birth is the spontaneous delivery of an infant before the end of the gestation period, or the intentional delivery (for reasons concerning the health of the mother or fetus) before that time. A premature infant is one that weighs less than 2500 grams (5.5 pounds.).

In terms of gestation time, an 8-month-old infant has a very good chance of surviving if good medical care is available. Infants of 7 months or less have respiratory distress, because their lungs have not yet produced enough surfactant to permit inflation of the alveoli. This is hyaline membrane disease, which was described in Chapter 15.

Infants as young as 24 weeks have been successfully treated and eventually sent home with their parents. Whether there will be any long-term detrimental effects of their very premature births will only be known in time.

Medical science may have reached its maximum capability in this area. In a fetus of 20 weeks, the cells of the alveoli and the cells of the pulmonary capillaries are just not close enough to each other to permit gas exchange. At present there is no medical intervention that can overcome this anatomical fact.

Second stage—delivery of the infant. More powerful contractions of the uterus are brought about by **oxytocin** released by the posterior pituitary gland and perhaps by the placenta itself. This stage may be prolonged by several factors. If the fetus is positioned other than head down, delivery may be difficult. This is called a breech birth and may necessitate a **cesarean section** (C-section), which is delivery of the fetus through a surgical incision in the abdominal wall and uterus. For some women, the central opening in the pelvic bone may be too small to permit a vaginal delivery. Fetal distress, as determined by fetal monitoring of heartbeat for example, may also require a cesarean section.

Third stage—delivery of the placenta (afterbirth). Continued contractions of the uterus expel the placenta and membranes, usually within 10 minutes after delivery of the infant. There is some bleeding at this time, but the uterus rapidly decreases in size, and the contractions compress the endometrium to close the ruptured blood vessels at the former site of the placenta. This is important to prevent severe maternal hemorrhage.

THE INFANT AT BIRTH

Immediately after delivery, the umbilical cord is clamped and cut, and the infant's nose and mouth are aspirated to remove any fluid that might interfere with breathing (see Box 21–6: Apgar Score). Now the infant is independent of the mother, and the most rapid changes occur in the respiratory and circulatory systems.

As the level of CO_2 in the baby's blood increases, the respiratory center in the medulla is stimulated and brings about inhalation to expand and inflate the lungs. Full expansion of the lungs may take up to 7 days following birth, and the infant's respiratory rate may be very rapid at this time, as high as 40 respirations per minute.

Breathing promotes greater pulmonary circulation, and the increased amount of blood returning to the left atrium closes the flap of the **foramen ovale.** The **ductus arteriosus** begins to constrict, apparently in response to the higher blood oxygen level. Full closure of the ductus arteriosus may take up to 3 months.

The **ductus venosus** no longer receives blood

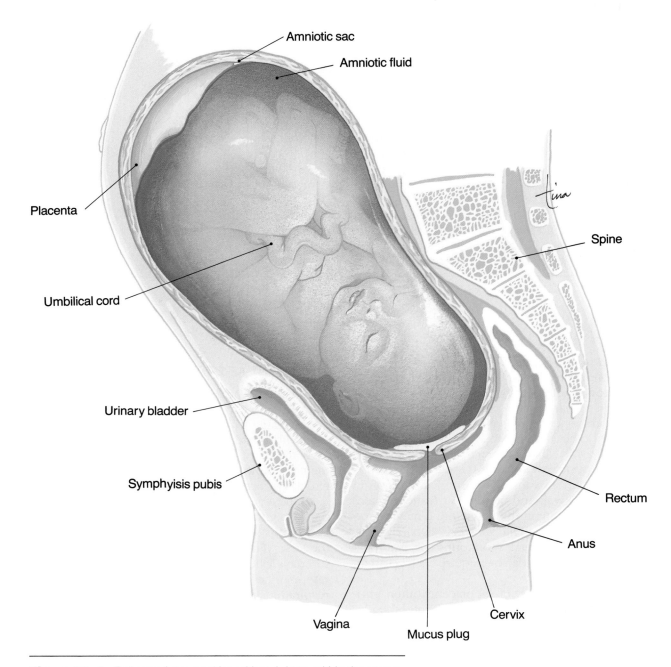

Figure 21–6 Full-term fetus positioned head down within the uterus.

Box 21–6   APGAR SCORE

The Apgar Score is an overall assessment of an infant and is usually made 1 minute after birth (may be repeated at 5 minutes if the first score is low). The highest possible score is 10. Infants who score less than 5 require immediate medical attention.

Characteristic	Description	Score
Heartbeat	• over 100 bpm • below 100 bpm • no heartbeat	2 1 0
Respiration	• strong, vigorous cry • weak cry • no respiratory effort	2 1 0
Muscle Tone	• spontaneous, active motion • some motion • no muscle tone	2 1 0
Reflex response to stimulation of sole of the foot	• a cry in response • a grimace in response • no response	2 1 0
Color	• healthy coloration • cyanotic extremities • cyanosis of trunk and extremities	2 1 0

---

from the umbilical vein and begins to constrict within a few minutes after birth. Within a few weeks the ductus venosus becomes a non-functional ligament.

The infant's liver is not fully mature at birth and may be unable to excrete bilirubin efficiently. This may result in jaundice, which may occur in as many as half of all newborns. Such jaundice is not considered serious unless there is another possible cause, such as Rh incompatibility (see Chapter 11).

GENETICS

Genetics is the study of inheritance. Most, if not virtually all, human characteristics are regulated at least partially by genes. We will first look at what

genes are, then describe some patterns of inheritance.

CHROMOSOMES AND GENES

Each of the cells of an individual (except mature RBCs and egg and sperm) contains 46 chromosomes, the diploid number. These chromosomes are in 23 pairs called **homologous pairs.** One member of each pair has come from the egg and is called maternal, the other member has come from the sperm and is called paternal. The autosomes are the chromosome pairs designated #1 to 22. The remaining pair is the sex chromosomes. In women these are designated XX and in men XY.

Chromosomes are made of DNA and protein; the DNA is the hereditary material. You may wish to refer to Chapter 3 to review DNA structure. The sequence of bases in the DNA of chromosomes is the genetic code for proteins; structural proteins as well as enzymes. The DNA code for one protein is called a gene. For example, a specific region of the DNA of chromosome #11 is the code for the beta chain of hemoglobin. Since an individual has two of chromosome #11, he or she will have two genes for this protein, a maternal gene inherited from the mother and a paternal gene inherited from the father. This is true for virtually all of the 50,000 to 100,000 genes estimated to be found in our chromosomes. In our genetic code, each of us has two genes for each protein.

GENOTYPE AND PHENOTYPE

For each gene of a pair, there may be two or more possibilities for its "expression," that is, its precise nature or how it will affect the individual. These possibilities are called **alleles.** A person, therefore, may be said to have two alleles for each protein or trait; the alleles may be the same or may be different.

If the two alleles are the same, the person is said to be **homozygous** for the trait. If the two alleles are different, the person is said to be **heterozygous** for the trait.

The **genotype** is the actual genetic makeup, that is, the alleles present. The **phenotype** is the appearance, or how the alleles are expressed. When a gene has two or more alleles, one allele may be **dominant** over the other, which is called **recessive.** For a person who is heterozygous for a trait, the dominant allele (or gene) is the one that will appear in the phenotype. The recessive allele (or gene) is hidden but may be passed to children. For a recessive trait to be expressed in the phenotype, the person must be homozygous recessive, that is, have two recessive alleles (genes) for the trait.

An example will be helpful here to put all this together and is illustrated in Fig. 21–7. When doing genetics problems, a **Punnett square** is used to show the possible combinations of genes in the egg and sperm for a particular set of parents and their children. Remember that an egg or sperm has only 23 chromosomes and, therefore, has only one gene for each trait.

In this example, the inheritance of eye color has been simplified. Although eye color is determined by many pairs of genes, with many possible phenotypes, one pair is considered the principal pair, with brown eyes dominant over blue eyes. A dominant gene is usually represented by a capital letter, and the corresponding recessive gene is represented by the same letter in lower case. The parents in Fig. 21–7 are both heterozygous for eye color. Their genotype consists of a gene for brown eyes and gene for blue eyes, but their phenotype is brown eyes.

Each egg produced by the mother has a 50% chance of containing the gene for brown eyes, or an equal 50% chance of containing the gene for blue eyes. Similarly, each sperm produced by the father has a 50% chance of containing the gene for brown eyes and a 50% chance of containing the gene for blue eyes.

Now look at the boxes of the Punnett square; these represent the possibilities for the genetic makeup of each child. For eye color there are three possibilities: a 25% (one of four) chance for homozygous brown eyes, a 50% (two of four) chance for heterozygous brown eyes, and a 25% (one of four) chance for homozygous blue eyes. Notice that BB and Bb have the same phenotype (brown eyes) despite their different genotypes, and that the phenotype of blue eyes is only possible with the genotype bb. Can brown-eyed parents have a blue-eyed child? Yes: if each parent is heterozygous for brown eyes, each child has a 25% chance of inheriting blue eyes. Could these parents have four children with blue eyes? What are the odds of this happening? The answers to these questions will be found in Box 21–7: Solution to Genetics Question.

INHERITANCE: DOMINANT–RECESSIVE

The inheritance of eye color just described is an example of a trait determined by a pair of alleles, one of which may dominate the other. Another example is sickle-cell anemia, which was discussed in Chapter 11. The gene for the beta chain of hemoglobin is on chromosome #11; an allele for normal hemoglobin is dominant, and an allele for sickle-cell hemoglobin is recessive. An individual who is

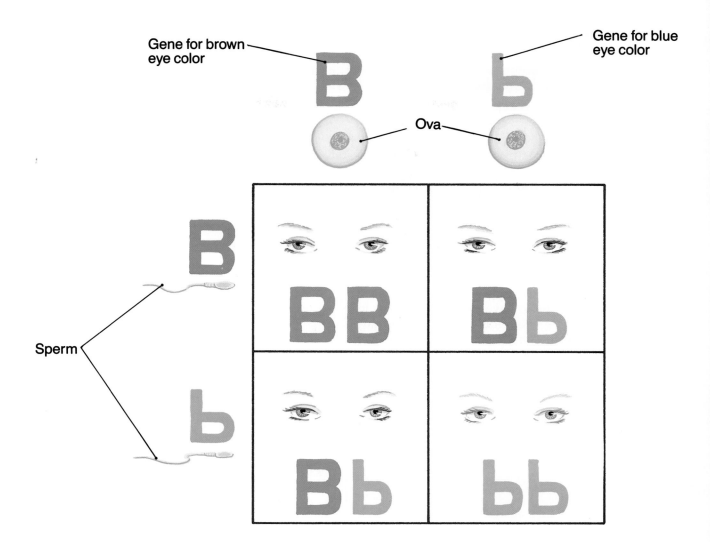

Key

BB   Genotype: homozygous brown (2 dominant genes)
        Phenotype: brown

Bb   Genotype: heterozygous (1 dominant and 1 recessive gene)
        Phenotype: brown (since brown is dominant)

bb   Genotype: homozygous blue (2 recessive genes)
        Phenotype: blue

Figure 21–7   Inheritance of eye color. Both mother and father are heterozygous for brown eyes. The Punnett square shows the possible combinations of genes for eye color in each child of these parents. See text for further description.

Box 21–7   SOLUTION TO GENETICS QUESTION

Question: Can parents who are both heterozygous for brown eyes have four
children with blue eyes? What are the odds of this happening?

Answer: Yes. For each child, the odds of having blue eyes are 1 in 4. To
calculate the odds of all four children having blue eyes, multiply the
odds for each child separately:

1st child   2nd child   3rd child   4th child

$\frac{1}{4}$ × $\frac{1}{4}$ × $\frac{1}{4}$ × $\frac{1}{4}$ = $\frac{1}{256}$

The odds are 256 to 1.

---

heterozygous is said to have sickle-cell trait; an individual who is homozygous recessive will have sickle-cell anemia. The Punnett square in Fig. 21–8 shows that if both parents are heterozygous, each child has a 25% chance of inheriting the two recessive genes. Table 21–4 lists some other human genetic diseases and their patterns of inheritance.

INHERITANCE: MULTIPLE ALLELES

The best example of this pattern of inheritance is human blood type of the ABO group. For each gene of this blood type, there are three possible alleles: A, B, or O. A person will have only two of these alleles, which may be the same or different. O is the

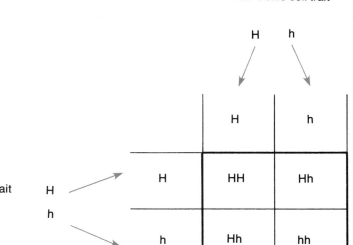

Figure 21–8 Inheritance of sickle cell anemia (dominant recessive pattern). See text for description.

Key: H   Gene for normal hemoglobin
       h   Gene for sickle cell hemoglobin

Table 21–4   HUMAN GENETIC DISEASES

Disease (Pattern of Inheritance)	Description
Sickle-cell anemia (R)	• The most common genetic disease among people of African ancestry. Sickle-cell hemoglobin forms rigid crystals that distort and disrupt RBCs; oxygen-carrying capacity of the blood is diminished.
Cystic fibrosis (R)	• The most common genetic disease among people of European ancestry. Production of thick mucus clogs the bronchial tree and pancreatic ducts. Most severe effects are chronic respiratory infections and pulmonary failure.
Tay-Sachs disease (R)	• The most common genetic disease among people of Jewish ancestry. Degeneration of neurons and the nervous system results in death by the age of 2 years.
Phenylketonuria or PKU (R)	• Lack of an enzyme to metabolize the amino acid phenylalanine leads to severe mental and physical retardation. These effects may be prevented by the use of a diet (beginning at birth) that limits phenylalanine.
Huntington's disease (D)	• Uncontrollable muscle contractions begin between the ages of 30–50 years; followed by loss of memory and personality. There is no treatment that can delay mental deterioration.
Hemophilia (x-linked)	• Lack of Factor 8 impairs chemical clotting; may be controlled with Factor 8 from donated blood.
Duchenne's muscular dystrophy (x-linked)	• Replacement of muscle by adipose or scar tissue, with progressive loss of muscle function; often fatal before age 20 years due to involvement of cardiac muscle.

R = recessive; D = dominant.

recessive allele: A and B are codominant alleles, that is, dominant over O but not over each other.

You already know that in this blood group there are four possible blood types: O, AB, A, and B. Table 21–5 shows the combinations of alleles for each type. Notice that for types O and AB there is only one possible genotype. For types A and B, however, there are two possible genotypes, since both A and B alleles are dominant over an O allele.

Let us now use a problem to illustrate the inheritance of blood type. The Punnett square in Fig. 21–9 shows that Mom has type O blood and Dad has type AB blood. The boxes of the square show the possible blood types for each child. Each child has a 50% chance of having type A blood, and a 50% chance of having type B blood. The genotype,

however, will always be heterozygous. Notice that in this example, the blood types of the children will not be the same as those of the parents.

Table 21–6 lists some other human genetic traits, with the dominant and recessive phenotype for each.

Table 21–5   ABO BLOOD TYPES: GENOTYPES

Blood Type	Possible Genotypes
O	OO
AB	AB
A	AA or OA
B	BB or OB

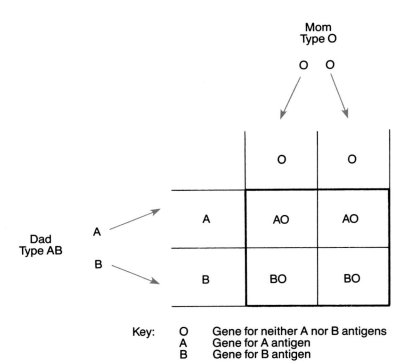

Key:
O	Gene for neither A nor B antigens
A	Gene for A antigen
B	Gene for B antigen

Figure 21–9 Inheritance of blood type (multiple alleles pattern). See text for description.

Table 21–6 HUMAN GENETIC TRAITS

Trait	Dominant Phenotype	Recessive Phenotype
ABO blood type	AB, A, B	O
Rh blood type	Rh positive	Rh negative
Hair color	Dark	Light (blond or red)
Change in hair color	Premature gray	Gray later in life
Hair texture	Curly	Straight
Hairline	Widow's peak	Straight
Eye color	Dark	Light
Color vision	Normal	Colorblind
Visual acuity	Nearsighted or farsighted	Normal
Skin color	Dark	Light
Freckles	Abundant	Few
Dimples	Present	Absent
Cleft chin	Present	Absent
Ear lobes	Unattached	Attached
Number of fingers/toes	Polydactyly (more than 5 digits)	5 per hand or foot
Mid-digital hair	Present	Absent
Double-jointed thumb	Present	Absent
Bent little finger	Present	Absent
Ability to roll tongue sides up	Able	Unable

INHERITANCE: SEX-LINKED TRAITS

Sex-linked traits may also be called X-linked traits because the genes for them are located only on the X chromosome. The Y chromosome is very small and has very few genes. The Y does not have corresponding genes for many of the genes on the X chromosome.

The genes for sex-linked traits are recessive, but since there are no corresponding genes on the Y chromosome to mask them, a man needs only one gene to express one of these traits in his phenotype. A woman who has one of these recessive genes on one X chromosome and a dominant gene for normal function on the other X chromosome, will not express this trait. She is called a carrier, however, because the gene is part of her genotype and may be passed to children.

Let us use as an example, red-green colorblindness. The Punnett square in Fig. 21–10 shows that Mom is carrier of this trait and that Dad has normal color vision. A Punnett square for a sex-linked trait uses the X and Y chromosomes with a lower case letter on the X to indicate the presence of the recessive gene. The possibilities for each child are divided equally into daughters and sons. In this example, each daughter has a 50% chance of being a carrier and a 50% chance of not being a carrier. In either case, a daughter will have normal color vision. Each son has a 50% chance of being red-green blind and a 50% chance of having normal color vision. Men can never be carriers of a trait such as this; they either have it or do not have it.

The inheritance of other characteristics is often not as easily depicted as are the examples shown above. Height, for example, is a multiple gene characteristic, meaning that many pairs of genes contribute. Many pairs of genes result in many possible combinations for genotype and many possible phenotypes. In addition, height is a trait that is influenced by environmental factors such as nutrition. These kinds of circumstances or influences are

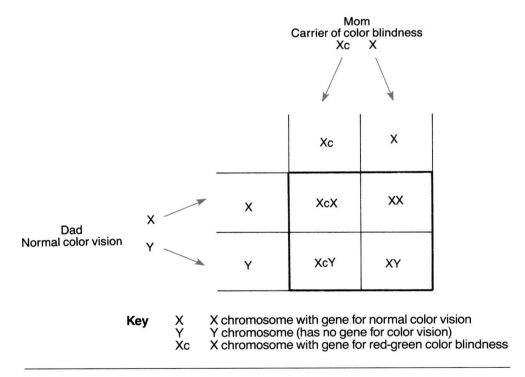

Key
X   X chromosome with gene for normal color vision
Y   Y chromosome (has no gene for color vision)
Xc   X chromosome with gene for red-green color blindness

Figure 21–10 Inheritance of red-green colorblindness (sex-linked pattern). See text for description.

probably important in many other human characteristics.

Another difficulty in predicting genetic outcomes is that we do not know what all our genes are for. Of the estimated 50,000 to 100,000 human genes, about 5000 are known. That is, we know the protein for which each gene is the code. Of these genes, about 2000 have been "mapped," which means that they have been precisely located on a particular chromosome. By the time you read this, many more genes will have been mapped, for this is a project that has been undertaken by many groups of researchers. Their goal is to map all the genes on our 23 pairs of chromosomes.

Someday it will be possible to cure genetic diseases by inserting correct copies of malfunctioning genes into the cells of affected individuals. The first such attempt was undertaken in September 1990, in an effort to supply a missing enzyme in an otherwise fatal disorder of the immune system. The following year, the child, now 5 years old, was able to start school with an immune system that seemed to be completely functional. Despite this success, gene therapy, because of its complexity and high cost, is still limited to federally funded experiments performed on individuals or small groups of people. Also unknown at this time, and yet another reason to proceed slowly, are any possible risks of gene replacement.

Other diseases that may eventually be cured or controlled with gene therapy include cystic fibrosis (for which clinical trials are already underway), Parkinson's disease, diabetes, muscular dystrophy, hemophilia, and sickle-cell anemia. Much more research and experimentation remain to be done before gene replacement becomes the standard treatment available to everyone with these genetic diseases, but the foundation of this remarkable therapy has been established.

STUDY OUTLINE

Human Development—growth of a fertilized egg into a human individual
Fertilization—the union of the nuclei of egg and sperm; usually takes place in the fallopian tube

1. Sperm undergo final maturation (capacitation) within the female reproductive tract; the acrosome secretes enzymes to digest the membrane of the ovum.
2. The 23 chromosomes of the sperm join with the 23 chromosomes of the egg to restore the diploid number of 46 in the zygote.
3. A zygote has 22 pairs of autosomes and one pair of sex chromosomes; XX in females, XY in males (see Fig. 21–1).

Implantation (see Fig. 21–2)

1. Within the fallopian tube, the zygote begins mitotic divisions called cleavage to form two-cell, four-cell, eight-cell stages, and so on.
2. A morula is a solid sphere of cells, which divides further to form a hollow sphere called a blastocyst.
3. A blastocyst consists of an outer layer of cells called the trophoblast and an inner cell mass that contains the potential embryo. The trophoblast secretes enzymes to form a crater in the endometrium into which the blastocyst sinks.

Embryo—weeks 1 through 8 of gestation (see Fig. 21–3)

1. In the embryonic disc, three primary germ layers develop: ectoderm, mesoderm, and endoderm (see Table 21–1).
2. By the eighth week of gestation (end of 2 months), all the organ systems are formed (see Table 21–2).

Embryonic Membranes (see Fig. 21–3)

1. The yolk sac forms the first blood cells and the cells that become spermatogonia or oogonia.
2. The amnion surrounds the fetus and contains amniotic fluid; this fluid absorbs shock around the fetus.
3. The chorion develops chorionic villi that will contain blood vessels that form the fetal portion of the placenta.

Fetus—weeks 9 through 40 of gestation (see Table 21–2)

1. The organ systems grow and mature.
2. The growing fetus brings about structural and functional changes in the mother (see Table 21–3).

Placenta and Umbilical Cord

1. The placenta is formed by the chorion of the embryo and the endometrium of the uterus; the umbilical cord connects the fetus to the placenta.
2. Fetal blood does not mix with maternal blood; fetal capillaries are within maternal blood sinuses (see Fig. 21–5); this is the site of exchanges between maternal and fetal blood.
3. Two umbilical arteries carry blood from the fetus to the placenta; fetal CO_2 and waste products diffuse into maternal blood; oxygen and nutrients enter fetal blood.
4. Umbilical vein returns blood from placenta to fetus.
5. The placenta is delivered after the baby and is called the afterbirth.

Placental Hormones

1. hCG—secreted by the chorion; maintains the corpus luteum so that it secretes estrogen and progesterone during the first few months of gestation. The corpus luteum is too small to maintain a full-term pregnancy.
2. Estrogen and progesterone secretion begins within 4 to 6 weeks and continues until birth in amounts great enough to sustain pregnancy.
3. Estrogen and progesterone inhibit FSH and LH secretion during pregnancy and prepare the mammary glands for lactation.
4. Progesterone inhibits contractions of the myometrium until just before birth, when progesterone secretion begins to decrease.

Parturition and Labor

1. Gestation period ranges from 37 to 42 weeks; the average is 40 weeks.
2. Labor: first stage—dilation of the cervix; uterine contractions force the amniotic sac into the cervix; amniotic sac ruptures and fluid escapes.
3. Labor: second stage—delivery of the infant; oxytocin causes more powerful contractions of the myometrium. If a vaginal delivery is not possible, a cesarean section may be performed.
4. Labor: third stage—delivery of the placenta; the uterus continues to contract to expel the placenta, then contracts further, decreases in size, and compresses endometrial blood vessels.

The Infant at Birth (see Box 21–6)

1. Umbilical cord is clamped and severed; increased CO_2 stimulates breathing, and lungs are inflated.
2. Foramen ovale closes, and ductus arteriosus constricts; ductus venosus constricts; normal circulatory pathways are established.
3. Jaundice may be present if the infant's immature liver cannot rapidly excrete bilirubin.

Genetics—the study of inheritance chromosomes—46 per human cell; in 23 homologous pairs

1. A homologous pair consists of a maternal and a paternal chromosome of the same type (#1 or #2, etc.).
2. There are 22 pairs of autosomes and one pair of sex chromosomes (XX or XY).
3. DNA—the hereditary material of chromosomes.
4. Gene—the genetic code for one protein; an individual has two genes for each protein or trait, one maternal and one paternal.
5. Alleles—the possibilities for how a gene may be expressed.

Genotype—the alleles present in the genetic makeup

1. Homozygous—having two similar alleles.
2. Heterozygous—having two different alleles.

Phenotype—the appearance, or expression of the alleles present

1. Depends on the dominance or recessiveness of alleles or the particular pattern of inheritance involved.

Inheritance—dominant-recessive

1. A dominant gene will appear in the phenotype of a heterozygous individual (who has only one dominant gene). A recessive gene will appear in

the phenotype only if the individual is homozygous, that is, has two recessive genes.
2. See Figs. 21–7 and 21–8 for Punnett squares.

Inheritance—multiple alleles

1. More than two possible alleles for each gene: human ABO blood type.
2. An individual will have only two of the alleles (same or different).
3. See Table 21–5 and Fig. 21–9.

Inheritance—sex-linked traits

1. Genes are recessive and found only on the X chromosome; there are no corresponding genes on the Y chromosome.
2. Women with one gene (and one gene for normal functioning) are called carriers of the trait.
3. Men cannot be carriers; they either have the trait or do not have it.
4. See Fig. 21–10.

REVIEW QUESTIONS

1. Where does fertilization usually take place? How many chromosomes are present in a human zygote? Explain what happens during cleavage, and describe the blastocyst stage. (pp. 479–480)

2. Describe the process of implantation, and state where this takes place. (p. 480)

3. How long is the period of embryonic growth? How long is the period of fetal growth? (pp. 480, 482)

4. Name two body structures derived from ectoderm, mesoderm, and endoderm. (p. 482)

5. Name the embryonic membrane with each of these functions: (p. 482)
   a. forms the fetal portion of the placenta
   b. contains fluid to cushion the embryo
   c. forms the first blood cells for the embryo

6. Explain the function of placenta, umbilical arteries, and umbilical vein. (pp. 482–483)

7. Explain the functions of the placental hormones: hCG, progesterone, and estrogen and progesterone (together). (pp. 483–484)

8. Describe the three stages of labor, and name the important hormone. (pp. 488–489)

9. Describe the major pulmonary and circulatory changes that occur in the infant after birth. (p. 489, 491)

10. What is the genetic material of chromosomes? Explain what a gene is. Explain why a person has two genes for each protein or trait. (pp. 491–492)

11. Define homologous chromosomes, autosomes, sex chromosomes. (p. 491)

12. Define allele, homozygous, heterozygous, genotype, phenotype. (p. 492)

13. Genetics Problem: Mom is heterozygous for brown eyes, and Dad has blue eyes. What is the % chance that a child will have blue eyes? brown eyes? (pp. 492–493)

14. Genetics Problem: Mom is homozygous for type A blood, and Dad is heterozygous for type B blood. What is the % chance that a child will have type AB blood? type A? type B? type O? (pp. 494–496)

15. Genetics Problem: Mom is red-green colorblind, and Dad has normal color vision. What is the % chance that a son will be colorblind? that a daughter will be colorblind? that a daughter will be a carrier? (p. 497)

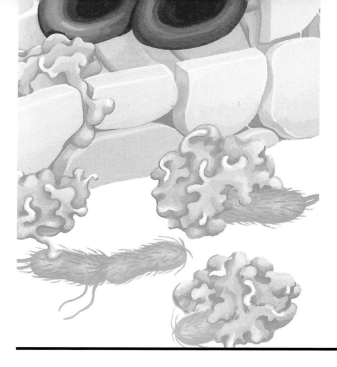

Chapter 22

Student Objectives

- Explain how microorganisms are classified and named.
- Describe the distribution of and benefits provided by normal flora.
- Explain what is meant by an infectious disease, and describe the different types of infection.
- Describe the ways in which infectious diseases may be spread.
- Explain how the growth of microorganisms may be controlled and the importance of this to public health.
- Describe the general structure of bacteria, viruses, fungi, and protozoa and the diseases they cause.
- Name the common worm infestations, and name the arthropods that are vectors of disease.

An Introduction to Microbiology and Human Disease

New Terminology

Bacillus (buh-**SILL**-us)

Coccus (**KOCK**-us)

Communicable (kuhm-**YOO**-ni-kah-b'l)

Contagious (kun-**TAY**-jus)

Epidemiology (EP-i-DEE-mee-**AH**-luh-jee)

Gram stain (**GRAM STAYN**)

Infestation (in-fess-**TAY**-shun)

Mycosis (my-**KOH**-sis)

Non-communicable (NON-kuhm-**YOO**-ni-kah-b'l)

Portal of entry (**POR**-tuhl of **EN**-tree)

Portal of exit (**POR**-tuhl of **EG**-zit)

Reservoir (**REZ**-er-vwor)

Spirillum (spih-**RILL**-uhm)

Spirochaete (**SPY**-roh-keet)

Vector (**VECK**-ter)

Zoonoses (ZOH-oh-**NOH**-seez)

Related Clinical Terminology

Antitoxin (AN-tee-**TOCK**-sin)

Broad spectrum (**BRAWD SPEK**-trum)

Culture and sensitivity testing (**KUL**-chur and SEN-si-**TIV**-i-tee)

Endotoxin (EN-doh-**TOCK**-sin)

Incubation period (IN-kew-**BAY**-shun)

Narrow spectrum (**NAR**-oh **SPEK**-trum)

Nosocomial infection (no-zoh-**KOH**-mee-uhl)

Opportunistic infection (OP-er-too-**NIS**-tick)

Secondary infection (**SECK**-un-dery)

Subclinical infection (sub-**KLIN**-i-kuhl)

Terms that appear in **bold type** in the chapter text are defined in the glossary, which begins on page 549.

Microbiology is the study of microorganisms (also called microbes) and of their place or role in their environment. Sometimes, the environment of microbes is us, people, and that will be our focus. Although there are many perspectives in the field of microbiology, we will concentrate on the microorganisms that affect the functioning of the human body. These microbes include our normal flora and those that are capable of causing human disease. A disease is any disruption of normal body functioning. Many diseases are not caused by microorganisms, but those that are may be called infectious diseases. The microorganisms that cause infectious diseases are called pathogens.

Pathogens may also be called parasites, that is, they live on another living organism called a host and cause harm to the host. Some parasites cause diseases that are fatal to the host, but many others live in a more balanced way with their hosts. These cause illnesses from which the host recovers, and the parasite often survives long enough to be spread to other hosts.

Our introduction to microbiology will begin with a brief description of the classification and naming of microorganisms, followed by a discussion of normal flora. We will then consider infectious diseases, types of infection, and the spread and control of infection. Last, we will describe the types of pathogens in more detail and include the methods we have to treat and control the diseases they cause. For a historical perspective on microbiology, see Box 22-1: The Golden Age of Microbiology, and Box 22-2: Microbiology in the 20th Century.

Box 22–1   THE GOLDEN AGE OF MICROBIOLOGY

Microorganisms were first seen in the 17th century when simple microscopes were developed. The roles of microorganisms, however, especially in relation to disease, were to remain largely unknown for another two centuries. The years between 1875 and 1900 are sometimes called "The Golden Age of Microbiology" because of the number and significance of the discoveries that were made during this time. The following is only a partial list.

1877 Robert Koch proves that anthrax is caused by a bacterium.
1878 Joseph Lister first grows bacteria in pure culture.
     The oil immersion lens for microscopes is developed.
1879 The bacterium that causes gonorrhea is discovered.
1880 Louis Pasteur develops a vaccine for chicken cholera.
1881 Discovery that staphylococci cause infections.
1882 The cause of tuberculosis is found to be a bacterium.
1883 Diphtheria is found to be caused by a bacterium.
1884 The bacteria that cause tetanus, typhoid fever, and cholera are each isolated.
     The first description of phagocytosis by white blood cells is published.
1885 Louis Pasteur first uses his vaccine for rabies.
1890 Development of antitoxins to treat tetanus and diphtheria.
1892 Discovery and demonstration of a virus.
1894 The bacterium that causes plague is discovered.
1897 Discovery of the cause of botulism.
     Rat fleas are found to be vectors of plague.
1900 Walter Reed and his associates demonstrate that yellow fever is caused by a virus and that the vector is a mosquito.

Box 22–2 MICROBIOLOGY IN THE 20TH CENTURY

Just a few of the many advances made in microbiology during this century are listed below. Many of them concerned diagnosis, prevention, or treatment of infectious diseases, and some involved using microorganisms and the new genetic technologies.

1928 Discovery of penicillin by Alexander Fleming.
1935 The first of the sulfa drugs is found to be effective against staphylococcal infections.
1938 Penicillin is purified and produced in large quantities.
1941 The fluorescent antibody test is developed.
1943 Streptomycin is discovered and is the first effective drug in the treatment of tuberculosis.
1953 Watson and Crick describe the structure of DNA.
1955 The Salk polio vaccine is first used.
1957 Interferon is discovered.
1959 A vaccine for whooping cough is available.
1962 The Sabin polio vaccine is marketed in the US.
1963 The measles vaccine becomes available.
1969 A vaccine for rubella is developed.
1976 Legionnaire's disease is discovered and described.
1980 Genetically engineered bacteria produce the hormone insulin.
1981 The first cases of AIDS are described.
1982 The first vaccine for hepatitis B is licensed.
1986 Genetically engineered yeast are used to produce a more effective vaccine for hepatitis B.
Genetically engineered bacteria produce human growth hormone.

CLASSIFICATION OF MICROORGANISMS

Bacteria are very simple single-celled organisms and are found virtually everywhere. The natural habitats of bacteria include fresh water, salt water, soil, and other living organisms. Most bacteria are not harmful to us, and within their normal environments, they have the vital role of decomposing dead organic material and recycling their nutrients. However, a number of bacteria cause human bacterial diseases, including strep throat, pneumonia, and meningitis.

Viruses are not cells; they are even smaller and simpler in structure than the bacteria. All viruses are parasites because they can reproduce only within the living cells of a host. Therefore, all viruses cause disease. Common human viral diseases are influenza, the common cold, and chickenpox.

Protozoa are single-celled animals such as amoebas. Most protozoa are freeliving in fresh or salt water, where they consume bacteria, fungi, and one another. Human protozoan parasites include those that cause malaria, amebic dysentery, and pneumocystis pneumonia (common in AIDS patients).

Fungi may be unicellular or multicellular. Molds and mushrooms are familiar fungi. They decompose organic matter in the soil and fresh water and help recycle nutrients. Fungal diseases of people include yeast infections, ringworm, and more serious diseases such as a type of meningitis.

Worms are multicellular animals. Most are free-living and non-pathogenic; within the soil they consume dead organic matter or smaller living things. Worm infestations of people include trichinosis, hookworm disease, and tapeworms.

Arthropods (the name means "jointed legs") are multicellular animals such as lobsters, shrimp, the insects, ticks, and mites. Some insects (such as mosquitoes and fleas) are **vectors** of disease, that is, they spread pathogens from host to host when they bite to obtain blood. Ticks are also vectors of certain diseases, and some mites may cause infestations of the skin.

BINOMIAL NOMENCLATURE

We refer to bacteria and all other living things using two names (binomial nomenclature), the genus and the species. The genus name is placed first, is always capitalized, and is the larger category. The species name is second, is not capitalized, and is the smaller category. Let us use as examples *Staphylococcus aureus* and *Staphylococcus epidermidis*. These two bacteria are in the same genus, *Staphylococcus,* which tells us that they are related or similar to one another. Yet they are different enough to be given their own species names: *aureus* or *epidermidis*. It may be helpful here to think of our own names. Each of us has a family name, which indicates that we are related to other members of our families, and each of us has a first name indicating that we are individuals in this related group. If we wrote our own names using the method of binomial nomenclature, we would write Smith Mary and Smith John.

In scientific articles and books, for the sake of convenience, the genus name is often abbreviated with its first letter. We might read of *S. aureus* as a cause of a food poisoning outbreak or see *E. coli* (E. for *Escherichia*) on a lab report as the cause of a patient's urinary tract infection. Therefore, it is important to learn both genus and species names of important pathogens.

NORMAL FLORA

Each of us has a natural population of microorganisms living on or within us. This is our normal flora. These microbes may be further categorized as residents or transients. **Resident flora** are those species that live on or in nearly everyone almost all the time. These residents live in specific sites, and we provide a very favorable environment for them. Some, such as *Staphylococcus epidermidis,* live on the skin. Others, such as *E. coli,* live in the colon and small intestine. When in their natural sites, resident flora do not cause harm to healthy tissue, and some are even beneficial to us. However, residents may become pathogenic if they are introduced into abnormal sites. If *E. coli,* for example, gains access to the urinary bladder, it causes an infection called cystitis. In this situation, *E. coli* is considered an **opportunist,** which is a normally harmless species that has become a pathogen in special circumstances.

Transient flora are those species that are found periodically on or in the body; they are not as well adapted to us as are the residents. *Streptococcus pneumoniae,* for example, is a transient in the upper respiratory tract, where it usually does not cause harm in healthy people. However, transients may become pathogenic when the host's resistance is lowered. In an elderly person with influenza, *S. pneumoniae* may invade the lower respiratory tract and cause a serious or even fatal pneumonia.

The distribution of our normal flora is summarized in Table 22–1. You can see that an important function of normal flora is to inhibit the growth of pathogens in the oral cavity, intestines, and in women, the vagina. The resident bacteria are believed to do this by simply being there and providing competition that makes it difficult for pathogens to establish themselves. An example may be helpful here. Let us use botulism. Typical food-borne botulism is acquired by ingesting the bacterial toxin that has been produced in food. Infants, however, may acquire botulism by ingesting the spores (dormant forms) of the botulism bacteria on foods such as honey or raw vegetables. The infant's colon flora is not yet abundant, and the botulism spores may

Table 22–1 DISTRIBUTION OF NORMAL FLORA IN THE HUMAN BODY

Body Site	Description of Flora
Skin	Exposed to the environment; therefore has a large bacterial population and small numbers of fungi, especially where the skin is often moist. Flora are kept in check by the continual loss of dead cells from the stratum corneum.
Nasal cavities	Bacteria, mold spores, and viruses constantly enter with inhaled air; the ciliated epithelium limits the microbial population by continuously sweeping mucus and trapped pathogens to the pharynx, where they are swallowed.
Trachea, bronchi, and lungs	The cilia of the trachea and large bronchial tubes sweep mucus and microbes upward toward the pharynx, where they are swallowed. Very few pathogens reach the lungs, and most of these are destroyed by alveolar macrophages.
Oral cavity	Large bacterial population and small numbers of yeasts and protozoa. Kept in check by lysozyme, the enzyme in saliva that inhibits bacterial reproduction. The resident flora help prevent the growth of pathogens.
Esophagus	Contains the microorganisms swallowed with saliva or food.
Stomach	The hydrochloric acid in gastric juice kills most bacteria. This may not be effective if large numbers of a pathogen or bacterial toxins are present in contaminated food.
Small intestine	The ileum, adjacent to the colon, has the largest bacterial population. The duodenum, adjacent to the stomach, has the smallest.
Large intestine	Contains an enormous population of bacteria, which inhibits the growth of pathogens and produces vitamins. The vitamins are absorbed as the colon absorbs water. Vitamin K is obtained in amounts usually sufficient to meet a person's daily need. Smaller amounts of folic acid, riboflavin, and other vitamins are also obtained from colon flora.
Urinary bladder	Is virtually free of bacteria, as is the upper urethra. The lower urethra, especially in women, has a flora similar to that of the skin.
Vagina	A large bacterial population creates an acidic pH that inhibits the growth of pathogens.
Tissue fluid	Small numbers of bacteria and viruses penetrate mucous membranes or get through breaks in the skin. Most are destroyed in lymph nodules or lymph nodes or by wandering macrophages in tissue fluid.
Blood	Should be free of microorganisms.

be able to germinate into active cells that produce toxin in the baby's own intestine. For older children or adults, botulism spores are harmless if ingested, because the normal colon flora prevents the growth of these bacteria.

Resident flora may be diminished by the use of antibiotics to treat bacterial infections. An antibiotic does not distinguish between the pathogen and the resident bacteria. In such circumstances, without the usual competition, yeasts or pathogenic bacteria may be able to overgrow and create new infections. This is most likely to occur on mucous membranes such as those of the oral cavity and vagina.

INFECTIOUS DISEASE

An infectious disease is one that is caused by microorganisms or by the products (toxins) of microorganisms. To cause an infection, a microorganism must enter and establish itself in a host and begin reproducing.

Several factors determine whether a person will develop an infection when exposed to a pathogen. These include the virulence of the pathogen and the resistance of the host. **Virulence** is the ability of the pathogen to cause disease. Host **resistance** is the total of the body's defenses against pathogens. Our defenses include intact skin and mucous membranes, the sweeping of cilia to clear the respiratory tract, adequate nutrition, and the immune responses of our lymphocytes and macrophages (see Chapter 14).

To illustrate these concepts, let us compare the measles virus and rhinoviruses (common cold). The measles virus has at least a 90% infectivity rate, meaning that for every 100 non-immune people exposed, at least 90 will develop clinical measles. Thus, the measles virus is considered highly virulent, even for healthy people. However, people who have recovered from measles or who have received the measles vaccine have developed an active immunity which increases their resistance to measles. Even if exposed many times, such people probably will not develop clinical measles.

In contrast, the rhinoviruses that cause the common cold are not considered virulent pathogens, and healthy people may have them in their upper respiratory tracts without developing illness. However, fatigue, malnutrition, and other physiological stresses may lower a person's resistance and increase the likelihood of developing a cold upon exposure to these viruses.

Once infected, a person may have a **clinical (apparent** or **symptomatic)** infection, in which symptoms appear. **Symptoms** are the observable or measurable changes that indicate illness. For some diseases, **subclinical (inapparent** or **asymptomatic)** infections are possible, in which the person shows no symptoms. Women with the sexually transmitted disease gonorrhea, for example, may have subclinical infections, that is, no symptoms at all. It is important to remember that such people are still **reservoirs** (sources) of the pathogen for others, who may then develop clinical infections.

COURSE OF AN INFECTIOUS DISEASE

When a pathogen establishes itself in a host, there is a period of time before symptoms appear. This is called the **incubation period.** Most infectious diseases have rather specific incubation periods (Table 22–2). Some diseases, however, have more variable incubation periods (see hepatitis in Table 22–2),

Table 22–2 INCUBATION PERIODS OF SOME INFECTIOUS DISEASES

Disease	Incubation Period
Chickenpox	14–16 days
Cholera	1–3 days
Diphtheria	2–6 days
Gas gangrene	1–5 days
Gonorrhea	3–5 days
Hepatitis A	2 weeks–2 months
Hepatitis B	6 weeks–6 months
Hepatitis C	2 weeks–6 months
Herpes simplex	4 days
Influenza	1–3 days
Leprosy	3 months–20+ years
Measles	10–12 days
Meningitis (bacterial)	1–7 days
Mumps	2–3 weeks
Pertussis	5 days–3 weeks
Pinworm	2–6 weeks
Plague	2–6 days
Polio	7–14 days
Rabies	2 weeks–2 months (up to 1 year)
Salmonella food poisoning	12–72 hours
Staphyloccus food poisoning	1–8 hours
Syphilis	10 days–3 months
Tetanus	3 days–5 weeks
Tuberculosis	2–10 weeks

which may make it difficult to predict the onset of illness after exposure or to trace outbreaks of a disease.

A short time called the prodromal period may follow the incubation period. During this time, vague, non-specific symptoms may begin. These include generalized muscle aches, lethargy and fatigue, or a feeling that "I'm coming down with something."

During the invasion period, the specific symptoms of the illness appear. These might include a high fever, rash, swollen lymph nodes, cough, diarrhea, or such things as the gradual paralysis of botulism. The acme is the height or worst of the disease, and this is followed by recovery or the death of the host.

Some diseases are **self-limiting;** that is, they typically last a certain length of time and are usually followed by recovery. The common cold, chickenpox, and mumps are illnesses that are considered self-limiting.

TYPES OF INFECTION

The terminology of infection may refer to the location of the pathogens in the body, to the general nature of the disease, or to how or where the pathogen was acquired.

A **localized** infection is one that is confined to one area of the body. Examples are the common cold of the upper respiratory tract, boils of the skin, and salmonella food poisoning which affects the intestines.

In a **systemic** infection, the pathogen is spread throughout the body by way of the lymph or blood. Typhoid fever, for example, begins as an intestinal infection, but the bacteria eventually spread to the liver, gallbladder, kidneys, and other organs. Bubonic plague is an infection that begins in lymph nodes, but again the bacteria are carried throughout the body, and fatal plague is the result of pneumonia.

Bacteremia and **septicemia** are terms that are often used synonymously in clinical practice; they mean that bacteria are present in the blood and are being circulated throughout the body. Septicemia is always serious, for it means that the immune defenses have been completely overwhelmed and are unable to stop the spread of the pathogen.

With respect to timing and duration, some infections may be called acute or chronic. An **acute** infection is one that usually begins abruptly and is severe. In contrast, a **chronic** infection often progresses slowly and may last for a long time.

A **secondary** infection is one that is made possible by a primary infection that has lowered the host's resistance. Influenza in an elderly person, for example, may be followed by bacterial pneumonia. This secondary bacterial infection might not have occurred had not the person first been ill with the flu.

Nosocomial infections are those that are acquired in hospitals or other institutions such as nursing homes. The hospital population includes newborns, the elderly, post-operative patients, people with serious chronic diseases, cancer patients receiving chemotherapy, and others whose resistance to disease is lowered. Some hospital-acquired pathogens, such as *Staphylococcus aureus,* are transmitted from patient to patient by healthy hospital personnel. These staff members are reservoirs for *S. aureus* and carry it on their skin or in their upper respiratory tracts. For this reason, proper hand-washing is of critical importance for all hospital staff.

Other nosocomial infections, however, are caused by the patient's own normal flora that has been inadvertently introduced into an abnormal body site. Such infections may be called **endogenous,** which literally means generated from within. Intestinal bacilli such as *E. coli* are now the number one cause of nosocomial infections. Without very careful aseptic technique (and sometimes in spite of it), the patient's own intestinal bacteria may contaminate urinary catheters, decubitus ulcers, surgical incisions, chest tubes, and intravenous lines. Such infections are a significant problem in hospitals, and all those involved in any aspect of patient care should be aware of this.

EPIDEMIOLOGY

Epidemiology is the study of the patterns and spread of disease within a population. As you see, this term is related to **epidemic,** which is an outbreak of disease, that is, more than the usual number of cases in a given time period. An **endemic** disease is one that is present in a population, with an expected or usual number of cases in a given time. Influenza, for example, is endemic in large cities during the winter, and public health personnel expect a certain number of cases. In some winters, however, the number of cases of influenza increases, often markedly, and this is an epidemic.

A **pandemic** is an epidemic that has spread throughout several countries. The bubonic plague pandemic of the 14th century affected nearly all of Europe and killed one fourth of the population. Just after World War I, in 1918 to 1920, an especially virulent strain of the influenza virus spread around the world and caused 20 million deaths. More recently, an epidemic of cholera began in Peru in January 1991, but soon became a pandemic as cholera spread to neighboring South American countries.

To understand the epidemiology of a disease, we must know several things about the pathogen.

These include where it lives in a host, the kinds of hosts it can infect, and whether it can survive outside of hosts.

PORTALS OF ENTRY AND EXIT

The **portal of entry** is the way the pathogen enters a host (Fig. 22–1). Breaks in the skin, even very small ones, are potential portals of entry, as are the natural body openings. Pathogens may be inhaled, consumed with food and water, or acquired during sexual activity. Most pathogens that enter the body by way of these natural routes are destroyed by the white blood cells found in and below the skin and mucous membranes, but some may be able to establish themselves and cause disease.

Insects such as mosquitoes, fleas, and lice, and other arthropods, such as ticks, are vectors of disease. They spread pathogens when they bite to obtain a host's blood. Mosquitoes, for example, are vectors of malaria, yellow fever, and encephalitis. Ticks are vectors of Lyme disease and Rocky Mountain spotted fever.

As mentioned previously, it is important to keep in mind that many hospital procedures may provide portals of entry for pathogens. Any invasive procedure, whether it involves the skin or the mucous membranes, may allow pathogens to enter the body. Thus it is essential that all health-care workers follow aseptic technique for such procedures.

The **portal of exit** (see Fig. 22–1) is the way the pathogen leaves the body or is shed from the host. Skin lesions, such as those of chickenpox, contain pathogens that may be transmitted to others by cutaneous contact. Intestinal pathogens such as the hepatitis A virus and the cholera bacteria are excreted in the host's feces, which may contaminate food or water and be ingested by another host (this is called the fecal-oral route of transmission). Respiratory pathogens such as influenza and measles viruses are shed in respiratory droplets from the mouth and nose and may be inhaled by another person. The pathogens of the reproductive tract, such as the bacteria that cause syphilis and gonorrhea, are transmitted to others by sexual contact. Notice that with respect to epidemiology, the pathogen travels from one host's portal of exit to another host's portal of entry.

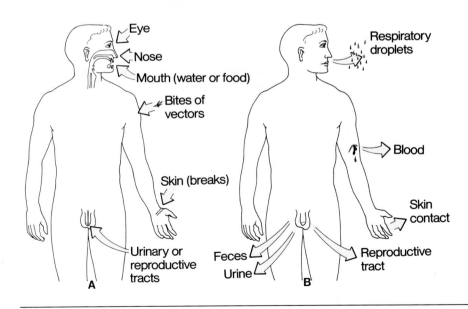

Figure 22–1 (**A**), Portals of entry. (**B**), Portals of exit.

RESERVOIRS OF INFECTION

Some pathogens cause disease only in people. Measles, whooping cough, syphilis, and bacterial meningitis are strictly human diseases. To acquire such a disease, a person must be exposed to someone who has the illness.

Also of importance is that upon recovery from some diseases, the host may continue to harbor the pathogen and thus be a reservoir of it for others. Such a person is called a **carrier.** Diseases for which the carrier state is possible include typhoid, diphtheria, and hepatitis B.

Many other diseases, however, are really animal diseases that people acquire in certain circumstances. These diseases are called **zoonoses** (singular **zoonosis**) and include plague, Lyme disease, encephalitis, and Rocky Mountain spotted fever, which are spread from animal to person by vectors such as ticks or fleas. Rabies is acquired by contact with infected animal saliva or infected tissue, the virus entering the new host through breaks in the skin. Salmonellosis is a type of food poisoning caused by the intestinal bacilli of animals that contaminate meats such as chicken and turkey. Prevention of such diseases depends upon knowledge of how they are spread. For example, people who live in areas where Lyme disease is endemic should be aware that the disease is acquired by way of a tick bite. If children and pets are examined for ticks after they have been out of doors, the chance of acquiring Lyme disease is greatly diminished.

Some bacteria are pathogenic only by accident, for their natural habitat is soil or water, where they act as decomposers. The bacteria that cause gas gangrene, tetanus, and botulism are normal soil flora and cause disease when they (or their toxins) contaminate a skin wound, or, in the case of botulism, the toxin is present in food.

SPREAD OF INFECTION

Based on our knowledge thus far, we can classify infectious diseases as non-communicable or communicable. A **non-communicable** disease is one in which a resident species causes disease under certain conditions or in which a non-resident species causes disease when it enters the body. Such diseases cannot be transmitted directly or indirectly from host to host. Cystitis caused by *E. coli* in a hospital patient, for example, is not communicable to the nurses who care for that patient. Similarly, a nurse caring for a patient with tetanus or botulism need not worry about acquiring these diseases; both are non-communicable.

A **communicable** disease is one in which the pathogen may be transmitted directly or indirectly from host to host. Direct spread of infection is by way of cutaneous contact (including sexual contact), respiratory droplets, contaminated blood, or placental transmission from mother to fetus. Indirect spread is by way of contaminated food or water, or vectors, or **fomites,** which are inanimate objects that carry the pathogen. Influenza and cold viruses, for example, can survive outside their hosts for a time, so that objects such as eating utensils may be vehicles of transmission for these pathogens.

Some communicable diseases may also be called **contagious,** which means that they are easily spread from person to person by casual cutaneous contact or by respiratory droplets. Chickenpox, measles, and influenza are contagious diseases. In contrast, AIDS is not contagious, because sexual contact, blood contact, or placental transmission is necessary to acquire the virus (HIV). HIV is not spread by cutaneous contact or by respiratory droplets.

METHODS OF CONTROL OF MICROBES

Microorganisms are everywhere in our environment, and although we need not always be aware of their presence, there are times when we must try to diminish or even eliminate them. These situations include the use of chemicals for disinfection, especially in hospitals, and the protection of our food and water supplies.

ANTISEPTICS, DISINFECTANTS, AND STERILIZATION

We are all familiar with the practice of applying iodine, hydrogen peroxide, or alcohol to minor cuts in the skin, and we know the purpose of this: to prevent bacterial infection. The use of such chemicals does indeed destroy many harmful bacteria, although it has no effect on bacterial spores. The chemicals used to prevent infection may be called antiseptics or disinfectants. An **antiseptic** (anti = against; septic = infection) is a chemical that destroys bacteria or inhibits their growth on a living being. The chemicals named above are antiseptics on skin surfaces. A **disinfectant** is a chemical that is used on inanimate objects. Chemicals with antibacterial effects may be further classified as bactericidal or bacteriostatic. **Bactericides** kill bacteria by disrupting important metabolic processes. **Bacteriostatic** chemicals do not destroy bacteria, but rather inhibit their reproduction and slow their growth. Alcohol, for example, is a bactericide that is both an antiseptic and a disinfectant, depending upon the particular surface on which it is used.

One other antiseptic deserves mention, silver nitrate. A 1% solution of silver nitrate is used as eyedrops for newborns to prevent gonococcal infections. This practice has virtually eliminated gonococcal conjunctivitis in newborns, which if untreated, can result in blindness.

Some chemicals are not suitable for use on human skin because they are irritating or damaging, but they may be used on environmental surfaces as disinfectants. Bleach, such as Clorox, and cresols, such as Lysol, may be used in bathrooms, on floors or countertops, and even on dishes and eating utensils (if rinsed thoroughly). These bactericides will also destroy certain viruses, such as those that cause influenza. A dilute (10%) bleach solution will inactivate HIV, the virus that causes AIDS.

In hospitals, environmental surfaces are disinfected, but materials such as surgical instruments, sutures, and dressings must be sterilized. **Sterilization** is a process that destroys all living organisms. Most medical and laboratory products are sterilized by autoclaving. An **autoclave** is a chamber in which steam is generated under pressure. This pressurized steam penetrates the contents of the chamber and kills all microorganisms present, including bacterial spores.

Materials such as disposable plastics that might be damaged by autoclaving are often sterilized by exposure to ionizing radiation. Foods such as meats may also be sterilized by this method. Such food products have a very long shelf life (equivalent to canned food), and this procedure is used for preparing some military field rations.

PUBLIC HEALTH MEASURES

Each of us is rightfully concerned with our own health and the health of our families. People who work in the public health professions, however, consider the health of all of us, that is, the health of a population. Two important aspects of public health are ensuring safe food and safe drinking water.

Food

The safety of our food depends on a number of factors. Most cities have certain standards and practices that must be followed by supermarkets and restaurants, and inspections are conducted on a regular basis.

Food companies prepare their products by using specific methods to prevent the growth of microorganisms. Naturally, it is in the best interests of these companies to do so, for they would soon be out of business if their products made people ill. Also of importance is the willingness of companies to recall products that are only suspected of being contaminated. This is all to the benefit of consumers. For example, since 1925 in the United States, only five fatal cases of botulism have been traced to commercially canned food. If we consider that billions of cans of food have been consumed during this time, we can appreciate the high standards the food industry has maintained.

Milk and milk products provide ideal environments for the growth of bacteria because they contain both protein and sugar (lactose) as food sources. For this reason, milk must be **pasteurized,** that is, heated to 145°F (62.9°C) for 30 minutes. Newer methods of pasteurization use higher temperatures for shorter periods of time, but the result is the same: the pathogens that may be present in milk are killed, although not all bacteria are totally destroyed. Milk products such as cheese and ice cream are also pasteurized, or are made from pasteurized milk.

When a food-related outbreak of disease does take place, public health workers try to trace the outbreak to its source. This stops the immediate spread of disease by preventing access to the contaminated food, and the ensuing publicity on television or in the newspapers may help remind everyone of the need for careful monitoring of food preparation.

Finally, the safety of our food may depend on something we often take for granted: our refrigerators. For example, a Thanksgiving turkey that was carved for dinner at 3 pm and left on the kitchen counter until midnight probably should not be used for turkey sandwiches the next day. Although we have to rely on others to assure that commercially prepared food will be safe, once food reaches our homes, all we really need (besides the refrigerator) is our common sense.

Water

When we turn on a faucet to get a glass of water, we usually do not wonder whether the water is safe to drink. It usually is. Having a reliable supply of clean drinking water depends on two things: diverting human sewage away from water supplies and chlorinating water intended for human consumption.

Large cities have sewer systems for the collection of waste water and its subsequent treatment in sewage plants. Once treated, however, the sludge (solid, particulate matter) from these plants must be disposed of. This is becoming more of a problem simply because there is so much sewage sludge (because there are so many of us). Although the sludge is largely free of pathogens, it ought not be put in landfills, and since ocean dumping is being prohibited in many coastal areas, this is a problem that will be with us for a long time.

Drinking water for cities and towns is usually chlorinated. The added chlorine kills virtually all the bacteria that may be present. The importance of chlorination is shown by a 1978 outbreak of enteritis (diarrhea) in a Vermont town of 10,000 people. The chlorination process malfunctioned for 2 days, and 2000 of the town's inhabitants became ill. (The bacterium was *Campylobacter*, a common intestinal inhabitant of animals).

You may now be wondering if all those bottled spring waters are safe to drink. The answer, in general, is yes, because the bottling companies do not wish to make people ill and put themselves out of business. Some bottled waters, however, do have higher mold spore counts than does chlorinated tap water. Usually these molds are not harmful when ingested; they are destroyed by the hydrochloric acid in gastric juice.

In much of North America, nearly everyone has easy access to safe drinking water. We might remind ourselves once in a while that our water will not give us typhoid, polio, or cholera. These diseases are still very common in other parts of the world, where the nearest river or stream is the laundry, the sewer, and the source of drinking water.

THE PATHOGENS

In the sections that follow, each group of pathogens will be described with a summary of important characteristics. Examples of specific pathogens will be given to help you become familiar with them. Tables of important human diseases caused by each group of pathogens are found at the end of this chapter.

BACTERIA (see Table 22–3, page 523)

Bacteria are very simple unicellular organisms. All are microscopic in size, and a magnification of 1000 times is usually necessary to see them clearly. A bacterial cell consists of watery cytoplasm and a single chromosome (made of DNA) surrounded by a cell membrane. Enclosing all of these structures is a cell wall, which is strong and often rigid, giving the bacterium its characteristic shape.

Based on shape, bacteria are classified as one of

three groups: coccus, bacillus, or spirillum (Fig. 22–2). A **coccus** (plural: **cocci**) is a sphere; under the microscope cocci appear round. Certain prefixes may be used to describe the arrangement of spheres. **Staphylo** means clusters; **strepto** refers to chains of cells, and **diplo** means pairs of cells.

A **bacillus** (plural: **bacilli**) is a rod-shaped bacterium; rods may vary in length depending on the genus. A **spirillum** (plural: **spirilla**) is a long cell with one or more curves or coils. Some spirilla, such as those that cause syphilis and Lyme disease, are called **spirochaetes.** Many of the bacilli and spirilla are capable of movement because they have **flagella.** These are long, thread-like structures that project from the cell and beat rhythmically.

Bacteria reproduce by the process of **binary fission,** in which the chromosome duplicates itself, and the original cell divides into two identical cells. The presence or absence of oxygen may be impor-tant for bacterial reproduction. **Aerobic** bacteria can reproduce only in the presence of oxygen, and **anaerobic** bacteria can reproduce only in the absence of oxygen. **Facultatively anaerobic** bacteria are not inhibited in either situation; they are able to reproduce in either the presence or absence of oxygen. This is obviously an advantage for the bacteria, and many pathogens and potential pathogens are facultative anaerobes.

The Gram Stain

Based on the chemicals in their cell walls, most bacteria can be put into one of two groups, called **gram positive** and **gram negative.** A simple lab-oratory procedure called the **Gram stain** shows us the shape of the bacteria and their gram reactions. Gram positive bacteria appear purple or blue, and gram negative bacteria appear pink or red. Some

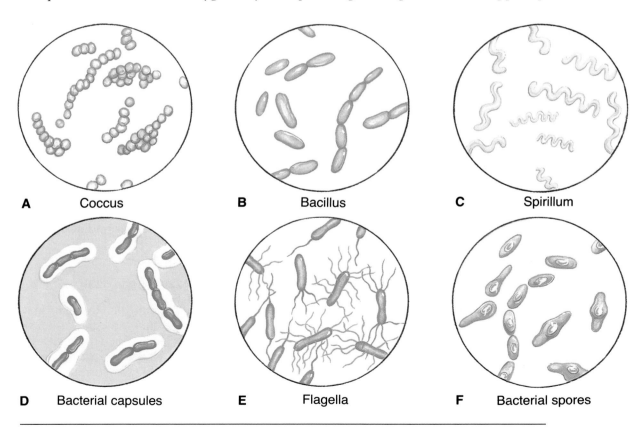

A Coccus   B Bacillus   C Spirillum

D Bacterial capsules   E Flagella   F Bacterial spores

Figure 22–2 Bacterial shapes and specialized structures (magnification × 2000).

bacteria do not stain with the gram method, but for those that do, each genus is either gram positive or gram negative. This does not change, just as the characteristic shape of the bacteria does not change. The genus *Streptococcus,* for example, is always a gram positive coccus; the genus *Escherichia* is always a gram negative bacillus. If a Gram stain is done on a sputum specimen from a patient with pneumonia, and a gram positive coccus is found, this eliminates all the gram negative cocci and bacilli that may also cause pneumonia. The Gram stain, therefore, is often an important first step in the indentification of the pathogen that is causing a particular infection. In Table 22–3 (at the end of this chapter), the gram reaction (where applicable) and shape are included for each pathogen.

Special Characteristics

Although bacteria are simple cells, many have special structural or functional characteristics that help them to survive. Some bacilli and cocci have capsules (see Fig. 22–2); a **capsule** is a gelatinous sheath that encloses the entire cell. Capsules are beneficial to the bacteria because they inhibit phagocytosis by the host's white blood cells. This gives the bacteria time to reproduce and possibly establish themselves in the host. This is *not* beneficial from our point of view (remember that we are the hosts), but bacterial capsules are also **antigenic,** which means that they stimulate antibody production by our lymphocytes. This starts the destruction of bacteria by our immune responses. We take advantage of this by using bacterial capsules in some of our vaccines, such as those used to prevent pneumonia and meningitis.

Some bacilli are able to survive unfavorable environments by forming spores. A **spore** is a dormant (inactive) stage that consists of the chromosome and a small amount of cytoplasm surrounded by a thick wall. Spores can survive conditions such as heat (even boiling), freezing, or dehydration, which would kill the vegetative (active) forms of the bacterial cells. Fortunately for us, most pathogens are unable to form spores, but some that do are the causative agents of gas gangrene, botulism, and tetanus. These bacteria are decomposers in the soil environment, and their spore-forming ability en-

ables them to survive the extremes of temperature and lack of water that may occur in the soil.

Many bacteria cause disease because they produce **toxins,** which are chemicals that are harmful to host tissues. Often these toxins are the equivalent of our digestive enzymes, which break down the food we eat. Some bacterial toxins such as hemolysins and proteases literally digest host tissues such as red blood cells and proteins. The bacteria then absorb the digested nutrients.

The toxins of other bacteria have very specific effects on certain cells of the host. Botulism and tetanus toxins, for example, are **neurotoxins** that disrupt the functioning of nerve cells, leading to the characteristic symptoms of each disease. The diphtheria toxin causes heart failure, the pertussis (whooping cough) toxin immobilizes the cilia of the respiratory tract, and the cholera enterotoxin causes diarrhea (see also Table 22–3).

The cell walls of gram negative bacteria are made of chemicals that are called endotoxins. **Endotoxins** all have the same effects on the host: they cause fever and circulatory shock (low blood pressure and heart failure). **Endotoxin shock** (also called **gram negative shock**) is a life-threatening condition that may accompany any serious infection with gram negative bacteria.

Rickettsias and Chlamydias

These two groups of bacteria differ from most other bacteria in that they are obligate intracellular parasites. This means that they can reproduce only within the living cells of a host.

The rickettsias are parasites of mammals (including people) and are often spread by arthropod vectors. In the United States, the most common rickettsial disease is Rocky Mountain spotted fever, which is spread by ticks. In other parts of the world, epidemic typhus, which is spread by body lice, is still an important disease. From a historical perspective, until World War I, more people died of epidemic typhus during times of war than were killed by weapons.

The chlamydias cause several human diseases, including ornithosis (parrot fever) and trachoma, which is the leading cause of blindness throughout the world. In the United States, chlamydial infection of the genitourinary tract has become the most prevalent sexually transmitted disease, with estimates of 4 million new cases each year.

Both rickettsial and chlamydial infections can be treated with antibiotics.

Antibiotics

Antibiotics are chemicals that are used to treat bacterial infections. A **broad-spectrum** antibiotic is one that affects many different kinds of bacteria; a **narrow-spectrum** antibiotic affects just a few kinds of bacteria.

The use of antibiotics is based on a very simple principle: certain chemicals can disrupt or inhibit the chemical reactions that bacteria must carry out to survive. An antibiotic such as penicillin blocks the formation of bacterial cell walls; without their cell walls, bacteria will die. Other antibiotics inhibit DNA synthesis or protein synthesis. These are vital activities for the bacteria, and without them bacteria cannot reproduce and will die.

It is very important to remember that our own cells carry out chemical reactions that are very similar to some of those found in bacteria. For this reason, our own cells may be damaged by antibiotics. This is why some antibiotics have harmful side effects. The most serious side effects are liver and kidney damage or depression of the red bone marrow. The liver is responsible for detoxifying the medication, which may accumulate and damage liver cells. Similar damage may occur in the kidneys, which are responsible for excreting the medication. The red bone marrow is a very active tissue, with constant mitosis and protein synthesis to produce RBCs, WBCs, and platelets. Any antibiotic that interferes with these processes may decrease production of all of these blood cells. Patients who are receiving any of the potentially toxic antibiotics should be monitored with periodic tests of liver and kidney function or with blood counts to assess the state of the red bone marrow.

Another problem with the use of antibiotics is that bacteria may become resistant to them, and so be unaffected. Bacterial **resistance** means that the bacteria are able to produce an enzyme that destroys the antibiotic, rendering it useless. This is a genetic capability on the part of bacteria, and it is,

therefore, passed to new generations of bacteria cells. Most strains of *Staphylococcus aureus,* for example, are resistant to penicillin and other antibiotics. Most of the gram negative intestinal bacilli are resistant to a great variety of antibiotics. This is why **culture and sensitivity testing** is so important before an antibiotic is chosen to treat these infections.

To counteract bacterial resistance, new antibiotics are produced that are not inactivated by the destructive bacterial enzymes. Within a few years, however, the usefulness of these new antibiotics will probably diminish as bacteria mutate and develop resistance. This is not a battle that we can ever truly win, because bacteria are living organisms that evolve as their environment changes.

Antibiotics have changed our lives, although we may not always realize that today. A child's strep throat will probably not progress to ear infections and meningitis, and bacterial pneumonia does not have the very high fatality rate that it once did. But, we must keep in mind that antibiotics are not a "cure" for any disease. An infection, especially a serious one, means that the immune system has been overwhelmed by the pathogen. An antibiotic diminishes the number of bacteria to a level with which the immune system can cope. Ultimately, however, the body's own white blood cells must eliminate the very last of the bacteria.

VIRUSES (see Table 22–4, page 527)

Viruses are not cells; their structure is even simpler than that of bacteria, which are the simplest cells. A virus consists of either DNA or RNA surrounded by a protein shell. The protein shell has a shape that is characteristic for each virus (Fig. 22–3). There are no enzymes, cytoplasm, cell membranes, or cell walls in viruses, and they can reproduce only when inside the living cells of a host. Therefore, all viruses are obligate intracellular parasites, and they cause disease when they reproduce inside cells. When a virus enters a host cell, it uses the cell's chromosomes, RNA, and enzymes to make new viruses. Several hundred new viruses may be produced from just one virus. The host cell ruptures and dies, releasing the new viruses, which then enter other cells and reproduce.

The severity of a viral disease depends upon the

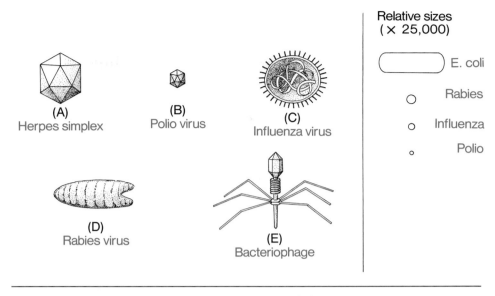

Figure 22–3 Viruses: representative shapes and relative sizes.

types of cells infected. If the virus affects skin cells, for example, the disease is usually mild and self-limiting, such as chickenpox. Small numbers of skin cells are not crucial to our survival, and these cells can be replaced by mitosis. If, however, the virus affects nerve cells, the disease is more serious and may be fatal. Rabies is such a disease. Neurons are much more vital to us, and they cannot be replaced once they die.

Some viruses, such as those that cause German measles (rubella) and chickenpox, are able to cross the placenta, that is, pass from maternal circulation to fetal circulation. Although the disease may be very mild for the pregnant woman, the virus may severely damage developing fetal organs and cause congenital birth defects such as blindness, heart malformations, and mental retardation. In the most serious cases, fetal infection may result in miscarriage or stillbirth.

There are some viruses that cause an initial infection, become dormant, then are reactivated, causing another infection months or years later. The herpes viruses that cause cold sores "hide out" in nerves of the face following the initial skin lesion. At some later time when the host's resistance is lowered, the viruses emerge from the nerves and cause another

cold sore. The chickenpox virus, which most of us acquire as children, is a herpes virus that may become dormant in nerves for years, and then be reactivated and cause shingles when we are adults.

A few human viruses are known to be tumor viruses, that is, they cause cells to develop abnormally and form tumors. The Epstein-Barr virus, which causes mononucleosis in North America, is associated with Burkitt's lymphoma in Africa and with nasopharyngeal carcinoma in China. There are environmental factors, as yet unknown, that contribute to the development of these cancers in specific parts of the world. Several of the human papilloma viruses have also been associated with cancers of the mouth or larynx, and three of these viruses are found in 90% of cervical carcinomas in women.

Important viral diseases are described in Table 22–4 at the end of this chapter.

Antiviral Medications

The treatment of viral diseases with chemicals poses some formidable challenges. First, viruses are active (reproducing) only within cells, so the medication must be able to enter infected cells to be effective. Second, viruses are such simple structures that the choice of which of their chemical processes to attempt to disrupt is limited. Third, viruses use the host cell's DNA and enzymes for self replication, and a medication that interferes with DNA or enzymes may kill the host cell even as it kills the virus.

These problems are illustrated by zidovudine (AZT), the first medication thought to be effective against HIV, the virus that causes AIDS. Zidovudine works by interfering with DNA synthesis, which the virus must carry out to reproduce. The side effects of zidovudine, which are experienced by a significant number of AIDS patients, are caused by the disruption of DNA synthesis in the person's own cells.

Despite these obstacles, a few successful antiviral drugs have been developed. Acyclovir, for example, has proved to be useful in the control (not cure) of herpes viruses. Ribavirin has been quite effective in the treatment of respiratory syncytial virus pneumonia in infants and young children. This is an area of intensive research, and more antiviral medications will undoubtedly be found within the next decade.

FUNGI (see Table 22–5, page 528)

Fungi may be unicellular, such as yeasts, or multicellular, such as the familiar molds and mushrooms. Most fungi are **saprophytes,** that is, they live on dead organic matter and decompose it to recycle the chemicals as nutrients. The pathogenic fungi cause infections that are called **mycoses** (singular: **mycosis**), which may be superficial or systemic.

Yeasts (Fig. 22–4) have been used by people for thousands of years in baking and brewing. In small numbers, yeasts such as *Candida albicans* are part of the resident flora of the skin, mouth, intestines, and vagina. In larger numbers, however, yeasts may cause superficial infections of mucous membranes or the skin, or very serious systemic infections of internal organs. An all-too-common trigger for oral or vaginal yeast infections is the use of an antibiotic to treat a bacterial infection. The antibiotic diminishes the normal bacterial flora, thereby removing competition for the yeasts, which are then able to overgrow. Yeasts may also cause skin infections in

diabetics, or in obese people who have skin folds that are always moist. In recent years, *Candida* has become an important cause of nosocomial infections. The resistance of hospital patients is often lowered because of their diseases or treatments, and they are more susceptible to systemic yeast infections in the form of pneumonia or endocarditis.

Another superficial mycosis is ringworm (Tinea), which may be caused by several species of fungi (see Table 22–5 at the end of this chapter). The name *ringworm* is misleading, since there are no worms involved. It is believed to have come from the appearance of the lesions: circular, scaly patches with reddened edges, the center clears as the lesion grows. Athlete's foot, which is probably a bacterial-fungal infection, is perhaps the most common form of ringworm.

The systemic mycoses are more serious diseases that occur when spores of some fungi gain access to the interior of the body. Most of these fungi grow in a mold-like pattern. The molds we sometimes see on stale bread or overripe fruit look fluffy or fuzzy. The fluff is called a mycelium and is made of many thread-like cellular structures called hyphae. The color of a mold is due to the spore cases (sporangia) in which spores are produced (see Fig. 22–4). Each spore may be carried by the air to another site, where it germinates and forms another mycelium.

Since spores of these fungi are common in the environment, they are often inhaled. The immune responses are usually able to prevent infection, however, and healthy people are usually not susceptible to systemic mycoses. Elderly people and those with chronic pulmonary diseases are much more susceptible, however, and they may develop lung infections. The importance of the immune system is clearly evident if we consider people with AIDS. Without the normal immune responses, AIDS patients are very susceptible to invasive fungal diseases, including meningitis caused by *Cryptococcus*.

Antifungal Medications

One of the most effective drugs used to treat serious, systemic mycoses, amphotericin B, has great potential to cause serious side effects. Patients receiving this medication should have periodic tests

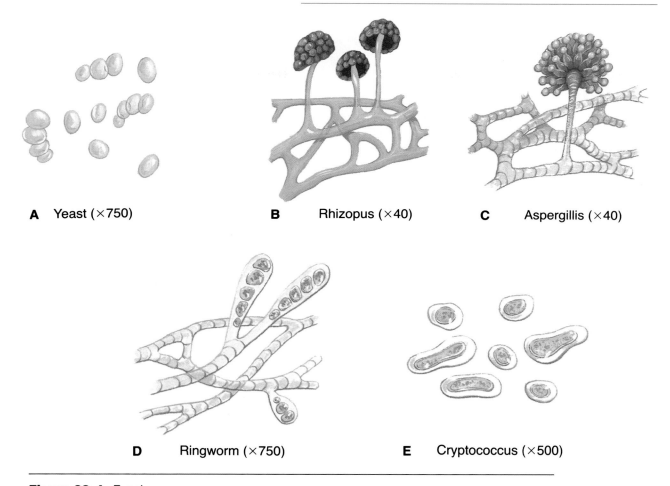

A   Yeast (×750)   **B**   Rhizopus (×40)   **C**   Aspergillis (×40)

D   Ringworm (×750)   **E**   Cryptococcus (×500)

Figure 22–4 Fungi.

of liver and kidney function. Newer medications include ketoconazole and fluconazole, which are less toxic to the recipient and may prove to be as effective as amphotericin B.

Superficial mycoses such as ringworm are treated with drugs such as griseofulvin. Taken orally, the drug is incorporated into living epidermal cells. When these cells die and reach the stratum corneum, they are resistant to the digestive action of the ringworm fungi.

There are several effective medications for mucosal yeast infections, but it is important that the trigger for the infection (such as antibiotic therapy) be resolved as well. If not, the yeast infection may recur when the medication is stopped.

PROTOZOA (see Table 22–6, page 529)

Protozoa are unicellular animals, single cells that are adapted to life in fresh water (including soil) and salt water. Some are human pathogens and are able to form cysts, which are resistant, dormant cells that are able to survive passage from host to host.

Intestinal protozoan parasites of people include *Entamoeba histolytica,* which causes amebic dysentery, and *Giardia lamblia,* which causes diarrhea called giardiasis (Fig. 22–5 and Table 22–6). People acquire these by ingesting food or water contaminated with the cysts of these species. Giardiasis can become a problem in day-care centers if the staff is

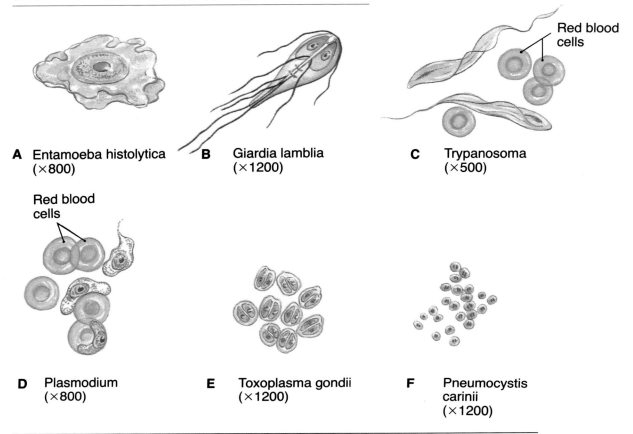

A Entamoeba histolytica
(×800)

B Giardia lamblia
(×1200)

C Trypanosoma
(×500)

Red blood
cells

Red blood
cells

D Plasmodium
(×800)

E Toxoplasma gondii
(×1200)

F Pneumocystis
carinii
(×1200)

Figure 22-5 Protozoa.

not careful concerning handwashing and food preparation.

Plasmodium, the genus that causes malaria, affects hundreds of millions of people throughout the world and is probably the most important protozoan parasite. The *Plasmodium* species are becoming increasingly resistant to the standard antimalarial drugs, which are used to prevent disease as well as cure it. Although work is progressing on malaria vaccines, one will probably not be available for several years.

One protozoan of which you have probably heard is *Pneumocystis carinii,* which causes pneumonia in people with AIDS. This species is usually not pathogenic, because the healthy immune system can easily control it. For AIDS patients, however, this form of pneumonia is often the cause of death.

Medications are available that can treat most protozoan infections. Intestinal protozoa, for example, may be treated with metronidazole or furazolidone. The drug pentamidine is used to treat pneumocystis pneumonia, although the underlying cause, AIDS, is not yet curable.

WORMS (HELMINTHS) (see Table 22–7, page 529)

Most worms are simple multicellular animals. The parasitic worms are even simpler than the familiar earthworm, because they live within hosts and use the host's blood or nutrients as food. Many of the parasitic worms have complex life cycles that involve two or more different host species.

The flukes are flatworms that are rare in most of North America but very common in parts of Africa

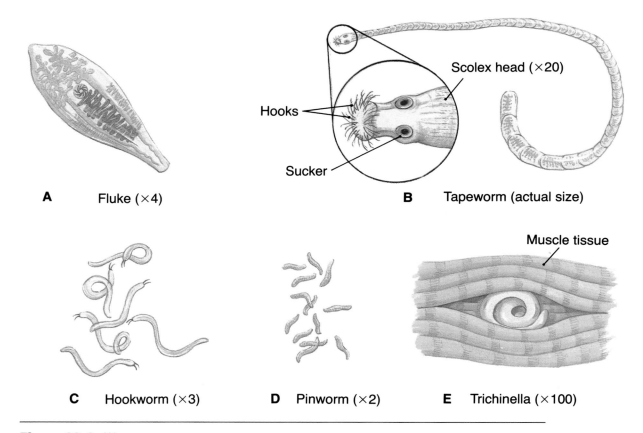

Figure 22–6 Worms.

and Asia. People acquire these species by eating aquatic plants or raw fish in which the larval worms have encysted. Within the person, each species lives in a specific site: the intestine, bile ducts, or even certain veins. Although rarely fatal, these chronic worm infestations are often debilitating, and the host person is a source of the eggs of the fluke, which may then infect others.

Tapeworms are also flatworms (Fig. 22–6). Some are 10 to 15 feet long, and the fish tapeworm can be as long as 60 feet. They are as flat as a ribbon, however, and one could easily be held in the palm of the hand. The tapeworm holds on to the lining of a host's small intestine with the suckers and hooks on its scolex (front end). The segments, called proglottids, are produced continuously in most species and absorb nutrients from the host's digested food. The only function of the proglottids is reproduction: eggs in one segment are fertilized by sperm from another segment. Mature proglottids containing fertilized eggs break off and are excreted in the host's feces. An intermediate host such as a cow or pig eats food contaminated with human feces, and the eggs hatch within this animal and grow into larval worms that encyst in the animal's muscle tissue. People become infected by eating poorly cooked beef or pork that contains cysts.

Parasitic roundworms of people include hookworm, pinworm, *Ascaris,* and *Trichinella* (see Table 22–7 at the end of this chapter). Medications are available that can eliminate worm infestations. In endemic areas, however, reinfestation is quite common.

ARTHROPODS (see Table 22–8, page 530)

Arthropods such as the scabies mite and head lice are **ectoparasites** that live on the surface of the

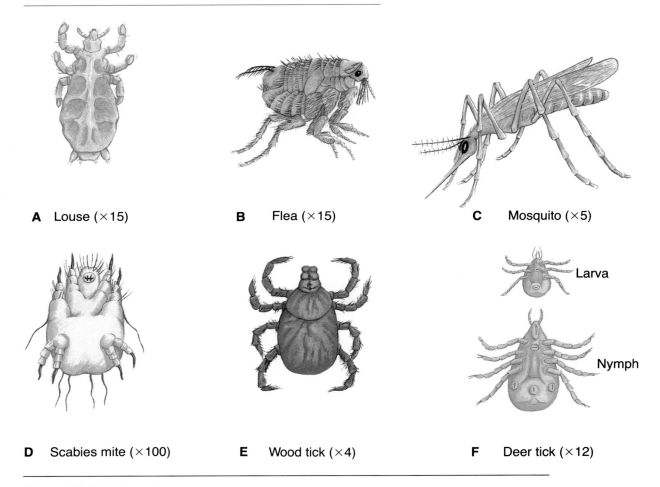

A Louse (×15)   **B** Flea (×15)   **C** Mosquito (×5)

D Scabies mite (×100)   **E** Wood tick (×4)   **F** Deer tick (×12)

Figure 22–7 Arthropods.

body. The infestations they cause are very itchy and uncomfortable but not debilitating or life threatening (Fig. 22–7). Of greater importance are the arthropods that are vectors of disease. These are listed in Table 22–8. Mosquitoes, fleas, lice, and flies are all insects. Ticks are not insects but are more closely related to spiders.

SUMMARY

The preceding discussion is an introduction to microorganisms and human disease, but it is only part of the story. The rest of this story is the remarkable ability of the human body to resist infection. Although we are surrounded and invaded by potential pathogens, most of us remain healthy most of the time. The immune responses that destroy pathogens and enable us to remain healthy are described in Chapter 14. Also in that chapter are discussions of vaccines. The development of vaccines represents the practical application of our knowledge of pathogens and of immunity, and it enables us to prevent many diseases. The availability of specific vaccines is noted in the tables of bacterial and viral diseases that follow.

Table 22-3   DISEASES CAUSED BY BACTERIA

Bacterial Species	Discussion/Disease(s) Caused
Staphylococcus aureus gram (+) coccus	Skin infections such as boils, pneumonia, toxic shock syndrome, osteomyelitis, septicemia, food poisoning. Most strains resistant to penicillin. Second-leading cause of nosocomial infections. No vaccine.
Staphylococcus epidermidis gram (+) coccus	Normal skin flora; potential pathogen for those with artificial internal prostheses such as heart valves and joints.
Streptococcus pyogenes gram (+) coccus	Strep throat, otitis media, scarlet fever, endocarditis, puerperal sepsis; possible immunologic complications are rheumatic fever (transient arthritis and permanent damage to heart valves) and glomerulonephritis (transient kidney damage, usually with complete recovery). No vaccine.
Streptococcus pneumoniae gram (+) coccus	Pneumonia: accumulation of fluids and white blood cells in the alveoli. The vaccine contains capsules of the most common strains; recommended for the elderly. Possible cause of meningitis in adults with predisposing factors such as sickle cell anemia, alcoholism, asplenism, or head trauma.
Streptococcus faecalis gram (+) coccus	Normal colon flora. Has become an important cause of nosocomial infections of the urinary tract.
Neisseria gonorrhoeae gram (−) coccus	Gonorrhea: inflammation of the mucous membranes of the reproductive and urinary tracts. May cause scarring of reproductive ducts and subsequent sterility; in women may cause pelvic inflammatory disease. Infants of infected women may acquire the bacteria during birth; this is ophthalmia neonatorum and is prevented by silver nitrate eyedrops. No vaccine.
Neisseria meningitidis gram (−) coccus	Meningitis: inflammation and edema of the meninges; pressure on the brain may cause death or permanent brain damage. Most common in older children and young adults. Most cases are sporadic, not part of epidemics. The vaccine is given to military recruits. Post-exposure prophylaxis (prevention) involves antibiotics.
Bacillus anthracis gram (+) bacillus (spore-forming)	Anthrax: spores in soil may be acquired by cattle or sheep. People acquire disease from these animals or from animal products such as wool or leather. Toxin causes death of tissue; may be fatal. Rare in the US, because grazing animals are vaccinated.
Clostridium perfringens gram (+) bacillus (spore-forming)	Gas gangrene: normal soil flora may contaminate wounds; spores require anaerobic environment (dead tissue); toxins destroy more tissue, permitting the bacteria to spread; gas produced collects as bubbles in dead tissue.
Clostridium tetani gram (+) bacillus (spore-forming)	Tetanus: normal soil flora may contaminate wounds; spores require anaerobic conditions. The toxin prevents muscle relaxation, resulting in muscle spasms. May be fatal if respiratory muscles are affected. The vaccine contains the toxoid (inactivated toxin) and has made this a rare disease in the US. Boosters are strongly recommended for older adults.
Clostridium botulinum gram (+) bacillus (spore-forming)	Botulism: normal soil flora; spores present in anaerobic food containers germinate and produce the toxin, which causes paralysis. Respiratory paralysis may be fatal without assisted ventilation. May cause infant botulism in children less than 2 years of age who have ingested spores. No vaccine. Treatment is antitoxin (antibodies).
Corynebacterium diphtheriae gram (+) bacillus	Diphtheria: toxin causes heart failure and paralysis; a pseudomembrane that grows in the pharynx may cover the larynx and cause suffocation. Vaccination of infants (DTP) has made this a very rare disease in the US. Older adults should receive boosters (combined with tetanus: DT).
Listeria monocytogenes gram (+) bacillus	Listeriosis: septicemia and meningitis in the elderly, infants, and unborn; may cause miscarriage or stillbirth. The bacteria are found in soil and in animals such as cattle. In the US, food poisoning outbreaks traced to contaminated milk or milk products. Sporadic cases traced to undercooked hot dogs or chicken or to cold cuts from delicatessen counters. No vaccine.

Table 22–3   DISEASES CAUSED BY BACTERIA (*Continued*)

Bacterial Species	Discussion/Disease(s) Caused
Salmonella typhi gram (−) bacillus	Typhoid fever: intestinal infection with erosion and septicemia; subsequent infection of liver, gallbladder, or kidneys. Upon recovery, the carrier state (bacteria in gallbladder) may occur. Rare in the US because of chlorination of drinking water. The vaccine is used in endemic areas of the world such as Asia.
Salmonella enteritidis and other species gram (−) bacillus	Salmonellosis: food poisoning following consumption of contaminated animal products such as poultry or eggs. Diarrhea is usually self-limiting, but it may be fatal for the elderly. In the US estimates are 4 million cases per year. No vaccine.
Shigella species gram (−) bacillus	Bacillary dysentery: mild to severe diarrhea; may be fatal because of dehydration and circulatory shock. Usually transmitted by food prepared by people with mild cases. No vaccine. An important cause of illness in day-care centers.
Escherichia coli, Serratia marcescens, Proteus vulgaris, and other genera of gram (−) bacilli	Normal colon flora; cause opportunistic infections when introduced into any other part of the body. This group is now the most common cause of nosocomial infections (urinary tract, pneumonia, skin infections).
Pseudomonas aeruginosa gram (−) bacillus	Normal soil and water flora; also transient in human intestines. A serious potential pathogen for patients with severe burns, cystic fibrosis (causes pneumonia), or cancer. May even survive in disinfectant solutions.
Yersinia pestis gram (−) bacillus	Bubonic plague: swollen lymph nodes, septicemia, and hemorrhagic pneumonia; often fatal. Animal reservoirs are prairie dogs, ground squirrels, and other rodents. Rats and people are infected by fleas (the vector). In the US, the few cases each year occur in the Southwest. The vaccine is not reliably protective.
Francisella tularensis gram (−) bacillus	Tularemia (rabbit fever): septicemia and pneumonia; not often fatal but very debilitating. Reservoirs are wild animals and birds. People are infected by vectors (ticks, lice, and biting flies), by ingestion of contaminated animal meat, or by inhalation. No vaccine.
Brucella species gram (−) bacillus	Brucellosis (undulant fever): extreme weakness and fatigue, anorexia, a fever that rises and falls. Reservoirs are cattle, sheep, goats, and pigs; people acquire infection by contact with contaminated animal products. In the US, this is an occupational disease: meat processing workers, vets, farmers. Vaccines are available for animals.
Haemophilis influenzae gram (−) bacillus	Meningitis in children, especially those less than 2 years of age. Older people may have mild upper respiratory infections. The vaccine (Hib) contains the capsules of the bacteria and is recommended for infants beginning at age 2 months. Prior to the vaccine this was the most common cause of meningitis in the US.
Haemophilis aegyptius gram (−) bacillus	Conjunctivitis: painful inflammation of the conjunctiva; spread by direct contact or formites; may occur in epidemics among groups of children.
Bordetella pertussis gram (−) bacillus	Whooping cough (pertussis): paroxysms of violent coughing that may last for several weeks. Pneumonia is a complication that may be fatal, especially for children less than 1 year of age. People are the only host, and the vaccine has eliminated epidemics in the US. Concern about the safety of the original vaccine has prompted the development of newer vaccines, which may further reduce the annual number of cases.

Table 22–3 DISEASES CAUSED BY BACTERIA (*Continued*)

Bacterial Species	Discussion/Disease(s) Caused
Vibrio cholerae gram (−) bacillus (comma shaped)	Cholera: profuse watery diarrhea; infection ranges from mild to fatal. Spread of infection is usually by way of water contaminated with human feces. Rare in the US; epidemic in Asia, Africa, and South America. The vaccine is not reliably protective.
Vibrio vulnificus gram (−) bacillus (comma shaped)	Gangrene and septicemia: acquired from ocean water that contaminates a wound or by the ingestion of raw shellfish. Illness is often severe and protracted, and it may be fatal.
Campylobacter species (new genus name: *Helicobacter*) gram (−) helical bacillus	Enteritis: diarrhea that is often self-limiting but may be severe in the elderly or very young. Reservoirs are animals such as poultry; people acquire infection from contaminated meat. In the US, estimates are 2 million cases per year. *Helicobacter pylori* has been linked with gastric ulcers and stomach cancer, but the exact relationship is still unknown.
Legionella pneumophilia gram (−) bacillus	Legionellosis, which occurs in two forms: Legionnaire's disease is a pneumonia that may be fatal; Pontiac fever is a mild upper respiratory infection that is usually self-limiting. The bacteria are found in natural water, including soil, and may contaminate air conditioning systems or water supplies. Person-to-person transmission does not seem to occur. Has become an important cause of nosocomial pneumonia. No vaccine.
Mycobacterium tuberculosis acid-fast bacillus	Tuberculosis (TB): formation of tubercles containing bacteria and white blood cells, usually in the lung. Lung tissue is destroyed (caseation necrosis) and is removed by macrophages, leaving large cavities. The bacteria are spread by respiratory droplets from people with active cases. Many people acquire a primary infection that becomes dormant and is without symptoms, yet may be triggered later into an active secondary infection. The BCG vaccine is not used in the US, but is in other parts of the world. In the US, TB cases are increasing among homeless people, those with AIDS, and in closed populations such as prisons. Strains of the bacteria resistant to the standard TB medications are becoming much more common and pose a difficult treatment problem.
Mycobacterium species acid-fast bacillus	Atypical mycobacterial infections: clinically similar to TB; usually in the lungs. These bacteria are pathogenic for people with AIDS or other forms of immunosuppression, and for those with chronic pulmonary diseases.
Mycobacterium leprae acid-fast bacillus	Leprosy (Hansen's disease): chronic disease characterized by disfiguring skin lesions and nerve damage that may cause paralysis or loss of sensation. The bacteria are acquired by cutaneous contact or respiratory droplets. The incubation period may be several years; children develop clinical disease more rapidly than do adults. A vaccine is in the testing stage.
Treponema pallidum spirochaete	Syphilis: a sexually transmitted disease that progresses in three stages. Primary syphilis: a painless, hard chancre at the site of entry on skin or mucous membrane. Secondary syphilis: a rash on the skin and mucous membranes (indicates systemic infection). Tertiary syphilis (5 to 40 years later): necrotic lesions (gummas) in the brain, heart valves, aorta, spinal cord, skin, or other organs. No vaccine.
Leptospira interrogans spirochaete	Leptospirosis: a disease of wild or domestic animals who excrete the bacteria in urine. People acquire the bacteria by contact with contaminated water. Disease is usually mild, resembling intestinal virus infection. Weil's disease is the serious form, with hemorrhages in the liver and kidneys. A vaccine is available for dogs.

Table 22–3   DISEASES CAUSED BY BACTERIA (*Continued*)

Bacterial Species	Discussion/Disease(s) Caused
Borrelia burgdorferi spirochaete	Lyme disease: begins as a flu-like illness, often with a bull's-eye rash at the site of the tick bite. May be followed by cardiac arrhythmias, self-limiting meningitis, or arthritis. Animal reservoirs are deer and field mice; the vector is the deer tick (genus *Ixodes*). Vaccines are in the testing stages.
Borrelia vincenti spirochaete	Trench mouth (Vicnent's gingivitis): an ulcerative infection of the gums and pharynx caused by overgrowth of *Borrelia* and other normal oral flora. Triggered by poor oral hygiene or oral infection, which must be corrected to make antibiotic therapy effective.
Rickettsia prowazekii rickettsia	Epidemic typhus: high fever and delirium, hemorrhagic rash; 40% fatality rate. Vector is the human body louse. Very rare in the US but still endemic in other parts of the world.
Rickettsia typhi rickettsia	Endemic typhus: similar to epidemic typhus but milder; 2% fatality rate. Reservoirs are rats and wild rodents; vectors are fleas. The few cases in the US each year usually occur in the Southeast.
Rickettsia rickettsii rickettsia	Rocky Mountain spotted fever (RMSF): high fever, hemorrhagic rash, and pneumonia; 20% fatality rate. Reservoirs are wild rodents and dogs; vectors are ticks. Despite its name, RMSF in the US is most prevalent in the Southeast coastal states (NC, SC) and in Oklahoma.
Chlamydia trachomatis, (serogroups D–K) chlamydia	Genitourinary infection (nongonococcal urethritis): in men, urethritis or epididymitis; in women, cervicitis, although many women are asymptomatic. Complications in women include pelvic inflammatory disease, ectopic pregnancy, and miscarriage. Newborns of infected women may develop conjunctivitis or pneumonia. This is now the most prevalent sexually transmitted disease in the US. No vaccine.
Chlamydia trachomatis, (serogroups A–C) chlamydia	Trachoma: conjunctivitis involving growth of papillae; vascular invasion of the cornea leading to scarring and blindness. Spread by direct contact and fomites. The leading cause of blindness throughout the world, especially in dry, dusty environments.

Table 22–4 DISEASES CAUSED BY VIRUSES

Virus	Discussion/Disease(s) Caused
Herpes simplex	Type 1: fever blisters (cold sores) on the lip or in oral cavity; the virus is dormant in nerves of the face between attacks. Spread in saliva; may cause eye infections (self-inoculation). Type 2: genital herpes; painful lesions in the genital area; a sexually transmitted disease. No vaccine.
Herpes varicella-zoster	Chickenpox: the disease of the first exposure; vesicular rash; pneumonia is a possible complication, especially in adults. The virus then becomes dormant in nerves. Shingles: painful, raised lesions on the skin above the affected nerves following reactivation of the dormant virus. Usually occurs in adults. A vaccine from Japan is currently under consideration for use in North America.
Cytomegalovirus (CMV)	Most people have asymptomatic infection; the virus does no harm but remains in the body. Fetal infection may result in mental retardation, blindness, or deafness. CMV is potentially serious for transplant recipients (pneumonia) and AIDS patients (blindness). No vaccine.
Epstein-Barr virus	Mononucleosis: swollen lymph nodes, fatigue, fever, possible spleen or liver enlargement. Spread by saliva. No vaccine.
Adenoviruses	Many different types: some cause acute respiratory disease (ARD) similar to the common cold; others cause pharyngoconjunctival fever and may occur in epidemics related to swimming pools. The ARD vaccine is used only in the military.
Rhinoviruses	Common cold: sore throat, runny nose, low fever; usually self-limiting. No vaccine (there are over 100 types of rhinoviruses).
Influenza viruses	Influenza: muscle aches, fever, fatigue, spread in respiratory droplets. Three types: A, B, and C. Type A is responsible for most epidemics. These are mutating viruses, and new vaccines are needed as the virus changes. The most serious complication is secondary bacterial pneumonia.
Measles virus	Measles (rubeola): fever, sore throat, Koplik's spots (white) on lining of mouth, rash. Complications are ear infections, pneumonia, and measles encephalitis, which may be fatal. The vaccine is given to infants in combination with mumps and rubella (MMR).
Rubella virus	German measles: mild upper respiratory symptoms; a rash may or may not be present. This virus may cross the placenta and cause congenital rubella syndrome (CRS): blindness, deafness, heart defects, mental retardation, or miscarriage. CRS is most likely to occur if the fetus is infected during the first trimester. The vaccine is given to infants (MMR).
Mumps virus	Mumps: fever, swelling of the parotid salivary glands and perhaps the others (asymptomatic infections do occur); the virus is spread in saliva. Complications are rare in children but include pancreatitis, nerve deafness and mumps encephalitis. Adult men may develop orchitis, inflammation of the testes. Adult women may develop oophoritis, inflammation of the ovaries. The vaccine is given to infants.
Polio viruses	Polio: most infections are asymptomatic or mild; major infection may result in paralysis. Two vaccines: IPV (Salk) contains a killed virus and cannot cause polio; booster injections are needed. OPV (Sabin) contains an attenuated virus, is given orally and carries a very small risk of causing polio. In the US, polio cases are vaccine related; polio is still endemic in other parts of the world. The WHO has set as a goal the eradication of polio by the year 2000.
Rabies virus	Rabies: headache, nausea, fever, spasms of the swallowing muscles; seizures; fatal because of respiratory or heart failure; virtually 100% fatal. Reservoirs are wild animals; the virus is present in their saliva. Post-exposure prevention requires Human Rabies Immune Globulin (antibodies) and the rabies vaccine.

Table 22–4 DISEASES CAUSED BY VIRUSES (*Continued*)

Virus	Discussion/Disease(s) Caused
Encephalitis viruses	Encephalitis: most infections are mild; CNS involvement is indicated by confusion, lethargy, or coma. Several types of these viruses occur in the US. Reservoirs are wild birds and small mammals; vectors are mosquitoes. Vaccines are available for horses and for people whose occupations put them at risk.
Yellow fever virus	Yellow fever: hemorrhages in the liver, spleen, kidneys and other organs. The vector is a mosquito. The vaccine is recommended for travelers to endemic areas: Central and South America and Africa.
Hepatitis viruses: types A, B, and C	Hepatitis: anorexia, nausea, fatigue, jaundice (may not be present in mild cases). HAV is spread by the fecal-oral route; contaminated shellfish or food prepared by people with mild cases. No carriers after recovery. HBV is spread by sexual activity or contact with blood or other body fluids. Carrier state is possible; may lead to liver cancer or cirrhosis. HCV was the most common cause of post-transfusion hepatitis and is spread by contact with blood. Carrier state is possible. There is a vaccine for hepatitis B. A vaccine for hepatitis A is in final testing stages.
Human immunodeficiency virus (HIV)	AIDS: destruction of helper T cells and suppression of the immune system; opportunistic infections; invariably fatal, often after many years. HIV is spread by sexual activity, contact with blood, or placental transmission. No vaccine.

Table 22–5 DISEASES CAUSED BY FUNGI

Fungus Genus	Discussion/Disease(s) Caused
Microsporum, Trichophyton, Epidermophyton	Ringworm (tinea): scaly red patches on the skin or scalp; loss of hair. Tinea pedis is athlete's foot. May also infect damaged nails. Spores of these fungi are acquired from people or animals.
Candida (*albicans* and other species)	Yeast infections: mucosal infections are called thrush; may be oral or vaginal; yeasts have come from resident flora. Systemic infections include pneumonia and endocarditis. Important nosocomial pathogens.
Cryptococcus	Cryptococcosis: pulmonary infection that may progress to meningitis, especially in AIDS patients. Spores are carried in the air from soil or pigeon droppings.
Histoplasma	Histoplasmosis: pulmonary infection that is often self-limiting. Progressive disease involves ulcerations of the liver, spleen, and lymph nodes; usually fatal. Spores are carried by the air from soil.
Coccidioides	Coccidioidomycosis: pulmonary infection that is often self-limiting. Progressive disease involves the meninges, bones, skin, and other organs; high mortality rate. Spores are carried by the air.

Table 22–6   DISEASES CAUSED BY PROTOZOA

Protozoan	Discussion/Disease(s) Caused
Entamoeba histolytica	Amebic dysentery; ulcerative lesions in the colon, bloody diarrhea; abscesses may form in the liver, lungs, or brain. Spread by the fecal-oral route in water or food.
Naegleria species	Amebic meningoencephalitis: inflammation of the meninges and brain; uncommon in the US but almost always fatal. Amebas in fresh water are acquired when swimmers sniff water into the nasal cavities; the amebas move along the olfactory nerves into the brain.
Balantidium coli	Balantidiasis: abdominal discomfort and diarrhea; often mild. Reservoirs are pigs and other domestic animals; spread by the fecal-oral route.
Giardia lamblia	Giardiasis: fatty diarrhea; may be mild. Reservoirs are wild and domestic animals and people. Spread by the fecal-oral route in water or food prepared by people with mild cases. An important cause of diarrhea in day-care centers.
Trichomonas vaginalis	Trichomoniasis: a sexually transmitted disease. Women: causes cervicitis and vaginitis; men are often asymptomatic.
Plasmodium species	Malaria: the protozoa reproduce in red blood cells, causing hemolysis and anemia. The vector is the *Anopheles* mosquito. No vaccine yet.
Toxoplasma gondii	Toxoplasmosis: asymptomatic infection in healthy people. Congenital infection: miscarriage or mental retardation, blindness. Reservoirs are cats and grazing animals. Pregnant women may acquire cysts from cat feces or from ingestion of rare beef or lamb.
Cryptosporidium species	Diarrhea: ranges from mild to severe; spread by the fecal-oral route. An important cause of diarrhea in day-care centers and in AIDS patients. May also contaminate municipal water supplies and cause extensive epidemics.
Pneumocystis carinii	Pneumonia: only in very debilitated or immunosuppressed persons. A frequent cause of death in AIDS patients.

Table 22–7   INFESTATIONS CAUSED BY WORMS

Worm (Genus)	Discussion/Disease(s) Caused
Chinese liver fluke (*Clonorchis*)	Abdominal discomfort; cirrhosis after many years. Adult worms (½ inch) live in bile ducts. Acquired by people from ingestion of raw fish that contains worm cysts.
Tapeworms (*Taenia, Diphyllobothrium*)	Bloating and abdominal discomfort; constipation or diarrhea. People acquire the worms by eating poorly cooked beef, pork, or fish (the alternate hosts) that contain worm cysts.
Pinworm (*Enterobius*)	Adult worms (⅛ inch) live in colon; females lay eggs on perianal skin while host is asleep, causing irritation and itching of skin. Eggs are spread to family members on hands and bed linens. In the US, this is probably the most common worm infestation.
Hookworm (*Necator*)	Adult worms (½ inch) live in the small intestine; their food is blood. Heavy infestations cause anemia and fatigue. Eggs are excreted in feces; larval worms burrow through the skin of a bare foot and migrate to the intestine.
Ascaris	Adults are 10–12 inch long, and live in the small intestine. Large numbers of worms may cause intestinal obstruction. Eggs are excreted in feces and are spread to others on hands or vegetation contaminated by human feces.
Trichinella spiralis	Trichinosis: severe muscle pain as migrating worms form cysts that become calcified. Acquired by eating poorly cooked pork (or wild animals) that contains cysts.

Table 22–8 ARTHROPOD VECTORS

Arthropod	Disease (Type of Pathogen)*
Mosquito	Malaria (protozoan)
	Encephalitis (virus)
	Yellow fever (virus)
Flea	Plague (bacterium)
	Endemic typhus (rickettsia)
Body louse	Epidemic typhus (rickettsia)
	Tularemia (bacterium)
	Relapsing fever (bacterium)
Tick	Lyme disease (bacterium)
	Rocky Mountain spotted fever (rickettsia)
	Tularemia (bacterium)
Tse tse fly	African sleeping sickness (protozoan)
Deer fly, horse fly	Tularemia (bacterium)

*These diseases are described in previous tables.

STUDY OUTLINE

Classification of Microorganisms
1. Bacteria—unicellular; some are pathogens.
2. Viruses—not cells; all are parasites.
3. Protozoa—unicellular animals; some are pathogens.
4. Fungi—unicellular (yeasts) or multicellular (molds); most are decomposers.
5. Worms—multicellular animals; a few are parasites.
6. Arthropods—insects, ticks, or mites that are vectors of disease or cause infestations.
   • Binomial Nomenclature—the genus and species names.

Normal Flora—see Table 22–1
1. Resident flora—the microorganisms that live on or in nearly everyone, in specific body sites; cause no harm when in their usual sites.
2. Transient flora—the microorganisms that periodically inhabit the body and usually cause no harm unless the host's resistance is lowered.

Infectious Disease
1. Caused by microorganisms or their toxins.

2. Clinical infections are characterized by symptoms; in a subclinical infection, the person shows no symptoms.
3. Course of an Infectious Disease: Incubation period—the time between the entry of the pathogen and the onset of symptoms. The acme is the worst stage of the disease, followed by recovery or death. A self-limiting disease typically lasts a certain period of time and is followed by recovery.
4. **Types of Infection**
   • Localized—the pathogen is in one area of the body.
   • Systemic—the pathogen is spread throughout the body by the blood or lymph.
   • Septicemia (Bacteremia)—bacteria in the blood.
   • Acute—usually severe or of abrupt onset.
   • Chronic—progresses slowly or is prolonged.
   • Secondary—made possible by a primary infection that lowered host resistance.
   • Nosocomial—a hospital-acquired infection.
   • Endogenous—caused by the person's own normal flora in an abnormal site.

Epidemiology—see Fig. 22–1

1. The study of the patterns and spread of disease.
2. Portal of Entry—the way a pathogen enters a host.
3. Portal of Exit—the way a pathogen leaves a host.
4. Reservoirs—persons with the disease, carriers after recovery, or animal hosts (for zoonoses).
5. Non-communicable disease—cannot be directly or indirectly transmitted from host to host.
6. Communicable disease—may be transmitted directly from host to host by respiratory droplets, cutaneous or sexual contact, placental transmission, or blood contact. May be transmitted indirectly by food or water, vectors, or fomites.
7. Contagious disease—easily spread from person to person by casual contact (respiratory droplets).

Methods of Control of Microbes

1. Antiseptics—chemicals that destroy or inhibit bacteria on a living being.
2. Disinfectants—chemicals that destroy or inhibit bacteria on inanimate objects.
3. Sterilization—a process that destroys all living organisms.
4. Public health measures include laws and regulations to ensure safe food and water.

Bacteria—see Fig. 22–2

1. Shapes: coccus, bacillus, spirillum.
2. Flagella provide motility for some bacilli and spirilla.
3. Aerobes require oxygen, anaerobes are inhibited by oxygen; facultative anaerobes grow in the presence or absence of oxygen.
4. The gram reaction (positive or negative) is based on the chemistry of the cell wall. The Gram stain is a laboratory procedure used in the identification of bacteria.
5. Capsules inhibit phagocytosis by white blood cells. Spores are dormant forms that are resistant to environmental extremes.
6. Toxins are chemicals produced by bacteria that are poisonous to host cells.
7. Rickettsias and Chlamydias differ from other bacteria in that they must be inside living cells to reproduce.
8. Antibiotics are chemicals used in the treatment of bacterial diseases. Broad-spectrum: affects many kinds of bacteria. Narrow-spectrum: affects only a few kinds of bacteria.
9. Bacteria may become resistant to certain antibiotics, which are then of no use in treatment. Culture and sensitivity testing may be necessary before an antibiotic is chosen to treat an infection.
10. Diseases—see Table 22–3.

Viruses—see Fig. 22–3

1. Not cells; a virus consists of either DNA or RNA surrounded by a protein shell.
2. Must be inside living cells to reproduce, which causes death of the host cell.
3. Severity of disease depends on the types of cells infected; some viruses may cross the placenta and infect a fetus.
4. Antiviral medications must interfere with viral reproduction without harming host cells; there are few such chemicals available.
5. Diseases—see Table 22–4.

Fungi—see Fig. 22–4

1. Most are saprophytes, decomposers of dead organic matter. May be unicellular yeasts or multicellular molds.
2. Mycoses may be superficial, involving the skin or mucous membranes, or systemic, involving internal organs such as the lungs or meninges.
3. Effective antifungal medications are available, but some are highly toxic.
4. Diseases—see Table 22–5.

Protozoa—see Fig. 22–5

1. Unicellular animals; some are pathogens.
2. Some are spread by vectors, others by fecal contamination of food or water.
3. Effective medications are available for most diseases.
4. Diseases—see Table 22–6.

Worms—see Fig. 22–6

1. Simple multicellular animals; the parasites are flukes, tapeworms, and some roundworms.
2. May have life cycles that involve other animal hosts as well as people.

3. Effective medications are available for most worm infestations.
4. Diseases—see Table 22–7.

Arthropods—see Fig. 22–7
1. Some cause superficial infestations.
2. Others are vectors of disease—see Table 22–8.

REVIEW QUESTIONS

1. Define resident flora, and explain its importance. (p. 506)

2. State the term described by each statement: (pp. 508, 509, 511, 514)

   a. an infection in which the persons shows no symptoms
   b. bacteria that are inhibited by oxygen
   c. a disease that lasts a certain length of time and is followed by recovery
   d. a disease that is usually present in a given population
   e. the presence of bacteria in the blood
   f. an infection made possible by a primary infection that lowers host resistance
   g. a disease of animals that may be acquired by people
   h. bacteria that are spherical in shape

3. Name these parts of a bacterial cell: (pp. 514–515)

   a. inhibits phagocytosis by white blood cells
   b. provides motility
   c. the basis for the gram reaction or Gram stain
   d. a form resistant to heat and drying
   e. chemicals produced that are poisonous to host cells

4. Explain what is meant by a nosocomial infection, and describe the two general kinds with respect to sources of the pathogen. (p. 509)

5. Name five potential portals of entry for pathogens. (p. 510)

6. Name five potential portals of exit for pathogens. (p. 510)

7. Explain the difference between a communicable disease and a contagious disease. (p. 511)

8. Explain the difference between pasteurization and sterilization. (p. 512)

9. Describe the structure of a virus, and explain how viruses cause disease. (pp. 516–517)

10. Describe the differences between yeasts and molds. (p. 518)

11. Describe the difference between superficial and systemic mycoses. (p. 518)

12. Name some diseases that are spread by vectors, and name the vector for each. (p. 530)

Appendix A

Units of Measure

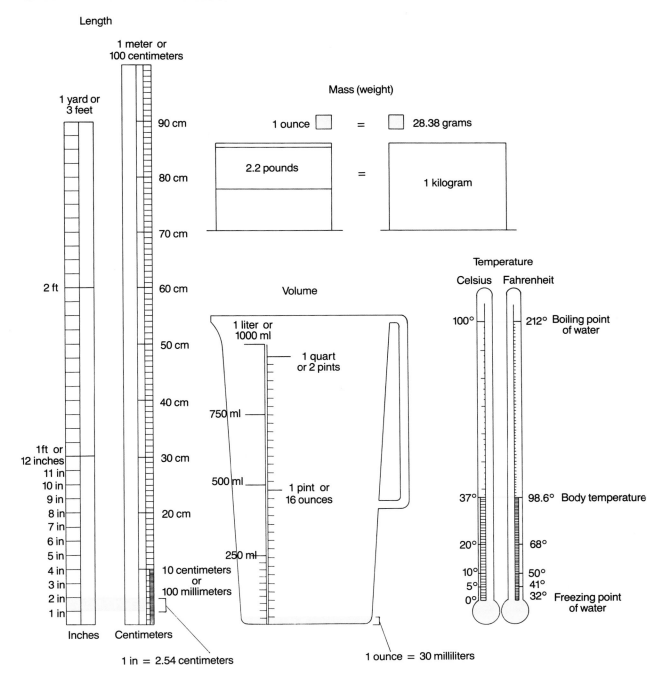

Length

1 meter or
100 centimeters

1 yard or
3 feet

Mass (weight)

1 ounce ☐ = ☐ 28.38 grams

2.2 pounds = 1 kilogram

90 cm

80 cm

70 cm

Temperature

Celsius Fahrenheit

60 cm

Volume

2 ft

50 cm

1 liter or
1000 ml

1 quart
or 2 pints

100° 212° Boiling point
of water

40 cm

750 ml

1ft or
12 inches
11 in
10 in
9 in
8 in
7 in
6 in
5 in
4 in
3 in
2 in
1 in

30 cm

500 ml

1 pint or
16 ounces

37° 98.6° Body temperature

20 cm

250 ml

20° 68°

10 centimeters
or
100 millimeters

10° 50°
5° 41°
0° 32° Freezing point
of water

Inches Centimeters

1 in = 2.54 centimeters

1 ounce = 30 milliliters

UNITS OF LENGTH

	mm	cm	in	ft	yd	M
1 millimeter =	1.0	0.1	0.04	0.003	0.001	0.001
1 centimeter =	10.0	1.0	0.39	0.032	0.011	0.01
1 inch =	25.4	2.54	1.0	0.083	0.028	0.025
1 foot =	304.8	30.48	12.0	1.0	0.33	0.305
1 yard =	914.4	91.44	36.0	3.0	1.0	0.914
1 meter =	1000.0	100.0	39.37	3.28	1.09	1.0

1 μ = 1 mu = 1 micrometer (micron) = 0.001 mm = 0.00004 in.
mm = millimeters; **cm** = centimeters; **in** = inches; **ft** = feet; **yd** = yards; **M** = meters.

UNITS OF WEIGHT

	mg	g	oz	lb	kg
1 milligram =	1.0	0.001	0.00004	0.000002	0.000001
1 gram =	1000.0	1.0	0.035	0.002	0.001
1 ounce =	28,380	28.4	1.0	0.06	0.028
1 pound =	454,000	454.0	16	1.0	0.454
1 kilogram =	1,000,000	1000.0	35.2	2.2	1.0

mg = milligrams; **g** = grams; **oz** = ounces; **lb** = pounds; **kg** = kilograms.

UNITS OF VOLUME

	ml	in³	oz	qt	l
1 milliliter =	1.0	0.06	0.034	0.001	0.001
1 cubic inch =	16.4	1.0	0.55	0.017	0.016
1 ounce =	29.6	1.8	1.0	0.03	0.029
1 quart =	946.3	57.8	32.0	1.0	0.946
1 liter =	1000.0	61.0	33.8	1.06	1.0

ml = milliliters; **in³** = cubic inches; **oz** = ounces; **qt** = quarts; **l** = liters.

TEMPERATURE   Centigrade and Fahrenheit

°C	IS EQUIVALENT TO	°F
0°C		32°F
5°C		41°F
10°C		50°F
15°C		59°F
20°C		68°F
25°C		77°F
30°C		86°F
35°C		95°F
40°C		104°F
45°C		113°F
50°C		122°F

Appendix B

Abbreviations

The use of abbreviations for medical and scientific terms is timesaving and often standard practice. Some of the most frequently used abbreviations have been listed here.

ABG	arterial blood gas	**ECG (EKG)**	electrocardiogram
ACh	acetylcholine	**EEG**	electroencephalogram
ACTH	adrenocorticotropic hormone	**EP**	ectopic pregnancy
ADH	antidiuretic hormone	**ER**	endoplasmic reticulum
AIDS	acquired immune deficiency syndrome	**ESR**	erythrocyte sedimentation rate
ALS	amyotrophic lateral sclerosis	**ESRD**	end-stage renal disease
ANS	autonomic nervous system	**FAS**	fetal alcohol syndrome
ARDS	adult respiratory distress syndrome	**FSH**	follicle-stimulating hormone
ARF	acute renal failure	**FUO**	fever of unknown origin
ATP	adenosine triphosphate	**GFR**	glomerular filtration rate
AV	atrioventricular	**GH**	growth hormone
BBB	blood-brain barrier	**GI**	gastrointestinal
BMR	basal metabolic rate	**HAV**	hepatitis A virus
BP	blood pressure	**Hb**	hemoglobin
BUN	blood urea nitrogen	**HBV**	hepatitis B virus
CAD	coronary artery disease	**hCG**	human chorionic gonadotropin
CBC	complete blood count	**HCV**	hepatitis C virus
CF	cystic fibrosis	**HDL**	high-density lipoprotein
CHD	coronary heart disease	**HLA**	human leukocyte antigen
CHF	congestive heart failure	**HR**	heart rate
CNS	central nervous system	**HSV**	herpes simplex virus
CO	cardiac output; carbon monoxide	**ICF**	intracellular fluid
COPD	chronic obstructive pulmonary disease	**ICP**	intracranial pressure
CPR	cardiopulmonary resuscitation	**ICU**	intensive care unit
CRF	chronic renal failure	**ID**	intradermal
C-section	cesarean section	**IDDM**	insulin-dependent diabetes mellitus
CSF	cerebrospinal fluid	**IM**	intramuscular
CT (CAT)	computed (axial) tomography	**IV**	intravenous
CVA	cerebrovascular accident	**LA**	left atrium
CVP	central venous pressure	**LDL**	low-density lipoprotein
CVS	chorionic villus sampling	**LH**	luteinizing hormone
D & C	dilation and curettage	**LLQ**	left lower quadrant
DMD	Duchenne muscular dystrophy	**LUQ**	left upper quadrant
DNA	deoxyribonucleic acid	**LV**	left ventricule
DNR	do not resuscitate	**mEq/L**	milliequivalents per liter
Dx	diagnosis	**MG**	myasthenia gravis
EBV	Epstein-Barr virus	**MI**	myocardial infarction
ECF	extracellular fluid	**mm³**	cubic millimeter

mmHg	millimeters of mercury	**RLQ**	right lower quadrant
MRI	magnetic resonance imaging	**RNA**	ribonucleic acid
MS	multiple sclerosis	**RV**	right ventricle
MVP	mitral valve prolapse	**RUQ**	right upper quadrant
NGU	non-gonococcal urethritis	**Rx**	prescription
NIDDM	non-insulin-dependent diabetes mellitus	**SA**	sinoatrial
NPN	non-protein nitrogen	**SIDS**	sudden infant death syndrome
OC	oral contraceptive	**SLE**	systemic lupus erythematosus
OTC	over the counter	**SPF**	sun protection factor
PE	pulmonary embolism	**STD**	sexually transmitted disease
PG	prostaglandin	**T$_3$**	triiodothyronine
PID	pelvic inflammatory disease	**T$_4$**	thyroxine
PKU	phenylketonuria	**TIA**	transient ischemic attack
PMN	polymorphonuclear leukocyte	**TMJ**	temporomandibular joint
PMS	premenstrual syndrome	**t-PA**	tissue plasminogen activator
PTH	parathyroid hormone	**TPN**	total parenteral nutrition
RA	right atrium	**TSS**	toxic shock syndrome
RBC	red blood cell	**Tx**	treatment
RBM	red bone marrow	**URI**	upper respiratory infection
RDS	respiratory distress syndrome	**UTI**	urinary tract infection
REM	rapid eye movement	**UV**	ultraviolet
RES	reticuloendothelial system	**VD**	venereal disease
Rh	*Rhesus*	**WBC**	white blood cell

Appendix C

Normal Values for Some Commonly Used Blood Tests

Test	Normal Value	Clinical Significance of Variations
Albumin	3.5–5.5 g/100 ml	• Decreases: kidney disease, severe burns
Bilirubin–Total Direct Indirect	0.3–1.4 mg/100 ml 0.1–0.4 mg/100 ml 0.2–1.0 mg/100 ml	• Increases: liver disease, rapid RBC destruction, biliary obstruction
Calcium	4.3–5.3 mEq/liter	• Increases: hyperparathyroidism • Decreases: hypoparathyroidism, severe diarrhea, malnutrition
Chloride	95–108 mEq/liter	• Decreases: severe diarrhea, severe burns, ketoacidosis
Cholesterol HDL cholesterol LDL cholesterol	150–250 mg/100 ml 29–77 mg/100 ml 62–185 mg/100 ml	• Increases: hypothyroidism, diabetes mellitus
Clotting time	5–10 minutes	• Increases: liver disease
Creatinine	0.6–1.5 mg/100 ml	• Increases: kidney disease
Globulins	2.3–3.5 g/100 ml	• Increases: chronic infections
Glucose	70–110 mg/100 ml	• Increases: diabetes mellitus, liver disease, hyperthyroidism, pregnancy
Hematocrit	38%–48%	• Increases: dehydration, polycythemia • Decreases: anemia, hemorrhage
Hemoglobin	12–18 g/100 ml	• Increases: polycythemia, high altitude, chronic pulmonary disease • Decreases: anemia, hemorrhage
P_{CO_2}	35–45 mmHg	• Increases: pulmonary disease • Decreases: acidosis, diarrhea, kidney disease
pH	7.35–7.45	• Increases: hyperventilation, metabolic alkalosis • Decreases: ketoacidosis, severe diarrhea, hypoventilation
P_{O_2}	75–100 mmHg	• Decreases: anemia, pulmonary disease
Phosphorus	1.8–4.1 mEq/liter	• Increases: kidney disease, hypoparathyroidism • Decreases: hyperparathyroidism

Test	Normal Value	Clinical Significance of Variations
Platelet count	150,000–300,000/mm³	• Decreases: leukemia, aplastic anemia
Potassium	3.5–5.0 mEq/liter	• Increases: severe cellular destruction • Decreases: diarrhea, kidney disease
Prothrombin time	11–15 seconds	• Increases: liver disease, vitamin K deficiency
Red blood cell count	4.5–6.0 million/mm³	• Increases: polycythemia, dehydration • Decreases: anemia, hemorrhage, leukemia
Reticulocyte count	0.5%–1.5%	• Increases: anemia, following hemorrhage
Sodium	136–142 mEq/liter	• Increases: dehydration • Decreases: kidney disease, diarrhea, severe burns
Urea nitrogen (BUN)	8–25 mg/100 ml	• Increases: kidney disease, high protein diet
Uric acid	3.0–7.0 mg/100 ml	• Increases: kidney disease, gout, leukemia
White blood cell count	5000–10,000/mm³	• Increases: acute infection, leukemia • Decreases: aplastic anemia, radiation sickness

Appendix D

Normal Values for Some Commonly Used Urine Tests

Test	Normal Value	Clinical Significance of Variations
Acetone and acetoacetic acid (ketones)	0	• Increases: ketoacidosis, starvation
Albumin	0–trace	• Increases: kidney disease, hypertension
Bilirubin	0	• Increases: biliary obstruction
Calcium	less than 250 mg/24 hrs	• Increases: hyperparathyroidism • Decreases: hypoparathyroidism
Creatinine	1.0–2.0 g/24 hrs	• Increases: infection • Decreases: kidney disease, muscle atrophy
Glucose	0	• Increases: diabetes mellitus
pH	4.5–8.0	• Increases: urinary tract infection, alkalosis, vegetarian diet • Decreases: acidosis, starvation, high protein diet
Protein	0	• Increases: kidney disease, extensive trauma, hypertension
Specific gravity	1.010–1.025	• Increases: dehydration • Decreases: excessive fluid intake, alcohol intake, severe kidney damage
Urea	25–35 g/24 hrs	• Increases: high protein diet; excessive tissue breakdown • Decreases: kidney disease
Uric acid	0.4–1.0 g/24 hrs	• Increases: gout, liver disease • Decreases: kidney disease
Urobilinogen	0–4 mg/24 hrs	• Increases: liver disease, hemolytic anemia • Decreases: biliary obstruction

Appendix E

Suggestions for Further Reading

Taber's Cyclopedic Medical Dictionary, 17th ed.
Clayton L. Thomas, Editor
F.A. Davis Company, Philadelphia, 1993

Melloni's Illustrated Medical Dictionary
Ida Box, Biagio J. Melloni, Gilbert M. Eisner
The Williams & Wilkins Company, Baltimore, 1979

Tissues and Organs: A Text-Atlas of Scanning Electron Microscopy
Richard G. Kessel and Randy H. Kardon
W.H. Freeman and Company, San Francisco, 1979

Atlas of Normal Histology, 6th ed.
Mariano S.H. diFiore, edited by Victor P. Eroschenko
Lea & Febiger, Philadelphia, 1989

Anatomy & Physiology
Arthur C. Guyton
W.B. Saunders College Publishing, Philadelphia, 1985

Principles of Anatomy & Physiology, 7th ed.
Gerard J. Tortora and Nicholas P. Anagnostakos
Harper & Row, New York, 1990

Introduction to Microbiology for the Health Sciences, 3rd ed.
Marcus M. Jensen and Donald N. Wright
Prentice-Hall, Englewood Cliffs, NJ, 1993

A Manual of Laboratory Diagnostic Tests, 4th ed.
Frances Fischbach
J.B. Lippincott Company, Philadelphia, 1992

Diagnostic Tests—Clinical Pocket Manual
Springhouse Corporation, Springhouse, 1985

Behold Man: A Photographic Journey Inside the Body
Lennart Nilsson
Little, Brown & Co, Boston, 1973

Life, Death, and in Between: Tales of Clinical Neurology
Harold L. Klawans
Paragon House Publishers, New York, 1992

Toscanini's Fumble and Other Tales of Clinical Neurology
Harold L. Klawans
Bantam Books, New York, 1989

New Guinea Tapeworms and Jewish Grandmothers: Tales of Parasites and People
Robert S. Desowitz
W.W. Norton and Company, New York, 1987

The Malaria Capers: Tales of Parasites and People
Robert S. Desowitz
W.W. Norton and Company, New York, 1993

How We Die
Sherwin B. Nuland
Alfred A. Knopf, New York, 1994

Appendix F

Prefixes, Combining Word Roots, and Suffixes Used in Medical Terminology

PREFIXES AND COMBINING WORD ROOTS

a-, an- absent, without (amenorrhea: absence of menstruation)

ab- away from (abduct: move away from the midline)

abdomin/o- abdomen (abdominal aorta: the portion of the aorta in the abdomen)

acou- hearing (acoustic nerve: the cranial nerve for hearing)

ad- toward, near, to (adduct: move toward the midline)

aden/o- gland (adenohypophysis: the glandular part of the pituitary gland)

af- to, toward (afferent: toward a center)

alba- white (albino: an animal lacking coloration)

alg- pain (myalgia: muscle pain)

ana- up, back (anabolism: the constructive phase of metabolism)

angi/o- vessel (angiogram: imaging of blood vessels, as in the heart)

ante- before (antenatal: before birth)

anti- against (antiemetic: an agent that prevents vomiting)

arthr/o- joint (arthritis: inflammation of a joint)

atel- imperfect, incomplete (atelectasis: incomplete expansion of a lung)

auto- self (autoimmune disease: a disease in which immune reactions are directed against part of one's own body)

bi- two, twice (biconcave: concave on each side, as a red blood cell)

bio- life (biochemistry: the chemistry of living organisms)

blasto- growth, budding (blastocyst: a rapidly growing embryonic stage)

brachi/o- arm (brachial artery: the artery that passes through the upper arm)

brachy- short (brachydactyly: abnormally short fingers or toes)

brady- slow (bradycardia: slow heart rate)

bronch- air passage (bronchioles: small air passages in the lungs)

carcin/o- cancer (carcinogen: cancer causing substance)

cardi/o- heart (cardiopathy: heart disease)

carp/o- wrist (carpals: bones of the wrist)

cata- down (catabolism: the breaking down phase of metabolism)

caud- tail (cauda equina: the spinal nerves that hang below the end of the spinal cord and resemble a horse's tail)

celi/o- abdomen (celiac artery: a large artery that supplies abdominal organs)

cephal/o- head (cephaledema: swelling of the head)

cerebr/o- brain (cerebrum: the largest part of the human brain)

cervic- neck (cervical nerves: the spinal nerves from the neck portion of the spinal cord)

chem/o- chemical (chemotherapy: the use of chemicals to treat disease)

chondr/o- cartilage (chondrocyte: cartilage cell)

circum- around (circumoral: around the mouth)

co-, com-, con- with, together (congenital: born with)

contra- opposite, against (contraception: the prevention of conception)

cost/o- ribs (intercostal muscles: muscles between the ribs)

crani/o- skull, head (cranial nerves: the nerves that arise from the brain)

cut- skin (cutaneous: pertaining to the skin)

cyan/o- blue (cyanosis: bluish discoloration of the skin due to lack of oxygen) cyst- bladder, sac (cystic duct: duct of the gallbladder)

cyt/o- cell (hepatocyte: cell of the liver)

dactyl/o- digits, fingers or toes (polydactyly: more than five fingers or toes)

de- down, from (dehydration: loss of water)

derm- skin (dermatologist: a specialist in diseases of the skin)

di- two, twice (disaccharide: a sugar made of two monosaccharides)

diplo- double (diplopia: double vision)

dis- apart, away from (dissect: to cut apart)

duct- lead, conduct (ductus arteriosus: a fetal artery)

dys- difficult, diseased (dyspnea: difficult breathing)

ecto- outside (ectoparasite: a parasite that lives on the body surface)

edem- swelling (edematous: affected with swelling)

endo- within (endocardium: the innermost layer of the heart wall)

enter/o- intestine (enterotoxin: a toxin that affects the intestine and causes diarrhea)

epi- on, over, upon (epidermis: the outer layer of the skin)

erythr/o- red (erythrocyte: red blood cell)

eu- normal, good (eupnea: normal breathing)

ex- out of (excise: to cut out or remove surgically)

exo- without, outside of (exopthalmia: protrusion of the eyeballs)

extra- outside of, in addition to, beyond (extraembryonic membranes: the membranes that surround the embryo-fetus)

fasci- band (fascia: a fibrous connective tissue membrane)

fore- before, in front (forehead: the front of the head)

gastr/o- stomach (gastric juice: the digestive secretions of the stomach lining)

gluco-, glyco- sugar (glycosuria: glucose in the urine)

gyn/o-, gyne/co- woman, female (gynecology: study of the female reproductive organs)

haplo- single, simple (haploid: a single set, as of chromosomes)

hema-, hemato-, hemo- blood (hemoglobin: the protein of red blood cells)

hemi- half (cerebral hemisphere: the right or left half of the cerebrum)

hepat/o- liver (hepatic duct: the duct that takes bile out of the liver)

hetero- different (heterozygous: having two different genes for a trait)

hist/o- tissue (histology: the study of tissues)

homeo- unchanged (homeostasis: the state of body stability)

homo- same (homozygous: having two similar genes for a trait)

hydr/o- water (hydrophobia: fear of water)

hyper- excessive, above (hyperglycemia: high blood glucose level)

hypo- beneath, under, deficient (hypodermic: below the skin)

idio- distinct, peculiar to the individual (idiopathic: of unknown cause, as a disease)

inter- between, among (interventricular septum: the wall between the ventricles of the heart)

intra- within (intracellular: within cells)

is/o- equal, the same (isothermal: having the same temperature)

kinesi/o- movement (kinesthetic sense: muscle sense)

labi- lip (herpes labialis: cold sores of the lips)

lacri- tears (lacrimal glands: tear-producing glands)

lact/o- milk (lactation: milk production)

leuc/o, leuk/o- white (leukocyte: white blood cell)

lip/o- fat (liposuction: removal of fat with a suctioning instrument)

macr/o- large (macromolecule: a large molecule such as a protein)

mal- poor, bad (malnutrition: poor nutrition)

medi- middle (mediastinum: a middle cavity, as in the chest)

mega- large (megacolon: abnormally dilated colon)

meta- next to, beyond (metatarsal: bone of the foot next to the ankle)

micr/o- small (microcephaly: small head)

mon/o- one (monozygotic twins: indentical twins, from one egg)

morph/o- shape, form (amorphous: without definite shape)

multi- many (multicellular: made of many cells)

my/o- muscle (myocardium: heart muscle)

narco- sleep (narcotic: a drug that produces sleep)

nat/a- birth (neonate: a newborn infant)

neo- new (neoplasty: surgical restoration of parts)

nephr/o- kidney (nephrectomy: removal of a kidney)

neur/o- nerve (neuron: nerve cell)

non- not (non-communicable: unable to spread)

ocul/o- eye (oculomotor nerve: a cranial nerve for eye movement) olig/o- few, scanty (oliguria: diminished amount of urine)

oo- egg (oogenesis: production of an egg cell)

ophthalmo- eye (ophthalmoscope: instrument to examine the eye)

orth/o- straight, normal, correct (orthostatic: related to standing upright)

oste/o- bone (osteocyte: bone cell)

ot/o- ear (otitis media: inflammation of the middle ear)

ovi-, ovo- egg (oviduct: duct for passage of an egg cell, fallopian tube)

path/o- disease (pathology: the study of disease)

ped/ia- child (pediatric: concerning the care of children)

per- through (permeate: to pass through)

peri- around (percardium: membranes that surround the heart

phag/o- eat (phagocyte: a cell that engulfs other cells)

phleb/o- vein (phlebitis: inflammation of a vein)

pleuro-, pleura- rib (pleurisy: inflammation of the pleural membranes of the chest cavity)

pneumo- lung (pneumonia: lung infection)

pod- foot (pseudopod: false foot, as in ameboid movement)

poly- many (polysaccharide: a carbohydrate made of many monosaccharides)

post- after (postpartum: after delivery of a baby)

pre- before (precancerous: a growth that probably will become malignant)

pro- before, in front of (progeria: premature old age, before its time)

pseudo- false (pseudomembrane: false membrane)

py/o- pus (pyogenic: pus producing)

pyel/o- renal pelvis (pyelogram: an x-ray of the renal pelvis and ureter)

quadr/i- four (quadriceps femoris: a thigh muscle with four parts)

retro- behind, backward (retroperitoneal: located behind the peritoneum)

rhin/o- nose (rhinoviruses that cause the common cold)

salping/o- fallopian tube (salpingitis: inflammation of a fallopian tube)

sarc/o- flesh, muscle (sarcolemma: membrane of a muscle cell)

sclero- hard (sclerosis: hardening of tissue with loss of function)

semi- half (semilunar valve: a valve shaped like a half moon)

steno- narrow (aortic stenosis: narrowing of the aorta)

sub- below, beheath (subcutaneous: below the skin)

supra- above (suprarenal gland: gland above the kidney, the adrenal gland)

sym- together (symphysis: a joint where two bones meet)

syn- together (synapse: the space between two nerve cells)

tachy- fast (tachycardia: rapid heart rate)

thorac/o- chest (thoracic cavity: chest cavity)

thromb/o- clot (thrombosis: formation of a blood clot)

tox- poison (toxicology: the study of poisons)

trans- across (transmural: across the wall of an organ)

tri- three (trigone: a three-sided area on the floor of the urinary bladder)

ultra- excessive, extreme (ultrasonic: sound waves beyond the normal hearing range)

un/i- one (unicellular: made of one cell)

uria-, uro- urine (urinary calculi: stones in the urine)

vas/o- vessel (vasodilation: dilation of a blood vessel)

viscera-, viscero- organ (visceral pleura: the pleural membrane that covers the lungs)

SUFFIXES

-ac pertaining to (cardiac: pertaining to the heart)

-al pertaining to (intestinal: pertaining to the intestine)

-an, -ian characteristic of, pertaining to, belonging to (ovarian cyst: a cyst of the ovary)

-ar relating to (muscular: relating to muscles)

-ary relating to, connected with (salivary: relating to saliva)

-ase enzyme (sucrase: an enzyme that digests sucrose)

-atresia abnormal closure (biliary atresia: closure or absence of bile ducts)

-blast grow, produce (osteoblast: a bone-producing cell)

-cele swelling, tumor (meningocele: a hernia of the meninges)

-centesis puncture of a cavity (thoracocentesis: puncture of the chest cavity to remove fluid)

-cide kill (bactericide: a chemical that kills bacteria)

-clast destroy, break down (osteoclast: a bone-reabsorbing cell)

-desis binding, stabilizing, fusion (arthrodesis: the surgical immobilization of a joint)

-dipsia thirst (polydipsia: excessive thirst)

-dynia pain (gastrodynia: stomach pain)

-ectasia, -ectasis expansion (atelectasis: without expansion)

-ectomy excision, cutting out (thyroidectomy: removal of the thyroid)

-emia pertaining to blood (hypokalemia: low blood potassium level)

-form structure (spongiform: resembling a sponge)

-gen producing (carcinogen: a substance that produces cancer)

-genesis production of, origin of (spermatogenesis: production of sperm)

-globin protein (myoglobin: a muscle protein)

-gram record, writing (electroencephalogram: a record of the electrical activity of the brain)

-graph an instrument for making records (ultrasonography: the use of ultrasound to produce an image)

-ia condition (pneumonia: condition of inflammation of the lungs)

-iasis diseased condition (cholelithiasis: gall stones)

-ic pertaining to (atomic: pertaining to atoms)

-ile having qualities of (febrile: feverish)

-ism condition, process (alcoholism: condition of being dependent on alcohol)

-ist practitioner, specialist (neurologist: a specialist in diseases of the nervous system)

-itis inflammation (hepatitis: inflammation of the liver)

-lepsy seizure (narcolepsy: a sudden onset of sleep)

-lith stone, crystal (otoliths: stones in the inner ear)

-logy study of (virology: the study of viruses)

-lysis break down (hemolysis: rupture of red blood cells)

-megaly enlargement (splenomegaly: enlargement of the spleen)

-meter a measuring instrument (spirometer: an instrument to measure pulmonary volumes)

-ness state of, quality (illness: state of being ill)

-oid the appearance of (ovoid: resembling an oval or egg)

-ole small, little (arteriole: small artery)

-oma tumor (carcinoma: malignant tumor)

-opia eye (hyperopia: farsightedness)

-ory pertaining to (regulatory: pertaining to regulation)

-ose having qualities of (comatose: having qualities of a coma)

-osis state, condition, action, process (keratosis: abnormal growth of the skin)

-ostomy creation of an opening (colostomy: creation of an opening between the intestine and the abdominal wall)

-otomy cut into (tracheotomy: cut into the trachea)

-ous pertaining to (nervous: pertaining to nerves)

-pathy disease (retinopathy: disease of the retina)

-penia lack of, deficiency (leukopenia: lack of white blood cells)

-philia love of, tendency (hemophilia: a clotting disorder, "love of blood")

-phobia an abnormal fear (acrophobia: fear of heights)

-plasia growth (hyperplasia: excessive growth)

-plasty formation, repair (rhinoplasty: plastic surgery on the nose)

-plegia paralysis (hemiplegia: paralysis of the right or left half of the body)

-poiesis production (erythropoiesis: production of red blood cells)

-ptosis dropping, falling (hysteroptosis: falling of the uterus)

-rrhage burst forth (hemorrhage: loss of blood from blood vessels)

-rrhea discharge, flow (diarrhea: frequent discharge of feces)

-scope instrument to examine (microscope: instrument to examine small objects)

-spasm involuntary contraction (blepharospasm: twitch of the eyelid)

-stasis to be still, control, stop (hemostasis: to stop loss of blood)

-sthenia strength (myasthenia: loss of muscle strength)

-stomy surgical opening (colostomy: a surgical opening in the colon)

-taxia muscle coordination (ataxia: loss of coordination)

-tension pressure (hypertension: high blood pressure)

-tic pertainig to (paralytic: pertaining to paralysis)

-tomy incision, cut into (phlebotomy: incision into a vein)

-tripsy crush (lithotripsy: crushing of stone such as gall stones)

-trophic related to nutrition or growth (autotrophic: capable of making its own food, such as a green plant)

-tropic turning toward (chemotropic: turning toward a chemical)

-ula, -ule small, little (venule: small vein)

-uria urine (hematuria: blood in the urine)

-y condition, process (healthy: condition of health)

Appendix G

Eponymous Terms

An eponym is a person for whom something is named, and an eponymous term is a term that uses that name or eponym. For example, fallopian tube is named for Gabriele Fallopio, an Italian anatomist of the sixteenth century.

In recent years it has been suggested that eponymous terms be avoided because they are not descriptive and that they be replaced with more informative terms. Such changes, however, occur slowly, because the older terms are so familiar to those of us who teach. Some of us may even use them as opportunities to impart a little history, also known as "telling stories."

In this edition, the most familiar eponymous terms have been retained, with the newer term in parentheses after the first usage. The list below is provided to show the extent of reclassification of eponymous terms as related to basic anatomy and physiology.

Eponymous Term	New Term
Achilles reflex	plantar reflex
Achilles tendon	calcaneal tendon
Adam's apple	thyroid cartilage
ampulla of Vater	hepatopancreatic ampulla
aqueduct of Sylvius	cerebral aqueduct
Auerbach's plexus	myenteric plexus
Bartholin's glands	greater vestibular glands
Bowman's capsule	glomerular capsule
Broca's area	Broca's speech area
Brunner's glands	duodenal submucosal glands
bundle of His	atrioventricular bundle
canal of Schlemm	scleral venous sinus
circle of Willis	cerebral arterial circle
Cowper's glands	bulbourethral glands
crypts of Lieberkuhn	intestinal glands
duct of Santorini	accessory pancreatic duct
duct of Wirsung	pancreatic duct
Eustachian tube	auditory tube
Fallopian tube	uterine tube
fissure of Rolando	central sulcus
fissure of Sylvius	lateral cerebral sulcus
Graafian follicle	vesicular ovarian follicle
Grave's disease	hyperthyroidism
Haversian canal	central canal
Haversian system	osteon
Heimlich maneuver	abdominal thrust maneuver
islet of Langerhans	pancreatic islet
Krebs cycle	citric acid cycle
Kupffer cells	stellate reticuloendothelial cells

Eponymous Term	New Term
Langerhans' cell	non-pigmented granular dendrocyte
Leydig cells	interstitial cells
loop of Henle	loop of the nephron
Meissner's corpuscles	tactile corpuscles
Meissner's plexus	submucosal plexus
nodes of Ranvier	neurofibral nodes
organ of Corti	spiral organ
Pacinian corpuscle	lamellated corpuscle
Peyer's patches	aggregated lymph nodules
Purkinje fibers	cardiac conducting myofibers
Schwann cell	neurolemmocyte
Sertoli cells	sustentacular cells
sphincter of Boyden	sphincter of the common bile duct
sphincter of Oddi	sphincter of the hepatopancreatic ampulla
Stensen's ducts	parotid ducts
Volkmann's canal	perforating canal, nutrient canal
Wernicke's area	posterior speech area
Wharton's duct	submandibular duct
Wormian bone	sutural bone

Glossary

PRONUNCIATION GUIDE

This pronunciation guide is intended to help you pronounce the words that appear below in the Glossary. Although it is not a true phonetic key, it does help to suggest the necessary sounds by spelling the sounds of the syllables of frequently encountered words and then using these familiar combinations to "spell out" a pronunciation of the new word being defined in the Glossary.

VOWELS

Long vowel sounds: ay, ee, eye or igh, oh, yoo

The sound spelled as . . .	Is pronounced as it appears in . . .
ay	a as in face
a	a as in atom
aw	au as in cause
	o as in frost
ah	o as in proper
ee	e as in beat
e	e as in ten

CONSONANTS

Consonants are pronounced just as they look, with the following equivalents.

The consonant . . .	Is pronounced as it appears in . . .
ph	f as in fancy
g	g as in gone

ACCENTS WITHIN WORDS

One accent: boldface capital letters
Two accents: primary accent is in boldface capital letters
secondary accent is in capital letters

—A—

Abdomen (**AB**–doh–men)—Portion of the body between the diaphragm and the pelvis (Chapter 1).

Abdominal cavity (ab–**DAHM**–in–uhl **KAV**–i–tee)—Part of the ventral cavity, inferior to the diaphragm and above the pelvic cavity (Chapter 1).

Abducens nerves (ab–**DEW**–senz)—Cranial nerve pair VI. Motor to an extrinsic muscle of the eye (Chapter 8).

Abduction (ab–**DUK**–shun)—Movement of a body part away from the midline of the body (Chapter 7).

ABO group (A–B–O **GROOP**)—The red blood cell types determined by the presence or absence of A and B antigens on the red blood cell membrane; the four types are A, B, AB, and O (Chapter 11).

Absorption (ab–**ZORB**–shun)—The taking in of materials by cells or tissues (Chapter 4).

Accessory nerves (ak–**SES**–suh–ree)—Cranial nerve pair XI. Motor to the larynx and shoulder muscles (Chapter 8).

Accessory organs (ak–**SES**–suh–ree)—The digestive organs that contribute to the process of digestion, although digestion does not take place within them; consist of the teeth, tongue, salivary glands, liver, gallbladder, and pancreas (Chapter 16).

Acetabulum (ASS–uh–**TAB**–yoo–lum)—The deep socket in the hip bone that articulates with the head of the femur (Chapter 6).

Acetylcholine (as–**SEE**–tull–KOH–leen)—A chemical neurotransmitter released at neuromuscular junctions, as well as by neurons in the central and peripheral nervous systems (Chapter 7).

Acid (**ASS**–id)—A hydrogen ion (H⁺) donor; when in solution has a pH less than 7 (Chapter 2).

Acidosis (Ass–i–**DOH**–sis)—The condition in which the pH of the blood falls below 7.35 (Chapter 2).

Acne (**ACK**–nee)—Inflammation of the sebaceous glands and hair follicles (Chapter 5).

Acoustic nerves (uh–**KOO**–stik)—Cranial nerve pair VIII. Sensory for hearing and equilibrium (Chapter 8).

Acquired immunity (uh–**KWHY**–erd im–**YOO**–ni–tee)—The immunity obtained upon exposure to a pathogen or a vaccine or upon reception of antibodies for a particular pathogen (Chapter 14).

Acromegaly (ACK–roh–**MEG**–ah–lee)—Hypersecretion of growth hormone in an adult, resulting in excessive growth of the bones of the face, hands, and feet (Chapter 10).

Acrosome (**AK**–roh–sohm)—The tip of the head of a sperm cell; contains enzymes to digest the membrane of the ovum (Chapter 20).

Actin (**AK**–tin)—A contractile protein in the sarcomeres of muscle fibers (Chapter 7).

Action potential (**AK**–shun poh–**TEN**–shul)—The changes in electrical charges on either side of a cell membrane in response to a stimulus; depolarization followed by repolarization (Chapter 7).

Active immunity (**AK**–tiv im–**YOO**–ni–tee)—The immunity provided by the production of antibodies after exposure to a foreign antigen; may be natural (recovery from disease) or artificial (reception of a vaccine) (Chapter 14).

Active site theory (**AK**–tiv SITE **THEER**–ree)—The process by which an enzyme catalyzes a specific reaction; depends on the shapes of the enzyme and the substrate molecules (Chapter 2).

Active transport (**AK**–tiv **TRANS**–port)—The process in which there is movement of molecules against a concentration gradient; that is, from an area of lesser concentration to an area of greater concentration. Requires energy (Chapter 3).

Acute (ah–**KEWT**)—1. Characterized by rapid onset 2. Sharp or severe, with respect to symptoms; not chronic. (Chapter 22).

Adaptation (A–dap–**TAY**–shun)—The characteristic of sensations in which awareness of the sensation diminishes despite a continuing stimulus (Chapter 9).

Addison's disease (**ADD**–i–sonz)—Hyposecretion of the hormones of the adrenal cortex, characterized by low blood pressure, dehydration, muscle weakness, and mental lethargy (Chapter 10).

Adduction (ad–**DUK**–shun)—The movement of a body part toward the midline of the body (Chapter 7).

Adenohypophysis (uh–DEN–oh–high–**POFF**–e–sis)—The anterior pituitary gland (Chapter 10).

Adipocyte (**ADD**–i–poh–site)—A cell of adipose tissue, specialized to store fat (Chapter 4).

Adipose tissue (**ADD**–i–pohz **TISH**–yoo)—A connective tissue composed primarily of adipocytes; function is fat storage as a source of potential energy (Chapter 4).

Adrenal cortex (uh–**DREE**–nuhl **KOR**–teks)—The outer layer of the adrenal glands, which secretes cortisol and aldosterone (Chapter 10).

Adrenal glands (uh–**DREE**–nuhl)—The endocrine glands located on the top of the kidneys; each consists of an adrenal cortex, which secretes cortisol and aldosterone, and an adrenal medulla, which secretes epinephrine and norepinephrine (Syn.—suprarenal glands) (Chapter 10).

Adrenal medulla (uh–**DREE**–nuhl muh–**DEW**–lah)—The inner layer of the adrenal glands, which secretes epinephrine and norepinephrine (Chapter 10).

Adrenocorticotropic hormone (ACTH) (uh–DREE-no–KOR–ti–koh–**TROH**–pik)—A hormone produced by the anterior pituitary gland that stimulates the adrenal cortex to secrete cortisol (Chapter 10).

Aerobic (air–**ROH**–bik)—Requiring oxygen (Chapter 3).

Afferent (**AFF**–uh–rent)—To carry toward a center or main part (Chapter 8).

Afferent arteriole (**AFF**–er–ent ar–**TIR**–ee–ohl)—The arteriole that takes blood from the renal artery into a glomerulus; within its wall are juxtaglomerular cells that secrete renin (Chapter 18).

Afterbirth (**AFF**–ter–berth)—The placenta delivered shortly after delivery of the infant (Chapter 21).

After-image (**AFF**–ter–IM–ije)—The characteristic of sensations in which a sensation remains in the consciousness even after the stimulus has stopped (Chapter 9).

Agglutination (uh–GLOO–ti–**NAY**–shun)—Clumping of blood cells or microorganisms; the result of an antigen-antibody reaction (Chapter 11).

AIDS (AYDS)—Acquired immune deficiency syndrome; caused by a virus (HIV) that infects helper T cells and depresses immune responses (Chapter 14).

Albumin (Al–**BYOO**–min)—A protein synthesized by the liver, which circulates in blood plasma; contributes to the colloid osmotic pressure of the blood (Chapter 11).

Aldosterone (al–**DAH**–ster–ohn)—A hormone (mineralocorticoid) secreted by the adrenal cortex that increases the reabsorption of sodium and the excretion of potassium by the kidneys (Chapter 10).

Alimentary tube (AL–i–**MEN**–tah–ree TOOB)—The series of digestive organs that extends from the mouth to the anus; consists of the oral cavity, pharynx, esophagus, stomach, small intestine, and large intestine (Chapter 16).

Allergen (**AL**–er–jen)—A substance capable of stimulating an allergic response (Chapter 14).

Allergy (**AL**–er–jee)—A hypersensitivity to a foreign antigen that usually does not stimulate an immune response in people; the immune response serves no useful purpose (Chapter 14).

Allele (uh–**LEEL**)—One of two or more different genes for a particular characteristic (Chapter 21).

Alopecia (AL–oh–**PEE**–she–ah)—Loss of hair, especially that of the scalp (Chapter 5).

Alpha cells (**AL**–fah SELLS)—The cells of the Islets of Langerhans of the pancreas that secrete the hormone glucagon (Chapter 10).

Alveoli (al–**VEE**–oh–lye)—The air sacs of the lungs, made of simple squamous epithelium, in which gas exchange takes place (Chapter 15).

Alzheimer's disease (**ALZ**–high–mers)—A progressive brain disease, of unknown cause, resulting in loss of memory, intellectual ability, speech, and motor control (Chapter 8).

Amenorrhea (ay–MEN–uh–**REE**–ah)—Absence of menstruation (Chapter 20).

Amino acid (ah–**MEE**–noh **ASS**–id)—An organic compound that contains an amino, or amine, group (NH_2) and a carboxyl group (COOH). Twenty different amino acids are the subunit molecules of which proteins are made (Chapter 2).

Amino group (ah–**MEE**–noh)—The NH_2 portion of a molecule such as an amino acid (Chapter 12).

Amniocentesis (AM–nee–oh–sen–**TEE**–sis)—A diagnostic procedure in which amniotic fluid is obtained for culture of fetal cells; used to detect genetic diseases or other abnormalities in the fetus (Chapter 21).

Amnion (**AM**–nee–on)—An embryonic membrane that holds the fetus suspended in amniotic fluid; fuses with the chorion by the end of the third month of gestation (Chapter 21).

Amniotic fluid (AM–nee–**AH**–tik **FLOO**–id)—The fluid contained within the amnion; cushions the fetus and absorbs shock (Chapter 21).

Amphiarthrosis (AM–fee–ar–**THROH**–sis)—A slightly movable joint, such as a symphysis (Chapter 6).

Amylase (**AM**–i–lays)—A digestive enzyme that breaks down starch to maltose; secreted by the salivary glands and the pancreas (Chapter 16).

Anabolic steroid (AN–ah–**BAH**–lik **STEER**–oid)—A chemical similar in structure and action to the male hormone testosterone; increases protein synthesis, especially in muscles (Chapter 7).

Anabolism (an–**AB**–uh–lizm)—Synthesis reactions, in which smaller molecules are bonded together to form larger molecules; require energy (ATP) and are catalyzed by enzymes (Chapter 17).

Anaerobic (AN–air–**ROH**–bik)—1. In the absence of oxygen. 2. Not requiring oxygen (Chapter 7).

Anaphase (**AN**–ah–fayz)—The third stage of mitosis, in which the separate chromatids move toward opposite poles of the cell (Chapter 3).

Anaphylactic shock (AN–uh–fi–**LAK**–tik SHAHK)—A type of circulatory shock that is the result of a massive allergic reaction (from the Greek "unguarded") (Chapter 13).

Anastomosis (a–NAS–ti–**MOH**–sis)—A connection or joining, especially of blood vessels (Chapter 13).

Anatomical position (AN–uh–**TOM**–ik–uhl pa–**ZI**–shun)—The position of the body used in anatomical descriptions: the body is erect and facing forward, the arms are at the sides with the palms facing forward (Chapter 1).

Anatomy (uh–**NAT**–uh–mee)—The study of the structure of the body and the relationships among the parts.

Anemia (uh–**NEE**–mee–yah)—A deficiency of red blood cells or hemoglobin (Chapter 11).

Aneurysm (**AN**–yur–izm)—A localized sac or bubble that forms in a weak spot in the wall of a blood vessel, usually an artery (Chapter 13).

Angiotensin II (AN–jee–oh–**TEN**–sin 2)—The final product of the renin-angiotensin mechanism; stimulates vasoconstriction and increased secretion of adolsterone, both of which help raise blood pressure (Chapter 13).

Anion (**AN**–eye–on)—An ion with a negative charge (Chapter 2).

Antagonistic muscles (an–**TAG**–on–ISS–tik **MUSS**–uhls)—Muscles that have opposite functions with respect to the movement of a joint (Chapter 7).

Anterior (an–**TEER**–ee–your)—Toward the front (Syn.—ventral) (Chapter 1).

Antibiotic (AN–ti–bye–**AH**–tick)—A chemical medication that stops or inhibits the growth of bacteria or fungi (Chapter 22).

Antibody (AN–ti–**BAH**–dee)—A protein molecule produced by plasma cells that is specific for and will bond to a particular foreign antigen (Syn.—gamma globulin, immune globulin) (Chapter 14).

Antibody titer (**AN**–ti–BAH–dee **TIGH**–ter)—A diagnostic test that determines the level or amount of a particular antibody in blood or serum (Chapter 14).

Anticodon (**AN**–ti–KOH–don)—A triplet of bases on tRNA that matches a codon on mRNA (Chapter 3).

Antidiuretic hormone (ADH) (AN–ti–DYE–yoo–**RET**–ik)—A hormone produced by the hypothalamus and stored in the posterior pituitary gland; increases the reabsorption of water by the kidney tubules (Chapter 8).

Antigen (**AN**–ti–jen)—A chemical marker that identifies cells of a particular species or individual. May be "self" or "foreign." Foreign antigens stimulate immune responses (Chapter 2).

Antigenic (An–ti–**JEN**–ik)—Capable of stimulating antibody production (Chapter 14).

Anti-inflammatory effect (AN–ti–in–**FLAM**–uh–tor–ee)—To lessen the process of inflammation; cortisol is the hormone that has this effect (Chapter 10).

Antipyretic (AN–tigh–pye–**RET**–ik)—A medication, such as aspirin, that lowers a fever (Chapter 17).

Antiseptic (AN–ti–**SEP**–tick)—A chemical that destroys bacteria or inhibits their growth on a living being (Chapter 22).

Antithrombin (AN–ti–THROM–bin)—A protein synthesized by the liver that inactivates excess thrombin to prevent abnormal clotting (Chapter 11).

Antitoxin (AN–tee–**TOCK**–sin)—Antibodies specific for a bacterial toxin; used in treatment of diseases such as botulism or tetanus (Chapter 7).

Anus (**AY**–nus)—The terminal opening of the alimentary tube for the elimination of feces; surrounded by the internal and external anal sphincters (Chapter 16).

Aorta (ay–**OR**–tah)—The largest artery of the body; emerges from the left ventricle; has four parts: ascending aorta, aortic arch, thoracic aorta, and abdominal aorta (Chapter 13).

Aortic body (ay–**OR**–tik **BAH**–dee)—The site of chemoreceptors in the aortic arch, which detect changes in blood pH and the blood levels of oxygen and carbon dioxide (Chapter 9).

Aortic semilunar valve (ay–**OR**–tik SEM–ee–**LOO**–nar VALV)—The valve at the junction of the left ventricle and the aorta; prevents backflow of blood from the aorta to the ventricle when the ventricle relaxes (Chapter 12).

Aortic sinus (ay–**OR**–tik **SIGH**–nus)—The location of pressoreceptors in the wall of the aortic arch (Chapter 9).

Apgar score (**APP**–gar SKOR)—A system of evaluating an infant's condition 1 minute after birth; includes heart rate, respiration, muscle tone, response to stimuli, and color (Chapter 21).

Aphasia (ah–**FAY**–zee–ah)—Impairment or absence of the ability to communicate in speech, reading, or writing. May involve word deafness or word blindness (Chapter 8).

Aplastic anemia (ay–**PLAS**–tik un–**NEE**–mee–yah)—Failure of the red bone marrow resulting in decreased numbers of red blood cells, white blood cells, and platelets; may be a side effect of some medications (Chapter 11).

Apneustic center (ap–**NEW**–stik **SEN**–ter)—The respiratory center in the pons that prolongs inhalation (Chapter 15).

Apocrine gland (**AP**–oh–krin)—The type of sweat gland (exocrine) found primarily in the axilla and genital area; actually a modified scent gland (Chapter 5).

Apparent (uh–**PAR**–ent)—1. Readily seen or visible. 2. An infection in which the patient exhibits the symptoms of the disease (Chapter 22).

Appendicitis (uh–PEN–di–**SIGH**–tis)—Inflammation of the appendix (Chapter 16).

Appendicular skeleton (AP–en–**DIK**–yoo–lar)—The portion of the skeleton that consists of the shoulder and pelvic girdles and the bones of the arms and legs (Chapter 6).

Appendix (uh–**PEN**–diks)—A small tubular organ that extends from the cecum; has no known function for people and is considered a vestigial organ (Chapter 16).

Aqueous (**AY**–kwee–us)—Pertaining to water; used especially to refer to solutions (Chapter 2).

Aqueous humor (**AY**–kwee–us **HYOO**–mer)—The tissue fluid of the eye within the anterior cavity of the eyeball; nourishes the lens and cornea (Chapter 9).

Arachnoid membrane (uh–**RAK**–noid)—The middle layer of the meninges, made of web-like connective tissue (Chapter 8).

Arachnoid villi (uh–**RAK**–noid **VILL**–eye)—Projections of the cranial arachnoid membrane into the cranial venous sinuses, through which cerebrospinal fluid is reabsorbed back into the blood (Chapter 8).

Areolar connective tissue (uh–**REE**–oh–lar)—A tissue that consists of tissue fluid, fibroblasts, collagen and elastin fibers, and wandering WBCs; found in all mucous membranes and in subcutaneous tissue (Syn.—loose connective tissue) (Chapter 4).

Arrhythmia (uh–**RITH**–me–yah)—An abnormal or irregular rhythm of the heart (Chapter 12).

Arteriole (ar–**TEER**–ee–ohl)—A small artery (Chapter 5).

Arteriosclerosis (ar–TIR–ee–oh–skle–**ROH**–sis)—Deterioration of arteries with loss of elasticity that is often a consequence of aging or hypertension; a contributing factor to aneurysm or stroke (Chapter 13).

Artery (**AR**–tuh–ree)—A blood vessel that takes blood from the heart toward capillaries (Chapter 13).

Arthropod (**AR**–throw–pod)—Invertebrate animals

characterized by an exoskeleton and jointed appendages; includes insects, spiders, ticks, mites, and crustaceans (Chapter 22).

Articular cartilage (ar–**TIK**–yoo–lar **KAR**–ti–lidj)—The cartilage on the joint surfaces of a bone; provides a smooth surface (Chapter 6).

Articulation (ar–TIK–yoo–**LAY**–shun)—A joint (Chapter 6).

Asthma (**AZ**–mah)—A respiratory disorder characterized by constriction of the bronchioles, excessive mucus production, and dyspnea; often caused by allergies (Chapter 15).

Astigmatism (uh–**STIG**–mah–TIZM)—An error of refraction caused by an irregular curvature of the lens or cornea (Chapter 9).

Astrocyte (**ASS**–troh–site)—A type of neuroglia that forms the blood–brain barrier to prevent potentially harmful substances from affecting brain neurons (Chapter 8).

Asymptomatic (AY–simp–toh–**MAT**–ick)—Without symptoms (Chapter 22).

Atherosclerosis (ATH–er–oh–skle–**ROH**–sis)—The abnormal accumulation of lipids and other materials in the walls of arteries; narrows the lumen of the vessel and may stimulate abnormal clot formation (Chapter 2).

Atlas (**AT**–las)—An irregular bone, the first cervical vertebra; supports the skull (Chapter 6).

Atmospheric pressure (AT–mus–**FEER**–ik)—The pressure exerted by the atmosphere on objects on the earth's surface; 760 mmHg at sea level (Chapter 15).

Atom (**A**–tom)—The unit of matter that is the smallest part of an element (Chapter 2).

Atomic number (a–**TOM**–ik)—Number of protons in the nucleus of an atom (Chapter 2).

Atomic weight (a–**TOM**–ik WAYT)—The weight of an atom determined by adding the number of protons and neutrons (Chapter 2).

ATP (Adenosine triphosphate)—A specialized nucleotide that traps and releases biologically useful energy (Chapter 2).

Atrial natriuretic hormone (ANH) (**AY**–tree–uhl NAY–tree–yu–**RET**–ick)—A peptide hormone secreted by the atria of the heart when blood pressure or blood volume increases; increases loss of sodium ions and water by the kidneys (Chapter 12).

Atrioventricular (AV) node (AY–tree–oh–ven–**TRIK**–yoo–lar NOHD)—The part of the cardiac conduction pathway located in the lower interatrial septum (Chapter 12).

Atrium (**AY**–tree–um)—One of the two upper chambers of the heart that receive venous blood from the lungs or the body (Pl.—atria) (Chapter 12).

Atrophy (**AT**–ruh–fee)—Decrease in size of a body part due to lack of use; a wasting (Chapter 7).

Attenuated (uh–**TEN**–yoo–AY–ted)—Weakened, or less harmful; used to describe the microorganisms contained in vaccines, which have been treated to reduce their pathogenicity (Chapter 14).

Auditory bones (**AW**–di–tor–ee)—The malleus, incus, and stapes in the middle ear (Chapter 6).

Auerbach's plexus (**OW**–er–baks **PLEK**–sus)—The autonomic nerve plexus in the external muscle layer of the organs of the alimentary tube; regulates the contractions of the external muscle layer (Chapter 16).

Auricle (**AW**–ri–kuhl)—The portion of the outer ear external to the skull; made of cartilage covered with skin (Syn.—pinna) (Chapter 9).

Autoclave (**AW**–toh–clayve)—A machine that uses steam under pressure for sterilization (Chapter 22).

Autoimmune disease (AW–toh–im–**YOON** di–**ZEEZ**)—A condition in which the immune system produces antibodies to the person's own tissue (Chapter 6).

Autonomic nervous system (AW–toh–**NOM**–ik **NER**–vuhs)—The portion of the peripheral nervous system that consists of visceral motor neurons to smooth muscle, cardiac muscle, and glands (Chapter 8).

Autosomes (**AW**–toh–sohms)—Chromosomes other than the sex chromosomes; for people there are 22 pairs of autosomes in each somatic cell (Chapter 21).

Axial skeleton (**ACK**–see–uhl)—The portion of the skeleton that consists of the skull, vertebral column, and rib cage (Chapter 6).

Axis (**AK**–sis)—An irregular bone, the second cervical vertebra; forms a pivot joint with the atlas (Chapter 6).

Axon (**AK**–sahn)—The cellular process of a neuron that carries impulses away from the cell body (Chapter 4).

Axon terminal (**AK**–sahn **TER**–mi–null)—The end of the axon of a motor neuron, part of the neuromuscular junction (Chapter 7).

—B—

B cell (B SELL)—A subgroup of lymphocytes, including memory B cells and plasma cells, both of which are involved in immune responses (Chapter 11).

Bacillus (buh–**SILL**–us) (pl.: bacilli)—A rod-shaped bacterium (Chapter 22).

Bacteremia (back–tah–**REE**–mee–ah)—The presence of bacteria in the blood, which is normally sterile (Chapter 22).

Bacteria (back–**TIR**–ee–yuh) (sing.: bacterium)—The simple unicellular microorganisms of the class Schizomycetes; may be free-living, saprophytic, or parasitic (Chapter 22).

Bactericide (back–**TEER**–i–sigh'd)—A chemical that kills bacteria (Chapter 22).

Bacteriostatic (back–TEE–ree–oh–**STAT**–ick)—Capable of inhibiting the reproduction of bacteria (Chapter 22).

Bacteruria (BAK–tur–**YOO**–ree–ah)—The presence of large numbers of bacteria in urine (Chapter 18).

Ball and socket joint (BAWL and **SOK**–et)—A diarthrosis that permits movement in all planes (Chapter 6).

Bartholin's glands (**BAR**–toh–linz)—The small glands in the wall of the vagina; secrete mucus into the vagina and vestibule (Syn.—vestibular glands) (Chapter 20).

Basal ganglia (**BAY**–zuhl **GANG**–Lee–ah)—Masses of gray matter within the white matter of the cerebral hemispheres; concerned with subconscious aspects of skeletal muscle activity, such as accessory movements (Chapter 8).

Basal metabolic rate (**BAY**–zuhl met–ah–**BAHL**–ik RAYT)—The energy required to maintain the functioning of the body in a resting condition (Chapter 17).

Base (BAYS)—A hydrogen ion (H$^+$) acceptor, or hydroxyl ion (OH$^-$) donor; when in solution has a pH greater than 7 (Chapter 2).

Basilar layer (bah–**SILL**–ar **LAY**–er)—The permanent vascular layer of the endometrium that is not lost in menstruation; regenerates the functional layer during each menstrual cycle (Chapter 20).

Basophil (**BAY**–so–fill)—A type of white blood cell (granular); contains heparin and histamine (Chapter 11).

Benign (bee–**NINE**)—Not malignant (Chapter 3).

Beta cells (**BAY**–tah sells)—The cells of the Islets of Langerhans of the pancreas that secrete the hormone insulin (Chapter 10).

Beta-oxidation (BAY–tah–OK–si–**DAY**–shun)—The process by which the long carbon chain of a fatty acid molecule is broken down into two-carbon acetyl groups to be used in cell respiration; takes place in the liver (Chapter 16).

Bile (BYL)—The secretion of the liver that is stored in the gallbladder and passes to the duodenum; contains bile salts to emulsify fats; is the fluid in which bilirubin and excess cholesterol are excreted (Chapter 16).

Bile salts (BYL SAWLTS)—The active component of bile which emulsifies fats in the digestive process (Chapter 16).

Bilirubin (**BILL**–ee–roo–bin)—The bile pigment produced from the heme portion of the hemoglobin of old red blood cells; excreted by the liver in bile (Chapter 11).

Binary fission (**BYE**–na–ree **FISH**–en)—The asexual reproductive process in which one cell divides into two identical new cells (Chapter 22).

Binocular vision (bye–**NOK**–yoo–lur **VI**–zhun)—Normal vision involving the use of both eyes; the ability of the brain to create one image from the slightly different images received from each eye (Chapter 9).

Biopsy (**BYE**–op–see)—Removal of a small piece of living tissue for microscopic examination; a diagnostic procedure (Chapter 5).

Birth canal (BERTH ka–**NAL**)—The vagina during delivery of an infant (Chapter 21).

Blastocyst (**BLAS**–toh–sist)—The early stage of embryonic development that follows the morula; consists of the outer trophoblast and the internal inner cell mass and blastocele (cavity) (Chapter 21).

Blister (**BLISS**–ter)—A collection of fluid below or within the epidermis (Chapter 5).

Blood (BLUHD)—The fluid that circulates in the heart and blood vessels; consists of blood cells and plasma (Chapter 4).

Blood-brain barrier (BLUHD BRAYN)—The barrier between the circulating blood and brain tissue, formed by astrocytes and brain capillaries, to prevent harmful substances in the blood from damaging brain neurons (Chapter 8).

Blood pressure (BLUHD **PRE**–shure)—The force exerted by the blood against the walls of the blood vessels; measured in mmHg (Chapter 13).

Bond (BAHND)—An attraction or force that holds atoms together in the formation of molecules (Chapter 2).

Bone (BOWNE)—1. A connective tissue made of osteocytes in a calcified matrix 2. An organ that is an individual part of the skeleton (Chapter 4).

Botulism (**BOTT**–yoo–lizm)—A disease, characterized by muscle paralysis, caused by the bacterium *Clostridum botulinum* (Chapter 7).

Bowman's capsule (**BOW**–manz **KAP**–suhl)—The expanded end of the renal tubule that encloses a glomerulus; receives filtrate from the glomerulus (Chapter 18).

Bradycardia (BRAY–dee–KAR–dee–yah)—An abnormally slow heart rate; less than 60 beats per minute (Chapter 12).

Brain (BRAYN)—The part of the central nervous system within the skull; regulates the activity of the rest of the nervous system (Chapter 8).

Brain stem (**BRAYN** STEM)—The portion of the brain that consists of the medulla, pons, and midbrain (Chapter 8).

Broad-spectrum (**BRAWD SPEK**–trum)—An antibiotic that is effective against a wide variety of bacteria (Chapter 22).

Bronchial tree (**BRONG**–kee–uhl TREE)—The entire system of air passageways formed by the branching of the bronchial tubes within the lungs; the smallest bronchioles terminate in clusters of alveoli (Chapter 15).

Bronchioles (**BRONG**–kee–ohls)—The smallest of the air passageways within the lungs (Chapter 15).

Buffer system (**BUFF**–er **SIS**–tem)—A pair of chemicals that prevents significant changes in the pH of a body fluid (Chapter 2).

Bulbourethral glands (BUHL–boh–yoo–**REE**–thruhl)—The glands on either side of the prostate gland that open into the urethra; secrete an alkaline fluid that becomes part of semen (Syn.—Cowper's glands) (Chapter 20).

Bundle of His (**BUN**–duhl of HISS)—The part of the cardiac conduction pathway located in the upper interventricular septum (Chapter 12).

Burn (BERN)—Damage caused by heat, flames, chemicals, or electricity, especially to the skin. Classified as first degree (minor), second degree (blisters), or third degree (extensive damage) (Chapter 5).

Bursa (**BURR**–sah)—A sac of synovial fluid that decreases friction between a tendon and a bone (Chapter 6).

Bursitis (burr–**SIGH**–tiss)—Inflammation of a bursa (Chapter 6).

—C—

Calcaneus (kal–**KAY**–nee–us)—A short bone, the largest of the tarsals; the heel bone (Chapter 6).

Calciferol (kal–**SIF**–er–awl)—A form of vitamin D (Chapter 18).

Calcitonin (KAL–si–**TOH**–nin)—A hormone secreted by the thyroid gland that decreases the reabsorption of calcium from bones (Chapter 10).

Callus (**KAL**–us)—Thickening of an area of epidermis (Chapter 5).

Calorie (**KAL**–oh–ree)—1. Small calorie: the amount of heat energy needed to change the temperature of 1 gram of water 1 degree centigrade; 2. Large calorie or Calorie: a kilocalorie, used to indicate the energy content of foods (Chapter 17).

Calyx (**KAY**–liks)—A funnel-shaped extension of the renal pelvis that encloses the papilla of a renal pyramid and collects urine. (Pl.—calyces) (Chapter 18).

Canal of Schlemm (ka–**NAL** of SHLEM)—Small veins at the junction of the cornea and iris of the eye; the site of reabsorption of aqueous humor into the blood (Chapter 9).

Canaliculi (KAN–a–**LIK**–yoo–lye)—Small channels, such as those in bone matrix, that permit contact between adjacent osteocytes (Chapter 6).

Cancer (**KAN**–ser)—A malignant tumor or growth of cells (Chapter 3).

Capillary (**KAP**–i–lar–ee)—A blood vessel that takes blood from an arteriole to a venule; walls are one cell in thickness to permit exchanges of materials (Chapter 13).

Capsule (**KAP**–suhl)—A gelatinous layer located outside the cell wall of some bacteria; provides resistance to phagocytosis (Chapter 22).

Carbohydrate (KAR–boh–**HIGH**–drayt)—An organic compound that contains carbon, hydrogen, and oxygen; includes sugars and starches (Chapter 2).

Carbonic anhydrase (kar–**BAHN**–ik an–**HIGH**–drays)—The enzyme present in red blood cells and other cells that catalyzes the reaction of carbon dioxide and water to form carbonic acid (Chapter 15).

Carboxyl group (kar–**BAHK**–sul)—The COOH portion of a molecule such as an amino acid (Chapter 19).

Carcinogen (kar–**SIN**–oh–jen)—A substance that increases the risk of developing cancer (Chapter 3).

Carcinoma (KAR–sin–**OH**–mah)—A malignant tumor of epithelial tissue (Chapter 5).

Cardiac cycle (**KAR**–dee–yak **SIGH**–kuhl)—The sequence of events in one heartbeat, in which simultaneous contraction of the atria is followed by simultaneous contraction of the ventricles (Chapter 12).

Cardiac muscle (**KAR**–dee–yak **MUSS**–uhl)—The muscle tissue that forms the walls of the chambers of the heart (Chapter 4).

Cardiac output (**KAR**–dee–yak **OUT**–put)—The amount of blood pumped by a ventricle in 1 minute; the resting average is 5 to 6 liters/min (Chapter 12).

Carotid body (kah–**RAH**–tid **BAH**–dee)—The site of chemoreceptors in the internal carotid artery, which detect changes in blood pH and the levels of oxygen and carbon dioxide in the blood (Chapter 9).

Carotid sinus (kah–**RAH**–tid **SIGH**–nus)—The location of pressoreceptors in the wall of the internal carotid artery, which detect changes in blood pressure (Chapter 9).

Carpals (**KAR**–puhls)—The eight short bones of each wrist (Chapter 6).

Carrier (**KAR**–ree–yur)—A person who recovers from a disease but continues to be a source of the pathogen and may infect others (Chapter 22).

Carrier enzyme (**KA**–ree–er **EN**–zime)—An enzyme that is part of a cell membrane and carries out the process of facilitated diffusion of a specific substance (Chapter 3).

Cartilage (**KAR**–ti–lidj)—A connective tissue made of chondrocytes in a protein matrix (Chapter 4).

Catabolism (kuh–**TAB**–uh–lizm)—Breakdown or degradation reactions, in which larger molecules are broken down to smaller molecules; often release energy (ATP) and catalyzed by enzymes (Chapter 17).

Catalyst (**KAT**–ah–list)—A chemical that affects the speed of a chemical reaction, while remaining itself unchanged (Chapter 2).

Cataract (**KAT**–uh–rackt)—An eye disorder in which the lens becomes opaque and impairs vision (from the Latin "waterfall") (Chapter 9).

Catecholamines (KAT–e–**KOHL**–ah–meens)—Epinephrine and norepinephrine, the hormones secreted by the adrenal medulla (Chapter 10).

Cation (**KAT**–eye–on)—An ion with a positive charge (Chapter 2).

Cauda equina (**KAW**–dah ee–**KWHY**–nah)—The lumbar and sacral spinal nerves that hang below the end of the spinal cord and before they exit from the vertebral canal (Chapter 8).

Cecum (**SEE**–kum)—The first part of the large intestine, the dead-end portion adjacent to the ileum (from the Latin "blindness") (Chapter 16).

Cell (SELL)—The smallest living unit of structure and function of the body (Chapter 1).

Cell body (SELL **BAH**–dee)—The part of a neuron that contains the nucleus (Chapter 4).

Cell mediated immunity (SELL **ME**–dee–ay–ted im–**YOO**–ni–tee)—The mechanism of immunity that does not involve antibody production, but rather the destruction of foreign antigens by the activities of T cells and macrophages (Chapter 14).

Cell (plasma) membrane (SELL **MEM**–brayn)—The membrane made of phospholipids, protein, and cholesterol that forms the outer boundary of a cell and regulates passage of materials into and out of the cell (Chapter 2).

Cell respiration (SELL RES–pi–**RAY**–shun)—A cellular process in which the energy of nutrients is released in the form of ATP and heat. Oxygen is required, and carbon dioxide and water are produced (Chapter 2).

Central (**SEN**–truhl)—The main part; or in the middle of (Chapter 1).

Central canal (**SEN**–truhl ka–**NAL**)—The hollow center of the spinal cord that contains cerebrospinal fluid (Chapter 8).

Central nervous system (**SEN**–tral **NER**–vuhs)—The part of the nervous system that consists of the brain and spinal cord (Chapter 8).

Centrioles (**SEN**–tree–ohls)—The cell organelles that organize the spindle fibers during cell division (Chapter 3).

Cerebellum (SER–e–**BELL**–uhm)—The part of the brain posterior to the medulla and pons; responsible for many of the subconscious aspects of skeletal muscle functioning, such as coordination and muscle tone (Chapter 7).

Cerebral aqueduct (se–**REE**–bruhl **A**–kwi–dukt)—A tunnel through the midbrain that permits cerebrospinal fluid to flow from the third to the fourth ventricle (Chapter 8).

Cerebral cortex (se–**REE**–bruhl **KOR**–teks)—The gray matter on the surface of the cerebral hemispheres. Includes motor areas, sensory areas, auditory areas, visual areas, taste areas, olfactory areas, speech areas, and association areas (Chapter 8).

Cerebrospinal fluid (se–**REE**–broh–**SPY**–nuhl)—The tissue fluid of the central nervous system; formed by choroid plexuses in the ventricles of the brain, circulates in and around the brain and spinal cord, and is reabsorbed into cranial venous sinuses (Chapter 8).

Cerebrovascular accident (SER–e–broh–**VAS**–kyoo–lur)—A hemorrhagic or ischemic lesion in the brain, often the result of aneurysm, arteriosclerosis, atherosclerosis, or hypertension (Syn.—stroke) (Chapter 8).

Cerebrum (se–**REE**–bruhm)—The largest part of the brain, consisting of the right and left cerebral hemispheres; its many functions include movement, sensation, learning, and memory (Chapter 8).

Cerumen (suh–**ROO**–men)—The waxy secretion of ceruminous glands (Chapter 5).

Ceruminous gland (suh–**ROO**–mi–nus)—An exocrine gland in the dermis of the ear canal that secretes cerumen (ear wax) (Chapter 5).

Cervical (**SIR**–vi–kuhl)—Pertaining to the neck (Chapter 1).

Cervical vertebrae (**SIR**–vi–kuhl **VER**–te–bray)—The seven vertebrae in the neck (Chapter 6).

Cervix (**SIR**–viks)—The most inferior part of the uterus that projects into the vagina (Chapter 20).

Cesarean section (se–**SAR**–ee–an **SEK**–shun)—Removal of the fetus by way of an incision through the abdominal wall and uterus (Chapter 21).

Chemical clotting (**KEM**–i–kuhl **KLAH**–ting)—A series of chemical reactions, stimulated by a rough surface or a break in a blood vessel, that results in the formation of a fibrin clot (Chapter 11).

Chemical digestion (**KEM**–i–kuhl dye–**JES**–chun)—The breakdown of food accomplished by digestive enzymes; complex organic molecules are broken down to simpler organic molecules (Chapter 16).

Chemoreceptors (KEE–moh–re–**SEP**–ters)—1. A sensory receptor that detects a chemical change. 2. Olfactory receptors, taste receptors, and the carotid and aortic chemoreceptors that detect changes in blood gases and blood pH (Chapter 9).

Chemotherapy (KEE–moh–**THER**–uh–pee)—The use of chemicals (medications) to treat disease (Chapter 3).

Chief cells (CHEEF SELLS)—The cells of the gastric pits of the stomach that secrete pepsinogen, the inactive form of the digestive enzyme pepsin (Chapter 16).

Chlamydia (kluh–**MID**–ee–ah)—A group of simple bacteria; *Chlamydia trachomatis* is a sexually transmitted pathogen that may cause conjunctivitis or pneumonia in infants born to infected women (Chapter 20).

Cholecystokinin (KOH–lee–SIS–toh–**KYE**–nin)—A hormone secreted by the duodenum when food enters; stimulates contraction of the gallbladder and secretion of enzyme pancreatic juice (Chapter 16).

Cholesterol (koh–**LESS**–ter–ohl)—A steroid that is synthesized by the liver and is part of cell membranes (Chapter 2).

Cholinesterase (KOH–lin–**ESS**–ter–ays)—The chemical inactivator of acetylcholine (Chapter 7).

Chondrocyte (**KON**–droh–site)—A cartilage cell (Chapter 4).

Chordae tendineae (**KOR**–day ten–**DIN**–ee–ay)—Strands of connective tissue that connect the flaps of an AV valve to the papillary muscles (Chapter 12).

Chorion (**KOR**–ee–on)—An embryonic membrane that is formed from the trophoblast of the blastocyst and will develop chorionic villi and become the fetal portion of the placenta (Chapter 21).

Chorionic villi (**KOR**–ee–ON–ik **VILL**–eye)—Projections of the chorion that will develop the fetal blood vessels that will become part of the placenta (Chapter 21).

Chorionic villus sampling (KOR–ee–ON–ik **VILL**–us)—A diagnostic procedure in which a biopsy of the chorionic villi is made; used to detect genetic diseases or other abnormalities in the fetus (Chapter 21).

Choroid layer (**KOR**–oid)—The middle layer of the eyeball, contains a dark pigment to absorb light and prevent glare within the eye (Chapter 9).

Choroid plexus (**KOR**–oid **PLEK**–sus)—A capillary network in a ventricle of the brain; forms cerebrospinal fluid (Chapter 8).

Chromatin (**KROH**–mah–tin)—The thread-like structure of the genetic material when a cell is not dividing; is not visible as individual chromosomes (Chapter 3).

Chromosomes (**KROH**–muh–sohms)—Structures made of DNA and protein within the nucleus of a cell. A human cell has 46 chromosomes (Chapter 3).

Chronic (**KRAH**–nick)—Characterized by long duration or slow progression (Chapter 22).

Chylomicron (KYE–loh–**MYE**–kron)—A small fat globule formed by the small intestine from absorbed fatty acids and glycerol (Chapter 16).

Cilia (**SILLY**–ah)—Thread-like structures that project through a cell membrane and sweep materials across the cell surface (Chapter 3).

Ciliary body (**SILLY**–air–ee **BAH**–dee)—A circular muscle that surrounds the edge of the lens of the eye and changes the shape of the lens (Chapter 9).

Ciliated epithelium (**SILLY**–ay–ted)—The tissue that has cilia on the free surface of the cells (Chapter 4).

Circle of Willis (**SIR**–kuhl of **WILL**–iss)—An arterial anastomosis that encircles the pituitary gland and supplies the brain with blood; formed by the two internal carotid arteries and the basilar (two vertebral) artery (Chapter 13).

Circulatory shock (**SIR**–kew–lah–TOR–ee SHAHCK)—The condition in which decreased cardiac output deprives all tissues of oxygen and permits the accumulation of waste products (Chapter 5).

Cisterna chyli (sis–**TER**–nah **KYE**–lee)—A large lymph vessel formed by the union of lymph vessels from the lower body; continues superiorly as the thoracic duct (Chapter 14).

Clavicle (**KLAV**–i–kuhl)—The flat bone that articulates with the scapula and sternum. (Syn.—collarbone) (Chapter 6).

Cleavage (**KLEE**–vije)—The series of mitotic cell divisions that take place in a fertilized egg; forms the early multicellular embryonic stages (Chapter 21).

Cleft palate (KLEFT **PAL**–uht)—A congenital disorder in which the bones of the hard palate do not fuse, leaving an opening between the oral and nasal cavities (Chapter 6).

Clinical infection (**KLIN**–i–kuhl)—An infection in which the patient exhibits the symptoms of the disease (Chapter 22).

Clitoris (**KLIT**–uh–ris)—An organ that is part of the vulva; a small mass of erectile tissue at the anterior junction of the labia minora; enlarges in response to sexual stimulation (Chapter 20).

Clot retraction (KLAHT ree–**TRAK**–shun)—The shrinking of a blood clot shortly after it forms due to the folding of the fibrin strands; pulls the edges of the ruptured vessel closer together (Chapter 11).

Coccus (**KOCK**–us) (pl.: cocci)—A spherical bacterium (Chapter 22).

Coccyx (**KOK**–siks)—The last four to five very small vertebrae; for humans a vestigial tail (Chapter 6).

Cochlea (**KOK**–lee–ah)—The snail-shell-shaped portion of the inner ear that contains the receptors for hearing in the organ of Corti (Chapter 9).

Codon (**KOH**–don)—The sequence of three bases in DNA or mRNA that is the code for one amino acid; also called a triplet code (Chapter 3).

Coenzyme (ko–**EN**–zime)—A non-protein molecule that combines with an enzyme and is essential for the functioning of the enzyme; some vitamins and minerals are coenzymes (Chapter 17).

Collagen (**KAH**–lah–jen)—A protein that is found in the form of strong fibers in many types of connective tissue (Chapter 4).

Collecting tubule (kah–**LEK**–ting)—The part of a renal tubule that extends from a distal convoluted tubule to a papillary duct (Chapter 18).

Colloid osmotic pressure (**KAH**–loid ahs–**MAH**–tik)—The force exerted by the presence of protein in a solution; water will move by osmosis to the area of greater protein concentration (Chapter 13).

Colon (**KOH**–lun)—The large intestine (Chapter 16).

Color blindness (**KUHL**–or **BLIND**–ness)—The inability to distinguish certain colors, a hereditary trait (Chapter 9).

Columnar (kuh–**LUM**–nar)—Shaped like a column; height greater than width; used especially in reference to epithelial tissue (Chapter 4).

Common bile duct (**KOM**–mon BYL DUKT)—The duct formed by the union of the hepatic duct from the liver and the cystic duct from the gallbladder, and joined by the main pancreatic duct; carries bile and pancreatic juice to the duodenum (Chapter 16).

Communicable disease (kuhm–**YOO**–ni–kah–b'l)—A disease that may be transmitted from person to person by direct or indirect contact (Chapter 22).

Compact bone (**KOM**–pakt BOWNE)—Bone tissue made of Haversian systems; forms the diaphyses of long bones and covers the spongy bone of other bones (Chapter 6).

Complement (**KOM**–ple–ment)—A group of plasma proteins that are activated by and bond to an antigen-antibody complex; complement fixation results in the lysis of cellular antigens (Chapter 14).

Complement fixation test (**KOM**–ple–ment fik–**SAY**–shun)—A diagnostic test that determines the presence of a particular antibody in blood or serum (Chapter 14).

Computed tomography (CT) scan (kom–**PEW**–ted toh–**MAH**–grah–fee SKAN)—A diagnostic imaging technique that uses x-rays integrated by computer (Chapter 1).

Concentration gradient (KON–sen–**TRAY**–shun **GRAY**–de–ent)—The relative amounts of a substance on either side of a membrane. Diffusion occurs with, or along, a concentration gradient, that is, from high concentration to low concentration (Chapter 3).

Conduction (kon–**DUK**–shun)—1. The heat loss process in which heat energy from the skin is transferred to cooler objects touching the skin. 2. The transfer of any energy form from one substance to another; includes nerve and muscle impulses, and the transmission of vibrations in the ear (Chapter 17).

Condyle (**KON**–dyel)—A rounded projection on a bone (Chapter 6).

Condyloid joint (**KON**–di–loyd)—A diarthrosis that permits movement in one plane and some lateral movement (Chapter 6).

Cones (KOHNES)—The sensory receptors in the retina of the eye that detect colors (the different wavelengths of the visible spectrum of light) (Chapter 9).

Congenital (kon–**JEN**–i–tuhl)—Present at birth (Chapter 21).

Conjunctiva (KON–junk–**TIGH**–vah)—The mucous membrane that lines the eyelids and covers the white of the eye (Chapter 9).

Conjunctivitis (kon–JUNK–ti–**VIGH**–tis)—Inflammation of the conjunctiva, most often due to an allergy or bacterial infection (Chapter 9).

Connective tissue (kah–**NEK**–tiv **TISH**–yoo)—Any of the tissues that connects, supports, transports, or stores materials. Consists of cells and matrix (Chapter 4).

Contagious disease (kun–**TAY**–jus)—A disease that is easily transmitted from person to person by casual contact (Chapter 22).

Contrast (**KON**–trast)—The characteristic of sensations in which a previous sensation affects the perception of a current sensation (Chapter 9).

Contusion (kon–**TOO**–zhun)—A bruise; the skin is not broken but may be painful, swollen, and discolored (Chapter 5).

Convection (kon–**VEK**–shun)—The heat loss process in which heat energy is moved away from the skin surface by means of air currents (Chapter 17).

Convolution (kon–voh–**LOO**–shun)—A fold, coil, roll, or twist; the surface folds of the cerebral cortex (Syn.— gyrus) (Chapter 8).

Cornea (**KOR**–nee–ah)—The transparent anterior portion of the sclera of the eye; the first structure that refracts light rays that enter the eye (Chapter 9).

Coronal (frontal) section (koh–**ROH**–nuhl **SEK**–shun)—A plane or cut from side to side, separating front and back parts (Chapter 1).

Coronary vessels (**KOR**–ah–na–ree **VESS**–uhls)—The blood vessels that supply the myocardium with blood; emerge from the ascending aorta and empty into the right atrium (Chapter 12).

Corpus callosum (**KOR**–pus kuh–**LOH**–sum)—The band of white matter that connects the cerebral hemispheres (Chapter 8).

Corpus luteum (**KOR**–pus **LOO**–tee–um)—The temporary endocrine gland formed from an ovarian follicle that has released an ovum; secretes progesterone and estrogen (Chapter 10).

Cortex (**KOR**–teks)—The outer layer of an organ, such as the cerebrum, kidney, or adrenal gland (Chapter 8).

Cortisol (**KOR**–ti–sawl)—A hormone secreted by the adrenal cortex that promotes the efficient use of nutrients in stressful situations and has an anti-inflammatory effect (Chapter 10).

Cough reflex (KAWF)—A reflex integrated by the medulla that expels irritating substances from the pharynx, larynx, or trachea by means of an explosive exhalation (Chapter 15).

Covalent bond (ko–**VAY**–lent)—A chemical bond formed by the sharing of electrons between atoms (Chapter 2).

Cranial cavity (**KRAY**–nee–uhl **KAV**–i–tee)—The cavity formed by the cranial bones; contains the brain; part of the dorsal cavity.

Cranial nerves (**KRAY**–nee–uhl NERVS)—The 12 pairs of nerves that emerge from the brain (Chapter 8).

Cranial venous sinuses (**KRAY**–nee–uhl **VEE**–nus **SIGH**–nuh–sez)—Large veins between the two layers of the cranial dura mater; the site of reabsorption of the cerebrospinal fluid (Chapter 8).

Cranium (**KRAY**–nee–um)—The cranial bones or bones of the skull that enclose and protect the brain (Chapter 6).

Creatine phosphate (**KREE**–ah–tin **FOSS**–fate)—An energy source in muscle fibers; the energy released is used to synthesize ATP (Chapter 7).

Creatinine (kree–**A**–ti–neen)—A waste product produced when creatine phosphate is used for energy; excreted by the kidneys in urine (Chapter 7).

Cretinism (**KREE**–tin–izm)—Hyposecretion of thyroxine in an infant; if uncorrected, the result is severe mental and physical retardation (Chapter 10).

Cross section (KRAWS **SEK**–shun)—A plane or cut perpendicular to the long axis of an organ (Chapter 1).

Crypts of Lieberkuhn (KRIPTS of **LEE**–ber–koon)—The digestive glands of the small intestine; secrete digestive enzymes (Chapter 16).

Cuboidal (kew–**BOY**–duhl)—Shaped like a cube; used especially in reference to epithelial tissue (Chapter 4).

Culture and sensitivity testing (**KUL**–chur and SEN–si–**TIV**–i–tee)—A laboratory procedure to determine the best antibiotic with which to treat a bacterial infection (Chapter 22).

Cushing's syndrome (**KOOSH**–ingz **SIN**–drohm)—Hypersecretion of the glucocorticoids of the adrenal cortex, characterized by fragility of skin, poor wound healing, truncal fat deposition, and thin extremities (Chapter 10).

Cutaneous senses (kew–**TAY**–nee–us)—The senses of the skin; the receptors are in the dermis (Chapter 9).

Cyanosis (SIGH–uh–**NOH**–sis)—A blue, gray, or purple discoloration of the skin caused by hypoxia and abnormal amounts of reduced hemoglobin in the blood (Chapter 15).

Cyclic AMP (**SIK**–lik)—A chemical that is the second messenger in the two-messenger theory of hormone action; formed from ATP and stimulates characteristic cellular responses to the hormone (Chapter 10).

Cystic duct (**SIS**–tik DUKT)—The duct that takes bile into and out of the gallbladder; unites with the hepatic duct of the liver to form the common bile duct (Chapter 16).

Cystitis (sis–**TIGH**–tis)—Inflammation of the urinary bladder; most often the result of bacterial infection (Chapter 18).

Cytochrome transport system (**SIGH**–toh–krohm)—The stage of cell respiration in which ATP is formed during reactions of cytochromes with the electrons of the hydrogen atoms that were once part of a food molecule, and metabolic water is formed; aerobic; takes place in the mitochondria of cells (Chapter 17).

Cytokinesis (SIGH–toh–ki–**NEE**–sis)—The division of the cytoplasm of a cell following mitosis (Chapter 3).

Cytoplasm (**SIGH**–toh–plazm)—The cellular material between the nucleus and the cell membrane (Chapter 3).

—D—

Deafness (**DEFF**–ness)—Impairment of normal hearing; may be caused by damage to the vibration conduction pathway (conduction), the acoustic nerve or cochlear receptors (nerve), or the auditory area in the temporal lobe (central) (Chapter 9).

Deamination (DEE–am–i–**NAY**–shun)—The removal of an amino (NH_2) group from an amino acid; takes place in the liver when excess amino acids are used for energy production; the amino groups are converted to urea (Chapter 16).

Decubitus ulcer (dee–**KEW**–bi–tuss **UL**–ser)—The breakdown and death of skin tissue due to prolonged pressure that interrupts blood flow to the area (Chapter 5).

Defecation reflex (DEF–e–**KAY**–shun)—The spinal cord reflex that eliminates feces from the colon (Chapter 16).

Dehydration (DEE–high–**DRAY**–shun)—Excessive loss of water from the body (Chapter 5).

Deltoid (**DELL**–toyd)—1. The shoulder region. 2. The large muscle that covers the shoulder joint (Chapter 1).

Dendrite (**DEN**–dright)—The cellular process of a neuron that carries impulses toward the cell body (Chapter 4).

Dentin (**DEN**–tin)—The bone-like substance that forms the inner crown and the roots of a tooth (Chapter 16).

Depolarization (DE–poh–lahr–i–**ZA**–shun)—The reversal of electrical charges on either side of a cell membrane in response to a stimulus; negative charge outside and a positive charge inside; brought about by a rapid inflow of sodium ions (Chapter 7).

Dermatology (DER–muh–**TAH**–luh–jee)—The study of the skin and skin diseases (Chapter 5).

Dermis (**DER**–miss)—The inner layer of the skin, made of fibrous connective tissue (Chapter 5).

Detached retina (dee–**TACHD RET**–in–nah)—The separation of the retina from the choroid layer of the eyeball (Chapter 9).

Detrusor muscle (de–**TROO**–ser)—The smooth muscle layer of the wall of the urinary bladder; contracts as part of the urination reflex to eliminate urine (Chapter 18).

Diabetes mellitus (DYE–ah–**BEE**–tis mel–**LYE**–tus)—Hyposecretion of insulin by the pancreas or the inability of insulin to exert its effects; characterized by hyperglycemia, increased urinary output with glycosuria, and thirst (Chapter 10).

Diagnosis (DYE–ag–**NOH**–sis)—The procedures used to identify the cause and nature of a person's illness (Chapter 1).

Diaphragm (**DYE**–uh–fram)—The skeletal muscle that separates the thoracic and abdominal cavities; moves downward when it contracts to enlarge the thoracic cavity to bring about inhalation (Chapter 15).

Diaphysis (dye–**AFF**–i–sis)—The shaft of a long bone; contains a narrow canal filled with yellow bone marrow (Chapter 6).

Diarthrosis (DYE–ar–**THROH**–sis)—A freely movable joint such as hinge, pivot, and ball and socket joints; all are considered synovial joints since synovial membrane is present (Chapter 6).

Diastole (dye–**AS**–tuh–lee)—In the cardiac cycle, the relaxation of the myocardium (Chapter 12).

Differential WBC count (**DIFF**–er–**EN**–shul KOWNT)—A laboratory test that determines the percentage of each of the five types of white blood cells present in the blood (Chapter 11).

Diffusion (di–**FEW**–zhun)—The process in which there is movement of molecules from an area of greater concentration to an area of lesser concentration; occurs because of the free energy (natural movement) of molecules (Chapter 2).

Digestive system (dye–**JES**–tiv **SIS**–tem)—The organ system that changes food into simpler organic and inorganic molecules that can be absorbed by the blood and lymph and used by cells; consists of the alimentary tube and accessory organs (Chapter 16).

Diploid number (**DIH**–ployd)—The characteristic or usual number of chromosomes found in the somatic (body) cells of a species (human = 46) (Chapter 3).

Disaccharide (dye–**SAK**–ah–ride)—A carbohydrate

molecule that consists of two monosaccharides bonded together; includes sucrose, maltose, and lactose (Chapter 2).

Disease (di–**ZEEZ**)—A disorder or disruption of normal body functioning (Chapter 1).

Disinfectant (DIS–in–**FECK**–tent)—A chemical that destroys microorganisms or limits their growth on inanimate objects (Chapter 22).

Dissociation (dih–SEW–see–**AY**–shun)—The separation of an inorganic salt, acid, or base into its ions when dissolved in water (Syn.—ionization) (Chapter 2).

Distal (**DIS**–tuhl)—Furthest from the origin or point of attachment (Chapter 1).

Distal convoluted tubule (**DIS**–tuhl KON–voh–**LOO**–ted)—The part of a renal tubule that extends from a loop of Henle to a collecting tubule (Chapter 18).

Diverticulitis (DYE–ver–tik–yoo–**LYE**–tis)—Inflammation of diverticula in the intestinal tract (Chapter 16).

DNA Deoxyribonucleic acid.—A nucleic acid in the shape of a double helix. Makes up the chromosomes of cells and is the genetic code for hereditary characteristics (Chapter 2).

DNA replication (REP–li–**KAY**–shun)—The process by which a DNA molecule makes a duplicate of itself. Takes place before mitosis or meiosis, to produce two sets of chromosomes within a cell (Chapter 3).

Dominant (**DAH**–ma–nent)—In genetics, a characteristic that will be expressed even if only one gene for it is present in the homologous pair (Chapter 21).

Dormant (**DOOR**–ment)—Temporarily inactive; a state of little metabolic activity (Chapter 22).

Dorsal (**DOR**–suhl)—Toward the back (Syn.—posterior) (Chapter 1).

Dorsal cavity (DOR–suhl **KAV**–i–tee)—Cavity that consists of the cranial and spinal cavities (Chapter 1).

Dorsal root (**DOR**–suhl ROOT)—The sensory root of a spinal nerve (Chapter 8).

Dorsal root ganglion (**DOR**–suhl ROOT **GANG**–lee–on)—An enlarged area of the dorsal root of a spinal nerve that contains the cell bodies of sensory neurons (Chapter 8).

Down syndrome (DOWN **SIN**–drohm)—A trisomy in which three chromosomes of number 21 are present; characterized by moderate to severe mental retardation and certain physical malformations (Chapter 20).

Duct (DUKT)—A tube or channel, especially one that carries the secretion of a gland (Chapter 4).

Ductus arteriosus (**DUK**–tus ar–TIR–ee–**OH**–sis)—A short fetal blood vessel that takes most blood in the pulmonary artery to the aorta, bypassing the fetal lungs (Chapter 13).

Ductus deferens (**DUK**–tus **DEF**–eer–enz)—The tubular organ that carries sperm from the epididymis to the ejaculatory duct (Syn.—vas deferens) (Chapter 20).

Ductus venosus (**DUK**–tus ve–**NOH**–sus)—A short fetal blood vessel that takes blood from the umbilical vein to the inferior vena cava (Chapter 13).

Duodenum (dew–**AH**–den–um)—The first 10 inches of the small intestine; the common bile duct enters (Chapter 16).

Dura mater (**DEW**–rah **MAH**–ter)—The outermost layer of the meninges, made of fibrous connective tissue (Chapter 8).

Dwarfism (**DWORF**–izm)—The condition of being abnormally small, especially small of stature due to hereditary or endocrine disorder. Pituitary dwarfism is caused by a deficiency of growth hormone (Chapter 10).

Dyspnea (**DISP**–nee–ah)—Difficult breathing (Chapter 15).

Dysuria (dis–**YOO**–ree–ah)—Painful or difficult urination (Chapter 18).

—E—

Ear (EER)—The organ that contains the sensory receptors for hearing and equilibrium; consists of the outer ear, middle ear, and inner ear (Chapter 9).

Eccrine gland (**ECK**–rin)—The type of sweat gland (exocrine) that produces watery sweat; important in maintenance of normal body temperature (Chapter 5).

Eczema (**ECK**–zuh–mah)—An inflammatory condition of the skin that may include the formation of vesicles or pustules (Chapter 5).

Ectoderm (**EK**–toh–derm)—The outer primary germ layer of cells of an embryo; gives rise to epidermis and nervous system (Chapter 21).

Ectoparasite (EK–toh–**PAR**–uh–sight)—A parasite that lives on the surface of the body (Chapter 22).

Ectopic focus (ek–**TOP**–ik **FOH**–kus)—The initiation of a heartbeat by part of the myocardium other than the SA node (Chapter 12).

Ectopic pregnancy (ek–**TOP**–ik **PREG**–nun–see)—Implantation of a fertilized ovum outside the uterus; usually occurs in the fallopian tube but may be in the ovary or abdominal cavity; often results in death of the embryo since a functional placenta cannot be formed in these abnormal sites (Chapter 20).

Edema (uh–**DE**–muh)—An abnormal accumulation of tissue fluid; may be localized or systemic (Chapter 19).

Effector (e–**FEK**–tur)—An organ such as a muscle or gland that produces a characteristic response after receiving a stimulus (Chapter 8).

Efferent (**EFF**–uh–rent)—To carry away from a center or main part (Chapter 8).

Efferent arteriole (**EFF**–er–ent ar–**TIR**–ee–ohl)—The arteriole that takes blood from a glomerulus to the peritubular capillaries that surround the renal tubule (Chapter 18).

Ejaculation (ee–JAK–yoo–**LAY**–shun)—The ejection of semen from the male urethra (Chapter 20).

Ejaculatory duct (ee–**JAK**–yoo–la–TOR–ee DUKT)—The duct formed by the union of the ductus deferens and the duct of the seminal vesicle; carries sperm to the urethra (Chapter 20).

Elastin (eh–**LAS**–tin)—A protein that is found in the form of elastic fibers in several types of connective tissue (Chapter 4).

Electrocardiogram (ECG or EKG) (ee–**LEK**–troh–**KAR**–dee–oh–GRAM)—A recording of the electrical changes that accompany the cardiac cycle (Chapter 12).

Electrolytes (ee–**LEK**–troh–lites)—Substances that, in solution, dissociate into their component ions; include acids, bases, and salts (Chapter 19).

Electron (e–**LEK**–trahn)—A subatomic particle that has a negative electrical charge; found orbiting the nucleus of an atom (Chapter 2).

Element (**EL**–uh–ment)—A substance that consists of only one type of atom; 92 elements occur in nature (Chapter 2).

Embolism (**EM**–boh–lizm)—Obstruction of a blood vessel by a blood clot or foreign substance that has traveled to and lodged in that vessel (Chapter 11).

Embryo (**EM**–bree–oh)—The developing human individual from the time of implantation until the eighth week of gestation (Chapter 21).

Embryonic disc (EM–bree–**ON**–ik DISK)—The portion of the inner cell mass of the early embryo that will develop into the individual (Chapter 21).

Emphysema (EM–fi–**SEE**–mah)—The deterioration of alveoli and loss of elasticity of the lungs; normal exhalation and gas exchange are impaired (Chapter 15).

Emulsify (e–**MULL**–si–fye)—To physically break up fats into smaller fat globules; the function of bile salts in bile (Chapter 16).

Enamel (en–**AM**–uhl)—The hard substance that covers the crowns of teeth and forms the chewing surface (Chapter 16).

Encapsulated nerve ending (en–**KAP**–sul–LAY–ted NERV **END**–ing)—A sensory nerve ending enclosed in a specialized cellular structure; the cutaneous receptors for touch, pressure, heat, and cold (Chapter 5).

Endemic (en–**DEM**–ick)—A disease that occurs continuously or expectedly in a given population (Chapter 22).

Endocardium (EN–doh–**KAR**–dee–um)—The simple squamous epithelial tissue that lines the chambers of the heart and covers the valves (Chapter 12).

Endocrine gland (**EN**–doh–krin)—A ductless gland that secretes its product (hormone) directly into the blood (Chapter 4).

Endocrine system (**EN**–doh–krin **SIS**–tem)—The organ system that consists of the endocrine glands that secrete hormones into the blood (Chapter 10).

Endoderm (**EN**–doh–derm)—The inner primary germ layer of cells of an embryo; gives rise to respiratory organs and the lining of the digestive tract (Chapter 21).

Endogenous (en–**DOJ**–en–us)—Coming from or produced within the body (Chapter 17).

Endogenous infection (en–**DOJ**–en–us)—An infection caused by a person's own normal flora that have been introduced into an abnormal body site (Chapter 22).

Endolymph (**EN**–doh–limf)—The fluid in the membranous labyrinth of the inner ear (Chapter 9).

Endometrium (EN–doh–**ME**–tree–um)—The vascular lining of the uterus that forms the maternal portion of the placenta (Chapter 20).

Endoplasmic reticulum (ER) (EN–doh–**PLAZ**–mik re–**TIK**–yoo–lum)—A cell organelle found in the cytoplasm; a network of membranous channels that transport materials within the cell and synthesize lipids (Chapter 3).

Endothelium (EN–doh–**THEE**–lee–um)—The simple squamous epithelial lining of arteries and veins, continuing as the walls of capillaries (Chapter 13).

Endotoxin (EN–doh–**TOCK**–sin)—The toxic portion of the cell walls of gram negative bacteria; causes fever and shock (Chapter 22).

Endotoxin shock (EN–doh–**TOCK**–sin SHAHK)—A state of circulatory shock caused by infection with gram negative bacteria (Chapter 22).

Energy levels (**EN**–er–jee **LEV**–els)—The position of electrons within an atom (Syn.—orbitals or shells) (Chapter 2).

Enzyme (**EN**–zime)—A protein that affects the speed of a chemical reaction. Also called an organic catalyst (Chapter 2).

Eosinophil (EE–oh–**SIN**–oh–fill)—A type of white blood cell (granular); active in allergic reactions (Chapter 11).

Epicardium (EP–ee–**KAR**–dee–um)—The serous membrane on the surface of the myocardium (Syn.—visceral pericardium) (Chapter 12).

Epidemic (EP–i–**DEM**–ick)—A disease that affects many people in a given population in a given time with more than the usual or expected number of cases (Chapter 22).

Epidemiology (EP–i–DEE–mee–**AH**–luh–jee)—The study of the spread of disease and the factors that determine disease frequency and distribution (Chapter 22).

Epidermis (EP–i–**DER**–miss)—The outer layer of the skin, made of stratified squamous epithelium (Chapter 5).

Epididymis (EP–i–**DID**–i–mis)—The tubular organ coiled on the posterior side of a testis; sperm mature here and are carried to the ductus deferens (Pl.—epididymides) (Chapter 20).

Epiglottis (EP–i–**GLAH**–tis)—The uppermost cartilage of the larynx; covers the larynx during swallowing (Chapter 15).

Epinephrine (EP–i–**NEFF**–rin)—A hormone secreted by the adrenal medulla that stimulates many responses to enable the body to react to a stressful situation (Syn.—adrenalin) (Chapter 10).

Epiphyseal disc (e–**PIFF**–i–se–al DISK)—A plate of cartilage at the junction of an epiphysis with the diaphysis of a long bone; the site of growth of a long bone (Chapter 6).

Epiphysis (e–**PIFF**–i–sis)—The end of a long bone (Chapter 6).

Epithelial tissue (EP–i–**THEE**–lee–uhl **TISH**–yoo)—The tissue found on external and internal body surfaces and which forms glands (Chapter 4).

Equilibrium (E–kwe–**LIB**–ree–um)—1. A state of balance. 2. The ability to remain upright and be aware of the position of the body (Chapter 9).

Erythema (ER–i–**THEE**–mah)—Redness of the skin (Chapter 5).

Erythroblastosis fetalis (e–RITH–roh–blass–**TOH**–sis fee–**TAL**–is)—Hemolytic anemia of the newborn, characterized by anemia and jaundice; the result of an Rh incompatibility of fetal blood and maternal blood (Chapter 11).

Erythrocyte (e–**RITH**–roh–site)—Red blood cell (Chapter 11).

Erythropoietin (e–RITH–roh–**POY**–e–tin)—A hormone secreted by the kidneys in a state of hypoxia; stimulates the red bone marrow to increase the rate of red blood cell production (Chapter 11).

Esophagus (e–**SOF**–uh–guss)—The organ of the alimentary tube that is a passageway for food from the pharynx to the stomach (Chapter 16).

Essential amino acids (e–**SEN**–shul ah–**ME**–noh **ASS**–ids)—The amino acids that cannot be synthesized by the liver and must be obtained from proteins in the diet (Chapter 16).

Estrogen (**ES**–troh–jen)—The female sex hormone secreted by a developing ovarian follicle; contributes to the growth of the female reproductive organs and the secondary sex characteristics (Chapter 10).

Ethmoid bone (**ETH**–moyd)—An irregular cranial bone that forms the upper part of the nasal cavities and a small part of the lower anterior braincase (Chapter 6).

Eustachian tube (yoo–**STAY**–shee–un TOOB)—The air passage between the middle ear cavity and the nasopharynx (Syn.—auditory tube) (Chapter 9).

Exocrine gland (**EK**–so–krin)—A gland that secretes its product into a duct to be taken to a cavity or surface (Chapter 4).

Expiration (EK–spi–**RAY**–shun)—Exhalation; the output of air from the lungs (Chapter 15).

Expiratory reserve (ek–**SPYR**–ah–tor–ee ree–**ZERV**)—The volume of air beyond tidal volume that can be exhaled with the most forceful exhalation; average: 1000–1500 ml (Chapter 15).

Extension (eks–**TEN**–shun)—To increase the angle of a joint (Chapter 7).

External (eks–**TER**–nuhl)—On the outside; toward the surface (Chapter 1).

External anal sphincter (eks–**TER**–nuhl **AY**–nuhl **SFINK**–ter)—The circular skeletal muscle that surrounds the internal anal sphincter and provides voluntary control of defecation (Chapter 16).

External auditory meatus (eks–**TER**–nuhl **AW**–di–TOR–ee me–**AY**–tuss)—The ear canal; the portion of the outer ear that is a tunnel in the temporal bone between the auricle and the ear drum (Chapter 9).

External respiration (eks–**TER**–nuhl RES–pi–**RAY**–shun)—The exchange of gases between the air in the alveoli and the blood in the pulmonary capillaries (Chapter 15).

External urethral sphincter (yoo–**REE**–thruhl **SFINK**–ter)—The skeletal muscle sphincter in the wall of the urethra; provides voluntary control of urination (Chapter 18).

Extracellular fluid (EX–trah–**SELL**–yoo–ler **FLOO**–id)—The water found outside cells; includes plasma, tissue fluid, lymph, and other fluids (Chapter 2).

Extrinsic factor (eks–**TRIN**–sik **FAK**–ter)—Vitamin B_{12}, obtained from food and necessary for DNA synthesis, especially by stem cells in the red bone marrow (Chapter 11).

Extrinsic muscles (eks–**TRIN**–sik)—The six muscles that move the eyeball (Chapter 9).

—F—

Facial bones (**FAY**–shul)—The 14 irregular bones of the face (Chapter 6).

Facial nerves (**FAY**–shul)—Cranial nerve pair VII; sensory for taste, motor to facial muscles and the salivary glands (Chapter 8).

Facilitated diffusion (fuh–**SILL**–ah–tay–ted di–**FEW**–zhun)—The process in which a substance is transported through a membrane in combination with a carrier molecule (Chapter 3).

Facultative anaerobe (**FAK**–uhl–tay–tive **AN**–air–robe)—A bacterium that is able to reproduce either in the presence or absence of oxygen (Chapter 22).

Fallopian tube (fuh–**LOH**–pee–an TOOB)—The tubular organ that propels an ovum from the ovary to the uterus by means of ciliated epithelium and peristalsis of its smooth muscle layer (Syn.—uterine tube) (Chapter 20).

Fascia (**FASH**–ee–ah)—A fibrous connective tissue membrane that covers individual skeletal muscles and certain organs (Chapter 4).

Fatty acid (**FA**–tee **ASS**–id)—A lipid molecule that consists of an even-numbered carbon chain of 12–24 carbons with hydrogens; may be saturated or unsaturated; an end product of the digestion of fats (Chapter 2).

Femur (**FEE**–mur)—The long bone of the thigh (Chapter 6).

Fertilization (FER–ti–li–**ZAY**–shun)—The union of the nuclei of an ovum and a sperm cell; restores the diploid number (Chapter 3).

Fetal alcohol syndrome (**FEE**–tuhl **AL**–koh–hol)—Birth defects or developmental abnormalities in infants born to women who chronically consumed alcohol during the gestation period (Chapter 21).

Fever (**FEE**–ver)—An abnormally high body temperature, caused by pyrogens; may accompany an infectious disease or severe physical injury (Chapter 17).

Fever blister (**FEE**–ver **BLISS**–ter)—An eruption of the skin caused by the Herpes simplex virus (Syn.—cold sore) (Chapter 5).

Fibrillation (fi–bri–**LAY**–shun)—Very rapid and uncoordinated heart beats; ventricular fibrillation is a life-threatening emergency due to ineffective pumping and decreased cardiac output (Chapter 12).

Fibrin (**FYE**–brin)—A thread-like protein formed by the action of thrombin on fibrinogen; the substance of which a blood clot is made (Chapter 11).

Fibrinogen (fye–**BRIN**–o–jen)—A protein clotting factor produced by the liver; converted to fibrin by thrombin (Chapter 11).

Fibrinolysis (FYE–brin–**AHL**–e–sis)—1. The dissolving of a fibrin clot by natural enzymes, after the clot has served its purpose. 2. The clinical use of clot-dissolving enzymes to dissolve abnormal clots (Chapter 11).

Fibroblast (**FYE**–broh–blast)—A connective tissue cell that produces collagen and elastin fibers (Chapter 4).

Fibrous connective tissue (**FYE**–brus)—The tissue that consists primarily of collagen fibers. Its most important physical characteristic is its strength (Chapter 4).

Fibula (**FIB**–yoo–lah)—A long bone of the lower leg; on the lateral side, thinner than the tibia (Chapter 6).

Filtration (fill–**TRAY**–shun)—The process in which water and dissolved materials move through a membrane from an area of higher pressure to an area of lower pressure (Chapter 3).

Fimbriae (**FIM**–bree–ay)—Finger-like projections at the end of the fallopian tube which encloses the ovary (Chapter 20).

Fissure (**FISH**–er)—A groove or furrow between parts of an organ such as the brain (Syn.—sulcus) (Chapter 8).

Flagellum (flah–**JELL**–um)—A long, thread-like projection through a cell membrane; provides motility for the cell (Chapter 3).

Flexion (**FLEK**–shun)—To decrease the angle of a joint (Chapter 7).

Flexor reflex (**FLEKS**–er **REE**–fleks)—A spinal cord reflex in which a painful stimulus causes withdrawal of a body part (Chapter 8).

Fluorescent antibody test (floor–**ESS**–ent **AN**–ti–BAH–dee)—A diagnostic test that uses fluorescently tagged antibodies to determine the presence of a particular pathogen in the blood or other tissue specimen (Chapter 14).

Follicle-stimulating hormone (FSH) (**FAH**–lik–uhl)—A gonadotropic hormone produced by the anterior pituitary gland, that initiates the production of ova in the ovaries or sperm in the testes (Chapter 10).

Fomites (**FOH**–mights; **FOH**–mi–teez)—Inanimate objects capable of transmitting infectious microorganisms from one host to another (Chapter 22).

Fontanel (FON–tah–**NELL**)—An area of fibrous connective tissue membrane between the cranial bones of an infant's skull, where bone formation is not complete (Chapter 6).

Foramen (for–**RAY**–men)—A hole or opening, as in a bone (Chapter 6).

Foramen ovale (for–**RAY**–men oh–**VAHL**–ee)—An opening in the interatrial septum of the fetal heart that permits blood to flow from the right atrium to the left atrium, bypassing the fetal lungs (Chapter 13).

Fossa (**FAH**–sah)—A shallow depression in a bone (Chapter 6).

Fovea (**FOH**–vee–ah)—A depression in the retina of the eye directly behind the lens; contains only cones and is the area of best color vision (Chapter 9).

Fracture (**FRAK**–chur)—A break in a bone (Chapter 6).

Free nerve ending (FREE NERV **END**–ing)—The end of a sensory neuron; the receptor for the sense of pain in the skin and viscera (Chapter 5).

Frontal bone (**FRUN**–tuhl)—The flat cranial bone that forms the forehead (Chapter 6).

Frontal lobes (**FRUN**–tuhl LOWBS)—The most anterior parts of the cerebrum; contain the motor areas for voluntary movement and the motor speech area (Chapter 8).

Frontal section (**FRUN**–tuhl **SEK**–shun)—A plane separating the body into front and back portions (Syn.—coronal section) (Chapter 1).

Frostbite (**FRAWST**–bite)—The freezing of part of the body, resulting in tissue damage or death (gangrene) (Chapter 17).

Fructose (**FRUHK**–tohs)—A monosaccharide, a six-carbon sugar that is part of the sucrose in food; converted to glucose by the liver (Chapter 2).

Functional layer (**FUNK**–shun-ul **LAY**–er)—The vascular layer of the endometrium that is lost in menstruation, then regenerated by the basilar layer (Chapter 20).

Fungus (**FUNG**–gus)—Any of the organisms of the kingdom Fungi; they lack chlorophyll; may be unicellular or multicellular; saprophytic or parasitic; include yeasts, molds, mushrooms (Chapter 22).

—G—

Galactose (guh–**LAK**–tohs)—A monosaccharide, a six-carbon sugar that is part of the lactose in food; converted to glucose by the liver (Chapter 2).

Gallbladder (**GAWL**–bla–der)—An accessory organ of digestion; a sac located on the undersurface of the liver; stores and concentrates bile (Chapter 16).

Gallstones (**GAWL**–stohns)—Crystals formed in the gallbladder or bile ducts; the most common type is made of cholesterol (Chapter 16).

Gametes (**GAM**–eets)—The male or female reproductive cells, sperm cells or ova, each with the haploid number of chromosomes (Chapter 3).

Gamma globulins (**GA**–mah **GLAH**–byoo–lins)—Antibodies (Chapter 14).

Ganglion (**GANG**–lee–on)—A group of neuron cell bodies located outside the CNS (Chapter 8).

Ganglion neurons (**GANG**–lee–on **NYOOR**–onz)—The neurons that form the optic nerve; carry impulses from the retina to the brain (Chapter 9).

Gastric juice (**GAS**–trik JOOSS)—The secretion of the gastric pits of the stomach; contains hydrochloric acid, pepsin, and mucus (Chapter 16).

Gastric pits (**GAS**–trik PITS)—The glands of the mucosa of the stomach; secrete gastric juice (Chapter 16).

Gastric ulcer (**GAS**–trik **UL**–ser)—An erosion of the gastric mucosa and submucosa (Chapter 16).

Gastrin (**GAS**–trin)—A hormone secreted by the gastric mucosa when food enters the stomach; stimulates the secretion of gastric juice (Chapter 16).

Gene (JEEN)—A segment of DNA that is the genetic code for a particular protein and is located in a definite position on a particular chromosome (Chapter 3).

Genetic code (je–**NET**–ik KOHD)—The sequence of bases of the DNA in the chromosomes of cells; is the code for proteins (Chapter 2).

Genetic disease (je–**NET**–ik di–**ZEEZ**)—A hereditary disorder that is the result of an incorrect sequence of bases in the DNA (gene) of a particular chromosome. May be passed to offspring (Chapter 3).

Genetic immunity (je–**NET**–ik im–**YOO**–ni–tee)—The immunity provided by the genetic makeup of a species; reflects the inability of certain pathogens to cause disease in certain host species (Chapter 14).

Genotype (**JEE**–noh–type)—The genetic makeup of an individual; the genes that are present (Chapter 21).

Gestation (jes–**TAY**–shun)—The length of time from conception to birth; the human gestation period averages 280 days (Chapter 21).

Giantism (**JIGH**–an–tizm)—Excessive growth of the body or its parts; may be the result of hypersecretion of growth hormone in childhood (Chapter 10).

Gingiva (jin–**JIGH**–vah)—The gums; the tissue that covers the upper and lower jaws around the necks of the teeth (Chapter 16).

Gland (GLAND)—A cell or group of epithelial cells that are specialized to secrete a substance (Chapter 4).

Glaucoma (glaw–**KOH**–mah)—An eye disease characterized by increased intraocular pressure due to excessive accumulation of aqueous humor (Chapter 9).

Gliding joint (**GLY**–ding)—A diarthrosis that permits a sliding movement (Chapter 6).

Globulins (**GLAH**–byoo–lins)—Proteins that circulate in blood plasma; alpha and beta globulins are synthesized by the liver; gamma globulins (antibodies) are synthesized by lymphocytes (Chapter 11).

Glomerular filtration (gloh–**MER**–yoo–ler fill–**TRAY**–shun)—The first step in the formation of urine; blood pressure in the glomerulus forces plasma, dissolved materials, and small proteins into Bowman's capsule; this fluid is then called renal filtrate (Chapter 18).

Glomerular filtration rate (gloh–**MER**–yoo–ler fill–**TRAY**–shun RAYT)—The total volume of renal filtrate that the kidneys form in 1 minute; average is 100–125 ml/minute (Chapter 18).

Glomerulus (gloh–**MER**–yoo–lus)—A capillary network that is enclosed by Bowman's capsule; filtration takes place from the glomerulus to Bowman's capsule (Chapter 18).

Glossopharyngeal nerves (GLAH–so–fuh–**RIN**–jee–uhl)—Cranial nerve pair IX. Sensory for taste and cardiovascular reflexes. Motor to salivary glands (Chapter 8).

Glottis (**GLAH**–tis)—The opening between the vocal cords; an air passageway (Chapter 15).

Glucagon (**GLOO**–kuh–gahn)—A hormone secreted by the pancreas that increases the blood glucose level (Chapter 10).

Glucocorticoids (GLOO–koh–**KOR**–ti–koids)—The hormones secreted by the adrenal cortex that affect the metabolism of nutrients; cortisol is the major hormone in this group (Chapter 10).

Gluconeogenesis (GLOO–koh–nee–oh–**JEN**–i–sis)—The conversion of excess amino acids to simple carbohydrates or to glucose to be used for energy production (Chapter 10).

Glucose (**GLOO**–kos)—A hexose monosaccharide that is the primary energy source for body cells (Chapter 2).

Glycerol (**GLISS**–er–ol)—A three-carbon molecule that is one of the end products of the digestion of fats (Chapter 2).

Glycogen (**GLY**–ko–jen)—A polysaccharide that is the storage form for excess glucose in the liver and muscles (Chapter 2).

Glycogenesis (GLIGH–koh–**JEN**–i–sis)—The conversion of glucose to glycogen to be stored as potential energy (Chapter 10).

Glycogenolysis (GLIGH–koh–jen–**OL**–i–sis)—The conversion of stored glycogen to glucose to be used for energy production (Chapter 10).

Glycolysis (gly–**KOL**–ah–sis)—The first stage of the cell respiration of glucose, in which glucose is broken down to two molecules of pyruvic acid and ATP is formed; anaerobic; takes place in the cytoplasm of cells (Chapter 17).

Glycosuria (GLY–kos–**YOO**–ree–ah)—The presence of glucose in urine; often an indication of diabetes mellitus (Chapter 18).

Goblet cell (**GAHB**–let)—Unicellular glands that secrete mucus; found in the respiratory and GI mucosa (Chapter 4).

Goiter (**GOY**–ter)—An enlargement of the thyroid gland, often due to a lack of dietary iodine (Chapter 10).

Golgi apparatus (**GOHL**–jee)—A cell organelle found in the cytoplasm; synthesizes carbohydrates and packages materials for secretion from the cell (Chapter 3).

Gonadotropic hormone (GAH–nah–doh–**TROH**–pik)—A hormone that has its effects on the ovaries or testes (gonads); FSH and LH (Chapter 10).

Gonorrhea (GAH–nuh–**REE**–ah)—A sexually transmitted disease caused by the bacterium *Neisseria gonorrhoeae;* may also cause conjunctivitis in newborns of infected women (Chapter 20).

Graafian follicle (**GRAFF**–ee–uhn **FAH**–li–kuhl)—A mature ovarian follicle that releases an ovum (Chapter 20).

Gram negative (**GRAM NEG**–uh–tiv)—Bacteria that appear red or pink after gram staining (Chapter 22).

Gram positive (**GRAM PAHS**–uh–tiv)—Bacteria that appear purple or blue after gram staining (Chapter 22).

Gram stain (**GRAM STAYN**)—A staining procedure for bacteria to make them visible microscopically and to determine their gram reaction, which is important in the identification of bacteria (Chapter 22).

Graves' disease (GRAYVES)—Hypersecretion of thyroxine, believed to be an autoimmune disease; symptoms reflect the elevated metabolic rate (Chapter 10).

Gray matter (GRAY)—Nerve tissue within the central nervous system that consists of the cell bodies of neurons (Chapter 8).

Growth hormone (GH) (GROHTH **HOR**–mohn)—A hormone secreted by the anterior pituitary gland that increases the rate of cell division and protein synthesis (Chapter 10).

Gyrus (**JIGH**–rus)—A fold or ridge, as in the cerebral cortex (Syn.—convolution) (Chapter 8).

—**H**—

Hair (HAIR)—An accessory skin structure produced in a hair follicle (Chapter 5).

Hair follicle (HAIR **FAH**–li–kull)—The structure within the skin in which a hair grows (Chapter 5).

Hair root (HAIR ROOT)—The site of mitosis at the base of a hair follicle; new cells become the hair shaft (Chapter 5).

Haploid number (**HA**–ployd)—Half the usual number of chromosomes found in the cells of a species. Characteristic of the gametes of the species (human = 23) (Chapter 3).

Hard palate (HARD **PAL**–uht)—The anterior portion of the palate formed by the maxillae and the palatine bones (Chapter 6).

Haustra (**HOWS**–trah)—The pouches of the colon (Chapter 16).

Haversian system (ha–**VER**–zhun)—The structural unit of compact bone, consisting of a central haversian canal surrounded by concentric rings of osteocytes within matrix (Chapter 4).

Heart murmur (HART **MUR**–mur)—An abnormal heart sound heard during the cardiac cycle; often caused by a malfunctioning heart valve (Chapter 12).

Heat exhaustion (HEET eks–**ZAWS**–chun)—A state of weakness and dehydration caused by excessive loss of body water and sodium chloride in sweat; the result of exposure to heat or of strenuous exercise (Chapter 17).

Heat stroke (HEET STROHK)—An acute reaction to heat exposure in which there is failure of the temperature-regulating mechanisms; sweating ceases, and body temperature rises sharply (Chapter 17).

Heimlich maneuver (**HIGHM**–lik ma–**NEW**–ver)—A procedure used to remove foreign material lodged in the pharynx, larynx, or trachea (Chapter 15).

Helix (**HEE**–liks)—A coil or spiral. Double helix is the descriptive term used for the shape of a DNA molecule: two strands of nucleotides coiled around each other and resembling a twisted ladder (Chapter 2).

Hematocrit (hee–**MAT**–oh–krit)—A laboratory test that determines the percentage of red blood cells in a given volume of blood; part of a complete blood count (Chapter 11).

Hematuria (HEM–uh–**TYOO**–ree–ah)—The presence of blood (RBCs) in urine (Chapter 18).

Hemodialysis (HEE–moh–dye–**AL**–i–sis)—A technique for providing the function of the kidneys by passing the blood through tubes surrounded by solutions that selectively remove waste products and excess minerals; may be life-saving in cases of renal failure (Chapter 18).

Hemoglobin (**HEE**–muh–GLOW–bin)—The protein in red blood cells that contains iron and transports oxygen in the blood (Chapter 7).

Hemolysis (he–**MAHL**–e–sis)—Lysis or rupture of red blood cells; may be the result of an antigen-antibody reaction or of increased fragility of red blood cells in some types of anemia (Chapter 11).

Hemophilia (HEE–moh–**FILL**–ee–ah)—A hereditary blood disorder characterized by the inability of the blood to clot normally; hemophilia A is caused by a lack of clotting factor 8 (Chapter 11).

Hemopoietic tissue (HEE–moh poy–**ET**–ik)—A blood-forming tissue; the red bone marrow and lymphatic tissue (Chapter 4).

Hemorrhoids (**HEM**–uh–royds)—Varicose veins of the anal canal (Chapter 13).

Hemostasis (HEE–moh–**STAY**–sis)—Prevention of blood loss; the mechanisms are chemical clotting, vascular spasm, and platelet plug formation (Chapter 11).

Heparin (**HEP**–ar–in)—A chemical that inhibits blood clotting, an anticoagulant; produced by basophils. Also used clinically to prevent abnormal clotting, such as following some types of surgery (Chapter 11).

Hepatic duct (hep–**PAT**–ik DUKT)—The duct that takes bile out of the liver; joins the cystic duct of the gallbladder to form the common bile duct (Chapter 16).

Hepatic portal circulation (hep–**PAT**–ik **POOR**–tuhl)—The pathway of systemic circulation in which venous blood from the digestive organs and the spleen circulates through the liver before returning to the heart (Chapter 13).

Hepatitis (HEP–uh–**TIGH**–tis)—Inflammation of the liver, most often caused by the hepatitis viruses A, B, or C (Chapter 16).

Herniated disc (**HER**–nee–ay–ted DISK)—Rupture of an intervertebral disc (Chapter 6).

Herpes simplex (**HER**–peez **SIM**–pleks)—A virus that causes lesions in the skin or mucous membranes of the mouth (usually type 1) or genital area (usually type 2); genital herpes may cause death or mental retardation of infants of infected women (Chapter 20).

Heterozygous (HET–er–oh–**ZYE**–gus)—Having two different alleles for a trait (Chapter 21).

Hexose sugar (**HEKS**–ohs)—A six-carbon sugar, such as glucose, that is an energy source (in the process of cell respiration) (Chapter 2).

Hilus (**HIGH**–lus)—An indentation or depression on the surface of an organ such as a lung or kidney (Chapter 15).

Hinge joint (HINJ)—A diarthrosis that permits movement in one plane (Chapter 6).

Hip bone (HIP BOWNE)—The flat bone that forms half of the pelvic bone; consists of the upper ilium, the lower posterior ischium, and the lower anterior pubis (Chapter 6).

Histamine (**HISS**–tah–meen)—An inflammatory chemical released by damaged tissues; stimulates increased capillary permeability and vasodilation (Chapter 5).

Hives (**HIGHVZ**)—A very itchy eruption of the skin, usually the result of an allergy (Chapter 5).

Hodgkin's disease (**HODJ**–kinz)—A malignancy of the lymphatic tissue; a lymphoma (Chapter 14).

Homeostasis (HOH–me–oh–**STAY**–sis)—The state in which the internal environment of the body remains relatively stable by responding appropriately to changes (Chapter 1).

Homologous pair (hoh–**MAHL**–ah–gus)—A pair of chromosomes, one maternal and one paternal, that contain genes for the same characteristics (Chapter 21).

Homozygous (HOH–moh–**ZYE**–gus)—Having two similar alleles for a trait (Chapter 21).

Hormone (**HOR**–mohn)—The secretion of an endocrine gland that has specific effects on particular target organs (Chapter 4).

Human leukocyte antigens (HLA) (**HYOO**–man **LOO**–koh–site **AN**–ti–jens)—The antigens on white blood cells that are representative of the antigens present on all the cells of the individual; the "self" antigens that are controlled by several genes on chromosome number 6; the basis for tissue-typing before an organ transplant is attempted (Chapter 11).

Humerus (**HYOO**–mer–us)—The long bone of the upper arm (Chapter 6).

Humoral immunity (**HYOO**–mohr–uhl im–**YOO**–ni–tee)—The mechanism of immunity that involves antibody production and the destruction of foreign antigens by the activities of B cells, T cells, and macrophages (Chapter 14).

Hyaline membrane disease (**HIGH**–e–lin **MEM**–brayn)—A pulmonary disorder of premature infants whose lungs have not yet produced sufficient pulmonary surfactant to permit inflation of the alveoli (Chapter 15).

Hydrochloric acid (HIGH–droh–**KLOR**–ik **ASS**–id)—An acid secreted by the parietal cells of the gastric pits of the stomach; activates pepsin and maintains a pH of 1–2 in the stomach (Chapter 16).

Hymen (**HIGH**–men)—A thin fold of mucous membrane that partially covers the vaginal orifice (Chapter 20).

Hypercalcemia (HIGH–per–kal–**SEE**–mee–ah)—A high blood calcium level (Chapter 10).

Hyperglycemia (HIGH–per–gligh–**SEE**–mee–ah)—A high blood glucose level (Chapter 10).

Hyperkalemia (HIGH–per–kuh–**LEE**–mee–ah)—A high blood potassium level (Chapter 19).

Hypernatremia (HIGH–per–nuh–**TREE**–mee–ah)—A high blood sodium level (Chapter 19).

Hyperopia (HIGH–per–**OH**–pee–ah)—Farsightedness; an error of refraction in which only distant objects are seen clearly (Chapter 9).

Hypertension (HIGH–per–**TEN**–shun)—An abnormally high blood pressure, consistently above 140/90 mmHg (Chapter 13).

Hypertonic (HIGH–per–**TOHN**–ik)—Having a greater concentration of dissolved materials than the solution used as a comparison (Chapter 3).

Hypertrophy (high–**PER**–troh–fee)—Increase in size of a body part, especially of a muscle following long-term exercise or overuse (Chapter 7).

Hypocalcemia (HIGH–poh–kal–**SEE**–mee–ah)—A low blood calcium level (Chapter 10).

Hypoglossal nerves (HIGH–poh–**GLAH**–suhl)—Cranial nerve pair XII. Motor to the tongue (Chapter 8).

Hypoglycemia (HIGH–poh–gligh–**SEE**–mee–ah)—A low blood glucose level (Chapter 10).

Hypokalemia (HIGH–poh–kuh–**LEE**–mee–ah)—A low blood potassium level (Chapter 19).

Hyponatremia (HIGH–poh–nuh–**TREE**–mee–ah)—A low blood sodium level (Chapter 19).

Hypophyseal portal system (high–POFF–e–**SEE**–al **POR**–tuhl)—The pathway of circulation in which releasing factors from the hypothalamus circulate directly to the anterior pituitary gland (Chapter 10).

Hypophysis (high–**POFF**–e–sis)—The pituitary gland (Chapter 10).

Hypotension (HIGH–poh–**TEN**–shun)—An abnormally low blood pressure, consistently below 90/60 mmHg (Chapter 13).

Hypothalamus (HIGH–poh–**THAL**–uh–muss)—The part of the brain superior to the pituitary gland and inferior to the thalamus; its many functions include regulation of body temperature and regulation of the secretions of the pituitary gland (Chapter 8).

Hypothermia (HIGH–poh–**THER**–mee–ah)—1. The condition in which the body temperature is abnormally low due to excessive exposure to cold. 2. A procedure used during some types of surgery to lower body temperature to reduce the patient's need for oxygen (Chapter 17).

Hypotonic (HIGH–po–**TOHN**–ik)—Having a lower concentration of dissolved materials than the solution used as a comparison (Chapter 3).

Hypovolemic shock (HIGH–poh–voh–**LEEM**–ik SHAHK)—A type of circulatory shock caused by a decrease in blood volume (Chapter 13).

Hypoxia (high–**POCK**–see–ah)—A deficiency or lack of oxygen (Chapter 2).

—I—

Idiopathic (ID–ee–oh–**PATH**–ik)—A disease or disorder of unknown cause (Chapter 11).

Ileocecal valve (ILL–ee–oh–**SEE**–kuhl VALV)—The tissue of the ileum that extends into the cecum and acts as a sphincter; prevents the backup of fecal material into the small intestine (Chapter 16).

Ileum (**ILL**–ee–um)—The third and last portion of the small intestine, about 11 feet long (Chapter 16).

Ilium (**ILL**–ee–yum)—The upper, flared portion of the hip bone (Chapter 6).

Immunity (im–**YOO**–ni–tee)—The state of being protected from an infectious disease, usually by having been exposed to the infectious agent or a vaccine (Chapter 11).

Impetigo (IM–pe–**TYE**–go)—A bacterial infection of the skin that occurs most often in children (Chapter 5).

Implantation (IM–plan–**TAY**–shun)—Embedding of the embryonic blastocyst in the endometrium of the uterus 6 to 8 days after fertilization (Chapter 21).

Inactivator (in–**AK**–ti–vay–tur)—A chemical that inactivates a neurotransmitter to prevent continuous impulses (Chapter 8).

Inapparent infection (**IN**–uh–PAR–ent)—An infection without symptoms (Chapter 22).

Incubation period (IN–kew–**BAY**–shun)—In the course of an infectious disease, the time between the entry of the pathogen and the onset of symptoms (Chapter 22).

Incus (**ING**–kuss)—The second of the three auditory bones in the middle ear; transmits vibrations from the malleus to the stapes (Chapter 9).

Infarct (**IN**–farkt)—An area of tissue that has died due to lack of a blood supply (Chapter 12).

Infection (in–**FECK**–shun)—A disease process caused by the invasion and multiplication of a microorganism (Chapter 22).

Inferior (in–**FEER**–ee–your)—Below or lower (Chapter 1).

Inferior vena cava (**VEE**–nah **KAY**–vah)—The vein that returns blood from the lower body to the right atrium (Chapter 12).

Infestation (in–fess–**TAY**–shun)—The harboring of parasites, especially worms or arthropods (Chapter 22).

Inflammation (in–fluh–**MAY**–shun)—The reactions of tissue to injury (Chapter 5).

Inguinal canal (**IN**–gwi–nuhl ka–**NAL**)—The opening in the lower abdominal wall that contains a spermatic cord in men and the round ligament of the uterus in women; a natural weak spot that may be the site of hernia formation (Chapter 20).

Inhibin (in–**HIB**–in)—A protein hormone secreted by the sustentacular cells of the testes in response to increased testosterone; inhibits secretion of FSH to help maintain a constant rate of spermatogenesis (Chapter 10).

Inorganic (**IN**–or–GAN–ik)—A chemical compound that does not contain carbon-hydrogen covalent bonds; includes water, salts, and oxygen (Chapter 1).

Insertion (in–**SIR**–shun)—The more movable attachment point of a muscle to a bone (Chapter 7).

Inspiration (in–spi–**RAY**–shun)—Inhalation; the intake of air to the lungs (Chapter 15).

Inspiratory reserve (in–**SPYR**–ah–tor–ee ree–**ZERV**)—The volume of air beyond tidal volume that can be inhaled with the deepest inhalation; average: 2000–3000 ml (Chapter 15).

Insulin (**IN**–syoo–lin)—A hormone secreted by the pancreas that decreases the blood glucose level by increasing storage of glycogen and use of glucose by cells for energy production (Chapter 10).

Integumentary system (in–TEG–yoo–**MEN**–tah–ree)—The organ system that consists of the skin and its accessory structures and the subcutaneous tissue (Chapter 5).

Intensity (in–**TEN**–si–tee)—The degree to which a sensation is felt (Chapter 9).

Intercostal muscles (IN–ter–**KAHS**–tuhl **MUSS**–uhls)—The skeletal muscles between the ribs; the external intercostals pull the ribs up and out for inhalation; the internal intercostals pull the ribs down and in for a forced exhalation (Syn.—spareribs) (Chapter 15).

Intercostal nerves (IN–ter–**KAHS**–tuhl NERVS)—The pairs of peripheral nerves that are motor to the intercostal muscles (Chapter 15).

Interferon (in–ter–**FEER**–on)—A chemical produced by T cells or by cells infected with viruses; prevents the reproduction of viruses (Chapter 14).

Internal (in–**TER**–nuhl)—On the inside, or away from the surface (Chapter 1).

Internal anal sphincter (in–**TER**–nuhl **AY**–nuhl **SFINK**–ter)—The circular smooth muscle that surrounds the anus; relaxes as part of the defecation reflex to permit defecation (Chapter 16).

Internal respiration (in–**TER**–nuhl RES–pi–**RAY**–shun)—The exchange of gases between the blood in the systemic capillaries and the surrounding tissue fluid and cells (Chapter 15).

Internal urethral sphincter (yoo–**REE**–thruhl **SFINK**–ter)—The smooth muscle sphincter at the junction of the urinary bladder and the urethra; relaxes as part of the urination reflex to permit urination (Chapter 18).

Interneuron (**IN**–ter–NYOOR–on)—A nerve cell entirely within the central nervous system (Chapter 8).

Interphase (**IN**–ter–fayz)—The period of time between mitotic divisions during which DNA replication takes place (Chapter 3).

Interstitial cells (In–ter–**STI**–shul SELLS)—The cells in the testes that secrete testosterone when stimulated by LH (Chapter 20).

Intestinal glands in–**TESS**–tin–uhl)—1. The glands of the small intestine that secrete digestive enzymes. 2. The glands of the large intestine that secrete mucus (Chapter 16).

Intracellular fluid (IN–trah–**SELL**–yoo–ler **FLOO**–id)—The water found within cells (Chapter 2).

Intramuscular injection (In–trah–**MUSS**–kuh–ler in–**JEK**–shun)—An injection of a medication into a muscle (Chapter 7).

Intrapleural pressure (In–trah–**PLOOR**–uhl)—The pressure within the potential pleural space; always slightly below atmospheric pressure, about 756 mmHg (Chapter 15).

Intrapulmonic pressure (In–trah–pull–**MAHN**–ik)—The air pressure within the bronchial tree and alveoli; fluctuates below and above atmospheric pressure during breathing (Chapter 15).

Intrinsic factor (in–**TRIN**–sik **FAK**–ter)—A chemical produced by the parietal cells of the gastric mucosa; necessary for the absorption of vitamin B_{12} (Chapter 11).

In vitro fertilization (IN **VEE**–troh FER–ti–li–**ZAY**–shun)—Fertilization outside the body, in which sperm and ova are mixed in laboratory glassware; early embryos may then be introduced into the uterus for implantation (Chapter 20).

Involuntary muscle (in–**VAHL**–un–tary **MUSS**–uhl)—Another name for smooth muscle tissue (Chapter 4).

Ion (**EYE**–on)—An atom or group of atoms with an electrical charge (Chapter 2).

Ionic bond (eye–**ON**–ik)—A chemical bond formed by the loss and gain of electrons between atoms (Chapter 2).

Iris (**EYE**–ris)—The colored part of the eye, between the cornea and lens; made of two sets of smooth muscle fibers that regulate the size of the pupil, the opening in the center of the iris (Chapter 9).

Ischemic (iss–**KEY**–mik)—Lack of blood to a body part, often due to an obstruction in circulation (Chapter 12).

Ischium (**ISH**–ee–um)—The lower posterior part of the hip bone (Chapter 6).

Islets of Langerhans (**EYE**–lets of **LAHNG**–er–hanz)—The endocrine portions of the pancreas that secrete insulin and glucagon (Chapter 10).

Isometric exercise (**EYE**–so–**MEH**–trik)—Contraction of muscles without movement of a body part (Chapter 7).

Isotonic (**EYE**–so–**TAHN**–ik)—Having the same concentration of dissolved materials as the solution used as a comparison (Chapter 3).

Isotonic exercise (**EYE**–so–**TAHN**–ik)—Contraction of muscles with movement of a body part (Chapter 7).

—J—

Jaundice (**JAWN**–diss)—A condition characterized by a yellow color in the whites of the eyes and the skin; caused by an elevated blood level of bilirubin. May be hepatic, pre-hepatic, or post-hepatic in origin (Chapter 11).

Jejunum (je–**JOO**–num)—The second portion of the small intestine, about 8 feet long (Chapter 16).

Joint capsule (JOYNT **KAP**–suhl)—The fibrous connective tisseue sheath that encloses a joint (Chapter 6).

Juxtaglomerular cells (JUKS–tah–gloh–**MER**–yoo–ler SELLS)—Cells in the wall of the afferent arteriole that secrete renin when blood pressure decreases (Chapter 18)

—K—

Keratin (**KER**–uh–tin)—A protein produced by epidermal cells; found in the epidermis, hair, and nails (Chapter 5).

Ketoacidosis (KEY–toh–ass–i–**DOH**–sis)—A metabolic acidosis that results from the accumulation of ketones in the blood when fats and proteins are used for energy production (Chapter 10).

Ketones (**KEY**–tohns)—Organic acid molecules that are formed from fats or amino acids when these nutrients are used for energy production; include acetone and acetoacetic acid (Chapter 10).

Ketonuria (KEY–ton–**YOO**–ree–ah)—The presence of ketones in urine (Chapter 18).

Kidneys (**KID**–nees)—The two organs on either side of the vertebral column in the upper abdomen that produce urine to eliminate waste products and to regulate the volume, pH, and fluid-electrolyte balance of the blood (Chapter 6).

Kilocalorie (KILL–oh–**KAL**–oh–ree)—One thousand calories; used to indicate the energy content of foods or the energy expended in activity (Chapter 17).

Kinesthetic sense (KIN–ess–**THET**–ik)—Muscle sense (Chapter 9).

Krebs cycle (KREBS **SIGH**–kuhl)—The stage of cell respiration comprised of a series of reactions in which pyruvic acid or acetyl CoA is broken down to carbon dioxide and ATP is formed; aerobic; takes place in the mitochondria of cells (Syn.—citric acid cycle) (Chapter 17).

Kupffer cells (**KUP**–fer SELLS)—The macrophages of the liver; phagocytize pathogens and old red blood cells (Chapter 16).

Kyphosis (kye–**FOH**–sis)—An exaggerated thoracic curvature of the vertebral column (Chapter 6).

—L—

Labia majora (**LAY**–bee–uh muh–**JOR**–ah)—The outer folds of skin of the vulva; enclose the labia minora and the vestibule (Chapter 20).

Labia minora (**LAY**–bee–uh min–**OR**–ah)—The inner folds of the vulva; enclose the vestibule (Chapter 20).

Labor (**LAY**–ber)—The process by which a fetus is expelled from the uterus through the vagina to the exterior of the body (Chapter 21).

Labyrinth (**LAB**–i–rinth)—1. A maze; an interconnected series of passageways. 2. In the inner ear: the bony labyrinth is a series of tunnels in the temporal bone lined with membrane called the membranous labyrinth (Chapter 9).

Lacrimal glands (**LAK**–ri–muhl)—The glands that secrete tears, located at the upper, outer corner of each eyeball (Chapter 9).

Lactase (**LAK**–tays)—A digestive enzyme that breaks down lactose to glucose and galactose; secreted by the small intestine (Chapter 16).

Lacteals (lak–**TEELS**)—The lymph capillaries in the villi of the small intestine, which absorb the fat-soluble end products of digestion (Chapter 14).

Lactic acid (**LAK**–tik **ASS**–id)—The chemical end product of anaerobic cell respiration; contributes to fatigue in muscle cells (Chapter 7).

Lactose (**LAK**–tohs)—A disaccharide made of one glucose and one galactose molecule (Syn.—milk sugar) (Chapter 2).

Lactose intolerance (**LAK**–tohs in–**TAHL**–er–ense)—The inability to digest lactose due to a deficiency of the enzyme lactase; may be congenital or acquired (Chapter 16).

Large intestine (LARJ in–**TESS**–tin)—The organ of the alimentary tube that extends from the small intestine to the anus; absorbs water, minerals, and vitamins and eliminates undigested materials (Syn.—colon) (Chapter 16).

Laryngopharynx (la–RIN–goh–**FA**–rinks)—The lower portion of the pharynx that opens into the larynx and the esophagus; a passageway for both air and food (Chapter 15).

Larynx (**LA**–rinks)—The organ between the pharynx and the trachea that contains the vocal cords for speech (Syn.—voice box) (Chapter 15).

Lateral (**LAT**–er–uhl)—Away from the midline, or at the side (Chapter 1).

Lens (LENZ)—The oval structure of the eye posterior to the pupil, made of transparent protein; the only adjustable portion of the refraction pathway for the focusing of light rays (Chapter 9).

Lesion (**LEE**–zuhn)—An area of pathologically altered tissue; an injury or wound (Chapter 5).

Leukemia (loo–**KEE**–mee–ah)—Malignancy of blood-forming tissues, in which large numbers of immature and non-functional white blood cells are produced (Chapter 11).

Leukocyte (**LOO**–koh–site)—White blood cell; the five kinds are neutrophils, eosinophils, basophils, lymphocytes, and monocytes (Chapter 11).

Leukocytosis (LOO–koh–sigh–**TOH**–sis)—An elevated white blood cell count, often an indication of infection (Chapter 11).

Leukopenia (LOO–koh–**PEE**–nee–ah)—An abnormally low white blood cell count; may be the result of aplastic anemia, or a side effect of some medications (Chapter 11).

Ligament (**LIG**–uh–ment)—A fibrous connective tissue structure that connects bone to bone (Chapter 6).

Lipase (**LYE**–pays)—A digestive enzyme that breaks down emulsified fats to fatty acids and glycerol; secreted by the pancreas (Chapter 16).

Lipid (**LIP**–id)—An organic chemical insoluble in water; includes true fats, phospholipids, and steroids (Chapter 2).

Lipoprotein (Li–poh–**PRO**–teen)—A large molecule that is a combination of proteins, triglycerides, and cholesterol; formed by the liver to circulate lipids in the blood (Chapter 16).

Lithotripsy (LITH–oh–**TRIP**–see)—Crushing of gallstones or renal calculi by an instrument that uses ultrasonic waves applied to the exterior of the body (Chapter 16).

Liver (**LIV**–er)—The organ in the upper right and center of the abdominal cavity; secretes bile for the emulsification of fats in digestion; has many other functions related to the metabolism of nutrients and the compsition of blood (Chapter 16).

Localized infection (**LOH**–kuhl–IZ'D)—An infection confined to one body organ or site (Chapter 22).

Longitudinal section (LAWNJ–i–**TOO**–din–uhl **SEK**–shun)—A plane or cut along the long axis of an organ or the body (Chapter 1).

Loop of Henle (LOOP of **HEN**–lee)—The part of a renal tubule that extends from the proximal convoluted tubule to the distal convoluted tubule (Chapter 18).

Lordosis (lor–**DOH**–sis)—An exaggerated lumbar curvature of the vertebral column (Chapter 6).

Lower esophageal sphincter (e–SOF–uh–**JEE**–uhl **SFINK**–ter)—The circular smooth muscle at the lower end of the esophagus; prevents backup of stomach contents (Syn.—cardiac sphincter) (Chapter 16).

Lower respiratory tract (**LOH**–er **RES**–pi–rah–TOR–ee TRAKT)—The respiratory organs located within the chest cavity (Chapter 15).

Lumbar puncture (**LUM**–bar **PUNK**–chur)—A diagnostic procedure that involves removal of cerebrospinal fluid from the lumbar meningeal sac to assess the pressure and constituents of cerebrospinal fluid (Chapter 8).

Lumbar vertebrae (**LUM**–bar **VER**–te–bray)—The five large vertebrae in the small of the back (Chapter 6).

Lungs (LUHNGS)—The paired organs in the thoracic cavity in which gas exchange takes place between the air in the alveoli and the blood in the pulmonary capillaries (Chapter 15).

Luteinizing hormone (LH or ICSH) (LOO–tee–in–**EYE**–zing)—A gonadotropic hormone produced by the anterior pituitary gland that, in men, stimulates secretion of testosterone by the testes or, in women, stimulates ovulation and secretion of progesterone by the corpus luteum in the ovary (Chapter 10).

Lymph (LIMF)—The water found within lymphatic vessels (Chapter 2).

Lymph node (LIMF NOHD)—A small mass of lymphatic tissue located along the pathway of a lymph vessel; produces lymphocytes and monocytes and destroys pathogens in the lymph (Chapter 14).

Lymph nodule (LIMF **NAHD**–yool)—A small mass of lymphatic tissue located in a mucous membrane; produces lymphocytes and monocytes and destroys pathogens that penetrate mucous membranes (Chapter 14).

Lymphatic tissue (lim–**FAT**–ik **TISH**–yoo)—A hemopoietic tissue that produces lymphocytes and monocytes; found in the spleen and lymph nodes and nodules (Chapter 11).

Lymphocyte (**LIM**–foh–site)—A type of white blood cell (agranular); the two kinds are T cells and B cells, both of which are involved in immune responses (Chapter 11).

Lymphokines (**LIMF**–oh–kines)—Chemicals released by activated T cells that attract macrophages (Chapter 14).

Lysosome (**LYE**–soh–zome)—A cell organelle found in the cytoplasm; contains enzymes that digest damaged cell parts or material ingested by the cell (Chapter 3).

Lysozyme (**LYE**–soh–zime)—An enzyme in tears and saliva that inhibits the growth of bacteria in these fluids (Chapter 9).

—M—

Macrophage (**MAK**–roh–fahj)—A phagocytic cell derived from monocytes; capable of phagocytosis of pathogens, dead or damaged cells, and old red blood cells (Chapter 11).

Magnetic resonance imaging (MRI) (mag–**NET**–ik **REZ**–ah–nanse **IM**–ah–jing)—A diagnostic imaging technique that uses a magnetic field and a computer to integrate the images (Chapter 1).

Malignant (muh–**LIG**–nunt)—Tending to spread and become worse; used especially with reference to cancer (Chapter 3).

Malleus (**MAL**–ee–us)—The first of the three auditory bones in the middle ear; transmits vibrations from the eardrum to the incus (Chapter 9).

Maltase (**MAWL**–tays)—A digestive enzyme that breaks down maltose to glucose; secreted by the small intestine (Chapter 16).

Maltose (**MAWL**–tohs)—A disaccharide made of two glucose molecules (Chapter 2).

Mammary glands (**MAM**–uh–ree)—The glands of the female breasts that secrete milk; secretion and release of milk are under hormonal control (Chapter 20).

Mammography (mah–**MOG**–rah–fee)—A diagnostic procedure that uses radiography to detect breast cancer (Chapter 20).

Mandible (**MAN**–di–buhl)—The lower jaw bone (Chapter 6).

Manubrium (muh–**NOO**–bree–um)—The upper part of the sternum (Chapter 6).

Marrow canal (**MA**–roh ka–**NAL**)—The cavity within the diaphysis of a long bone; contains yellow bone marrow (Chapter 4).

Mastoid sinus (**MASS**–toyd)—An air cavity within the mastoid process of the temporal bone (Chapter 6).

Matrix (**MAY**–tricks)—The non-living intercellular material that is part of connective tissues (Chapter 4).

Matter (**MAT**–ter)—Anything that occupies space; may be solid, liquid, or gas; may be living or non-living (Chapter 2).

Maxilla (mak–**SILL**–ah)—The upper jaw bone (Chapter 6).

Mechanical digestion (muh–**KAN**–i–kuhl dye–**JES**–chun)—The physical breakdown of food into smaller pieces, which increases the surface area for the action of digestive enzymes (Chapter 16).

Medial (**MEE**–dee–uhl)—Toward the midline, or in the middle (Chapter 1).

Mediastinum (ME–dee–ah–**STYE**–num)—The area or space between the lungs; contains the heart and great vessels (Chapter 12).

Medulla (muh–**DEW**–lah) (muh–**DULL**–ah)—1. The part of the brain superior to the spinal cord; regulates vital functions such as heart rate, respiration, and blood pressure. 2. The inner part of an organ, such as the renal medulla or the adrenal medulla (Chapter 8).

Megakaryocyte (MEH–ga–**KA**–ree–oh–site)—A cell in the red bone marrow that breaks up into small fragments called platelets, which then circulate in peripheral blood (Chapter 11).

Meiosis (my–**OH**–sis)—The process of cell division in which one cell with the diploid number of chromosomes divides twice to form four cells, each with the haploid number of chromosomes (Chapter 3).

Meissner's plexus (**MIZE**–ners **PLEK**–sus)—The autonomic nerve plexus in the submucosa of the organs of the alimentary tube; regulates secretions of the glands in the mucosa of these organs (Chapter 16).

Melanin (**MEL**–uh–nin)—A protein pigment produced by melanocytes. Absorbs ultraviolet light; gives color to the skin, hair, iris, and choroid layer of the eye (Chapter 5).

Melanocyte (muh–**LAN**–o–site)—A cell in the lower epidermis that synthesizes the pigment melanin (Chapter 5).

Melanoma (MEL–ah–**NO**–mah)—Malignant pigmented mole or nevus (Chapter 5).

Membrane (**MEM**–brayn)—A sheet of tissue; may be made of epithelial tissue or connective tissue (Chapter 4).

Meninges (me–**NIN**–Jeez)—The connective tissue membranes that line the dorsal cavity and cover the brain and spinal cord (Chapter 1).

Meningitis (MEN–in–**JIGH**–tis)—Inflammation of the meninges, most often the result of bacterial infection (Chapter 8).

Menopause (**MEN**–ah–paws)—The period during life in which menstrual activity ceases; usually occurs between the ages of 45 and 55 years (Chapter 20).

Menstrual cycle (**MEN**–stroo–uhl **SIGH**–kuhl)—The periodic series of changes that occur in the female reproductive tract; the average cycle is 28 days (Chapter 20).

Menstruation (MEN–stroo–**AY**–shun)—The periodic discharge of a bloody fluid from the uterus that occurs at regular intervals from puberty to menopause (Chapter 20).

Mesentery (**MEZ**–en–TER–ee)—The visceral peritoneum (serous) that covers the abdominal organs; a large fold attaches the small intestine to the posterior abdominal wall (Chapter 1).

Mesoderm (**MEZ**–oh–derm)—The middle primary germ layer of cells of an embryo; gives rise to muscles, bones, and connective tissues (Chapter 21).

Metabolic acidosis (MET–uh–**BAH**–lik ass–i–**DOH**–sis)—A condition in which the blood pH is lower than normal, caused by any disorder that increases the number of acidic molecules in the body or increases the loss of alkaline molecules (Chapter 15).

Metabolic alkalosis (MET–uh–**BAH**–lik al–kah–**LOH**–sis)—A condition in which the blood pH is higher than normal, caused by any disorder that decreases the number of acidic molecules in the body or increases the number of alkaline molecules (Chapter 15).

Metabolism (muh–**TAB**–uh–lizm)—All the reactions that take place within the body; includes anabolism and catabolism (Chapter 17).

Metacarpals (MET–uh–**KAR**–puhls)—The five long bones in the palm of the hand (Chapter 6).

Metaphase (**MET**–ah–fayz)—The second stage of mitosis, in which the pairs of chromatids line up on the equator of the cell (Chapter 3).

Metastasis (muh–**TASS**–tuh–sis)—The spread of disease from one part of the body to another (Chapter 3).

Metatarsals (MET–uh–**TAR**–suhls)—The five long bones in the arch of the foot (Chapter 6).

Microglia (mye–kroh–**GLEE**–ah)—A type of neuroglia capable of movement and phagocytosis of pathogens (Chapter 8).

Micron (**MY**–kron)—A unit of linear measure equal to 0.001 millimeter (Syn.—micrometer) (Chapter 3).

Microvilli (MY–kro–**VILL**–eye)—Folds of the cell membrane on the free surface of an epithelial cell; increase the surface area for absorption (Chapter 4).

Micturition (MIK–tyoo–**RISH**–un)—Urination; the voiding or elimination of urine from the urinary bladder (Chapter 18).

Midbrain (**MID**–brayn)—The part of the brain between the pons and hypothalamus; regulates visual, auditory, and righting reflexes (Chapter 8).

Mineral (**MIN**–er–al)—An inorganic element or compound; many are needed by the body for normal metabolism and growth (Chapter 17).

Mineralocorticoids (MIN–er–al–oh–**KOR**–ti–koidz)—The hormones secreted by the adrenal cortex that affect fluid-electrolyte balance; aldosterone is the major hormone in this group (Chapter 10).

Minute respiratory volume (**MIN**–uht RES–pi–rah–**TOR**–ee **VAHL**–yoom)—The volume of air inhaled and exhaled in 1 minute; calculated by multiplying tidal volume by number of respirations per minute (Chapter 15).

Mitochondria (MY–to–**KON**–dree–ah)—The cell organelles in which aerobic cell respiration takes place and energy (ATP) is produced; found in the cytoplasm of a cell (Chapter 3).

Mitosis (my–**TOH**–sis)—The process of cell division in which one cell with the diploid number of chromosomes divides once to form two identical cells, each with the diploid number of chromosomes (Chapter 3).

Mitral valve (**MYE**–truhl VALV)—The left AV valve (bicuspid valve), which prevents backflow of blood from the left ventricle to the left atrium when the ventricle contracts (Chapter 12).

Mixed nerve (MIKSD NERV)—A nerve that contains both sensory and motor neurons (Chapter 8).

Molecule (**MAHL**–e–kuhl)—A chemical combination of two or more atoms (Chapter 2).

Monocyte (**MAH**–no–site)—A type of white blood cell (agranular); differentiates into a macrophage, which is capable of phagocytosis of pathogens and dead or damaged cells (Chapter 11).

Monosaccharide (MAH–noh–**SAK**–ah–ride)—A carbohydrate molecule that is a single sugar; includes the hexose and pentose sugars (Chapter 2).

Morula (**MOR**–yoo–lah)—An early stage of embryonic development, a solid mass of cells (Chapter 21).

Motility (moh–**TILL**–e–tee)—The ability to move (Chapter 3).

Motor neuron (**MOH**–ter **NYOOR**–on)—A nerve cell that carries impulses from the central nervous system to an effector (Syn.—efferent neuron) (Chapter 8).

Mucosa (mew–**KOH**–suh)—A mucous membrane, the epithelial lining of a body cavity that opens to the environment (Chapter 4).

Mucous membrane (**MEW**–kuss **MEM**–brayn)—The epithelial tissue lining of a body tract that opens to the environment (Chapter 4).

Mucus (**MEW**–kuss)—The thick fluid secreted by mucous membranes or mucous glands (Chapter 4).

Multicellular (MULL–tee–**SELL**–yoo–lar)—Consisting of more than one cell; made of many cells (Chapter 4).

Multiple sclerosis (**MULL**–ti–puhl skle–**ROH**–sis)—A progressive nervous system disorder, possibly an autoimmune disease, characterized by the degeneration of the myelin sheaths of CNS neurons (Chapter 8).

Muscle fatigue (**MUSS**–uhl fah–**TEEG**)—The state in which muscle fibers cannot contract efficiently, due to a lack of oxygen and the accumulation of lactic acid (Chapter 7).

Muscle fiber (**MUSS**–uhl **FYE**–ber)—A muscle cell (Chapter 7).

Muscle sense (**MUSS**–uhl SENSE)—The conscious or unconscious awareness of where the muscles are, and their degree of contraction, without having to look at them (Chapter 7).

Muscle tissue (**MUSS**–uhl **TISH**–yoo)—The tissue specialized for contraction and movement of parts of the body (Chapter 4).

Muscle tone (**MUSS**–uhl TONE)—The state of slight contraction present in healthy muscles (Chapter 7).

Muscular dystrophy (**MUSS**–kyoo–ler **DIS**–truh–fee)—A genetic disease characterized by the replacement of muscle tissue by fibrous connective tissue or adipose tissue, with progressive loss of muscle functioning; the most common form is Duchenne's muscular dystrophy (Chapter 7).

Muscular system (**MUSS**–kew–ler)—The organ system that consists of the skeletal muscles and tendons; its functions are to move the skeleton and produce body heat (Chapter 7).

Mutation (mew–**TAY**–shun)—A change in DNA; a genetic change that may be passed to offspring (Chapter 3).

Myalgia (my–**AL**–jee–ah)—Pain or tenderness in a muscle (Chapter 7).

Myasthenia gravis (MY–ass–**THEE**–nee–yuh **GRAH**–viss)—An autoimmune disease characterized by extreme muscle weakness and fatigue following minimal exertion (Chapter 7).

Mycosis (my–**KOH**–sis) (pl.: mycoses)—An infection caused by a pathogenic fungus (Chapter 22).

Myelin (**MY**–uh–lin)—A phospholipid produced by Schwann cells and oligodendrocytes that forms the myelin sheath of axons and dendrites (Chapter 2).

Myelin sheath (**MY**–uh–lin SHEETH)—The white, segmented, phospholipid sheath of most axons and dendrites; provides electrical insulation and increases the speed of impulse transmission (Chapter 4).

Myocardial infarction (MI) (MY–oh–**KAR**–dee–uyhl in–**FARK**–shun)—Death of part of the heart muscle due to lack of oxygen; often the result of an obstruction in a coronary artery (Syn.—heart attack) (Chapter 12).

Myocardium (MY–oh–**KAR**–dee–um)—The cardiac muscle tissue that forms the walls of the chambers of the heart (Chapter 4).

Myofibril (MY–oh–**FYE**–bril)—A linear arrangement of sarcomeres within a muscle fiber (Chapter 7).

Myoglobin (**MYE**–oh–GLOW–bin)—The protein in muscle fibers that contains iron and stores oxygen in muscle fibers (Chapter 7).

Myometrium (MY–oh–**ME**–tree–uhm)—The smooth muscle layer of the uterus; contracts for labor and delivery of an infant (Chapter 20).

Myopathy (my–**AH**–puh–thee)—A disease or abnormal condition of skeletal muscles (Chapter 7).

Myopia (my–**OH**–pee–ah)—Nearsightedness; an error of refraction in which only near objects are seen clearly (Chapter 9).

Myosin (**MYE**–oh–sin)—A contractile protein in the sarcomeres of muscle fibers (Chapter 7).

Myxedema (MICK–suh–**DEE**–mah)—Hyposecretion of thyroxine in an adult; decreased metabolic rate results in physical and mental lethargy (Chapter 10).

—N—

Nail follicle (NAYL **FAH**–li–kull)—The structure within the skin of a finger or toe in which a nail grows; mitosis takes place in the nail root (Chapter 5).

Narrow-spectrum (**NAR**–oh **SPEK**–trum)—An antibiotic that is effective against only a few kinds of bacteria (Chapter 22).

Nasal cavities (**NAY**–zuhl **KAV**–i–tees)—The two air cavities within the skull through which air passes from the nostrils to the nasopharynx; separated by the nasal septum (Chapter 15).

Nasal mucosa (NAY–zuhl mew–**KOH**–sah)—The lining of the nasal cavities; made of ciliated epithelium that warms and moistens the incoming air and sweeps mucus, dust, and pathogens toward the nasopharynx (Chapter 15).

Nasal septum (NAY–zuhl **SEP**–tum)—The verticle plate made of bone and cartilage that separates the two nasal cavities (Chapter 15).

Nasolacrimal duct (NAY–zo–**LAK**–ri–muhl)—A duct that carries tears from the lacrimal sac to the nasal cavity (Chapter 9).

Nasopharynx (NAY–zo–**FA**–rinks)—The upper portion of the pharynx above the level of the soft palate; an air passageway (Chapter 15).

Negative feedback mechanism (**NEG**–ah–tiv **FEED**–bak)—A control system in which a stimulus initiates a response that reverses or reduces the stimulus, thereby stopping the response until the stimulus occurs again (Chapter 10).

Nephritis (ne–**FRY**–tis)—Inflammation of the kidney; may be caused by bacterial infection or toxic chemicals (Chapter 18).

Nephron (**NEFF**–ron)—The structural and functional unit of the kidney that forms urine; consists of a renal corpuscle and a renal tubule (Chapter 18).

Nerve (NERV)—A group of neurons, together with blood vessels and connective tissue (Chapter 8).

Nerve tissue (NERV **TISH**–yoo)—The tissue specialized to generate and transmit electrochemical impulses that have many functions in the maintenance of homeostasis (Chapter 4).

Nerve tract (NERV TRAKT)—A group of neurons that share a common function within the central nervous system. A tract may be ascending (sensory) or descending (motor) (Chapter 8).

Nervous system (**NERV**–us **SIS**–tem)—The organ system that regulates body functions by means of electrochemical impulses; consists of the brain, spinal cord, cranial nerves, and spinal nerves (Chapter 8).

Neuralgia (new–**RAL**–jee–ah)—Sharp, severe pain along the course of a nerve (Chapter 8).

Neuritis (new–**RYE**–tis)—Inflammation of a nerve (Chapter 8).

Neuroglia (new–**ROG**–lee–ah)—The non-neuronal cells of the central nervous system (Chapter 4).

Neurohypophysis (NEW–roo–high–**POFF**–e–sis)—The posterior pituitary gland (Chapter 10).

Neurolemma (NEW–roh–**LEM**–ah)—The sheath around peripheral axons and dendrites, formed by the cytoplasm and nuclei of Schwann cells; is essential for the regeneration of damaged peripheral neurons (Chapter 8).

Neuromuscular junction (NYOOR–oh–**MUSS**–kuhl–lar **JUNK**–shun)—The termination of a motor neuron on the sarcolemma of a muscle fiber; the synapse is the microscopic space between the two structures (Chapter 7).

Neuron (**NYOOR**–on)—A nerve cell; consists of a cell body, an axon, and dendrites (Chapter 4).

Neuropathy (new–**RAH**–puh–thee)—Any disease or disorder of the nerves (Chapter 8).

Neurotoxin (NEW–roh–**TOK**–sin)—A chemical that disrupts an aspect of the functioning of the nervous system (Chapter 7).

Neurotransmitter (NYOOR–oh–**TRANS**–mih–ter)—A chemical released by the axon of a neuron, which crosses a synapse and affects the electrical activity of the post-synaptic membrane (neuron or muscle cell or gland) (Chapter 4).

Neutron (**NEW**–trahn)—A sub-atomic particle that has no electrical charge; found in the nucleus of an atom (Chapter 2).

Neutrophil (**NEW**–troh–fill)—A type of white blood cell (granular); capable of phagocytosis of pathogens (Chapter 11).

Nevus (**NEE**–vus)—A pigmented area of the skin; a mole (Chapter 5).

Night blindness (NITE **BLIND**–ness)—The inability to see well in dim light or at night; may result from a vitamin A deficiency (Chapter 9).

Nine areas (NYNE)—The subdivision of the abdomen into nine equal areas to facilitate the description of locations (Chapter 1).

Non-communicable disease (NON–kuhm–**YOO**–ni–kah–b'l)—A disease that cannot be directly or indirectly transmitted from host to host (Chapter 22).

Non-essential amino acids (NON–e–**SEN**–shul ah–**ME**–noh **ASS**–ids)—The amino acids that can be synthesized by the liver (Chapter 16).

Norephinephrine (NOR–ep–i–**NEFF**–rin)—A hormone secreted by the adrenal medulla that causes vasoconstriction throughout the body, which raises blood pressure in stressful situations (Chapter 10).

Normal flora (**NOR**–muhl **FLOOR**–uh)—1. The population of microorganisms that is usually present in certain parts of the body. 2. In the colon, the bacteria that produce vitamins and inhibit the growth of pathogens (Chapter 16).

Normoblast (**NOR**–mow–blast)—A red blood cell with a nucleus, an immature stage in red blood cell formation; usually found in the red bone marrow and not in peripheral circulation (Chapter 11).

Nosocomial infection (no–zoh–**KOH**–mee–uhl)—An infection acquired in a hospital or other health-care institution (Chapter 22).

Nuclear membrane (**NEW**–klee–er **MEM**–brain)—The double-layer membrane that encloses the nucleus of a cell (Chapter 3).

Nucleic acid (new–**KLEE**–ik **ASS**–id)—An organic chemical that is made of nucleotide sub-units. Examples are DNA and RNA (Chapter 2).

Nucleolus (new–**KLEE**–oh–lus)—A small structure made of DNA, RNA, and protein. Found in the nucleus of a cell; produces ribosomal RNA (Chapter 3).

Nucleotide (**NEW**–klee–oh–tide)—An organic compound that consists of a pentose sugar, a phosphate group, and one of five nitrogenous bases (adenine, guanine, cytosine, thymine, or uracil). The sub-units of DNA and RNA (Chapter 2).

Nucleus (**NEW**–klee–us)—1. The membrane bound part of a cell that contains the hereditary material in chromosomes. 2. The central part of an atom containing protons and neutrons (Chapter 2, 3).

—O—

Occipital bone (ok–**SIP**–i–tuhl)—The flat bone that forms the back of the skull (Chapter 6).

Occipital lobes (ok–**SIP**–i–tuhl LOWBS)—The most posterior part of the cerebrum; contain the visual areas (Chapter 8).

Oculomotor nerves (OK–yoo–loh–**MOH**–tur)—Cranial nerve pair III. Motor to the extrinsic muscles of the eye, the ciliary body, and the iris (Chapter 8).

Olfactory nerves (ohl–**FAK**–tuh–ree)—Cranial nerve pair I. Sensory for smell (Chapter 8).

Olfactory receptors (ohl–**FAK**–tuh–ree ree–**SEP**–ters)—The sensory receptors in the upper nasal cavities that detect vaporized chemicals, providing a sense of smell (Chapter 9).

Oligodendrocyte (ah–li–goh–**DEN**–droh–site)—A type of neuroglia that produces the myelin sheath around neurons of the central nervous system (Chapter 8).

Oligosaccharide (ah–lig–oh–**SAK**–ah–ride)—A carbohydrate molecule that consists of from 3–20 monosaccharides bonded together; form "self" antigens on cell membranes (Chapter 2).

Oliguria (AH–li–**GYOO**–ree–ah)—Decreased urine formation and output (Chapter 18).

Oogenesis (Oh–oh–**JEN**–e–sis)—The process of meiosis in the ovary to produce an ovum (Chapter 3).

Opportunistic infection (OP–er–too–**NIS**–tick)—An infection caused by a microorganism that is usually a saprophyte but may become a parasite under certain conditions, such as lowered host resistance (Chapter 22).

Opsonization (OP–sah–ni–**ZAY**–shun)—The action of antibodies or complement that upon binding to a foreign antigen attracts macrophages and facilitates phagocytosis (from the Greek "to purchase food") (Chapter 14).

Optic chiasma (**OP**–tik kye–**AS**–muh)—The site of the crossing of the medial fibers of each optic nerve, anterior to the pituitary gland; important for binocular vision (Chapter 9).

Optic disc (**OP**–tik DISK)—The portion of the retina where the optic nerve passes through; no rods or cones are present (Syn.—blind spot) (Chapter 9).

Optic nerves (**OP**–tik)—Cranial nerve pair II. Sensory for vision (Chapter 8).

Oral cavity (**OR**–uhl **KAV**–i–tee)—The cavity in the skull bounded by the hard palate, cheeks, and tongue (Chapter 16).

Orbit (**OR**–bit)—The cavity in the skull that contains the eyeball (Syn.—eyesocket) (Chapter 9).

Organ (**OR**–gan)—A structure with specific functions; made of two or more tissues (Chapter 1).

Organ of Corti (**KOR**–tee) (spiral organ)—The structure in the cochlea of the inner ear that contains the receptors for hearing (Chapter 9).

Organ system (**OR**–gan **SIS**–tem)—A group of related organs that work together to perform specific functions (Chapter 1).

Organelle (OR–gan–**ELL**)—An intracellular structure that has a specific function (Chapter 3).

Organic (or–**GAN**–ik)—A chemical compound that contains carbon-hydrogen covalent bonds; includes carbohydrates, lipids, proteins, and nucleic acids (Chapter 1).

Origin (**AHR**–i–jin)—1. The more stationary attachment point of a muscle to a bone. 2. The beginning (Chapter 7).

Oropharynx (OR–oh–**FA**–rinks)—The middle portion of the pharynx behind the oral cavity; a passageway for both air and food (Chapter 15).

Osmolarity (ahs–moh–**LAR**–i–tee)—The concentration of osmotically active particles in a solution (Chapter 19).

Osmoreceptors (AHS–moh–re–**SEP**–ters)—Specialized cells in the hypothalamus that detect changes in the water content of the body (Chapter 10).

Osmosis (ahs–**MOH**–sis)—The diffusion of water through a selectively permeable membrane (Chapter 3).

Osmotic pressure (ahs–**MAH**–tik)—Pressure that develops when two solutions of different concentration are separated by a selectively permeable membrane. A hypertonic solution that would cause cells to shrivel has a higher osmotic pressure. A hypotonic solution that would cause cells to swell has a lower osmotic pressure (Chapter 3).

Ossification (AHS–i–fi–**KAY**–shun)—The process of bone formation; bone matrix is produced by osteoblasts during the growth or repair of bones (Chapter 6).

Osteoarthritis (AHS–tee–oh–ar–**THRY**–tiss)—The inflammation of a joint, especially a weight-bearing joint, that is most often a consequence of aging (Chapter 6).

Osteoblast (**AHS**–tee–oh–BLAST)—A bone-producing cell; produces bone matrix for the growth or repair of bones (Chapter 6).

Osteoclast (**AHS**–tee–oh–KLAST)—A bone-destroying cell; reabsorbs bone matrix as part of the growth or repair of bones (Chapter 6).

Osteocyte (**AHS**–tee–oh–SITE)—A bone cell (Chapter 4).

Osteomyelitis (AHS–tee–oh–my–uh–**LYE**–tiss)—Inflammation of a bone caused by a pathogenic microorganism (Chapter 6).

Osteoporosis (AHS–tee–oh–por–**OH**–sis)—A condition in which bone matrix is lost and not replaced, resulting in weakened bones which are then more likely to fracture (Chapter 6).

Otitis media (oh–**TIGH**–tis **MEE**–dee–ah)—Inflammation of the middle ear (Chapter 9).

Oval window (**OH**–vul **WIN**–doh)—The membrane-covered opening through which the stapes transmit vibrations to the fluid in the inner ear (Chapter 9).

Ovary (**OH**–vuh–ree)—The female gonad that produces ova; also an endocrine gland that produces the hormones estrogen and progesterone (Chapter 10).

Ovum (**OH**–vuhm)—An egg cell, produced by an ovary (Pl.—ova) (Chapter 20).

Oxygen debt (**OX**–ah–jen DET)—The state in which there is not enough oxygen to complete the process of cell respiration; lactic acid is formed, which contributes to muscle fatigue (Chapter 7).

Oxytocin (OK–si–**TOH**–sin)—A hormone produced by the hypothalamus and stored in the posterior pituitary gland; stimulates contraction of the myometrium and release of milk by the mammary glands (Chapter 8).

—P—

Palate (**PAL**–uht)—The roof of the mouth, which separates the oral cavity from the nasal cavities (Chapter 16).

Palpitation (pal–pi–**TAY**–shun)—An irregular heart beat of which the person is aware (Chapter 12).

Pancreas (**PAN**–kree–us)—1. An endocrine gland located between the curve of the duodenum and the spleen; secretes insulin and glucagon. 2. An exocrine gland that secretes digestive enzymes for the digestion of starch, fats, and proteins (Chapter 10).

Pancreatic duct (PAN–kree–**AT**–ik DUKT)—The duct that takes pancreatic juices to the common bile duct (Chapter 16).

Pandemic (pan–**DEM**–ick)—An epidemic that affects several countries at the same time (Chapter 22).

Papillae (pah–**PILL**–ay)—1. Elevated, pointed projections. 2. On the tongue, the projections that contain taste buds (Chapter 16).

Papillary layer (**PAP**–i–lar–ee **LAY**–er)—The uppermost layer of the dermis; contains capillaries to nourish the epidermis (Chapter 5).

Papillary muscles (**PAP**–i–lar–ee **MUSS**–uhls)—Columns of myocardium that project from the floor of a ventricle and anchor the flaps of the AV valve by way of the chordae tendineae (Chapter 12).

Paralysis (pah–**RAL**–i–sis)—Complete or partial loss of function, especially of a muscle (Chapter 7).

Paralytic ileus (**PAR**–uh–LIT–ik **ILL**–ee–us)—Paralysis of the intestines that may occur following abdominal surgery (Chapter 16).

Paraplegia (PAR–ah–**PLEE**–gee–ah)—Paralysis of the legs (Chapter 8).

Paranasal sinus (PAR–uh–**NAY**–zuhl **SIGH**–nus)—An air cavity in the frontal, maxilla, sphenoid, or ethmoid bones; opens into the nasal cavities (Chapter 6).

Parasite (**PAR**–uh–sight)—An organism that lives on or in another living organism, called a host, to which it causes harm (from the Greek for "to eat at another's table") (Chapter 22).

Parasympathetic (PAR–ah–SIM–puh–**THET**–ik)—The division of the autonomic nervous system that dominates during non-stressful situations (Chapter 8).

Parathyroid glands (PAR–ah–**THIGH**–roid)—The four endocrine glands located on the posterior side of the thyroid gland; secrete parathyroid hormone (Chapter 10).

Parathyroid hormone (PTH) (PAR–ah–**THIGH**–roid)—A hormone secreted by the parathyroid glands; increases the reabsorption of calcium from bones and the absorption of calcium by the small intestine and kidneys (Chapter 10).

Parietal (puh–**RYE**–uh–tuhl)—1. Pertaining to the walls of a body cavity (Chapter 1). 2. The flat bone that forms the crown of the cranial cavity (Chapter 6).

Parietal cells (puh–**RYE**–uh–tuhl SELLS)—The cells of the gastric pits of the stomach that secrete hydrochloric acid and the intrinsic factor (Chapter 16).

Parietal lobes (puh–**RYE**–uh–tuhl LOWBS)—The parts of the cerebrum posterior to the frontal lobes; contain the sensory areas for cutaneous sensation and conscious muscle sense (Chapter 8).

Parkinson's disease (**PAR**–kin–sonz)—A progressive disorder of the basal ganglia, characterized by tremor, muscle weakness and rigidity, and a peculiar gait (Chapter 8).

Parotid glands (pah–**RAH**–tid)—The pair of salivary glands located just below and in front of the ears (Chapter 16).

Partial pressure (**PAR**–shul **PRES**–shur)—1. The pressure exerted by a gas in a mixture of gases. 2. The value used to measure oxygen and carbon dioxide concentrations in the blood or other body fluid (Chapter 15).

Parturition (PAR–tyoo–**RISH**–uhn)—The act of giving birth (Chapter 21).

Passive immunity (**PASS**–iv im–**YOO**–ni–tee)—The immunity provided by the reception of antibodies from another source; may be natural (placental, breast milk) or artificial (injection of gamma globulins) (Chapter 14).

Pasteurization (PAS–tyoor–i–**ZAY**–shun)—The process of heating a fluid to moderate temperatures in order to destroy pathogenic bacteria (Chapter 22).

Patella (puh–**TELL**–ah)—The kneecap, a short bone (Chapter 6).

Patellar reflex (puh–**TELL**–ar **REE**–fleks)—A stretch reflex integrated in the spinal cord, in which a tap on the patellar tendon causes extension of the lower leg (Syn.—kneejerk reflex) (Chapter 8).

Pathogen (**PATH**–oh–jen)—A microorganism capable of producing disease; includes bacteria, viruses, fungi, protozoa, and worms (Chapter 14).

Pathophysiology (PATH–oh–FIZZ–ee–**AH**–luh–jee)—The study of diseases as they are related to functioning (Chapter 1).

Pelvic cavity (**PELL**–vik **KAV**–i–tee)—Inferior portion of the ventral cavity, below the abdominal cavity (Chapter 1).

Penis (**PEE**–nis)—The male organ of copulation when the urethra serves as a passage for semen; an organ of elimination when the urethra serves as a passage for urine (Chapter 20).

Pentose sugar (**PEN**–tohs)—A five-carbon sugar (monosaccharide) that is a structural part of the nucleic acids DNA and RNA (Chapter 2).

Pepsin (**PEP**–sin)—The enzyme found in gastric juice that begins protein digestion; secreted by chief cells (Chapter 16).

Peptidases (**PEP**–ti–day–ses)—Digestive enzymes that break down polypeptides to amino acids; secreted by the small intestine (Chapter 16).

Peptide bond (**PEP**–tide)—A chemical bond that links two amino acids in a protein molecule (Chapter 2).

Pericardium (PER–ee–**KAR**–dee–um)—The three membranes that enclose the heart, consisting of an outer fibrous layer and two serous layers (Chapter 12).

Perichondrium (PER–ee–**KON**–dree–um)—The fibrous connective tissue membrane that covers cartilage (Chapter 4).

Perilymph (**PER**–i–limf)—The fluid in the bony labyrinth of the inner ear (Chapter 9).

Periodontal membrane (PER–ee–oh–**DON**–tal)—The membrane that lines the tooth sockets in the upper and lower jaws; produces a bone-like cement to anchor the teeth (Chapter 16).

Periosteum (PER–ee–**AHS**–tee–um)—The fibrous connective tissue membrane that covers bone; contains osteoblasts for bone growth or repair (Chapter 4).

Peripheral (puh–**RIFF**–uh–ruhl)—Extending from a main part; closer to the surface (Chapter 1).

Peripheral nervous system (puh–**RIFF**–uh–ruhl **NERV**–vuhs)—The part of the nervous system that consists of the cranial nerves and spinal nerves (Chapter 8).

Peripheral resistance (puh–**RIFF**–uh–ruhl ree–**ZIS**–tense)—The resistance of the blood vessels to the flow of blood; changes in the diameter of arteries have effects on blood pressure (Chapter 13).

Peristalsis (per–i–**STALL**–sis)—Waves of muscular contraction (one-way) that propel the contents through a hollow organ (Chapter 2).

Peritoneum (PER–i–toh–**NEE**–um)—The serous membrane that lines the abdominal cavity (Chapter 1).

Peritonitis (per–i–toh–**NIGH**–tis)—Inflammation of the peritoneum (Chapter 16).

Peritubular capillaries (PER–ee–**TOO**–byoo–ler)—The capillaries that surround the renal tubule and receive the useful materials reabsorbed from the renal filtrate; carry blood from the efferent arteriole to the renal vein (Chapter 18)

Pernicious anemia (per–**NISH**–us uh–**NEE**–mee–yah)—An anemia that is the result of a deficiency of vitamin B_{12} or the intrinsic factor (Chapter 11).

Peyer's patches (**PYE**–erz)—The lymph nodules in the mucosa of the small intestine, especially in the ileum (Chapter 14).

pH —A symbol of the measure of the concentration of hydrogen ions in a solution. The pH scale extends from 0–14, with a value of 7 being neutral. Values lower than 7 are acidic, values higher than 7 are alkaline (basic) (Chapter 2).

Phagocytosis (FAG–oh–sigh–**TOH**–sis)—The process by which a cell engulfs a particle; especially, the ingestion of microorganisms by white blood cells (Chapter 3).

Phalanges (fuh–**LAN**–jees)—The long bones of the fingers and toes. There are 14 in each hand or foot (Chapter 6).

Phantom pain (**FAN**–tum PAYN)—Pain following amputation of a limb that seems to come from the missing limb (Chapter 9).

Pharynx (**FA**–rinks)—A muscular tube located behind the nasal and oral cavities; a passageway for air and food (Chapter 15).

Phenotype (**FEE**–noh–type)—The appearance of the individual as related to genotype; the expression of the genes that are present (Chapter 21).

Phlebitis (fle–**BY**–tis)—Inflammation of a vein (Chapter 13).

Phospholipid (**FOSS**–foh–LIP–id)—An organic compound in the lipid group that is made of one glycerol, two fatty acids, and a phosphate molecule (Chapter 2).

Phrenic nerves (**FREN**–ik NERVZ)—The pair of peripheral nerves that are motor to the diaphragm (Chapter 15).

Physiology (FIZZ–ee–**AH**–luh–jee)—The study of the functioning of the body and its parts (Chapter 1).

Pia mater (**PEE**–ah **MAH**–ter)—The innermost layer of the meninges, made of thin connective tissue on the surface of the brain and spinal cord (Chapter 8).

Pilomotor muscle (**PYE**–loh–MOH–ter)—A smooth muscle attached to a hair follicle; contraction pulls the follicle upright, resulting in "goose bumps" (Syn.—arrector pili muscle) (Chapter 5).

Pinocytosis (PIN–oh–sigh–**TOH**–sis)—The process by which a stationary cell ingests very small particles or a liquid (Chapter 3).

Pituitary gland (pi–**TOO**–i–TER–ee)—An endocrine gland located below the hypothalamus, consisting of anterior and posterior lobes (Syn.—hypophysis) (Chapter 10).

Pivot joint (**PI**–vot)—A diarthrosis that permits rotation (Chapter 6).

Placenta (pluh–**SEN**–tah)—The organ formed in the uterus during pregnancy, made of both fetal and maternal tissue; the site of exchanges of materials between fetal blood and maternal blood (Chapter 13).

Plane (PLAYN)—An imaginary flat surface that divides the body in a specific way (Chapter 1).

Plasma (**PLAZ**–mah)—The water found within the blood vessels. Plasma comprises 52%–62% of the total blood (Chapter 2).

Plasma cell (**PLAZ**–mah SELL)—A cell derived from an

activated B cell that produces antibodies to a specific antigen (Chapter 14).

Plasma proteins (**PLAZ**–mah **PRO**–teenz)—The proteins that circulate in the liquid portion of the blood; include albumin, globulins, and clotting factors (Chapter 11).

Platelets (**PLAYT**–lets)—Blood cells that are fragments of larger cells (megakaryocytes) of the red bone marrow; involved in blood clotting and other mechanisms of hemostasis (Syn.—thrombocytes) (Chapter 4).

Pleural membranes (**PLOOR**–uhl **MEM**–braynz)—The serous membranes of the thoracic cavity (Chapter 1).

Plica circulares (PLEE–ka SIR–kew–**LAR**–es)—The circular folds of the mucosa and submucosa of the small intestine; increase the surface area for absorption (Chapter 16).

Pneumonia (new–**MOH**–nee–ah)—Inflammation of the lungs caused by bacteria, viruses, or chemicals (Chapter 15).

Pneumotaxic center (NEW–moh–**TAK**–sik **SEN**–ter)—The respiratory center in the pons that helps bring about exhalation (Chapter 15).

Pneumothorax (NEW–moh–**THAW**–raks)—The accumulation of air in the potential pleural space, which increases intrapleural pressure and causes collapse of a lung (Chapter 15).

Polarization (POH–lahr–i–**ZA**–shun)—The distribution of ions on either side of a membrane; in a resting neuron or muscle cell, sodium ions are more abundant outside the cell, and potassium and negative ions are more abundant inside the cell, giving the membrane a positive charge outside and a relative negative charge inside (Chapter 7).

Polypeptide (PAH–lee–**PEP**–tide)—A short chain of amino acids, not yet a specific protein (Chapter 2).

Polysaccharide (PAH–lee–**SAK**–ah–ride)—A carbohydrate molecule that consists of many monosaccharides (usually glucose) bonded together; includes glycogen, starch, and cellulose (Chapter 2).

Polyuria (PAH–li–**YOO**–ree–ah)—Increased urine formation and output (Chapter 18).

Pons (PONZ)—The part of the brain anterior and superior to the medulla; contributes to the regulation of respiration (Chapter 8).

Pore (POR)—An opening on a surface to permit the passage of materials (Chapter 3).

Portal of entry (**POR**–tuhl of **EN**–tree)—The way a pathogen enters the body, such as natural body openings or breaks in the skin (Chapter 22).

Portal of exit (**POR**–tuhl of **EG**–zit)—The way a pathogen leaves a host, such as in respiratory droplets, feces, or reproductive secretions (Chaper 22).

Posterior (poh–**STEER**–ee–your)—Toward the back (Syn.—dorsal) (Chapter 1).

Postganglionic neuron (POST–gang–lee–**ON**–ik)—In the autonomic nervous system, a neuron that extends from a ganglion to a visceral effector (Chapter 8).

Pre-capillary sphincter (pree–**KAP**–i–lar–ee **SFINK**–ter)—A smooth muscle cell at the beginning of a capillary network that regulates the flow of blood through the network (Chapter 13).

Preganglionic neuron (PRE–gang–lee–**ON**–ik)—In the autonomic nervous system, a neuron that extends from the CNS to a ganglion and synapses with a post-ganglionic neuron (Chapter 8).

Presbyopia (PREZ–bee–**OH**–pee–ah)—Farsightedness that is a consequence of aging and the loss of elasticity of the lens (Chapter 9).

Pressoreceptors (**PRESS**–oh–ree–SEP–ters)—The sensory receptors in the carotid sinuses and aortic sinus that detect changes in blood pressure (Chapter 9).

Primary bronchi (**PRY**–ma–ree **BRONG**–kye)—The two branches of the lower end of the trachea; air passageways to the right and left lungs (Chapter 15).

Prime mover (PRIME **MOO**–ver)—The muscle responsible for the main action when a joint is moved (Chapter 7).

Progesterone (proh–**JESS**–tuh–rohn)—The female sex hormone secreted by the corpus luteum of the ovary; contributes to the growth of the endometrium and the maintenance of pregnancy (Chapter 10).

Projection (proh–**JEK**–shun)—The characteristic of sensations in which the sensation is felt in the area where the receptors were stimulated (Chapter 9).

Prolactin (proh–**LAK**–tin)—A hormone produced by the anterior pituitary gland, that stimulates milk production by the mammary glands (Chapter 10).

Pronation (pro–**NAY**–shun)—Turning the palm downward, or lying face down (Chapter 7).

Prophase (**PROH**–fayz)—The first stage of mitosis, in which the pairs on chromatids become visible (Chapter 3).

Proprioceptor (**PROH**–pree–oh–SEP–ter)—A sensory receptor in a muscle that detects stretching of the muscle (Syn.—stretch receptor) (Chapter 7).

Prostaglandins (PRAHS–tah–**GLAND**–ins)—Locally acting hormone-like substances produced by virtually all cells from the phospholipids of their cell membranes; the many types have many varied functions (Chapter 10).

Prostate gland (**PRAHS**–tayt)—A muscular gland that surrounds the first inch of the male urethra; secretes an alkaline fluid that becomes part of semen; its smooth muscle contributes to ejaculation (Chapter 20).

Prostatic hypertrophy (prahs–**TAT**–ik high–**PER**–truh–fee)—Enlargement of the prostate gland; may be benign or malignant (Chapter 20).

Protein (**PRO**–teen)—An organic compound made of amino acids linked by peptide bonds (Chapter 2).

Proteinuria (PRO–teen–**YOO**–ree–ah)—The presence of protein in urine (Chapter 18).

Prothrombin (proh–**THROM**–bin)—A clotting factor synthesized by the liver and released into the blood; converted to thrombin in the process of chemical clotting (Chapter 11).

Proton (**PRO**–tahn)—A sub-atomic particle that has a positive electrical charge; found in the nucleus of an atom (Chapter 2).

Protozoa (PROH–tuh–**ZOH**–ah) (Sing.: Protozoan)—The simplest animal-like microorganisms in the Kingdom Protista; usually unicellular, some are colonial; may be free-living or parasitic (Chapter 22).

Proximal (**PROCK**–si–muhl)—Closest to the origin or point of attachment (Chapter 1).

Proximal convoluted tubule (**PROK**–si–muhl KON–voh–**LOO**–ted)—The part of a renal tubule that extends from Bowman's capsule to the loop of Henle (Chapter 18).

Pruritus (proo–**RYE**–tus)—Severe itching (Chapter 5).

Puberty (**PEWO**–ber–tee)—The period during life in which members of both sexes become sexually mature and capable of reproduction; usually occurs between the ages of 10 and 14 years (Chapter 20).

Pubic symphysis (**PEW**–bik **SIM**–fi–sis)—The joint between the right and left pubic bones, in which a disc of cartilage separates the two bones (Chapter 6).

Pubis (**PEW**–biss)—The lower anterior part of the hip bone (Syn.—pubic bone) (Chapter 6).

Pulmonary artery (**PULL**–muh–NER–ee **AR**–tuh–ree)—The artery that takes blood from the right ventricle to the lungs (Chapter 12).

Pulmonary edema (**PULL**–muh–NER–ee uh–**DEE**–muh)—Accumulation of tissue fluid in the alveoli of the lungs (Chapter 15).

Pulmonary semilunar valve (**PULL**–muh–NER–ee SEM–ee–**LOO**–nar VALV)—The valve at the junction of the right ventricle and the pulmonary artery; prevents backflow of blood from the artery to the ventricle when the ventricle relaxes (Chapter 12).

Pulmonary surfactant (**PULL**–muh–NER–ee sir–**FAK**–tent)—A lipid substance secreted by the alveoli in the lungs; reduces the surface tension within alveoli to permit inflation (Chapter 15).

Pulmonary veins (**PULL**–muh–NER–ee VAYNS)—The four veins that return blood from the lungs to the left atrium (Chapter 12).

Pulp cavity (PUHLP)—The innermost portion of a tooth that contains blood vessels and nerve endings (Chapter 16).

Pulse (PULS)—The force of the heartbeat detected at an arterial site such as the radial artery (Chapter 12).

Pulse deficit (PULS DEF–i–sit)—The condition in which the radial pulse count is lower than the rate of the heartbeat heard with a stethoscope; may occur in some types of heart disease in which the heartbeat is weak (Chapter 13).

Pulse pressure (PULS **PRES**–shur)—The difference between systolic and diastolic blood pressure; averages about 40 mmHg (Chapter 13).

Punnett square (**PUHN**–net SKWAIR)—A diagram used to determine the possible combinations of genes in the offspring of a particular set of parents (Chapter 21).

Pupil (**PYOO**–pil)—The opening in the center of the iris; light rays pass through the aqueous humor in the pupil (Chapter 9).

Purkinje fibers (purr–**KIN**–jee)—Specialized cardiac muscle fibers that are part of the the cardiac conduction pathway (Chapter 12).

Pyloric sphincter (pye–**LOR**–ik **SFINK**–ter)—The circular smooth muscle at the junction of the stomach and the duodenum; prevents backup of intestinal contents into the stomach (Chapter 16).

Pyloric stenosis (pye–**LOR**–ik ste–**NOH**–sis)—Narrowing of the opening between the stomach and duodenum caused by hypertrophy of the pyloric sphincter; a congenital disorder (Chapter 16).

Pyrogen (**PYE**–roh–jen)—Any microorganism or substance that causes a fever; include bacteria, viruses, or chemicals released during inflammation (called endogenous pyrogens); activate the heat production and conservation mechanisms regulated by the hypothalamus (Chapter 17).

—Q—

QRS wave —The portion of an ECG that depicts depolarization of the ventricles (Chapter 12).

Quadrants (**KWAH**–drants)—A division into four parts, used especially to divide the abdomen into four areas to facilitate description of locations (Chapter 1).

Quadriplegia (KWA–dri–**PLEE**–jee–ah)—Paralysis of all four limbs (Chapter 17).

—R—

Radiation (RAY–dee–**AY**–shun)—1. The heat loss process in which heat energy from the skin is emitted to the cooler surroundings. 2. The emissions of certain radioactive elements; may be used for diagnostic or therapeutic purposes (Chapter 17).

Radius (**RAY**–dee–us)—The long bone of the forearm on the thumb side (Chapter 6).

Range of motion exercises (RANJE of **MOH**–shun)—Movements of joints through their full range of motion; used to preserve mobility or to regain mobility following an injury (Chapter 7).

Receptor (ree–**SEP**–tur)—A specialized cell or nerve ending that responds to a particular change such as light, sound, heat, touch, or pressure (Chapter 5).

Receptor site (ree–**SEP**–ter SITE)—An arrangement of molecules, often part of the cell membrane, that will accept only molecules with a complementary shape (Chapter 3).

Recessive (ree–**SESS**–iv)—In genetics, a characteristic that will be expressed only if two genes for it are present in the homologous pair (Chapter 21).

Red blood cells (RED BLUHD SELLS)—The most numerous cells in the blood; carry oxygen bonded to the hemoglobin within them (Syn.—erythrocytes) (Chapter 4).

Red bone marrow (RED BOWN **MAR**–row)—A hemopoietic tissue found in flat and irregular bones; produces all the types of blood cells (Chapter 6).

Reduced hemoglobin (re–**DOOSD HEE**–muh–GLOW–bin)—Hemoglobin that has released its oxygen in the systemic capillaries (Chapter 11).

Referred pain (ree–**FURD** PAYNE)—Visceral pain that is projected and felt as cutaneous pain (Chapter 9).

Reflex (**REE**–fleks)—An involuntary response to a stimulus (Chapter 8).

Reflex arc (**REE**–fleks ARK)—The pathway nerve impulses follow when a reflex is stimulated (Chapter 8).

Refraction (ree–**FRAK**–shun)—The bending of light rays as they pass through the eyeball; normal refraction focuses an image on the retina (Chapter 9).

Releasing hormones (ree–**LEE**–sing **HOR**–mohns)—Hormones released by the hypothalamus that stimulate secretion of hormones by the anterior pituitary gland (SYN-releasing factors) (Chapter 10).

Remission (ree–**MISH**–uhn)—Lessening of severity of symptoms (Chapter 8).

Renal artery (**REE**–nuhl **AR**–te–ree)—The branch of the abdominal aorta that takes blood into a kidney (Chapter 18).

Renal calculi (**REE**–nuhl **KAL**–kew–lye)—Kidney stones; made of precipitated minerals in the form of crystals (Chapter 18).

Renal corpuscle (**REE**–nuhl **KOR**–pusl)—The part of a nephron that consists of a glomerulus enclosed by a Bowman's capsule; the site of glomerular filtration (Chapter 18).

Renal cortex (**REE**–nuhl **KOR**–teks)—The outermost area of the kidney; consists of renal corpuscles and convoluted tubules (Chapter 18).

Renal failure (**REE**–nuhl **FAYL**–yer)—The inability of the kidneys to function properly and form urine; causes include severe hemorrhage, toxins, and obstruction of the urinary tract (Chapter 18).

Renal fascia (**REE**–nuhl **FASH**–ee–ah)—The fibrous connective tissue membrane that covers the kidneys and the surrounding adipose tissue and helps keep the kidneys in place (Chapter 18).

Renal filtrate (**REE**–nuhl **FILL**–trayt)—The fluid formed from blood plasma by the process of filtration in the renal corpuscles; flows from Bowman's capsules through the renal tubules where most is reabsorbed; the filtrate that enters the renal pelvis is called urine (Chapter 18).

Renal medulla (**REE**–nuhl muh–**DEW**–lah)—The middle area of the kidney; consists of loops of Henle and collecting tubules; the triangular segments of the renal medulla are called renal pyramids (Chapter 18).

Renal pelvis (**REE**–nuhl **PELL**–vis)—The innermost area of the kidney; a cavity formed by the expanded end of the ureter within the medial side of the kidney (Chapter 18).

Renal pyramids (**REE**–nuhl **PEER**–ah–mids)—The triangular segments of the renal medulla; the papillae of the pyramids empty urine into the calyces of the renal pelvis (Chapter 18).

Renal tubule (**REE**–nuhl **TOO**–byool)—The part of a nephron that consists of a proximal convoluted tubule, loop of Henle, distal convoluted tubule, and collecting tubule; the site of tubular reabsorption and tubular secretion (Chapter 18).

Renal vein (**REE**–nuhl VAYN)—The vein that returns blood from a kidney to the inferior vena cava (Chapter 18).

Renin-angiotensin mechanism (**REE**–nin AN–jee–oh–**TEN**–sin)—A series of chemical reactions initiated by a decrese in blood pressure that stimulates the kidneys to secrete the enzyme renin; culminates in the formation of angiotensin II (Chapter 10).

Repolarization (RE–pol–lahr–i–**ZA**–shun)—The restoration of electrical charges on either side of a cell membrane following depolarization; positive charge outside and a negative charge inside brought about by a rapid outflow of potassium ions (Chapter 7).

Reproductive system (REE–proh–**DUK**–tive **SIS**–tem)—The male or female organ system that produces gametes, ensures fertilization, and in women, provides a site for the developing embryo-fetus (Chapter 20).

Reservoir (**REZ**–er–vwor)—A person or animal who harbors a pathogen and is a source of the pathogen for others (Chapter 22).

Resident flora (**REZ**–i–dent **FLOOR**–uh)—Part of normal flora; those microorganisms on or in nearly everyone in specific body sites nearly all the time (Chapter 22).

Residual air (ree–**ZID**–yoo–al)—The volume of air that remains in the lungs after the most forceful exhalation; important to provide for continuous gas exchange; average: 1000–1500 ml (Chapter 15).

Resistance (re–**ZIS**–tenss)—The total of all of the body's defenses against pathogens; includes non-specific barriers such as unbroken skin and specific mechanisms such as antibody production (Chapter 22).

Respiratory acidosis (RES–pi–rah–**TOR**–ee ass–i–**DOH**–sis)—A condition in which the blood pH is lower than normal, caused by disorders that decrease the rate or efficiency of respiration and permit the accumulation of carbon dioxide (Chapter 15).

Respiratory alkalosis (RES–pi–rah–**TOR**–ee al–kah–**LOH**–sis)—A condition in which the blood pH is higher than normal, caused by disorders that increase the rate of respiration and decrease the level of carbon dioxide in the blood (Chapter 15).

Respiratory pump (RES–pi–rah–**TOR**–ee)—A mechanism that increases venous return; pressure changes during breathing compress the veins that pass through the thoracic cavity (Chapter 13).

Respiratory system (**RES**–pi–rah–TOR–ee **SIS**–tem)—The organ system that moves air into and out of the lungs so that oxygen and carbon dioxide may be exchanged between the air and the blood (Chapter 15).

Resting potential (**RES**–ting poh–**TEN**–shul)—The difference in electrical charges on either side of a cell membrane not transmitting an impulse; positive charge outside and a negative charge inside (Chapter 7).

Reticulocyte (re–**TIK**–yoo–loh–site)—A red blood cell that contains remnants of the ER, an immature stage in red blood cell formation; makes up about 1% of the red blood cells in peripheral circulation (Chapter 11).

Reticuloendothelial system (re–TIK–yoo–loh–en–doh–**THEE**–lee–al)—Former name for the tissue macrophage system, the organs or tissues that contain macrophages which phagocytize old red blood cells; the liver, spleen, and red bone marrow (Chapter 11).

Retina (**RET**–i–nah)—The innermost layer of the eyeball that contains the photoreceptors, the rods, and the cones (Chapter 9).

Retroperitoneal (RE–troh–PER–i–toh–**NEE**–uhl)—Located behind the peritoneum (Chapter 18).

Rh factor (R–H **FAK**–ter)—The red blood cell types determined by the presence or absence of the Rh (D) antigen on the red blood cell membranes; the two types are Rh positive and Rh negative (Chapter 11).

Rheumatoid arthritis (**ROO**–muh–toyd ar–**THRY**–tiss)—Inflammation of a joint; believed to be an autoimmune disease. The joint damage may progress to fusion and immobility of the joint (Chapter 6).

Rhodopsin (roh–**DOP**–sin)—The chemical in the rods of the retina that breaks down when light waves strike it; this chemical change initiates a nerve impulse (Chapter 9).

RhoGam (**ROH**–gam)—The trade name for the Rh (D) antibody administered to an Rh negative woman who has delivered an Rh positive infant; it will destroy any fetal red blood cells that may have entered maternal circulation (Chapter 11).

Ribosome (**RYE**–boh–sohme)—A cell organelle found in the cytoplasm; the site of protein synthesis (Chapter 3).

Ribs (RIBZ)—The 24 flat bones that, together with the sternum, form the rib cage. The first seven pairs are true ribs, the next three pairs are false ribs, and the last two pairs are floating ribs (Chapter 6).

Rickets (**RICK**–ets)—A deficiency of vitamin D in children, resulting in poor and abnormal bone growth (Chapter 6).

RNA —Ribonucleic acid. A nucleic acid that is a single strand of nucleotides. Essential for protein synthesis within cells. Messenger RNA (mRNA) is a copy of the genetic code of DNA. Transfer RNA (tRNA) aligns amino acids in the proper sequence on the mRNA (Chapter 2).

Rods (RAHDZ)—The sensory receptors in the retina of the eye that detect the presence of light (Chapter 9).

Rugae (**ROO**–gay)—Folds of the mucosa of organs such as the stomach, urinary bladder, and vagina; permit expansion of these organs (Chapter 16).

—S—

Saccule (**SAK**–yool)—The membranous sac in the vestibule of the inner ear that contains receptors for static equilibrium (Chapter 9).

Sacrum (**SAY**–krum)—The five fused sacral vertebrae at the base of the spine (Chapter 6).

Sacroiliac joint (SAY–kroh–**ILL**–ee–ak)—The slightly movable joint between the sacrum and the ilium (Chapter 6).

Saddle joint (**SA**–duhl)—The carpometacarpal joint of the thumb, a diarthrosis (Chapter 6).

Sagittal section (**SAJ**–i–tuhl **SEK**–shun)—A plane or cut from front to back, separating right and left parts (Chapter 1).

Saliva (sah–**LYE**–vah)—The secretion of the salivary glands; mostly water and containing the enzyme amylase (Chapter 16).

Salivary glands (**SAL**–i–va–ree)—The three pairs of exocrine glands that secrete saliva into the oral cavity; parotid, submandibular, and sublingual pairs (Chapter 16).

Salt (SAWLT)—A chemical compound that consists of a positive ion other than hydrogen and a negative ion other than hydroxyl (Chapter 2).

Saltatory conduction (**SAWL**–tah–taw–ree kon–**DUK**–shun)—The rapid transmission of a nerve impulse from one node of Ranvier to the next; characteristic of myelineated neurons (Chapter 8).

Saprophyte (**SAP**–roh–fight)—An organism that lives on dead organic matter; a decomposer (Chapter 22).

Sarcolemma (SAR–koh–**LEM**–ah)—The cell membrane of a muscle fiber (Chapter 7).

Sarcomere (**SAR**–koh–meer)—The unit of contraction in a skeletal muscle fiber; a precise arrangement of myosin and actin filaments between two Z lines (Chapter 7).

Sarcoplasmic reticulum (SAR–koh–**PLAZ**–mik re–**TIK**–yoo–lum)—The endoplasmic reticulum of a muscle fiber; is a reservoir for calcium ions (Chapter 7).

Saturated fat (**SAT**–uhr–ay–ted)—A true fat that is often solid at room temperature and of animal origin (Chapter 2).

Scapula (**SKAP**–yoo–luh)—The flat bone of the shoulder that articulates with the humerus (Syn.—shoulderblade) (Chapter 6).

Schwann cell (SHWAHN SELL)—A cell of the peripheral nervous system that forms the myelin sheath and neurolemma of peripheral axons and dendrites (Chapter 4).

Sclera (**SKLER**–ah)—The outermost layer of the eyeball, made of fibrous connective tissue; the anterior portion is the transparent cornea (Chapter 9).

Scoliosis (SKOH–lee–**OH**–sis)—A lateral curvature of the vertebral column (Chapter 6).

Scrotum (**SKROH**–tum)—The sac of skin between the upper thighs in males; contains the testes, epididymides, and part of the ductus deferens (Chapter 20).

Sebaceous gland (suh–**BAY**–shus)—An exocrine gland in the dermis that produces sebum (Chapter 5).

Sebum (**SEE**–bum)—The lipid (oil) secretion of sebaceous glands (Chapter 5).

Secondary infection (**SECK**–un–dery)—An infection made possible by a primary infection that has lowered the host's resistance (Chapter 22).

Secondary sex characteristics (**SEK**–un–DAR–ee SEKS)—The features that develop at puberty in males or females; they are under the influence of the sex hormones but are not directly involved in reproduction. Examples are growth of facial or body hair and growth of muscles.

Secretin (se–**KREE**–tin)—A hormone secreted by the duodenum when food enters; stimulates secretion of bile by the liver and secretion of bicarbonate pancreatic juice (Chapter 16).

Secretion (see–**KREE**–shun)—The production and release of a cellular product with a useful purpose (Chapter 4).

Section (**SEK**–shun)—The cutting of an organ or the body to make internal structures visible (Chapter 1).

Selectively permeable (se–**LEK**–tiv–lee **PER**–me–uh–buhl)—A characteristic of cell membranes; permits the passage of some materials but not of others (Chapter 3).

Self-limiting disease (sellf–**LIM**-i–ting)—A disease that typically lasts a certain period of time and is followed by recovery (Chapter 22).

Semen (**SEE**–men)—The thick, alkaline fluid that contains sperm and the secretions of the seminal vesicles, prostate gland, and bulbourethral glands (Chapter 20).

Semicircular canals (SEM–eye–**SIR**–kyoo–lur)—Three oval canals in the inner ear that contain the receptors that detect motion (Chapter 9).

Seminal vesicles (**SEM**–i–nuhl **VESS**–i–kulls)—The glands located posterior to the prostate gland and inferior to the urinary bladder; secrete an alkaline fluid that enters the ejaculatory ducts and becomes part of semen (Chapter 20).

Seminiferous tubules (sem–i–**NIFF**–er–us)—The site of spermatogenesis in the testes (Chapter 20).

Sensation (sen–**SAY**–shun)—A feeling or awareness of conditions outside or inside the body, resulting from the stimulation of sensory receptors (Chapter 9).

Sensory neuron (**SEN**–suh–ree **NYOOR**–on)—A nerve cell that carries impulses from a receptor to the central nervous system. (Syn.—afferent neuron) (Chapter 8).

Septic shock (**SEP**–tik SHAHK)—A type of circulatory shock that is a consequence of a bacterial infection (Chapter 13).

Septicemia (SEP–tih–**SEE**–mee–ah)—The presence of bacteria in the blood (Chapter 5).

Septum (**SEP**–tum)—A wall that separates two cavities, such as the nasal septum between the nasal cavities or the interventricular septum between the two ventricles of the heart (Chapter 12).

Serous fluid (**SEER**–us **FLOO**–id)—A fluid that prevents friction between the two layers of a serous membrane (Chapter 4).

Serous membrane (**SEER**–us **MEM**–brayn)—An epithelial membrane that lines a closed body cavity and covers the organs in that cavity (Chapter 4).

Sex chromosomes (**SEKS** KROH–muh–sohms)—The pair of chromosomes that determines the gender of an individual; designated XX in females and XY in males (Chapter 21).

Sex-linked trait (**SEKS** LINKED TRAYT)—A genetic characteristic in which the gene is located on the X chromosome (Chapter 7).

Simple (**SIM**–puhl)—Having only one layer, used especially to describe certain types of epithelial tissue (Chapter 4).

Sinoatrial (SA) node (**SIGH**–noh–AY–tree–al NOHD)—The first part of the cardiac conduction pathway, located in the wall of the right atrium; initiates each heartbeat (Chapter 12).

Sinusoid (**SIGH**–nuh–soyd)—A large, very permeable capillary; permits proteins or blood cells to enter or leave the blood (Chapter 13).

Skeletal muscle pump (**SKEL**–e–tuhl **MUSS**–uhl)—A mechanism that increases venous return; contractions of the skeletal muscles compress the deep veins, especially those of the legs (Chapter 13).

Skeletal system (**SKEL**–e–tuhl)—The organ system that consists of the bones, ligaments, and cartilage; supports the body and is a framework for muscle attachment (Chapter 6).

Skin (SKIN)—An organ that is part of the integumentary system; consists of the outer epidermis and the inner dermis (Chapter 5).

Sliding filament theory (**SLY**–ding **FILL**–ah–ment)—The sequence of events that occurs within sarcomeres when a musle fiber contracts (Chapter 7).

Small intestine (SMAWL in–**TESS**–tin)—The organ of the alimentary tube between the stomach and the large intestine; secretes enyzmes that complete the digestive process and absorbs the end products of digestion (Chapter 16).

Smooth muscle (SMOOTH **MUSS**–uhl)—The muscle tissue that forms the walls of hollow internal organs. Also called visceral or involuntary muscle (Chapter 4).

Sneeze reflex (SNEEZ)—A reflex integrated by the

medulla that expels irritating substances from the nasal cavities by means of an explosive exhalation (Chapter 15).

Sodium-potassium pumps (**SEW**–dee–um pa–**TASS**–ee–um)—The active transport mechanisms that maintain a high sodium ion concentration outside the cell and a high potassium ion concentration inside the cell (Chapter 7).

Soft palate (SAWFT **PAL**–uht)—The posterior portion of the palate that is elevated during swallowing to block the nasopharynx (Chapter 15).

Solute (**SAH**–loot)—The substance that is dissolved in a solution (Chapter 3).

Solution (suh–**LOO**–shun)—The dispersion of one or more compounds (solutes) in a liquid (solvent) (Chapter 2).

Solvent (**SAHL**–vent)—A liquid in which substances (solutes) will dissolve (Chapter 2).

Somatic (sew–**MA**–tik)—Pertaining to structures of the body wall, such as skeletal muscles and the skin (Chapter 8).

Somatostatin (**GHIH**) (SOH–mat–oh–**STAT**–in)—Growth hormone inhibiting hormone, produced by the hypothalamus (Chapter 10).

Somatotropin (SOH–mat–oh–**TROH**–pin)—Growth hormone (Chapter 10).

Specialized fluids (**SPEH**–shul–eyezd **FLUIDS**)—Specific compartments of extracellular fluid (ECF) which include cerebrospinal fluid, synovial fluid, aqueous humor in the eye, and others.

Spermatic cord (sper–**MAT**–ik KORD)—The cord that suspends the testis; composed of the ductus deferens, blood vessels, and nerves (Chapter 20).

Spermatogenesis (SPER–ma–toh–**JEN**–e–sis)—The process of meiosis in the testes to produce sperm cells (Chapter 3).

Spermatozoa (sper–MAT–oh–**ZOH**–ah)—Sperm cells; produced by the testes (Sing.—spermatozoon) (Chapter 20).

Sphenoid bone (**SFEE**–noyd)—The flat bone that forms part of the anterior floor of the cranial cavity and encloses the pituitary gland (Chapter 6).

Spinal cavity (**SPY**–nuhl **KAV**–i–tee)—The cavity within the vertebral column that contains the spinal cord; part of the dorsal cavity (Syn.—vertebral canal or cavity) (Chapter 1).

Spinal cord (**SPY**–nuhl KORD)—The part of the central nervous system within the vertebral canal; transmits impulses to and from the brain (Chapter 8).

Spinal cord reflex (**SPY**–nuhl KORD **REE**–fleks)—A reflex integrated in the spinal cord, in which the brain is not directly involved (Chapter 8).

Spinal nerves (**SPY**–nuhl NERVS)—The 31 pairs of nerves that emerge from the spinal cord (Chapter 8).

Spinal shock (**SPY**–nuhl SHAHK)—The temporary or permanent loss of spinal cord reflexes following injury to the spinal cord (Chapter 8).

Spirillum (spih–**RILL**–uhm) (Pl.: spirilla)—A bacterium with a spiral shape (Chapter 22).

Spirochaete (**SPY**–roh–keet)—Spiral bacteria of the order Spirochaetales (Chapter 22).

Spleen (SPLEEN)—An organ located in the upper left abdominal quadrant behind the stomach; consists of lymphatic tissue that produces lymphocytes and monocytes; also contains macrophages that phagocytize old red blood cells (Chapter 14).

Spongy bone (**SPUN**–jee BOWNE)—Bone tissue not organized into Haversian systems; forms most of short, flat, and irregular bones and forms epiphyses of long bones (Chapter 6).

Spontaneous fracture (spahn–**TAY**–nee–us)—A fracture that occurs without apparent trauma; often a consequence of osteoporosis (Chapter 6).

Spore (SPOOR)—1. A bacterial form that is dormant and highly resistant to environmental extremes such as heat. 2. A unicellular fungal reproductive form (Chapter 22).

Squamous (**SKWAY**–mus)—Flat or scale-like; used especially in reference to epithelial tissue (Chapter 4).

Stapes (**STAY**–peez)—The third of the auditory bones in the middle ear; transmits vibrations from the incus to the oval window of the inner ear (Chapter 9).

Starling's Law of the Heart (**STAR**–lingz LAW)—The force of contraction of cardiac muscle fibers is determined by the length of the fibers; the more cardiac muscle fibers are stretched, the more forcefully they contract (Chapter 12).

Stem cell (STEM SELL)—The immature cell found in red bone marrow and lymphatic tissue that is the precursor cell for all the types of blood cells (Chapter 11).

Stenosis (ste–**NO**–sis)—An abnormal constriction or narrowing of an opening or duct (Chapter 12).

Sterilization (STIR–ill–i–**ZA**–shun)—The process of completely destroying all of the microorganisms on or in a substance or object (Chapter 22).

Sternum (**STIR**–num)—The flat bone that forms part of the anterior rib cage; consists of the manubrium, body, and xiphoid process (Syn.—breastbone) (Chapter 6).

Steroid (**STEER**–oid)—An organic compound in the lipid group; includes cholesterol and certain hormones (Chapter 2).

Stimulus (**STIM**–yoo–lus)—A change, especially one that affects a sensory receptor or which brings about a response in a living organism (Chapter 9).

Stomach (**STUM**–uk)—The sac-like organ of the alimentary tube between the esophagus and the small intestine; is a reservoir for food and secretes gastric juice to begin protein digestion (Chapter 16).

Stratified (**STRA**–ti–fyed)—Having two or more layers (Chapter 4).

Stratum corneum (**STRA**–tum **KOR**–nee–um)—The outermost layer of the epidermis, made of many layers of dead, keratinized cells (Chapter 5).

Stratum germinativum (**STRA**–tum JER–min–ah–**TEE**–vum)—The innermost layer of the epidermis; the cells undergo mitosis to produce new epidermis (Chapter 5).

Streptokinase (STREP–toh–**KYE**–nase)—An enzyme produced by bacteria of the genus *Streptococcus* that is used clinically to dissolve abnormal clots, such as those in coronary arteries (Chapter 11).

Stretch receptor (STRETCH ree–**SEP**–ter)—A sensory receptor in a muscle that detects stretching of the muscle (Syn.—proprioceptor) (Chapter 7).

Stretch reflex (STRETCH **REE**–fleks)—A spinal cord reflex in which a muscle that is stretched will contract (Chapter 8).

Striated muscle (**STRY**–ay–ted **MUSS**–uhl)—The muscle tissue that forms the skeletal muscles that move bones (Chapter 4).

Stroke volume (STROHK **VAHL**–yoom)—The amount of blood pumped by a ventricle in one beat; the resting average is 60–80 ml/beat (Chapter 12).

Subarachnoid space (SUB–uh–**RAK**–noid)—The space between the arachnoid membrane and the pia mater; contains cerebrospinal fluid (Chapter 8).

Subclinical infection (sub–**KLIN**–i–kuhl)—An infection in which the person shows no symptoms (Chapter 22.)

Subcutaneous (SUB–kew–**TAY**–nee–us)—Below the skin; the tissues between the dermis and the muscles (Chapter 5).

Sublingual glands (sub–**LING**–gwal)—The pair of salivary glands located below the floor of the mouth (Chapter 16).

Submandibular glands (SUB–man–**DIB**–yoo–lar)—The pair of salivary glands located at the posterior corners of the mandible (Chapter 16).

Submucosa (SUB–mew–**KOH**–sah)—The layer of connective tissue and blood vessels located below the mucosa (lining) of a mucous membrane (Chapter 16).

Substrates (SUB–strayts)—The substances acted upon, as by enzymes (Chapter 2).

Sucrase (SOO–krays)—A digestive enzyme that breaks down sucrose to glucose and fructose; secreted by the small intestine (Chapter 16).

Sucrose (SOO–krohs)—A disaccharide made of one glucose and one fructose molecule (Syn.—cane sugar, table sugar) (Chapter 2).

Sulcus (**SUHL**–kus)—A furrow or groove, as between the gyri of the cerebrum (Syn.—fissure) (Chapter 8).

Superficial (soo–per–**FISH**–uhl)—Toward the surface (Chapter 1).

Superficial fascia (soo–per–**FISH**–uhl **FASH**–ee–ah)—The subcutaneous tissue, between the dermis and the muscles. Consists of areolar connective tissue and adipose tissue (Chapter 4).

Superior (soo–**PEER**–ee–your)—Above, or higher (Chapter 1).

Superior vena cava (**VEE**–nah **KAY**–vah)—The vein that returns blood from the upper body to the right atrium (Chapter 12).

Suspensory ligaments (suh–**SPEN**–suh–ree **LIG**–uh–ments)—The strands of connective tissue that connect the ciliary body to the lens of the eye (Chapter 9).

Suture (**SOO**–cher)—A synarthrosis, an immovable joint between cranial bones or facial bones (Chapter 6).

Supination (SOO–pi–**NAY**–shun)—Turning the palm upward, or lying face up (Chapter 7).

Sympathetic (SIM–puh–**THET**–ik)—The division of the autonomic nervous system that dominates during stressful situations (Chapter 8).

Sympathomimetic (SIM–pah–tho–mi–**MET**–ik)—Having the same effects as sympathetic impulses, as has epinephrine, a hormone of the adrenal medulla (Chapter 10).

Symphysis (**SIM**–fi–sis)—An amphiarthrosis in which a disc of cartilage is found between two bones, as in the vertebral column (Chapter 6).

Symptomatic infection (**SIMP**–toh–MAT–ick)—An infection in which the patient exhibits the symptoms of the disease (Chapter 22).

Synapse (**SIN**–aps)—The space between the axon of one neuron and the cell body or dendrite of the next neuron or between the end of a motor neuron and an effector cell (Chapter 4).

Synaptic knob (si–**NAP**–tik NOB)—The end of an axon of a neuron that releases a neurotransmitter (Chapter 8).

Synarthrosis (SIN–ar–**THROH**–sis)—An immovable joint, such as a suture (Chapter 6).

Synergistic muscles (SIN–er–**JIS**–tik **MUSS**–uhls)—Muscles that have the same function, or a stabilizing function, with respect to the movement of a joint (Chapter 7).

Synovial fluid (sin–**OH**–vee–uhl **FLOO**–id)—A thick slippery fluid that prevents friction within joint cavities (Chapter 6).

Synovial membrane (sin–**OH**–ve–uhl **MEM**–brayn)—The connective tissue membrane that lines joint cavities and secretes synovial fluid (Chapter 4).

Synthesis (**SIN**–the–siss)—The process of forming complex molecules or compounds from simpler compounds or elements (Chapter 2).

Syphilis (**SIFF**–i–lis)—A sexually transmitted disease caused by the bacterium *Treponema pallidum;* may also cause congenital syphilis in newborns of infected women (Chapter 20).

Systemic infection (sis–**TEM**–ick)—An infection that has spread throughout the body from an initial site (Chapter 22).

Systole (**SIS**–tuh–lee)—In the cardiac cycle, the contraction of the myocardium; ventricular systole pumps blood into the arteries (Chapter 12).

—T—

T cell (T SELL)—A sub-group of lymphocytes; include helper T cells, killer T cells, and suppressor T cells, all of which are involved in immune responses (Chapter 11).

Tachycardia (TAK–ee–**KAR**–dee–yah)—An abnormally rapid heart rate; more than 100 beats per minute (Chapter 12).

Taenia coli (**TAY**–nee–uh **KOH**–lye)—The longitudinal muscle layer of the colon; three bands of smooth muscle fibers that extend from the cecum to the sigmoid colon (Chapter 16).

Talus (**TAL**–us)—One of the tarsals; articulates with the tibia (Chapter 6).

Target organ (**TAR**–get **OR**–gan)—The organ (or tissue) in which a hormone exerts its specific effects. (Chapter 10).

Tarsals (**TAR**–suhls)—The seven short bones in each ankle (Chapter 6).

Taste buds (TAYST BUDS)—Structures on the papillae of the tongue that contain the chemoreceptors for the detection of chemicals (food) dissolved in saliva (Chapter 9).

Tears (TEERS)—The watery secretion of the lacrimal glands; wash the anterior surface of the eyeball and keep it moist (Chapter 9).

Teeth (TEETH)—Bony projections in the upper and lower jaws that function in chewing (Chapter 16).

Telophase (**TELL**–ah–fayz)—The fourth stage of mitosis, in which two nuclei are reformed (Chapter 3).

Temporal bone (**TEM**–puh–ruhl)—The flat bone that forms the side of the cranial cavity and contains middle and inner ear structures (Chapter 6).

Temporal lobes (**TEM**–puh–ruhl LOWBS)—The lateral parts of the cerebrum; contain the auditory, olfactory, and taste areas (Chapter 8).

Tendon (**TEN**–dun)—A fibrous connective tissue structure that connects muscle to bone (Chapter 7).

Teratogen (te–**RAH**–toh–jen)—Anything that causes developmental abnormalities in an embryo; may be a chemical or microorganism to which an embryo is exposed by way of the mother (Chapter 21).

Testes (**TES**–teez)—The male gonads that produce sperm cells; also endocrine glands that secrete the hormone testosterone (Sing.—testis) (Chapter 10).

Testosterone (tes–**TAHS**–ter–ohn)—The male sex hormone secreted by the interstitial cells of the testes; responsible for the growth of the male reproductive organs and the secondary sex characteristics (Chapter 10).

Tetanus (**TET**–uh–nus)—1. A sustained contraction of a muscle fiber in response to rapid nerve impulses. 2. A disease, characterized by severe muscle spasms, caused by the bacterium *Clostridium tetani* (Chapter 7).

Thalamus (**THAL**–uh–muss)—The part of the brain superior to the hypothalamus; regulates subconscious aspects of sensation (Chapter 8).

theory (**THEER**–ree)—A statement that is the best explanation of all the available evidence on a particular action or mechanism. A theory is *not* a guess (Chapter 3).

Thoracic cavity (thaw–**RASS**–ik **KAV**–i–tee)—Part of the ventral cavity, superior to the diaphragm (Chapter 1).

Thoracic duct (thaw–**RASS**–ik DUKT)—The lymph vessel that empties lymph from the lower half and upper left quadrant of the body into the left subclavian vein (Chapter 14).

Thoracic vertebrae (thaw–**RASS**–ik **VER**–te–bray)—The 12 vertebrae that articulate with the ribs (Chapter 6).

Threshold level–renal (**THRESH**–hold **LE**–vuhl)—The concentration at which a substance in the blood *not* normally excreted by the kidneys begins to appear in the urine. For several substances, such as glucose, in the renal filtrate, there is a limit to how much the renal tubules can reabsorb (Chapter 18).

Thrombocyte (**THROM**–boh–site)—Platelet, a fragment of a megakaryocyte (Chapter 11).

Thrombocytopenia (THROM–boh–SIGH–toh–**PEE**–nee–ah)—An abnormally low platelet count (Chapter 11).

Thrombus (**THROM**–bus)—A blood clot that obstructs blood flow through a blood vessel (Chapter 11).

Thymus (**THIGH**–mus)—An organ made of lymphatic tissue located inferior to the thyroid gland; large in the fetus and infant, and shrinks with age; produces T cells and hormones necessary for the maturation of the immune system (Chapter 14).

Thyroid cartilage (**THIGH**–roid **KAR**–ti–ledj)—The largest and most anterior cartilage of the larynx; may be felt in the front of the neck (Chapter 15).

Thyroid gland (**THIGH**–roid)—An endocrine gland on the anterior side of the trachea below the larynx; secretes thyroxine, triiodothyronine, and calcitonin (Chapter 10).

Thyroid-stimulating hormone (TSH) —A hormone secreted by the anterior pituitary gland that causes the thyroid gland to secrete triiodothyronine, and T_3 (Chapter 10).

Thyroxine (T_4) (thigh–**ROK**–sin)—A hormone secreted by the thyroid gland that increases energy production and protein synthesis (Chapter 10).

Tibia (**TIB**–ee–yuh)—The larger long bone of the lower leg (Syn.—shinbone) (Chapter 6).

Tidal volume (**TIGH**–duhl **VAHL**–yoom)—The volume of air in one normal inhalation and exhalation; average: 400–600 ml (Chapter 15).

Tissue (**TISH**–yoo)—A group of cells with similar structure and function (Chapter 1).

Tissue fluid (**TISH**–yoo **FLOO**–id)—The water found in intercellular spaces. Also called interstitial fluid (Chapter 2).

Tissue macrophage system (**TISH**–yoo **MACK**–roh–fayj)—The organs or tissues that contain macrophages which phagocytize old red blood cells: the liver, spleen, and red bone marrow (Chapter 11).

Tissue typing (**TISH**–yoo **TIGH**–ping)—A laboratory procedure that determines the HLA types of a donated organ, prior to an organ transplant (Chapter 11).

Tongue (TUHNG)—A muscular organ on the floor of the oral cavity; contributes to chewing and swallowing and contains taste buds (Chapter 16).

Tonsillectomy (TAHN–si–**LEK**–toh–mee)—The surgical removal of the palatine tonsils and/or adenoid (Chapter 14).

Tonsils (**TAHN**–sills)—The lymph nodules in the mucosa of the pharynx, the palatine tonsils, and the adenoid; also the lingual tonsils on the base of the tongue (Chapter 14).

Toxin (**TOCK**–sin)—A chemical that is poisonous to cells (Chapter 22).

Toxoid (**TOCK**–soid)—An inactivated bacterial toxin that is no longer harmful yet is still antigenic; used as a vaccine (Chapter 14).

Trace element (TRAYS **EL**–uh–ment)—Those elements needed in very small amounts by the body for normal functioning (Chapter 2).

Trachea (**TRAY**–kee–ah)—The organ that is the air passageway between the larynx and the primary bronchi (Syn.—windpipe) (Chapter 15).

Transamination (TRANS–am–i–**NAY**–shun)—The transfer of an amino (NH₂) group from an amino acid to a carbon chain to form a non-essential amino acid; takes place in the liver (Chapter 16).

Transient flora (**TRAN**–zee–ent **FLOOR**–uh)—Part of normal flora; those microorganisms that may inhabit specific sites in the body for short periods of time (Chapter 22).

Transitional (trans–**ZI**–shun–uhl)—Changing from one form to another (Chapter 4).

Transitional epithelium (tran–**ZI**–shun–uhl)—A type of epithelium in which the surface cells change from rounded to flat as the organ changes shape (Chapter 4).

Transverse section (trans–**VERS SEK**–shun)—A plane or cut from front to back, separating upper and lower parts (Chapter 1).

Tricuspid valve (try–**KUSS**–pid VALV)—The right AV valve, which prevents backflow of blood from the right ventricle to the right atrium when the ventricle contracts (Chapter 12).

Trigeminal nerves (try–**JEM**–in–uhl)—Cranial nerve pair V. Sensory for the face and teeth. Motor to chewing muscles (Chapter 8).

Trigone (**TRY**–gohn)—Triangular area on the floor of the urinary bladder bounded by the openings of the two ureters and the urethra (Chapter 18).

Triglyceride (tri–**GLI**–si–ride)—An organic compound, a true fat, that is made of one glycerol and three fatty acids (Chapter 2).

Triiodothyronine (T₃) (TRY–eye–oh–doh–**THIGH**–roh–neen)—A hormone secreted by the thyroid gland that increases energy production and protein synthesis (Chapter 10).

Trisomy (**TRY**–suh–mee)—In genetics, having three homologous chromosomes instead of the usual two (Chapter 20).

Trochlear nerves (**TROK**–lee–ur)—Cranial nerve pair IV. Motor to an extrinsic muscle of the eye (Chapter 8).

Trophoblast (**TROH**–foh–blast)—The outermost layer of the embryonic blastocyst; will become the chorion, one of the embryonic membranes (Chapter 21).

Tropomyosin (TROH–poh–**MYE**–oh–sin)—A protein that inhibits the contraction of sarcomeres in a muscle fiber (Chapter 7).

Troponin (**TROH**–poh–nin)—A protein that inhibits the contraction of the sarcomeres in a muscle fiber (Chapter 7).

True fat (TROO FAT)—An organic compound in the lipid group that is made of glycerol and fatty acids (Chapter 2).

Trypsin (**TRIP**–sin)—A digestive enzyme that breaks down proteins into polypeptides; secreted by the pancreas (Chapter 16).

Tubal ligation (**TOO**–buhl lye–**GAY**–shun)—A surgical procedure to remove or sever the fallopian tubes; usually done as a method of contraception in women (Chapter 20).

Tubular reabsorption (**TOO**–byoo–ler REE–ab–**SORP**–shun)—The processes by which useful substances in the renal filtrate are returned to the blood in the peritubular capillaries (Chapter 18).

Tubular secretion (**TOO**–byoo–ler se–**KREE**–shun)—The processes by which cells of the renal tubules secrete substances into the renal filtrate to be excreted in urine (Chapter 18).

Tunica (**TOO**–ni–kah)—A layer or coat (Chapter 13).

Tympanic membrane (tim–**PAN**–ik)—The eardrum, the membrane that is stretched across the end of the ear canal; vibrates when sound waves strike it (Chapter 9).

Typing and cross matching (**TIGH**–ping and **KROSS**–match–ing)—A laboratory test that determines whether or not donated blood is compatible, with respect to the red blood cell types.

—U—

Ulna (**UHL**–nuh)—The long bone of the forearm on the little finger side (Chapter 6).

Ultrasound (**UHL**–tra–sownd)—1. Inaudible sound. 2.

A technique used in diagnosis in which ultrasound waves provide outlines of the shapes of organs or tissues (Chapter 21).

Umbilical arteries (uhm–**BILL**–i–kull **AR**–tuh–rees)—The fetal blood vessels contained in the umbilical cord that carry deoxygenated blood from the fetus to the placenta (Chapter 13).

Umbilical cord (um–**BILL**–i–kull KORD)—The structure that connects the fetus to the placenta; contains two umbilical arteries and one umbilical vein (Chapter 13).

Umbilical vein (uhm–**BILL**–i–kull VAIN)—The fetal blood vessel contained in the umbilical cord that carries oxygenated blood from the placenta to the fetus (Chapter 13).

Unicellular (YOO–nee–**SELL**–yoo–lar)—Composed of one cell (Chapter 4).

Unsaturated fat (un–**SAT**–uhr–ay–ted)—A true fat that is often liquid at room temperature; of plant origin (Chapter 2).

Upper respiratory tract (**UH**–per **RES**–pi–rah–TOR–ee TRAKT)—The respiratory organs located outside the chest cavity (Chapter 15).

Urea (yoo–**REE**–ah)—A nitrogenous waste product formed in the liver from the deamination of amino acids or from ammonia (Chapter 5).

Uremia (yoo–**REE**–me–ah)—The condition in which blood levels of nitrogenous waste products are elevated; caused by renal insufficiency or failure (Chapter 18).

Ureter (**YOOR**–uh–ter)—The tubular organ that carries urine from the renal pelvis (kidney) to the urinary bladder (Chapter 18).

Urethra (yoo–**REE**–thrah)—The tubular organ that carries urine from the urinary bladder to the exterior of the body (Chapter 18).

Urinary bladder (**YOOR**–i–NAR–ee **BLA**–der)—The organ that stores urine temporarily and contracts to eliminate urine by way of the urethra (Chapter 18).

Urinary system (**YOOR**–i–NAR–ee **SIS**–tem)—The organ system that produces and eliminates urine; consists of the kidneys, ureters, urinary bladder, and urethra (Chapter 18).

Urine (**YOOR**–in)—The fluid formed by the kidneys from blood plasma (Chapter 18).

Uterus (**YOO**–ter–us)—The organ of the female reproductive system in which the placenta is formed to nourish a developing embryo-fetus (Chapter 20).

Utricle (**YOO**–tri-kuhl)—The membranous sac in the vestibule of the inner ear that contains receptors for static equilibrium (Chapter 9).

—**V**—

Vaccine (vak–**SEEN**)—A preparation of a foreign antigen that is administered by injection or other means in order to stimulate an antibody response to provide immunity to a particular pathogen (Chapter 14).

Vagina (vuh–**JIGH**–nah)—The muscular tube that extends from the cervix of the uterus to the vaginal orifice; serves as the birth canal (Chapter 20).

Vagus nerves (**VAY**–gus)—Cranial nerve pair X. Sensory for cardiovascular and respiratory reflexes. Motor to larynx, bronchioles, stomach, and intestines (Chapter 8).

Valence (**VAY**–lens)—The combining power of an atom when compared to a hydrogen atom. Expressed as a positive or negative number (Chapter 2).

Varicose vein (**VAR**–i–kohs VAIN)—An enlarged, abnormally dilated vein; most often occurs in the legs (Chapter 13).

Vasectomy (va–**SEK**–tuh–me)—A surgical procedure to remove or sever the ductus deferens; usually done as a method of contraception in men (Chapter 20).

Vasoconstriction (VAY–so–kon–**STRICK**–shun)—A decrease in the diameter of a blood vessel caused by contraction of the smooth muscle in the wall of the vessel (Chapter 5).

Vasodilation (VAY–so–dye–**LAY**–shun)—An increase in the diameter of a blood vessel caused by relaxation of the smooth muscle in the wall of the vessel (Chapter 5).

Vector (**VECT**–ter)—An arthropod that transmits pathogens from host to host, usually when it bites to obtain blood (Chapter 22).

Vein (VAYN)—A blood vessel that takes blood from capillaries back to the heart (Chapter 13).

Venous return (**VEE**–nus ree–**TURN**)—The amount of blood returned by the veins to the heart; is directly related to cardiac output, which depends on adequate venous return (Chapter 12).

Ventilation (VEN–ti–**LAY**–shun)—The movement of air into and out of the lungs (Chapter 15).

Ventral (**VEN**–truhl)—Toward the front (Syn.—anterior) (Chapter 1).

Ventral cavity (**VEN**–truhl **KAV**–i–tee)—Cavity that consists of the thoracic, abdominal, and pelvic cavities (Chapter 1).

Ventral root (**VEN**–truhl ROOT)—The motor root of a spinal nerve (Chapter 8).

Ventricle (VEN–tri-kul)—1. A cavity, such as the four ventricles of the brain that contain cerebrospinal fluid. 2. One of the two lower chambers of the heart that pump blood to the body or to the lungs (Chapter 8).

Venule (**VEN**–yool)—A small vein (Chapter 13).

Vertebra (**VER**–te–brah)—One of the bones of the spine or backbone (Chapter 6).

Vertebral canal (**VER**–te–brahl ka–**NAL**)—The spinal cavity that contains and protects the spinal cord (Chapter 6).

Vertebral column (**VER**–te–brahl **KAH**–luhm)—The spine or backbone (Chapter 6).

Vestibule (**VES**–ti–byool)—1. The bony chamber of the inner ear that contains the utricle and saccule (Chapter

9). 2. The female external genital area between the labia minor that contains the openings of the urethra, vagina, and Bartholin's glands (Chapter 20).

Vestigial organ (ves–**TIJ**–ee–uhl)—An organ that is reduced in size and function when compared with that of evolutionary ancestors; includes the appendix, ear muscles that move the auricle, and wisdom teeth (Chapter 16).

Villi (**VILL**–eye)—1. Folds of the mucosa of the small intestine that increase the surface area for absorption; each villus contains a capillary network and a lacteal (Chapter 16). 2. Projections of the chorion, an embryonic membrane that forms the fetal portion of the placenta (Chapter 21).

Virulence (**VIR**–yoo–lents)—The ability of a microorganism to cause disease; the degree of pathogenicity (Chapter 22).

Virus (**VIGH**–rus)—The simplest type of microorganism, consisting of either DNA or RNA within a protein shell; all are obligate intracellular parasites (Chapter 14).

Visceral (**VISS**–er–uhl)—Pertaining to organs within a body cavity, especially thoracic and abdominal organs (Chapter 8).

Visceral effectors (**VISS**–er–uhl e–**FEK**–turs)—Smooth muscle, cardiac muscle, and glands; receive motor nerve fibers of the autonomic nervous system; responses are involuntary (Chapter 8).

Visceral muscle (**VIS**–ser–uhl **MUSS**–uhl)—Another name for smooth muscle tissue (Chapter 4).

Vital capacity (**VY**–tuhl kuh–**PASS**–i–tee)—The volume of air involved in the deepest inhalation followed by the most forceful exhalation; average: 3500–5000 ml (Chapter 15).

Vitamin (**VY**–tah–min)—An organic molecule needed in small amounts by the body for normal metabolism or growth (Chapter 17).

Vitreous humor (**VIT**–ree–us **HYOO**–mer)—The semisolid, gelatinous substance in the posterior cavity of the eyeball; helps keep the retina in place (Chapter 9).

Vocal cords (**VOH**–kul KORDS)—The pair of folds within the larynx that are vibrated by the passage of air, producing sounds that may be turned into speech (Chapter 15).

Voluntary muscle (**VAHL**–un–tary **MUSS**–uhl)—Another name for striated or skeletal muscle tissue (Chapter 4).

Vomiting (**VAH**–mi–ting)—Ejection through the mouth of stomach and intestinal contents (Chapter 16).

Vulva (**VUHL**–vah)—The female external genital organs (Chapter 20).

—W–X–Y–Z—

Wart (WART)—An elevated, benign skin lesion caused by a virus (Chapter 5).

White blood cells (WIGHT BLUHD SELLS)—The cells that destroy pathogens that enter the body and provide immunity to some diseases. The five types are neutrophils, eosinophils, basophils, lymphocytes, and monocytes (Syn.—leukocytes) (Chapter 4).

White matter (WIGHT)—Nerve tissue within the central nervous system that consists of myelinated axons and dendrites of interneurons (Chapter 9).

Worm (WURM)—An elongated invertebrate; parasitic worms include tapeworms and hookworm (Chapter 22).

Xiphoid process (**ZYE**–foyd)—The most inferior part of the sternum (Chapter 6).

Yellow bone marrow (**YELL**–oh BOWN **MAR**–roh)—Primarily adipose tissue, found in the marrow cavities of the diaphyses of long bones and in the spongy bone of the epiphyses of adult bones (Chapter 6).

Yolk sac (YOHK SAK)—An embryonic membrane that forms the first blood cells for the developing embryo (Chapter 21).

Zoonoses (ZOH–oh–**NOH**–seez) (Sing.: zoonosis)—Diseases of animals that may be transmitted to people under certain conditions (Chapter 22).

Zygote (**ZYE**–goht)—A fertilized egg, formed by the union of the nuclei of egg and sperm; the diploid number of chromosomes (46 for people) is restored (Chapter 20).

Index

Page numbers followed by "t" or "f" indicate tables or figures, respectively. Page numbers followed by "b" indicate boxed material.